I writing
II grammar
III idiomatic English
IV sentences/words
V punctuation
VI mechanics
VII research
VIII MLA
IX APA/other
X projects
XI appendix

Your situation	What to do	Where to look
You know what you're looking for.	Make a search for key words.	➤ Look for topics in the Tab Guide (the reverse of this page); then go to tab sections to find detailed tables of contents. Find section numbers leading to your topic. ➤ Look for topics in the Index, and if you don't see your term, follow cross-references ("See" or "See also") to find synonyms for your topic. ➤ Look for topic markers and correction symbols at the top of each page. ➤ Look in the Brief Contents at the front of the book.
You want quick help on a specific part of a writing process.	Look for the right "How-to" box.	➤ Look at the Writing Processes chart inside the front cover to locate a "How-to" box that fits your writing situation. ➤ Read the accompanying text for more detail and examples.
You want background explanations to understand your instructor's comments.	Look for correction symbols or key words that appear in the comments.	➤ Find correction symbols identified at the back of the book, and follow references to pages indicated. ➤ Look for topic markers and correction symbols at the top of each page. ➤ Do a search for key words in the Tab Guide, Index, or Brief Contents. Find section numbers leading to your topic.
You're unsure what you're looking for.	Browse.	➤ Look at the Writing Processes chart inside the front cover to locate a "How-to" box that fits your writing situation. ➤ Scan the Tab Guide (the reverse of this page); follow leads to the Brief Contents, individual tabs, and Detailed Contents for each section. ➤ Check out topic markers and correction symbols at the top of each page.

How to Find Information on a Handbook Page

Find topic markers and correction symbols at the top ———

"Computer Tip" boxes give advice on using the computer as a critical thinking tool ———

Headings describe guidelines for writing, revising, or editing ———

Section numbers provide a reference for each topic ———

Explanations give positive help, guidelines, and advice ———

Examples show the revisions and edits to make in this situation ———

Cross-references lead to Section Numbers or page numbers for related topics elsewhere in the book ———

"How-to" boxes give immediate help for most writing processes ———

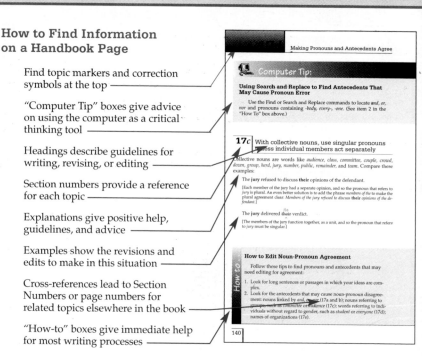

The Ready Reference Handbook

WRITING, REVISING, EDITING

SECOND CANADIAN EDITION

JACK DODDS
William Rainey Harper College

JUDI JEWINSKI
Renison College, University of Waterloo

Toronto

For Danielle, Nicole and Ed,
especially

Canadian Cataloguing in Publication Data

Dodds, Jack
      The ready reference handbook : writing, revising, editing

2nd Canadian ed.
ISBN 0-205-31917-3

1. English language - Rhetoric - Handbooks, manuals, etc.
2. English language - Grammar - Handbooks, manuals, etc.
I. Jewinksi, Judi. II. Title.

PE1408.D59 2001   808'.042   C00-930759-1

ISBN 0-13-027246-9

Vice-President, Editorial Director: Michael Young
Executive Editor: David Stover
Marketing Manager: Sophia Fortier
Executive Developmental Editor: Marta Tomins
Production Editor: Julia Hubble
Copy Editor: Nancy Mucklow
Production Coordinator: Wendy Moran
Page Layout: B.J. Weckerle
Art Direction: Julia Hall
Interior Design: Julia Hall
Cover Design: Dwayne Dobson
Cover Image: Photodisc

Original English-language edition published by Allyn and Bacon, Needham Heights, MA 02494, USA
© 2000, 1998, 1997

5 6 7 8   05 04 03 02

Printed and bound in Canada

A Brief Contents and Browsing Guide

Editing Grammar and Usage

part III Idiomatic English

part IV Crafting Sentences, Choosing Words

Crafting Sentences

Contents | vii

part VII Research and the Internet

part VIII MLA Documentation

part IX APA and Other Documentation Styles

APA Documentation

Other Styles

part X Other Writing Projects

Appendix

Index

Preface

Poet, journalist, and teacher Donald Murray once remarked that a wise composition instructor looks for what is best in students' writing and then shows these developing writers how to make their best even better. The students, teachers, and reviewers who have made suggestions for the second edition of *The Ready Reference Handbook* have done us that favour. In the first edition, we aimed for a book that was easy to use, practical, and as comprehensive as possible for a brief handbook. Their comments and suggestions have shown us how to make this new edition easier to use, more practical, and more comprehensive.

An easier-to-use design

- The binding makes the book sturdier for everyday use and preserves the lie-flat, ready-reference format.

- Eleven tabbed dividers organize *The Ready Reference Handbook* into the quick-access topics student writers need to consult most often as they write and revise.

- A more open page layout makes individual sections easier to locate and examples easier to see.

More practical advice for practising writers

- The "How-To" boxes (see inside cover) that students and teachers have found so useful for guiding the writing process have been simplified and focussed to provide essential tips, guidelines, questions, and checklists when and where writers need them most.

- New "How-To" boxes provide advice on critical thinking and reading, annotating a text, profiling an audience, peer reviewing, proofreading a final draft, writing summaries, searching the World Wide Web, and evaluating sources.

- "Computer Tip" boxes are placed throughout *The Ready Reference Handbook* to provide students with advice for doing efficient word processing and for using the computer as a critical-thinking tool.

- Chapters on composing, grammar, usage, and style have been sharpened to provide students with the most practical advice possible for inventing, drafting, revising, and editing—without, however, sacrificing the user-friendly tone of that advice, which students have found encouraging.

- Increased coverage is given to the key rhetorical choices that direct a writer's writing: analyzing an audience, crafting thesis statements to fulfill specific rhetorical purposes, and writing effective introductions and conclusions.

- Increasingly, students are becoming multi-media learners and writers. To meet their needs, this edition of *The Ready Reference Handbook* uses visuals to illustrate critical reading and online research. For their own writing, students are provided with illustrated examples of common graphics.

- An Appendix provides a topical list of URLs helpful to students learning Internet research.

More comprehensive coverage

- A new first chapter, "Becoming a Critical Writer," provides an important frame of reference for all that follows in *The Ready Reference Handbook*. The critical-thinking skills of analysis, interpretation, evaluation, and synthesis aid students as they investigate a topic, read, plan for readers, write, and revise.

- In chapters on the research paper, discussion of computerized research has been expanded with additional guidance to library search tools, Boolean searching, and note-taking.

- A new Chapter 50, "Searching the Internet," gives a clear, non-jargon, step-by-step introduction to the possibilities and challenges of Internet research.

- Chapter 50 and Section 48e introduce students to communicating online, observing Internet "Netiquette," and creating Web sites.

- In Chapter 51, the new mnemonic "CASE" method for evaluating sources (currency, authority, suitability, and ease of use) provides students with a comprehensive yet easy-to-remember procedure for judging the quality of their reading.

- Chapters 53–58 provide the latest guidance for online documentation using the MLA, APA, CM, and CBE documentation styles.

Other helpful features of *The Ready Reference Handbook*

- The insides of the front and back covers give writers an overview and access to key features: the "How-To" boxes, the tabs leading to each section, the book's reference features, and common correction symbols with page references.

- Section numbers and letters provide rapid references to headings and subheadings that summarize practical writing guidelines.

- *The Ready Reference Handbook* emphasizes all stages of the writing process, gives developing writers practical activities to meet their objectives at each stage, and provides numerous options so that writers can tailor their writing to their own styles or to the requirements of a particular situation.

- Students will find thorough introductions to the common forms of academic and public writing: the essay, formal report, and business writing.
- Special projects—arguments, persuasion, the literary essay, and the essay exam—are covered in depth and detail.
- Problems of grammar are treated not only as errors but also as unsuccessful strategies in specific rhetorical situations. The best solutions are shown as process-oriented responses to these situations.
- A special section on idioms and brief notes throughout the handbook offer specific advice for writers whose first language is not English.
- Annotated, full-length student writing samples illustrate an informative essay, MLA-style research project, formal report (APA), persuasive essay, literary essay, speech, business letter, résumé, and memo.
- Throughout, the user-friendly tone, numerous examples, and positive advice encourage writers to practise and experiment until they discover what to say and the best way of saying it.

Acknowledgments

The work of preparing this Canadian edition was simplified immeasurably by many people. I especially appreciate the contributions of the following:

My students have always been prepared to keep me on top of trends and current usage. Some of them have graciously permitted their work to appear in these pages; others have improved the text with their critical insights. Particular thanks go to Anouk Henry, Serge Krug, Stephen Noel, Kellie Siegner, Heather Sparling, and Joe Visser. To this list, I must add the names of my two pre-university daughters, Nicole and Danielle, who have been marvellous Internet tutors.

My colleagues too have been remarkably supportive. Special thanks go to Gail Cuthbert Brandt, Dawn Bailey, Tom Brenner, Darrol Bryant, Susan Hodges Bryant, Ian Campbell, Jim Chalmers, Hsiao d'Ailly, Joy Harris-Krpan, Grace Logan, Jane Mitchell, Mark Nagler, Stefan Rehm, Janet Stubbs, John Vardon and Mary Merikle for their assistance and encouragement. I had special help from the staff at our university libraries. There is one other colleague—my husband, Ed, who is this year celebrating with me the 23rd anniversary of our last argument about restrictive and non-restrictive clauses. . . .

And I am very glad to have had the editorial input of reviewers Matthew Clark, York University; Pat Rogin, Durham College; and Devon Galway, Algonquin College, who read the first Canadian edition and made useful recommendations. The people at Prentice Hall have been exceptionally easy to work with. In getting this manuscript to its final polished state, I was fortunate to have had the assistance of such fine editors as David Stover, Marta Tomins, Julia Hubble, and Nancy Mucklow.

Composing

The Ready Reference Handbook is designed not only for student writers but also for anyone who wants practical suggestions for writing effectively. What follows is based on the experience of writers of all kinds. At the outset, you should have some basic understanding about writers and the writing they do.

Writers write. Some people assume that writers are different from everyone else. They are inspired, they have a touch of the poet, or at least they have the gift of gab. But the truth is that writers are simply people who write. If they're inspired, they have worked hard for that flash of insight. If they sound poetic, they've probably had writer William Zinsser's experience of "endlessly rewriting what I had endlessly rewritten." When you write, you, too, are a writer.

Writing is a process. Writing is not a straightforward transcription of your thoughts. That would be dull work. It's a more exciting and experimental process of creating thoughts through written words. It's exciting because it involves discovery; writers don't always know what they'll say when they begin writing. It's experimental because writers play with words and ideas until they find what they want to say.

Writing is more than communication. Successful writers write first for themselves, to see what they think, and then for their readers, to communicate. Your writing will always be read by someone, of course. Even if you write only in a diary, you write for an audience of one—yourself. But before it is communication, writing is exploration, discovery, and self-expression. Successful writers almost always work in this two-step way: first, finding something to say and, second, finding a way to communicate it.

Good writing satisfies both writers and readers. Good writing is more than good grammar or impressive-sounding words. Yes, most successful public writing is polished, well laid out, and correct. But it also carries the sound of a writer's voice speaking to readers, it contains good ideas worth writing and reading about, and it is written with power and conviction.

There are many ways to write well. Looking at a book like this, you might think that it preaches the one right way to successful writing. But every successful writer has his or her own habits and techniques. Some writers are genuinely quirky. Ernest Hemingway sharpened precisely eight pencils before he began each writing day, and the German writer Schiller required the smell of apples rotting in his desk drawer to set him to work. Most successful writers, however, have more practical ways of doing their writing. This book describes many of these strategies. Consider them as options. Explore and experiment to find what works for you.

chapter

1 Becoming a Critical Writer

For many people, "critical" is a word with a bad reputation, associated in their minds with faultfinding, nit-picking, and negativity. But it has a much broader meaning, one important to writers of all kinds. *Critical* comes from a Greek word meaning "to discern or perceive, to separate, to understand." To be critical, therefore, means to look carefully at something, to discover its parts and what it's made of, and then, sometimes, to evaluate—positively or negatively.

In this day of political "spin doctors" who twist the truth, of computer-manipulated images, of competing authorities with conflicting opinions on nearly everything, it's sometimes difficult to tell fact from fiction, the virtual from the real. Skepticism and common sense may not be enough for deciding what to believe, whom, or how much. What can help are the methods of critical thinking, reading, and writing described in this and the following chapters.

1*a* | Think critically about information, ideas, and opinions

What goes into your writing may come from your own knowledge, imagination, or observation, or from a book or some other source. Whatever the source, these facts, ideas, and opinions will come to you in clumps or in bits and pieces, and you may be uncertain about their meaning or doubtful about their value. To sort things out, see the connections, and decide what things add up to, you'll use four methods of critical thinking: analysis, interpretation, evaluation, and synthesis.

In school and out, in research papers and other academic writing, in job applications, in business and professional writing of all kinds, even in your personal writing, you'll use these methods. This chapter introduces them to you and provides critical questions for you to ask as you think about a topic and prepare to write about it. Later chapters will show you how to apply these methods in specific kinds of writing. (See Chapters 2–6, 49–52, 60–63.)

1 Analyzing

When you analyze something, you take it apart and describe it, according to some specific interest, in order to understand it. If a literature teacher asks you to analyze a short story, you may describe the roles that the characters play, divide the plot into a series of related events, or explain why the characters behave as they do. Your interest in character relationships, the action of the story, or human motivation determines what you see as you make your analysis. If you are asked to analyze a business issue, you may describe the options, consider an orderly process for adopting one of them, and explain the beneficial effects of following your recommendations. Here you would be applying all three basic types of analysis.

How to Think Critically

From the following list, choose relevant questions to ask about the topics of your writing. If necessary, reword the questions to fit the topic and your interests, and then look for answers. Study the examples to see how to modify the questions.

1. What are the parts of (your topic)? How do they fit or work together? What larger topic is (your topic) a part of? How is it similar to or different from other topics?
   What are the duties of the Governor General? [a question about parts]
   How do the duties of the Governor General compare to those of the provincial Lieutenant-Governor? [a question of comparison]
2. What is the environment or background of (your topic)? Where does it come from?
   What is the history of the separatist movement in Quebec?
3. What is happening to (your topic)? What are the causes of its change? What are the effects of this change? Who is affected? How? What will stop the process?
   What is causing the increase in serious accidents on major highways?
   How do smoking bans affect people? What are the responses of restaurant and tavern owners?
4. What is known for a fact about (your topic)? What do the experts or eyewitnesses think? What assumptions or biases influence their view of the facts? Where do they disagree? Which opinions are best supported or most reasonable?
   How do children learn language? Why is this process seemingly effortless?
5. What is missing from the information about (your topic)?
   Why do we never actually meet Big Brother in George Orwell's 1984?
6. How are you involved with (your topic)? What bias might influence your thinking?
   Why do I automatically become suspicious and skeptical when panhandlers ask me for spare change?
7. What should be done about (your topic)? Who will do it? What will it cost?
   What will repair the environmental harm caused by visitors to our national parks?

- *Descriptive analysis.* When you describe the roles of the various characters in a play, for example, you're making a descriptive analysis.
  You are assigning each character a part and describing how each
  character plays that part, based on the plot of the play. A botanist who
  describes a newly discovered plant species part by part—root, stem,
  leaves, and flower—is also making a descriptive analysis.

- *Process analysis.* To divide an event or action into its stages or steps
  and then to describe their relationships is to make a process analysis.
  A recipe for macaroni and cheese is a kind of process analysis: first
  cook the noodles, then add the sauce, and then bake. A sports reporter who writes a goal-by-goal account of a hockey game is writing
  a process analysis.

- *Causal analysis.* To examine events as patterns of cause and effect is to
  make a causal analysis. An environmentalist who sets out to explain
  why the forests of Algonquin Park are slowly dying and discovers the
  reasons in acid rain has made a causal analysis, reasoning backward
  from effects to causes. An urban planner who considers the traffic
  consequences of a new highway is reasoning forward, from causes to
  their potential effects.

When you want to analyze a topic, think in terms of its parts, steps,
stages, causes, or effects. To begin thinking analytically, choose from questions 1, 2, and 3 in the "How to Think Critically" box (p. 3). As you analyze
a topic, be sure to describe *all* of its parts and to apply your interests—your
principles of analysis—consistently. For example, your analysis of the
death of a forest would be incomplete and ineffective if you neglected to
mention some of the regions affected or some of the causes, or if you confused the effects of acid rain with those of harmful insects.

2   Interpreting

To interpret means to explain or bring to light. When analysis alone
doesn't produce understanding, interpretation becomes necessary. When
you interpret something, you're reading between the lines, whether those
"lines" are the actual lines of a difficult poem, the confusing behaviour of a
person you know, or the reasons for some mysterious event. You're looking for "hidden meanings" that will remain hidden until you reveal them
through interpretation. Where are you likely to find these hidden meanings?

- *Assumptions.* To read printed texts—or people—successfully, try to
  discover their assumptions, the basic, often untested beliefs that influence their outlook and behaviour. The person who argues that "the
  federal government should increase the numbers of new immigrants

because the economy will benefit" is assuming, but not actually saying, that immigrants are hard-working.

- *Patterns.* When you're trying to understand something, look for patterns—regularities or repetitions in information, design, language, or
  occurrence. Patterns often reveal the meaning of the thing you're
  studying. Imagine an acquaintance who, you have noticed, speaks
  constantly about money: how much he has or doesn't have, how
  much other people earn, what everything costs, what risks there are
  of inflation. You may well base your interpretation of his personality
  on his overriding concern with money, guessing his values and pre-
  dicting his future behaviour accordingly.

- *Implications.* An implication is a connection, usually unstated, between one thing and another. Often printed texts and people don't
  come right out and state exactly what they mean. Instead, they imply
  something—that is, they suggest or point in a certain direction. To
  discover implications, ask yourself, "Where is this train of thought
  going? What is the next logical step?" What, for, example, are the implications of a provincial welfare policy that requires people to work
  in order to qualify for financial aid but cannot provide jobs for them?

When your subject matter requires interpretation, choose from questions 2 through 7 in the "How to Think Critically" box (p. 3). You'll express
the results of interpretation as an **inference**—that is, a statement of meaning based upon your understanding of the available information. To
state—or "draw"—an inference, you bring together all assumptions, patterns, and implications to see what they add up to. Using reasoning, you
state an idea that didn't exist or wasn't apparent before your interpretation. For example, in a literary essay interpreting a poem (see 60g), student
Leslie Kelly investigates the language, assumptions, and actions of a character in the poem to discover why he commits what appears to be a cold,
heartless act. What she discovers (her interpretation) is summed up in her
inference about what motivates his behaviour.

3   Evaluating information and opinions

When you evaluate, you do more than state your opinions or subjective preferences regarding a topic—a movie, an automobile, a book, a
political speech. When you evaluate, you measure something against
widely shared **standards of value** that indicate whether it is good or not so
good. To write effectively, you'll evaluate all that goes into your writing to
see that it is useful and trustworthy.

- *Facts and statistics.* A fact is something that can be verified. The
  statement "The value of tobacco products manufactured in Canada

actually doubled from 1985 to 1996," sounds like a fact, as does "Young people make up the majority of smokers today." You can check such statements in history books and public records to see whether they're true. To decide whether you or other writers are using facts effectively, apply these four standards (known as *Rules of Evidence*): (1) **sufficiency**—are there enough facts to support the point being made? (2) **relevance**—do these facts actually apply to the situation being considered? (3) **timeliness**—are these facts up to date? (4) **variety**—do these facts come from or are they verified by a variety of sources? The fourth standard acknowledges that people who disagree are likely to disagree about the facts. When such is the case, the more sources that accept something as true, the more confident you can be that it is.

- *Opinions.* Consider these two statements: "Gambling causes an increase of the same hormones in the blood that are seen in drug addicts. Gambling, like drug use, is addictive." These statements may sound like facts. The first can be verified by observation and is a fact. The second, however, is an inference—an opinion—based on the first. An opinion is a statement of belief or a conclusion. In your writing, you'll use both facts and opinions, and you'll have to distinguish between them. When you identify an opinion, evaluate its usefulness with these questions: (1) Is this opinion supported by sufficient facts? If not, you should mistrust it. (2) Is the source of this opinion an expert or eyewitness? Be careful with opinions from unqualified sources. (3) What are the opinions of other experts or eyewitnesses? See how they compare.

- *Examples and anecdotes.* An **example** describes one member of a group in order to explain the whole group (see also 8b5). Here is an example of an example: In order to explain the economic effects of a comprehensive smoking ban on small business owners, a writer looks at one city, Victoria, as an example. By showing what happens in Victoria, the writer can generalize to predict what might happen elsewhere. An **anecdote** is a brief story that makes a point. Examples and anecdotes are vivid ways to explain or support a point because they help people see what you mean. To use them effectively, ask yourself this question: does your example or anecdote really represent what it is supposed to illustrate? Now take another look at the example at the beginning of this paragraph and ask yourself this: is Victoria really representative of Canadian cities in terms of its population mix and its economic level?

When you write about important topics, you'll evaluate frequently, both information and the sources of that information. Questions 4, 5, and 6 in the "How to Think Critically" box (p. 3) will help you begin. To evaluate the sources of information, follow the guidelines in 51a and b. For more on evaluation, see 5c "Testing an Argument" and 60c "Writing about Literature: The Review."

4 Synthesizing

When information and opinions come from a variety of sources, you have to synthesize them to make them useful to you. *Synthesis* comes from the Greek word meaning "to put together, to integrate, to blend." When you synthesize facts, ideas, and opinions, you choose among them and put together your choices to express *your* ideas and support *your* opinions. *Your* thinking becomes the focus.

To prepare a research paper on problems in Canada's national parks, student Heather Sparling (see Chapter 55) read books, articles and Internet sources, interviewed officials, and drew on her own experiences. She gathered information about the effects visitors were having on the environment, park facilities, and one another. She also gathered a variety of opinions, some conflicting, about what should be done about the problems. She didn't reject conflicting opinions or eliminate those she disagreed with. She evaluated them, selected the best supported and most reasonable, and showed what was wrong with the others. From all her research, she drew inferences and formed her own opinions about the most economical, efficient solutions. Like most research papers, hers is a result of synthesis.

To synthesize effectively, follow these guidelines:

- *Make a working bibliography.* When you take materials from more than two or more sources, keep a list of your sources, including complete publication information (see 49e2). You may make this list an annotated bibliography by adding brief statements about the contents and quality of each source. (See 49e3.)

- *Compare sources.* Note similarities and differences in your sources' use of key terms, in their thinking, and in their use of facts and opinions. Try to classify or group your sources. To help yourself make useful comparisons, ask question 4 in the "How to Think Critically" box (p. 3).

- *Choose the best sources.* Follow the guidelines in 51a and b. Consider how your readers will respond to the sources you've chosen. Decide how to respond to sources you disagree with.

- As you write, blend your sources smoothly, so they support your ideas and opinions clearly and coherently (see 52c, d and e).

A note on the differences between synthesis and summary: When you synthesize, you gather information from a variety of sources to support your ideas. When you summarize, you present a brief digest of another person's ideas in your own words. A good synthesis makes frequent use of summary. (See also 51e2.)

1*b* | Read critically

Some reading you can do in the relaxed, casual way you watch television. But the reading you do for school, on the job, or about important issues calls for greater attention and care. Ideas won't leap off the page with dramatic clarity, and you won't always be able to tell at a glance whether something that looks plausible really is.

1 Previewing

Before you begin reading a book, article, or other source, look it over briefly to get a sense of its content and to see whether it meets your needs. Previewing will help you read with efficiency and understanding. Look for the following:

- The major topics of the source.
- Patterns of organization. Common patterns of organization are time order, part by part or step by step, comparison, thesis/support, problem/solution.
- Information about the author. Try to discover the writer's experiences, opinions, or organizational affiliations that reveal point of view or possible bias.
- The purpose of the source and whether it suits your purpose.

How to . . .

How to Preview Your Reading

To preview a source effectively, follow these tips:

1. Skim titles, prefaces, introductions, headings, boxed text, graphics and captions for information about a source's subject matter, author, and organization.
2. Check title pages, headnotes, endnotes, and book jacket biographies for information about the author.
3. If a source is lengthy, challenging, or controversial, take extra time to read about the author in periodicals like *Current Biography*. Read reviews of the source in *Quill & Quire*, *Book Review Digest*, or *Book Review Index*. Your librarian will direct you to these and other review sources.

- Quality indicators that reveal whether a source is trustworthy and whether readers will respond favourably to it if you refer to it in your writing. Evaluate a source according to the guidelines in 51a and b.

2 Reading to understand

If you read in the active, attentive way recommended here, you'll be doing the analyzing, interpreting, evaluating, and synthesizing described earlier in this chapter. Use the questions in the "How to Think Critically" box (p. 3). Be especially aware of whether you're reading facts, opinions, examples, or anecdotes, and whether they actually support the author's ideas. Listen for the charged language, name-calling, irony, or sarcasm that signals bias. Would you trust the following opinion? "One of the bigger lies about secondary school reform relates to improved literacy skills. The last time the province 'improved' upon these skills, major sections of curriculum were slashed." Do you hear the bias in words like *"lies," "improved,"* and *"slashed"*?

While reading your source, you should also be reading yourself. The material before you, no matter how fair or objective its author may be, has been selected and organized to represent a point of view or support an opinion. It is not neutral, and neither are you. When you read, you don't merely absorb the meaning of a source; you select and organize the materials to make them meaningful to you. And you use your own assumptions, outlook, knowledge, and opinions to help you make this meaning. Therefore, as you read, you should pay close attention to your responses and to their causes. Note what you don't understand, where you agree or disagree, whether your responses are emotional or intellectual. Ask yourself whether your thoughts and reactions are fair, relevant, and complete.

3 Annotating your reading

People who do a lot of reading know that the way to read for greatest understanding is to annotate what they read—highlighting important passages and jotting brief notes. Of course, they don't annotate everything they read, but if it's important or challenging, they do. If you annotate what you read, you begin a dialogue with the authors that will deepen your understanding of their words and ideas. You'll find that your annotations—the record of your critical thinking—will be useful to you when you borrow materials from a source to include in your own writing.

Certainly, you won't write in library materials or other people's books. Notes for these sources you might jot on a sheet of paper, a note card, a "stickie note," or a computerized notes file. But if you own the source, if it's a photocopy or a computer file, you should annotate it. You don't have to be elaborate or use coloured highlighters, but you should keep a record of your understanding of a source and your reactions to it.

How to . . .

How to Annotate Your Reading

Highlighting: Use the following symbols to highlight sources you own, photocopies, and, when possible, computer files.

_____	Underline key words and phrases. Also underline "clue" words and phrases that indicate relationships between ideas, suggest the importance of a passage, or indicate the author's evaluation: *to conclude, fortunately, in all fairness, on the other hand,* and so on.
|	Draw a vertical line next to important passages that you may want to quote or summarize in your own writing.
?	Place a question mark next to unfamiliar words or passages you don't understand.
+ or −	Use a plus or minus sign for passages you agree or disagree with.
*	Use an asterisk for passages an author wants you to respond to.
1, 2, 3, etc.	Number ideas in sequence or use arrows to connect related ideas.
Z	Identify where your attention drifts or you lose interest, and ask yourself why.
X-ref	Note cross-references to other sources containing related ideas. Marginally note the author of the cross-reference or other identifying information.

Notes: In the text's margins, or elsewhere if the source does not belong to you, jot brief summaries of important passages, questions you have, musings, reactions, ideas about how you'll use information from your reading in your writing.

Computer Tip:

Annotating Computer Files.

Print out Internet files; then annotate them as you would a photocopy. Or copy and paste Internet files into a word processing file. Then you can open them and add highlighting symbols or insert notes as you would to any other text file. However, be sure to use some clearly identifiable method of separating your words from your source's words, such as a row of asterisks (********) or some other keyboard symbol typed at the beginning and end of a note. If you wish to take detailed notes, then you should create a second file and divide your computer screen into two windows to switch between, one containing your source, the other, your notes. Some word processing files even have posting utilities you can use to attach notes to computer files.

On page 12 is an example of an annotated reading. In a writing class emphasizing research, student Anouk Henry investigated environmental problems in Canada's national parks. While doing her research, she learned of a controversial proposal to build a resort community to accommodate the increasing number of visitors to a national park. Looking into the debate over this proposal, she discovered a Web site supporting the construction of this community.

Consider how Anouk's underlining and marginal notes reveal her critical thinking as she analyzes, interprets, and evaluates the information in this document. She raises questions for further investigation, notes charged language that adds an air of urgency to the document, looks for relationships and bias in the various organizations involved, and considers the consequences of the proposed construction. Through annotated reading and the critical thinking it stimulates, this student comes to a deeper understanding of her topic and begins to form opinions that she may present in her own writing. Annotating your reading will help you prepare to write as well.

This solution to accommodation issues may be too expensive for the average family visiting the park. [Interpretation]

Note charged language. [Evaluation]

Are there other solutions? [Interpretation]

Did she say this in the context of Wilderness Forest Village? [Evaluation]

What do these terms mean? [Analysis]

Who is this "partnership"? [Analysis]

What does this mean? [Analysis]

Who are they and why are they adding their support? [Analysis]

---

http://www.Wildernessvillage.ca   A Village in the Forest   Friday, Oct. 29, 1999

A VILLAGE IN THE FOREST:
A Brighter Tomorrow for
BANFF NATIONAL PARK

A Time of Crisis: A Park Under Siege
Banff National Park confronts an awesome crisis.

- Park visits have exploded by 85% since 1987 to over 10,000 per day during peak season.
- By 2010, over 5 million visitors will throng the park annually.
- Visitors wait in long lines to enter the park, clogging entrances, and are often turned away from hotels and campsites.
- Local community services and retail facilities are ill-equipped to handle the crush of visitors.

> Minister of Canadian Heritage, the Hon. Sheila Copps has said, "Our national parks are treasures that we must protect for all Canadians and for future generations." What can we do to alleviate problems in Canada's premier national park?

A Timely Solution: Wilderness Forest Village

An ecologically designed gateway resort community one km. from the south entrance to Banff National Park, Wilderness Forest Village is the result of six years of effort by a public/private partnership. No tax dollars will be spent in its construction.

- Nestled on 25 hectares in the pines between Wolfville and Mary Lake, Wilderness Forest Village will be a sustainable development community.
- Wilderness Forest Village will double the number of locally available hotel rooms and add nearly 30,000 square metres of retail space.
- The community will offer visitors a year-round conference centre.
- Parking spaces for up to 1,000 cars will be provided.
- As mandated by the updated National Parks Act (1999), there will be no net negative environmental impact on the area.

Join Parks Canada employees and the members of nine environmental groups in supporting Wilderness Forest Village!

Wilderness Village Services Bureau—Last updated: October 25, 1999

1c Write critically: survey the writing situation

When you have a project to write, make preliminary plans by looking carefully at what you need to do. Ask yourself these questions to help you analyze and evaluate a project before you actually begin writing. You may not be able to answer them all at once, and some of your answers may change as your project unfolds. That's reasonable. But use the answers to guide your writing.

1 The subject and the assignment

- Has your topic been given to you as part of an assignment? Can you adapt the topic to your interests? If you have to choose a topic, what is suitable for the assignment?

- What kind of writing does the assignment require: a letter, essay, report, review, or some other form?

- What is the scope of the assignment? Do you have to cover a broad subject? How focussed must your writing be because of reader interest or length and time restrictions? How much detail will you have to use? A note for students: most writing assignments ask you to focus on a limited, specific subject and to go into it in as much detail as the time allows.

- What do you know about the subject? According to the assignment, what kinds of information should be included: personal experience, facts and figures, expert opinion? Where will you get your information: from memory, observation, reading, discussion? What experience or bias may affect your view of what you find? If you borrow others' words or ideas, what system of documentation are you required to use?

2 Your purpose and role

- What purpose does the wording of the assignment set for you? Consider such phrases as "Write a personal narrative . . . ," "Write an informative essay . . . ," "Explain . . . ," "Evaluate . . . ," and "Take a position . . . ." (To learn to interpret the instructions given in writing assignments, see 62a.)

- What writer's role have your knowledge and personal experience prepared you for? Can you play the role of an **autobiographer** and write about yourself? Are you a **reporter** informing readers, a **teacher** explaining ideas or procedures, a **critic** making an evaluation, a **persuader** arguing a position, or some combination of these?

3   Audience

When you are writing academic assignments, you know that you have a limited audience—your instructor. Often you may be told to imagine you are writing for a "general audience." This is good advice for writers first learning to write publicly. But the more you write, the more you will recognize that, actually, no audience is "general." Audiences may be large or small, one or a million readers, but all come to their reading with knowledge, expectations, opinions, and experiences that influence what they read and how they respond. As you plan your writing, envision your target audience—who they are, what they know about your topic, what they want or need from you. Ask the questions in the "How to Profile an Audience" box (below). Then use your answers to plan how you'll express your ideas to meet your audience's interests and needs.

Consider the situation of a student writing an informative persuasive essay promoting bicycle commuting. Recognizing that most readers would likely be motorists, the writer must identify the need to convince

---

How to . . .

How to Profile an Audience

As you begin planning your writing, answer these questions to help you envision your readers and plan how to communicate with them.

1. How can you classify your readers? Are they (1) **allies** who will accept almost anything you write, (2) **potential allies** who need only to be informed to accept your ideas, (3) **disinterested observers** who want information above all else, (4) **skeptics** who expect careful reasoning and detailed support, (5) **opponents** who may not accept your ideas even if you provide abundant proof?

2. What do these readers know about your topic? What assumptions, biases, or knowledge gaps will influence their responses? What illustrations will help them understand?

3. What do readers expect from you: personal experience, information, explanation, evaluation, proof, entertainment? What writing style is appropriate for addressing them, informal or formal?

4. What do these readers believe about your sources of information? Which ones will they accept as authoritative? Which might they reject as superficial, biased, or inaccurate?

---

the audience that bicycles and motor vehicles could share the same road safely. Similarly, Joe Visser, the writer of the evaluative essay on language imperialism (see 4f), recognized that his audience would likely speak only one language—English. His readers would need many examples before being convinced of the value of learning another language.

Be careful though. Sometimes, it's not wise to think too much about your audience early in a project, when you're exploring a topic or trying to discover your opinions. Doing so may cramp your reasoning or creativity. But as soon as you begin thinking of the actual writing you'll do, think carefully about your readers. Your supporting details, focus, organization, style, and word choice all depend upon who your readers are and the response you want from them.

4 The final draft

- Are there length specifications?

- When is the final draft due? How much time do you have for each stage of your writing: gathering materials, planning, writing, revising, editing, typing, and proofreading?

- What is the appropriate format for your final copy? (For academic writing, see 48a; for business writing, see 63.)

 Computer Tip:

Creating Templates

You can create a master computer file, called a template, that lists all the questions you'll need to ask yourself as you survey a writing assignment. Use the questions here in 1c, or make shorter files focussing on a specific set of questions about, for example, your audience. Then, at the beginning of a writing project, open this master file and answer the questions. Be sure to save your file of answered questions under a new and appropriate file name, such as "Survey#1" or "Audience: Autobiography."

chapter

2 "Inventing" Your Writing

Writers, like inventors, create their work not all at once but in stages, through trial and error, reflection, and discovery. As you begin this creative process, guide your writing by making the critical survey recommended in 1c. Then use the tips and options in this chapter to turn the results of your survey into the actual subject matter of your writing. Because this process differs from one writer to another and one kind of writing to another, you'll

Computer Tip:

Writing Successfully with Computers

Computers are an especially powerful tool for doing the exploratory, multi-stage writing recommended here. To write successfully with computers, use the tips offered here and throughout *The Ready Reference Handbook*.

- *Saving your work.* Save your writing frequently. If you lose power or your program crashes, anything not saved into permanent memory—on floppy or hard disk—will be lost.
- *Backing up your files.* To protect against damaged disks, save files on backup disks.
- *Making templates.* For frequent assignments, make templates. These are files that you create to reuse every time you begin a new project. They may contain questions or other prompts that guide you through each writing project. Consider templates for audience profiles, questions to answer about your topics, note-taking formats, outline formats, thesis or purpose statements, revision and editing checklists, formats for final drafts. Once you've created and saved an empty template file (named "Outline," for example), all you have to do is open it and begin typing at the appropriate prompt. If you want to save your work, save it under a new file name (for example, "Outline1"). The original, empty template will stay in place for your next project.

    <http://www.writers.com>
    <http://www.inkspot.com>
    <http://www.andromeda.rutgers.edu/~jlynch/writing/links.html>

2*a* dev

want to practise and experiment to discover which invention strategies are right for you and the writing you do.

2*a* | Explore possible topics

As you make a critical survey of a writing assignment and begin to see what to do (see 1c), create choices for yourself. The British novelist E. M. Forster once asked, "How can I know what I think till I see what I say?" Help yourself see what you think about possible topics by doing exploratory writing. Examine the following kinds of exploratory writing, and adapt them to your style and habits. Some may be more useful than others or only appropriate for certain kinds of writing.

If you have time to explore the Internet in search of topics, try these two websites:

<http://www.yorku.ca/admin/cawc/strategies/contents.html>
<http://www.rpi.edu/dept/llc/writecenter/web/handouts.html>

1 Keeping a journal or diary

These daily records of experience, reflection, and opinion can be a valuable source of personally important topics that may be transformed into public or academic writing.

2 Brainstorming

To **brainstorm,** simply make free-association lists. Start with a topic or whatever first comes to mind. Follow wherever your mind leads. Don't worry if you can't think of much the first time. Lists should be easy and fast. When you finish, underline key words or phrases to explore further.

> Bicycled to school again today—6 km there and back!
>
> Felt good, keeps me fit—<u>good exercise</u>.
>
> Biking's <u>good for everybody—less pollution</u>, one less car.
>
> More and more people are biking, but it's <u>nothing like China</u>—now there are a lot of bikes!
>
> <u>Unforgettable experience</u> living in China and <u>teaching English</u> last work term.
>
> Loved my students—so hardworking, so patient as I struggled with <u>Mandarin, a hard language</u>! The world's hardest?
>
> Lots of English teachers, so I didn't get too homesick—<u>everyone wants to learn English</u>.
>
> Nobody resented us . . . except that one guy—calling us <u>language imperialists</u>, out to conquer the world with our English . . . food for thought.

This example may make little sense to anyone but the writer, but if you look, you can see several topics that might be explored further, expanded, rearranged, and turned into the materials for a full-length writing project.

3   Topic mapping (clustering and branching)

If you like to visualize what to say before you write, draw a **topic map.** Put a topic in the middle of a sheet of paper, draw a circle around it, and then draw branches that lead to related topics and subtopics. Leave room in case you think of other branches and topics to add later.

4   Freewriting

Like brainstorming and mapping, **freewriting** is free association on paper. The difference is that, for most people, freewriting expresses thoughts more fully in sentence- and paragraph-length statements and may lead more deeply into a subject. Many writers find it a useful activity throughout the writing process as a way to explore new or challenging ideas. In freewriting, your aim is to loosen up your mind, go where it leads you, and record what you get.

Looping, an expanded form of freewriting, will help you focus your thinking and narrow a topic. When you finish one piece of freewriting, read it and look for the central thought or most interesting point. Use it as the opening for a new piece. When you finish this second exploration, look again for the central thought or most interesting point. Use that to begin a third exploration. Sometimes, you'll circle around a topic, examining it from different perspectives; at other times, you'll spiral into a topic, probing it more deeply each time you write.

5 Choosing a topic

If you've surveyed the writing situation (see 1c) and explored possible topics, you have probably given yourself a good choice—or, if you already had a topic, you'll see more clearly what is most interesting about it. A good writing topic has these characteristics:

- It is important. A good topic is important to you and your readers.

- It is fresh. A good topic is new to you or your readers, or your approach to a familiar topic is fresh. Don't reject topics that seem quirky or strange at first. They may lead to your freshest writing.

- It is a challenge. Choose topics that challenge your thinking, curiosity, or feeling. Easy topics may lead to boredom for you and your readers.

How to . . .

How to Explore a Topic

Follow these tips for doing exploratory writing. Notice that some tips apply to some kinds of exploration more than to others.

1. You can do exploratory writing in two ways. In unfocussed explorations, write whatever comes to mind, whether everything connects or not. In focussed explorations, try to focus on one topic, unless you get pulled to something more interesting.
2. Set a time limit, usually 7 to 15 minutes. Start writing about whatever comes to mind the moment you begin. Freewrite by hand, on a typewriter, or at a computer.
3. Don't stop. If your mind suddenly goes blank, write "blank, blank, blank" or repeat your last word until thoughts begin flowing again.
4. Don't censor. Write whatever comes to mind, however strange it sounds. It may lead to something important or powerful. If you don't like what you've written when you finish, you can throw it away.
5. Don't change anything. If you write something one way and think of another way, put a slash (/) and write the second version.
6. Don't stop to correct mistakes. Don't worry about them. You're only exploring.

Computer Tip:

Exploratory Writing

If you're having trouble getting started, try darkening the screen and writing out your thoughts without looking at them. Or try online brainstorming through e-mail, Internet chat rooms, or networked computers; toss ideas back and forth with other people to see how they evolve.

2b Focus your writing

Most topics will first come to you as an inviting—sometimes perplexing—array of possibilities. They'll be open-ended, broad, general—unfocussed. To **focus** a project means to become clear about your subject, what you want to do with it, and the point you want to make about it. A reminder: You may not be able to decide everything at once. In fact, if you focus on too much too soon, you may not see important parts of your topic. But before you begin a first draft, try using the following strategies.

1 Narrowing your topic

Most topics discovered in exploratory writing or listed in assignments will be too broad to cover adequately in the space and time available for the assignment. Therefore, focus on one narrow but important part of your topic and the significance of that part.

BROAD TOPICS				NARROW TOPICS
My life on the move: from the city to the country	→	What I learned moving 5 times in 18 years	→	What moving has taught me about good people and good communities
My co-op work terms	→	My co-op work term in China	→	Lessons taught and learned in China
Bicycling	→	Bicycle commuting	→	How to increase bicycle commuting

BROAD TOPICS			NARROW TOPICS
Canada's national parks	→	Tourism in national parks	→ Restrictions on tourism in national parks
Sinclair Ross's short story, "The Painted Door"	→	The door as a theme	→ The door as welcome mat or barrier

2 Writing a statement of purpose

After surveying the requirements of the assignment and exploring your ideas, write a tentative **statement of purpose.** Briefly tell yourself what you want to accomplish in your writing. This purpose may change as your project unfolds, but writing it out early will guide you.

> I want to tell students and, maybe, teachers that teaching English in another country is a worthwhile cross-cultural experience.

This writer's purpose is "to inform"; the writer's roles are those of a reporter and a teacher.

3 Asking questions

Jot down questions based on the reporter's *Who? What? When? Where? Why? How?* Or use the critical thinking questions listed in the "How to Think Critically" box (p. 3). Ask other questions relevant to your topic. Your answers may become the materials for your project.

> Where is English spoken most?
> How many people speak English worldwide?
> Who wants to learn English these days?
> Why do people want to learn English?
> What are the effects of having a global language?
> When is language teaching destructive, not instructive?
> What can we learn from our experiences abroad?

2c | Think about your writing voice

Everything you write speaks with your voice. Whether it is personal or public, informal or formal, opinionated or objective, whether you appear in your writing (as "I") or not, your voice comes through in your words and sentences, in your attitude to your subject, and in your relationship to your readers. This voice is the sound of your personality on paper, and you should write and revise with it in mind. Managing your voice is one of the great challenges and pleasures of writing.

Just as you adapt your speaking voice to suit the occasion, so too will you want to adapt your writing voice. This means adjusting its features in the same way that you adjust the volume, tone, and balance on a sound system. Here are the features of a writer's personality, each of which can be adjusted toward the opposite ends of the spectrum:

FORMALITY	Informal vocabulary	◄───●───►	Formal vocabulary
TONE	Negative attitude	◄───●───►	Positive attitude
BALANCE	Understatement	◄───●───►	Overstatement
APPROACH	Indirectness, irony, sarcasm	◄───●───►	Plain speaking

1 The voice for formal writing

In academic and professional writing, aim at sounding fair, objective, and relatively serious. Your style should generally be direct and to the point. Focus on your subject, and use "I" sparingly. Avoid slang and most contractions. Watch that you don't sound pompous or stuffy, however. Whatever you write should sound like you speaking in a voice that suits the subject and the occasion. (See also 32.)

How to . . .

How to Manage Your Writing Voice

Follow these guidelines as you write and revise.

1. As you write, listen for your voice. It should sound like you, speaking in a way suitable to the occasion, formal or informal (see 32). Writing and speaking are different, of course, but good writing almost always sounds like speech. "Talk" to readers as you write.
2. Choose words true to your knowledge and experience. Don't worry about writing impressively. What will impress is your accuracy, honesty, and command of the facts.
3. Choose words formal or informal enough for the occasion, but also words you can imagine yourself saying. (See 32a and d.)
4. Choose positive, negative, or neutral words that accurately express your feelings but that also express the amount of objectivity appropriate to the occasion. (See 32e.)
5. As you revise, read aloud and listen to your sentences. If necessary, rewrite your sentences so that they emphasize your most important words but have the rhythms of speech. (See 26a–e.)

2 The voice for personal or informal writing

The more personal your subject, the more informal you can be. There is plenty of room for variety in vocabulary, attitude, and expression. Remember the knowledge and interests of your readers though. You have to use a voice that will strike them as appropriate, too.

2d Write a tentative thesis

When you know enough about your subject and purpose, write a tentative statement of the point you want to make—your **thesis**. Usually a sentence but sometimes longer, a thesis in its final form will be the primary controlling idea holding your writing together, the basic message you want your writing to express. It may be any kind of assertion: a factual statement, a generalization, a cause-and-effect statement, an evaluation, a prediction, or a proposal. Consider these thesis statements:

- An informative thesis (an evaluation):

  Bicycles are a safe, practical, economical solution to the problems of rush-hour commuting.

- A personal discovery (cause and effect):

  While teaching English in China, I learned a valuable lesson about cultural and language exchanges.

Whatever its subject or purpose, a thesis is usually the most important statement of a piece of writing. At the beginning of a project, it will help you to decide what to say. In a later, more detailed version based on the

How to Write a Tentative Thesis

Early in a writing project, use the following formula to help you write a tentative thesis. Begin with the words *My point is that ...*, and then follow with a statement that identifies your topic and makes an assertion about it.

My point is that Canadians who plan to teach English abroad should be prepared to be learners as well as teachers, so that this cross-cultural experience will be valuable for everyone.

If you can't write a thesis early in your project because you don't yet know enough about your topic, write it later, after you've learned what you need to know.

How to . . .

information you've gathered, it will act as a reference point to keep you on course as you write a draft. Still later, as you revise your project, you'll compare your thesis to what you've actually written to see whether your point has remained the same or has changed. If it has changed, you'll rewrite it to fit your new discoveries. In this final version, it will help answer the one question readers almost always ask: "So, what's the point?"

1 Guidelines for writing an effective thesis

As your knowledge grows and your thinking changes, rewrite your thesis following these guidelines:

- *Make assertions instead of asking questions.* Write a sentence that makes a point or, if necessary, several sentences, but not a question. If all you can write is a question, you're not ready to write a thesis. Answer your question first. Compare these original and revised statements.

  Original: Are homeschooled students as well educated as students who attend public schools?

  Revised: Standardized test results and post-secondary graduation figures indicate that homeschooled students are as well educated as those who attend public schools.

  [The revised statement is an assertion that answers the question in the original version and identifies the subject matter the writer will cover in the essay.]

- *Write a thesis instead of a purpose statement.* A **thesis statement** focusses on your topic and says something about it. A **purpose statement** focusses on your paper and says something about it rather than your topic. Compare these statements:

  Purpose: In my paper, I intend to compare living in residence to living off campus.

  Thesis: For the student leaving home for the first time, a residence offers convenient room and board as well as plenty of opportunity for socializing.

  [The purpose statement focusses primarily on what the writer intends to do in the paper rather than on the topic of the paper. The thesis statement makes two assertions that the writer will attempt to prove. The thesis gives the paper focus and direction.]

- *Avoid "So?" statements.* A "So?" thesis is a statement that prompts readers to ask, "So? What's the point?" Do more than announce your topic or state a fact. Make a complete assertion about your topic. Compare these thesis statements:

  Original: Many people die each year from accidental poisoning.

  Revised: The many deaths each year from accidental poisoning can be prevented by more detailed consumer education, more extensive employee training in the handling of toxic materials, and stricter regulation of the disposal of toxic waste.

[The first version may state a tragic fact, but it lacks a point. The revised version makes three assertions—or points—about how to prevent this tragedy.]

- *Use accurate and specific words.* Replace broad, vague words with specific words that say precisely what you mean. Compare the original thesis and a revised version:

Original: In Margaret Atwood's *Cat's Eye*, the narrator's husband does many things that drive her crazy.

Revised: The narrator of Margaret Atwood's *Cat's Eye* is driven to leave her husband because of his self-obsession in his painting and his indifference to her need for intimacy.

[In the original version, the words *many things* and *crazy* are broad and vague. Readers don't know what the husband does and whether his wife is merely angry or actually insane. The revised version is both specific and accurate in its language.]

- *Match your thesis and supporting information.* Be sure the facts and other details that you've gathered support your thesis. Revise the thesis and the body of your writing until they fit each other point by point.

- *Write a reader's thesis.* After writing your essay, cut the *My point is that* … formula as you revise, keeping only your actual assertion. The formula helps you focus your subject, but it is too mechanical to leave for your readers. With the formula removed, what remains is a workable thesis to get started with: *Canadians who plan to teach English abroad should be prepared to be learners as well as teachers, so that this cross-cultural experience will be valuable for everyone.*

2 Unwritten thesis statements

In some kinds of writing, the writer decides not to state a thesis directly. In cases where it is unnecessary, impossible, or unwise to come right out and state a point, the writer makes the point implicitly. Readers will still "get the message," because everything supports that unwritten thesis, develops a dominant mood, and fulfills the overall purpose. Note, however, that in most academic writing you're expected to state your thesis clearly and explicitly.

3 Placement of your thesis

Thesis statements usually appear early in writing. If they're clear and especially dramatic, they may come in the first sentence. But more often they appear at the end of an introduction, after the writer prepares the reader for the main point. Placed in the introduction, a thesis guides writers as they write and readers as they read. (See the introduction to student Joe Visser's essay in 4f.)

Sometimes the thesis doesn't appear until the conclusion, revealing an important discovery or summing up what has come before. If you place a thesis at the end of a paper, your introduction must point the way to it, perhaps hinting at its message, describing the problem it solves, or posing the question it answers. (See the conclusion to Heather Sparling's project in 55.)

4 Other thesis-like statements

Thesis statements are usually associated with informative and explanatory essays. But other kinds of writing also depend upon thesis-like statements to give them unity, focus, and direction. Most of the writing you do will make a point of some kind or other.

- Personal narratives frequently contain a **discovery statement** to sum up the meaning or lesson of the experiences that the writer describes. Often this statement appears near the end of the story, at a moment of discovery or revelation.

- Reviews generally contain a **dominant impression statement** that gives the reviewer's overall judgment of the movie, book, product, or other topic under review. This statement may appear at the beginning or the end of the writing.

- **Arguments** and **persuasive writing** contain a **claim** that the writer intends to prove or to demonstrate as plausible. (See 5a.)

- **Reports** contain a **conclusion** that sums up the meaning, significance, or uses of the information in the body of the report. (See 56d.)

$2e$ | Gather the materials for your writing

Gather the information for your project by remembering, reflecting, observing, reading, or discussing. If the project will be brief, you can keep most of your ideas in your head or jot down a list of points to cover. But if your subject is complex or unfamiliar—as is likely in most academic projects—you'll have to take notes (see 51c, d and e). Here are ways you can approach a topic. The types of information you end up using will depend on your purpose and your readers' interests. (See 8b.)

- Gather facts and figures to inform, evaluate, or argue. (See 8b4.)
- Quote or summarize eyewitnesses, experts, or others involved with your subject. Use quotations to add life, variety, and authority to your writing. (Be sure to credit your sources when you borrow words or ideas. See 52d and e.)
- Describe scenes, people, features, traits, processes, and events. (See 8b3.)
- Tell stories or anecdotes. (See 8b1.)

- Give examples (8b5), compare and contrast (8b6), classify (8b9), and define (8b10).
- Explain. Restate unfamiliar ideas in familiar words, give instructions, or add details to expand a subject and make it clear. (See 31b.)
- Create metaphors and similes to dramatize feelings and ideas. (See 31c.)
- Interpret your subject. State its meaning or significance, and describe its implications—where it leads. Draw conclusions that tell what everything adds up to. (See 4f.)

 Computer Tip:

A Template for Taking Notes

Use the columns or tables feature of your word processing program to create a note-taking template. Adjust margins and spacing so you can take several notes on each printed page. As you begin taking notes for a new project, save your file under an appropriate name—for example, "Notes1" or "Notes: Hist107." Be sure to document the sources of your notes (see 51d). When you finish taking notes, print the file and cut the pages into individual slips that you can arrange and rearrange to help you organize your ideas.

chapter

3 Planning and Organizing

3a Refocus your writing

Because writing is a process of discovery, your topic and what you intend to say about it will probably change as you write. New information will lead to new ideas, or perhaps a new thesis; your original purpose may change; you may change your relation to your audience. Therefore, before you begin a first draft—or later, after completing a draft—pause, step back, and reconsider your project in light of all you've learned. Compare what you have so far with the survey you made when you began (see 1c). Answer these questions:

- At this point in your project, what is your exact subject?

- What will your paper contain? Facts, feelings, opinions, personal experiences, or observations? Are they reliable and suitable to the occasion? For most kinds of serious informative writing, personal experience or observation may not be suitable or sufficient. Consider your audience's interests and needs.

- Do you have what you need to fulfill your purpose? If not, should you gather more information or change your purpose?

- Do you have enough to support your point (your thesis) and communicate its message? If not, what do you need? Should you rewrite your thesis to fit what you've found?

3b | Plan a strategy

Experienced writers usually make detailed plans for communicating with readers. You'll write more effectively if you plan a communications strategy that includes the following elements.

1 Organization

Arrange the contents to fulfill your purpose and satisfy readers' needs. You can organize your writing to achieve many aims:

- Tell a story (personal narrative, how-to writing, steps in a process). (See 8b1 and 2.)
- Present causes and effects. (See 8b8.)
- Describe (scenic arrangement, part-by-part analysis). (See 8b3–5.)
- Compare or contrast (point by point or the block method). (See 8b6.)
- Classify. (See 8b9.)
- Emphasize what is most important (organizing from least to most important or most to least). (See 7a.)
- Give the pros and cons of an issue and then, perhaps, state your opinion. (See 4f.)
- Explain a problem and propose a solution.

For additional organizing patterns, see the research projects (55, 56d), the argument (6d), and the short report (63d).

2 Introduction

Think of an opening to attract and focus your readers' interest. (See 8c.) It should identify your topic, suggest your purpose, and, usually, state your thesis.

3 Lead

As you plan an introduction, try to think of an opening line, your **lead**, to start you writing and draw readers into your introduction.

4 Title

Think of an original title that is informative, intriguing, or both, but don't make it a baffling mystery. Come up with a word or phrase that arouses curiosity and, if possible, suggests your topic, even your thesis.

5 Conclusion

Good writing doesn't just stop, nor does it slowly unravel. Bring your writing to a satisfying close that ties up loose ends and leaves readers with the feeling that everything has come together. (See 8d.)

3c | Write an outline, if necessary

For many kinds of writing, especially on difficult or unfamiliar topics, outlines are essential. Especially for informative, technical, and research writing, you use outlines to organize ideas, guide your writing, and later reveal the actual design of various drafts. Depending on your project, you may write three related kinds of outlines, each a version of the others: a sketch, working, and final-draft formal outline. For some papers, a sketch outline is all you'll need; for others, you'll need all three.

1 Sketch outline

A **sketch outline** is just that—an outline of an outline, a list of major points in the order you want to cover them. As you begin organizing, experiment with sketch outlines until you find one that is right for your ideas and purpose.

Canadians who plan to teach English abroad should be prepared to be learners as well as teachers, so that this cross-cultural experience will be valuable for everyone.

I. The pervasiveness of English

  A. English as a global language
  B. English as a conquering language

II. The lessons for teachers

2 Working outline

A **working outline** is developed from a sketch outline and divided into topics and subtopics. The most detailed of the three outlines, it functions as a map to follow as you write. As a kind of rough draft of a rough draft, a good working outline has a place for almost everything:

- An introduction
- The thesis or main idea

How to Organize Your Ideas and Write an Outline

Arrange your notes or other exploratory writing in a suitable order to follow as you write. Look for organizing clues in key words in the sequence of ideas in your thesis, or in the questions readers might ask about your topic. Use one of these strategies:

1. If your exploratory writing doesn't follow a logical sequence, number the topics in the order you'll write about them.
2. Jot down a list of topics you'll cover (a sketch outline).
3. Draw a **flow chart,** a conceptual diagram showing relations and connections. Put topics in boxes arranged in sequence, connected by lines that trace the path of your writing. Use other boxes and lines to insert advice to yourself about details to remember, quotations, facts, transitional statements, and ideas about introductions and conclusions.
4. Create a working outline that includes most of what you want to say:
    - Sort your materials to see whether everything fits under the major headings of a sketch outline. Revise your sketch outline if necessary.
    - Arrange your materials in the order you want to follow as you write your paper. Write a detailed working outline that reflects this order.
    - Look for relationships among ideas and group them as subheadings under headings. Beware of long "shopping lists" of topics.
    - If you can't decide where to put something, put it in two or more places in your outline and trust your writing to show you where it belongs.
    - If an important idea doesn't fit, write a new outline with a place for it. If you're uncertain whether an element is necessary, write a reminder to see whether it belongs after you've written a draft.

How to . . .

- Major topics and subtopics, including facts, key details, illustrations, explanations, and quotations
- Major transitional statements
- A conclusion

You will, no doubt, think of other things to say while drafting, but the clearer and more detailed your plans now, the easier your first draft will be to write.

3 Final-draft formal outline

Your instructor may require you to hand in a **formal outline** with the final draft of some projects. Base the outline on the organization of your finished paper, and prepare it for your readers, to give them an overview of your project. It will probably be longer than a sketch outline but shorter than a working outline, often about a page. Include your thesis statement, list your major topics, and follow the guidelines for formal outlines listed here and illustrated in 3c4.

- Include at least two subheadings under each heading. Because subheadings divide up the ideas in a heading, you must have at least two subheadings under each heading. You can't divide a topic into only one subtopic. If you have, you may have simply restated the original heading.

- Be sure your subheadings are logical. Because subheadings break up or divide ideas in the headings they stand under, they must reflect the ideas and even the language of those broader headings.

- Make all your headings grammatically parallel. If heading *I.* is a complete sentence, headings *II.* and *III.* must also be complete sentences. If *A.* under heading *II.* is a noun phrase, *B.* must also be a noun phrase, and so forth. (See 21.)Use standard outline subdivisions.

  I.
    A.
    B.
      1.
      2.
        a.
        b.
          (1)
          (2)
            (a)
            (b)
  II.

Computer Tip:

An Outline Template

Create an outline template to use whenever you write an outline. Use the correct numerals, letters, and spacing for the standard outline subdivisions (see 3c3). Include enough subheading numbers and letters for a lengthy, detailed outline. Later, as you use the template to outline a project, cut unnecessary subheadings. Save each new outline under an appropriate file name.

4   Sample formal outline

Note how the following example follows the guidelines for formal outlines given above in 3c3. (For a sample formal outline arranged in the format for a typed paper, see 55.)

Thesis statement

Thesis: Canadians who plan to teach English abroad should be prepared to be learners as well as teachers, so that this cross-cultural experience will be valuable for everyone.

Logical sub-divisions: Every heading has two or more sub-heads clearly related to the headings.

I. The pervasiveness of English

   A. English is a global language.

      1. It is a native language for 350 000 people.

      2. It is an official language in many countries.

      3. Many learn English as a foreign language.

   B. English seems to be taking over.

      1. Many languages are dying.

      2. People worry about language "imperialism."

Parallel grammatical form: Co-ordinate headings are grammatically parallel. For example, I. and II. are noun phrases; all the other subdivisions are complete sentences.

      3. But there is no cause for alarm.

II. The lessons to be learned.

   A. We need to be open to other cultures and languages when we go abroad.

   B. Linguistic give-and-take breaks down barriers.

4

Writing, Revising, and Editing

4a | Write a first draft

Like experienced writers, you should expect to write more than one draft of important, complex projects. Each revision provides an opportunity for rethinking, rearranging, and rewording based on the discoveries of the preceding draft. When you write a first draft, let yourself go—you don't have to get everything right the first time. If you have the information you need and have planned your project, writing a first draft should feel almost like doing some freewriting once you get going.

If you're struck by writer's block as you stare at that blank first page, try these tips:

- Reread your plans and start writing with the first thing that comes to mind, as if you were doing some freewriting. The words and ideas will start to flow.

- If you can't begin at the beginning, start in the middle. Come back and write your opening later, after you're warmed up.

- Instead of beginning your project, write a letter to your audience. Tell them what you'd like to write about. Or write a letter to yourself about what you want to say and your frustrations.

- Try visualizing something to do with your subject. Start by writing about what you see.

- Write an advance summary of your essay. "In this essay I have . . . ." Pretend you're finished. Describe what you would like to have written.

4b | Revise to say what you want to say

Novice writers think they're nearly finished when they complete a first draft. For them, revision is correcting or touchup work. Experienced writers, however, know that a single draft rarely says all they want it to say or says it in the best way. The discovery process they began with, exploratory writing, continues as they revise. For them, revision means "reseeing" and then rewriting based on what they've seen. How do you revise? Consider these strategies.

1 Letting your writing cool off

Don't confuse the elation of ending a draft—or your frustrations—with a judgment of its quality. If you can, wait a while before you revise. Your perspective and objectivity will improve.

How to . . .

How to Write a First Draft

1. Write major sections or a complete draft at one sitting. Give yourself time to get warmed up.
2. Whether you write by hand, typewriter, or computer, leave lots of room to revise. Double- or triple-space; leave wide margins.
3. Don't bother editing or correcting. If you're unsure of a word or phrase, write out several versions separated by slashes (/). Put a ✓ in the margin to mark passages to check later.
4. If you have to stop, give yourself a thread to pick up when you return. Start writing a sentence or paragraph you know how to finish and stop in the middle.
5. Use a row of asterisks (*****) to mark easy-to-find places to fill in missing words or information as you revise.

 Computer Tip:

Writing a First Draft

Write revision notes to yourself surrounded by the pound sign (######) or another easy-to-see symbol. Your word processing program may even have a posting feature, enabling you to attach notes to your text. Or you can create a "Notes" file as you draft, split your computer screen, and switch between your draft and your notes. If you're unsure whether to keep something you've written, cut and paste it to the end of your file, where you can reconsider it as you revise.

2 Identifying the status of your draft

Ask yourself, "Is this draft a dress rehearsal, complete except for finishing touches?" "Is it exploratory, still searching for a point or something to hold it together?" "Is it experimental, trying out topics and styles?" Your answers here will help you see what to do next.

3 Changing your focus from distance to close up

Imagine you're a camera with a telephoto lens. Look at the "big picture" first. Decide on the status of major elements such as your thesis, its support, and your overall design. Add information, cut, rearrange, condense, or substitute to make your point and fulfill your purpose. When you're satisfied with the big picture, zoom in and focus on individual paragraphs, sentences, and words. Don't waste time fixing small problems before the big ones.

4 Comparing plans and results

- Compare the draft of your paper with the original plans you made as you first surveyed the situation. (See 1c.) Have you fulfilled the requirements of the assignment or met your readers' needs? Revise accordingly.

- Compare your original thesis with what you've written in your conclusion. Look for "Ah hah!" statements. Often, near the end of a draft, writers write something that makes them say, "Ah hah!" They think they've found a conclusion, but what they may have found is the real point of their paper—a new thesis, different from the original. If you find such a statement, rewrite it as your new thesis, move it to the introduction of your essay, and revise to support it.

- Compare your outline with your draft. If the two are different, which makes more sense of your ideas?

Computer Tip:

Revising with a Computer

(1) Revise on hard copy. Experienced computer users move from "on-screen" text to printed "hard copy" of their writing when they begin revising. Revision is easier when you can lay your projects out before you, page by page, rather than scrolling back and forth through a document on-screen. Revise and reprint as often as necessary.

(2) Save multiple versions. If you make significant changes to a draft but are unsure whether they're the right ones, save several versions of your draft under different file names—for example, "Essay 1a" and "Essay 1b." Compare printed versions and choose the best.

4c | Ask your peers to review your writing

Professional writers have reviewers to help them evaluate their writing. So should you. In many writing classes, peer review is a frequent activity. Outside class, you can get together with friends to share and improve your writing.

1 Reading as a peer reviewer

When you review someone else's writing, you help most when you are honest, tactful, sensitive to your experiences of reading, and aware of the writer's purpose. Your aim is not to tell the writer how to write the way you would, but to help the person say what he or she wants to say. As a reviewer, you may play three roles:

- As a **respondent**, you give the writer feedback about your experience of reading. Tell what you thought and felt as you read, what you understood or didn't, where you followed or lost the writer's thread. This role helps writers see the impact of their writing.

- As an **editor** you show the writer how to fulfill his or her intenions. If asked, you may give advice about subject matter, organization, style, and grammatical matters. Be specific, detailed, and practical.

- As a **critic** you evaluate. The best critics are the most descriptive and factual. They describe what something is or not, what it does or doesn't do, rather than labelling it good or bad. As critic Milton Shulman put it, "You simply have to be able to separate your objective reactions from your subjective reactions." Play the role only when asked by people you know well. Tell them what you see as the status of their writing. Is it a dress rehearsal, nearly finished? Or does it seem exploratory or experimental? Explain your answer.

2 Sharing your writing with peer reviewers

If you share your writing with readers outside class, check with your instructor for a definition of fair editorial assistance. If you know what you want, ask for specific feedback. But don't talk too much, don't explain, and don't apologize for what you've written. You'll colour readers' views and prevent honest responses. As you listen, remember that this is your paper and you have the final say. If their advice makes sense, use it. If it doesn't—keep to your original.

How to Make a Peer Review

Use these questions to help you review others' writing—and your own. Tell reviewers which questions to answer about your writing, or ask them to respond to the ones they think important. First consider the project as a whole.

1. What is the subject? Does it change from one page to the next? If so, which subject is right for this project? (See 2a5 and 2b1.)

2. Is the purpose of the writing autobiographical, informative, persuasive, or critical? Does it change? If so, what purpose is appropriate? (See 1c2 and 2b2.)

3. Given the content, who is the audience for this project? Are readers supposed to respond with sympathy, understanding, evaluation, agreement, or enjoyment? Will this project achieve its purpose? What changes would make it more effective? (See 1c3.)

4. Does this project have a thesis, main idea, or overall mood? Point it out or describe it. Does the writing provide enough detail to illustrate, explain, or support its point? What should be added? (See 2d and 3.)

5. Can you follow this project from start to finish? What reorganization would make its ideas clearer or easier to follow? (See 3b and c.)

When the project seems to say all that is necessary to fulfill its purpose, consider how effectively it will communicate with its intended audience.

6. Does the project have a distinctive writer's voice? What changes would make this voice more emphatic or appropriate? (See 2c.)

7. What does the opening do to attract readers and help them predict the project's subject, purpose, thesis, organization, or style? What changes would make the opening more interesting to readers? (See 8c.)

8. Consider whether each paragraph focusses on a single topic and says all that needs to be said about it. What changes would improve the paragraphs in this project or make them fit more smoothly with preceding or following paragraphs? (See Chapters 7–9.)

9. Are any sentences hard to follow? What additions, cuts, or rearrangements would make them clearer or more emphatic? (See Chapters 25–29.)

10. Are any words inaccurate, vague, abstract, or ambiguous? Are any charged with inappropriate feeling or bias? What are better alternatives? Can any words be cut without loss of meaning or feeling? (See Chapters 30–34.)

11. Does the project appear to be correct in grammar, punctuation, and spelling? Is it appropriately formatted? What changes are necessary? (See Chapters 13–21 and 35–48.)

3 Creating discussion agendas for peer reviewers

The following list will direct you to "How to" lists of questions that will help you read as a peer reviewer or provide your reviewers with questions to answer about your writing.

- General questions for revision and editing. See "How to Make a Peer Review," p. 37.

- Research projects. See "How to Revise and Edit a Research Project," p. 383.

- Argument and persuasion. See "How to Revise and Edit Persuasive Writing," p. 61.

- Writing about literature. See "How to Revise and Edit a Literary Essay," p. 450.

4d | Edit for your readers

1 The aims of editing

When you revise, you're focussing primarily on your ideas and message. When you edit, you're focussing on your readers and rewriting to help them get your message. Editing is a paragraph-by-paragraph, line-by-line process. Consider the edited paragraph about bicycle commuting that follows. The student writer, John Chen, made typical editorial improvements, the kinds you'll make in your writing.

- Improving accuracy and brevity. The writer cut and added words throughout to increase precision and brevity.

- Adding important information and details. He inserted additional information and details to develop and clarify his proposal.

- Adapting the contents for the intended audience. He cut a sentence that might offend readers who are motorists.

- Increasing precision and vividness. He cut vague, general words and substituted descriptive details.

- Rearranging for clarity and emphasis. He moved one passage to appear earlier in the paragraph for emphasis.

What will end commuters' rush-hour nightmare

~~The cycling solution to the problem of commuters' gridlock already~~

solution for all, however.

~~exists in sketch form. What it consists of~~ is not a single ~~one way for~~

~~all plan~~ Commuting problems and needs differ from community to

community, region to region. The best solutions will be local. Each will

specific

have a number of parts, and each part will solve a local travel problem.

All that may be needed is public service announcements to encourage bicycle commuting.
In some communities, few changes are required. In other communities,

belts   *park paths or*

converting abandoned railroad lines to green ~~paths~~ or improving other off-road

bikeways is the right solution. In others, parking might be restricted along

busy streets during peak travel times. ~~The police might begin ticketing~~

~~and the courts prosecuting drivers who harass bicyclists exercising their~~

~~right to the road.~~ In still other ~~communities, where highways have long~~

s,

~~been crumbling, aging~~ highways might be ~~widened to provide wide~~

repaved with widened

dangerous sewer grates might be removed, and high curbs eliminated. Larger,
shoulders, ~~or eliminate high curbs. Clearer~~, more frequent signs would

guide motorists and cyclists alike. In almost every community, *well-placed* bicycle

would   *commuting.*

racks and storage facilities ~~will help~~ encourage more bicycle ~~commuters~~,

~~as will public service announcements to promote bicycle awareness.~~

2 Readability tests

The Flesch test has long been a method for determining how easy
something is to read. But until the word processor came along, this test just
wasn't easy to apply. Now, calculating the number of syllables, words, sentences, and paragraphs is a simple matter of clicking the mouse.

Most grammar checkers now include a version of the Flesch test,
which either names the grade level a passage is written for or measures
readability on a scale of 1 to 80. It works best with writing samples of 100
words and longer, and it instantly calculates important measures like average sentence length.

You can use such calculations as guides for revisions. The paragraph
below, for example, was originally 101 words long with an average of 25.3
words per sentence. (The standard for formal documents is around 15
words per sentence.) At the same time, two separate tests gave low ratings

(20 and 27) and established the Flesch grade level at 16. These indicators call for some editing. Once the writer tightens the sentences and chooses some simpler, shorter words, the average sentence length drops to 17, and the reading ease increases to 54/80, or Grade 10.

> *Let's not measure the value of* ~~The importance of~~ an education ~~should not be measured solely~~ *just* in terms of ~~anyone's~~ career ~~advancement~~. Probably the greatest ~~contribution an~~ *Its* ~~education can offer a person rests in~~ its ability to ~~reinforce~~ *asset* the experience *is more likely* ~~of all human beings~~. Our understanding of everything around us—a ~~magnificent~~ painting, a ~~powerful literary work~~, a ~~heart-rending~~ song, a *novel* ~~clever~~ pun, a ~~persuasive political~~ speech, even a revolution~~ary uprising~~ *rousing* ~~somewhere far away~~—energizes us and ~~makes us ever more aware of our~~ *opens our eyes to the* world. ~~The value of~~ an education, ~~therefore, must be that it~~ ultimately *An* ~~assists~~ us ~~in utilizing~~ our hearts as well as our minds. *helps* *use*

To improve your own readability index, you can do as this writer has done: reduce your dependence on big words, unnecessary modifiers, and lengthy sentences. But don't let statistics control your writing to the point that it no longer sounds natural. Readability tests are not a diagnostic service for writing problems. As with everything, trust yourself to be the ultimate judge.

3 Editing symbols

As you edit, use the following proofreader's symbols to make your final draft easier to prepare.

insᵉrt

addspace

delete letter or ~~word~~

clos e up

transpose

let it stand as written: *stet*

new paragraph: ¶

remove paragraph: no ¶

cAPITALIZE A LETTeR OR word

Lower case a Letter or WORD

move left

move right

Computer Tip:

Editing with a Computer

Use these tips to make your editing easier and more effective.

- *Hard copy.* Edit your writing on a printed—hard—copy of your draft, using the editorial symbols in 4d3. Then transfer these changes to your computer file. Changes on hard copy are easier to see than changes on screen.
- *Find commands.* Use Search and Replace or Find commands to locate words, punctuation, blank lines, or symbols such as asterisks that you inserted at places where you want to add or change things.
- *Spell checkers.* Spell checkers point out a mistake only when the word does not appear in their dictionary. They won't recognize a slip of the typing finger that results in a word like *casual* instead of *causal*, *friend* instead of *fiend*, *our* instead of *out*. They also won't point out confused words when both appear in the dictionary: *there* and *their*, *whether* and *weather*, *by* and *bye*. If you typically confuse words like these, you cannot count on the spell checker to help. At the same time, if your word processor is American, you will need to get used to seeing—and ignoring corrections of—Canadian spellings that are called into question. While spell checkers are a blessing if you aren't the best typist, they are far from perfect proofreaders. Always read the text over slowly and out loud to yourself—and get a second opinion—if you want to catch every spelling mistake.
- *Grammar checkers.* Grammar and style checkers are a little more refined than the basic spell checker, for they flag typically confused words like *principal* and *principle* or *there, they're,* and *their*. No grammar or style checker can read your intentions, appreciate your audience, or understand your context. Be sure a recommended change will actually improve your writing before you accept it. If you are not sure of what the grammar checker is proposing, ignore its suggestions completely.
- *Manuscript form.* For information about the manuscript form of computer-produced papers, see 48a1.

4 How to know when you've finished revising and editing

You may have to write several drafts before you say what you want to say in the way you want to say it. But some writers tinker and tinker, changing and changing, never sure when they've finished. When your changes aren't making your writing noticeably better, you've finished. You've written as well as you can.

4e Prepare and proofread your final draft

As you prepare your final draft, use the appropriate manuscript format. (See 48c for the Modern Language Association format for writing in the humanities and 48d for the American Psychological Association format for writing in the social sciences.)

Proofread your final copy slowly and carefully. When many readers proofread, they miss typos because they're reading as they normally do, for the meaning, or looking for the parts they like.

How to . . .

How to Proofread a Final Draft

Follow these guidelines for systematic proofreading:

1. Read your final draft aloud, slowly pronouncing each word as you've written it. Use a pencil eraser to point at each word, or lay a ruler beneath each line to guide your eyes.
2. Once you spot and correct an error, return to the beginning of the line to begin proofreading anew in case you missed a second error on that line.
3. If you find it hard to concentrate on your words or if you're a poor speller, read your writing backward, looking at each word. Use a dictionary to check any word you don't write frequently. (See 47.)
4. If you use a computer, always proofread on hard copy (the printed version). Errors are harder to detect on a screen.

4f A sample student essay

The writer of the following project was asked to "write a 3- to 5-page essay about a topic many people misunderstand." An **essay** (a frequent assignment) is generally a brief piece of nonfiction on one subject unified by a specific purpose, thesis, or mood. The writer of this essay chose to write about what he had learned from a co-op work experience. For other sample essays, see the research project (55), the persuasive essay (6d), and the literary essay (60g). The writers of these essays have followed the Modern Language Association format for papers in the humanities. (See 48c.)

Joe Visser

Professor M.L. Hurst

English 377R–02

March 1, 2000

International English Teachers: Instructors or Imperialists?

I was sitting in a café in Yunnan Province, Southwestern China, with some English teachers when a Norwegian traveller accused us in almost unaccented English of being "language imperialists." His point was that countless cultures and languages around the world are being threatened by the unprecedented spread of a global language—English—the language of choice in international business, music and entertainment, tourism, technology, diplomacy, and so on. I found this comment ironic coming from someone who had successfully acquired a second language that, among other things, permitted him to communicate with people around the world while travelling. For him it was a catastrophe; for me, it raised more than a few interesting questions.

Is a culture weakened because many of its people also speak English? Why does English, this global language, this *lingua franca*, have even more learners than native speakers? Are we accessories to "language imperialism" when we teach our language abroad? The issues are hardly new, but they are pressing. On the whole, they mean that there are tremendous advantages and disadvantages to having more than one language to work in, something that is worth remembering for Anglophones like me.

The 330 million or so people who speak English as a mother tongue (Bryson 181) live chiefly in those remnants of the British Empire where large numbers of immigrants soon outnumbered

Modern Language Association format (see 48c)

Standard heading information

Centred title

Double spacing throughout

Anecdotal introduction to attract interest

Summary: Here are the issues

Implied thesis: Statement of problem

Topic sentence: People speak English here

Visser 2

the indigenous populations: Canada, the United States, Australia, and New Zealand. The Celtic languages of Ireland, Wales, and Scotland have mostly disappeared in favour of English after centuries of political and economic domination.

According to the British Council, English is an official language (used in government and education) for about 1.6 billion people (qtd. in English Today 23) who also live in places like India and numerous African countries like Kenya, Nigeria, and Liberia. Such countries have several of their own languages, but to prefer one of them for government administration would be to alienate the other language groups. English is thus a neutral language and generally inoffensive. In countries like these, English is essential for those aspiring to any good job. Elsewhere, for example in Scandinavia and the Netherlands—countries that were never colonized or dominated by English-speaking people—many people have an excellent command of English. Such countries have simply recognized the international importance of English and made it a fundamental of their education systems.

Topic sentence: English is official here

Following their lead are the tigers of Asia: influential countries like Japan, China, and Korea, as well as emerging powers like Indonesia and Thailand—even former French colonies like Vietnam and Cambodia. The importance of international trade has made English necessary. English is also increasingly useful for communicating from country to country. Many speakers of English as a second language may never actually talk to a native speaker. Instead they use their new language as a cross-cultural communications tool.

Transition and topic sentence: These countries promote English as a second language

The current popularity of English is due, in large part, to the rise of the United States as an economic superpower and the pervasiveness of American culture as portrayed in music and the movies. The American "empire" has replaced the British colonial one (McCrum 351). People in poorer countries admire the American culture and language because it is glamorized in the media. In the process, "American-ness" is becoming the global culture and language. Here is the essence of the concern about "language imperialism" as voiced by the Norwegian we met in Yunnan. He fears that cultures and languages are being lost forever, obliterated by a globalization of the English language.

Undoubtedly, there is plenty of support for his claim. Linguists are busy recording languages before they disappear, because, "in general, worldwide non-European languages have been disappearing at a rapid rate whenever they come in contact with European ones" (Chaika 59). In North America, it seems that immigrant languages are abandoned in favour of English within a generation or two. The different strains of Gaelic have been all but lost in Ireland, Wales, Scotland, and France despite efforts to save them from extinction (Bryson 45).

On the surface, the problem is that English seems not to be challenged. There is resistance, however. Passive, but effective resistance. People learning English to communicate internationally or cross-culturally do not tend to take the language home with them. Any language will survive "where there are large enough populations so that social activities can be carried on in that language" (Chaika 58). People are not about to speak English at home just because they are fluent in it. Even in countries where such fluency abounds, people prefer to read books and watch television in their own languages (Bryson 187). The power, vibrancy, and vitality of the local non-English-

Parenthetical in-text documentation of borrowed information (see 53)

Reiteration of the problem

Direct quotation: Word-for-word support from secondary source

Contrast transition

Fragment for effect

Visser 4

speaking communities should never be underestimated. They keep to their business, in their own languages. Even an intrusion of anglicisms in their languages will not mean the demise of their forms of speech and culture, any more than the Norman conquest of 1066 caused the death of English.

The Norwegian in the Yunnan café still had a point. When we teach English abroad, the exchange should always be a cross-cultural one. We Canadians may embody the culture and one of the languages of Canada—especially when we teach English. But to retain the potency and richness of cultures we share while interacting with our students and other local people, we must learn not only something of their culture but also something of their language. Our aim should not be to go abroad only to impose our language like conquerors or imperialists, but to go precisely because we want to expand our own understanding of the world—by also learning the languages of other cultures.

Reiteration of main point and transition to conclusion: Lessons for teachers

Conclusion echoes points made earlier and dramatizes the writer's thesis

Learning a foreign language requires work, perseverance, personal sacrifice, and expense. If we are going to teach English abroad, it makes sense to go to a country where the language we want to learn dominates. No one is trying to turn this into an English-speaking world. Admittedly, if a global language did not exist, we would need to invent one, and English appears to be serving that need. We who already speak English are therefore quite fortunate. In admitting as much to our Norwegian fellow traveller, I finally appreciated the importance of having more than one language to learn in this world. "Language imperialism" exists when language teaching is a one-way process. It is when languages and cultures are shared that we make global communication—and global sensitivity—easier than ever.

Summary of general implications and lessons for the writer too

WORKS CITED

Bryson, Bill. <u>The Mother Tongue: English & How It Got That Way</u>.

New York: William Morrow, 1990.

Chaika, Elaine. <u>Language: The Social Mirror</u>. 3rd ed. Boston:

Heinle & Heinle, 1994.

"English 2000." <u>English Today</u> Jan. 1997:23.

McCrum, Robert, William Cran, and Robert MacNeil. <u>The Story of</u>

<u>English</u>. London: Faber & Faber, 1986.

An alphabetical list of sources for this essay (see 54a)

Argument and Persuasion

5 Creating Logical Arguments

In most people's minds, argument involves anger and other heated emotions. But here, and in most academic writing, it is nothing more—and nothing less—than a process of reasoning about an issue whose truth or plausibility is in doubt. In its simplest form, argument consists of an assertion supported by factual information and logic.

Consider, for example, two friends planning a vacation. One says, "If it's real wilderness you want, let's go canoeing in Pukaskwa National Park, north of Superior. RVs and buses can't get there, so there won't be tourists and souvenir stands cluttering the landscape. That's about as close to my definition of wilderness as we're going to get." What we have here is a capsule argument (and note that in its classic definition an argument requires only one participant):

- *Assertion.* "If it's real wilderness you want, let's go canoeing in Pukaskwa National Park."

- *Factual information.* "RVs and buses can't get there, so there won't be tourists and souvenir stands cluttering the landscape."

- *Logic.* A definition of wilderness shows that the factual information supports the assertion.

As you will see in this chapter, this process of reasoning in its more fully developed form is a feature of many kinds of writing you do, in school, on the job, in public. In essays, reports, business writing, and elsewhere, it provides a way to determine the truth, make sound judgments, and decide on the best course of action.

5a | Write arguable claims

1 Identifying the point of an argument

An argument begins when someone makes an assertion—a claim—needing support before others will accept it. Like the thesis of an essay, a **claim** is the point of an argument, what it is all about. Just as the contents of an essay provide support for the thesis, the factual information and logic of an argument provide support for the claim. There are four kinds of claims. Knowing what they assert will help you see how to support them.

- Factual claims. A **factual claim** asserts that something about a subject is true or plausible. For example: *Standardized achievement tests are biased against minorities.* The subject of this claim is *standardized tests.* The claim asserts that these tests are biased. To prove the truth of this claim, an argument would have to provide factual information about standardized test score distributions to show that these scores reveal bias.

- Cause/effect claims. A **cause/effect claim** makes an assertion about the causes of an effect or, conversely, the effects resulting from a cause. For example: *Television advertising targeted to children raises unattainable expectations and promotes their unhappiness.* This claim asserts that a cause, television advertising, has two effects on children. An argument supporting it would have to demonstrate that young viewers of television advertising are affected in these ways.

- Value judgments. A **value judgment** is a claim that evaluates a subject for its usefulness, beauty, desirability, or rightness or wrongness. For example: *The Dynacomp Personal Computer has the internal memory, disk space, and speed to meet the needs of most students.* An argument supporting this evaluation of a computer's usefulness would have to present information about the needs of students and then show that the features of this computer meet those needs.

- Proposals. A **proposal** is a claim advocating a course of action or a policy. It may assert a need for action, the benefits of action, or both. For example: *To protect endangered species, Parks Canada should restrict admission to parks during the spring breeding season.* An argument supporting this proposal would have to show a need for action, including information about threats to endangered species, the benefits of restricted use, and the practicality of limiting admission.

2 Writing a tentative claim

When you have a project requiring an argument, begin by writing a tentative claim that you hope to support. Write it as you would a tentative thesis, using the formula *My point is that. . . .* (See 2d.)

> My point is that immersion is the most effective and economical method for teaching English to nonnative speakers.

As you gather support for your claim, revise the claim to fit that support. Later, as you write the actual argument, remove the formula phrase. Here is the result: *Immersion is the most effective and economical method for teaching English to nonnative speakers.*

3   Converting a tentative claim to an arguable assertion

As you write a claim, make it an arguable assertion, one whose truth or plausibility is in doubt but that can be supported by factual information and logic. Follow these guidelines.

- Avoid subjective assertions of personal preference. An arguable claim is more than an expression of personal preference or taste.

  > Our *so overcrowded that visitor enjoyment and the environment are suffering.*
  > ~~I think our~~ national parks are ~~too crowded.~~

  [The original claim may have meant only that the writer doesn't like all those others visiting national parks. This is why so many writers avoid the "I" point of view. The revision makes a value judgment claim that can be supported by factual information and logic.]

- Avoid easily verifiable statements of fact. Statements that are obviously true or easily shown to be true do not require argument.

  > *have an innate sense of*
  > Even before they attend kindergarten, most children ~~speak in complete~~
  > *grammar that allows them to learn additional languages.*
  > ~~sentences.~~

  [The original claim is obvious. The revision is a cause/effect claim whose truth must be established by an argument showing that children unconsciously understand grammar.]

- Use exact, specific language. You and your audience must know exactly what your words refer to.

  > *devote more funds to protect wildlife and preserve the natural habitat*
  > Environment Canada must ~~act now to save the treasures~~ of our national
  > parks.

  [The meaning of the words *act*, *save*, and *treasures* is imprecise and vague. The revision makes a proposal in which the subject is well focussed and clear.]

5*b* Gather two kinds of support for your claim

1   Collecting evidence

Evidence consists of factual information presented to support a claim. (For methods of research to help you gather evidence, see 49, 50 and 51.) You'll probably collect three kinds.

- **Data** may be facts, statistics, experimental data, research findings, or reliable observation.

- **Examples** are specific instances or illustrations of the point being made.

- As evidence, you may use the **opinion of an expert** based on an examination of the facts unless the opinion is challenged. In that case, the truth must be established independently.

2   Establishing warrants

A **warrant** makes a connection between evidence and a claim, showing how or why the two connect. For an argument to be effective, there must be a link, and it must be clear and logical. Consider this example: Two people are driving down a busy street, late for a concert. As they approach an intersection, the passenger says, "Here, turn right on Highland Avenue. There's less traffic, and it's shorter." In a diagram of this passenger's argument, the evidence is connected to the claim by the warrant, an assumption anyone might make when choosing a route.

| **Evidence:** Highland Avenue is the shorter route and has less traffic. | **Unspoken implicit warrant:** The best route is the shortest one with the least traffic. | **Claim:** Turn right on Highland Avenue. |

In simple arguments like this, the logic is so clear that the warrant need not be explicitly stated. In other arguments, however, the link between evidence and claim may not be clear, or more than one warrant may be at work, and people who have trouble following the line of reasoning will say, "I don't see the connection." Consider another argument:

EVIDENCE

Agricultural, industrial, and household pollutants eventually end up in our waterways—both above and below ground. Those that are not neutralized end up contaminating drinking water supplies, increasing health risks for all living creatures.

CLAIM

Canada needs to establish a national clean water policy that legislates protection of our water resources before they are polluted.

Even if the claim is one you could agree with, it may not be clear why the evidence calls for the action the claim proposes, and so the link must be identified. Here is the way this argument looks written out, with several warrants connecting the evidence to the claim.

> [*Evidence*] Agricultural, industrial, and household pollutants eventually end up in our waterways—both above and below ground. Those that are not neutralized contaminate drinking water supplies for human beings as well as for animals, increasing health risks for all living creatures. [*Partial claim*] Something needs to be done. [*Warrant 1: an ecological principle*] After all, clean, fresh water is vital to the ecosystem; the balance of nature depends on it. [*Warrant 2: the principle of self-interest*] The pleasure we get from the recreational opportunities we take for granted—swimming, boating, fishing—is equally threatened. [*Warrant 3: an economic principle*] Existing anti-pollution and water purification programs notwithstanding, it is extraordinarily expensive, and sometimes impossible, to decontaminate water supplies. [*Warrant 4: a moral principle*] Even more important, we have no existing legal means of assuring our own compliance with the international water quality commitments we have made. [*Complete claim*] For all these reasons, then, it makes sense for Canada to establish a national clean water policy that legislates protection of our water resources from pollution.

Singly and together, these warrants reveal the logic of the argument, showing how evidence and claim are related.

As this example shows, we take warrants from many sources: natural laws (like gravity or photosynthesis), scientific and mathematical formulas (πr^2), theories (evolution), human laws, institutional policies, standards of artistic taste, moral values, principles of human nature, rules of thumb, proverbs ("Waste not, want not"), basic assumptions ("All people are created equal"), and precedent (the assumption that past events may be a guide to future events).

3   Building logic into your argument

As you construct an argument and look for warrants linking evidence to your claim, follow these guidelines.

- *Writing a claim based on evidence.* If you're unsure what to claim about a body of evidence, ask yourself what laws, policies, principles, assumptions, or procedures apply to that evidence. They will act as warrants leading you to a logical claim.

- *Identifying the link between evidence and claim.* If you already have a claim and evidence and need the link to tie the two together, ask what laws, policies, principles, assumptions, or procedures explain the connection. These are your warrants.

- *Stating warrants in an argument.* As you design an argument for an audience, ask whether the connection between evidence and claim is clear and logical. If you have doubts, express your warrant or warrants directly in your argument. If you're certain the relationship is clear, they can remain unstated.

5c | Test your argument; modify it, if necessary

1 Testing an argument

Throughout the process of building an argument, check its accuracy, logic, and strength by applying the following tests. Some will apply only to certain parts or to certain kinds of arguments. But the more tests your argument can pass, the more confident you can be that your reasoning is sound.

- *The truth test.* Is everything supporting your claim true or plausible? Facts must be facts, opinions must be accepted as true, and assumptions must be plausible. If your evidence and warrants are unreliable, you cannot be confident your claim is true.

- *Relevance.* Do your evidence and warrants actually apply to the case you're arguing? Your support must be relevant to your claim. Evidence about tourist overcrowding in a provincial park like Algonquin Park will not be relevant to an argument about overcrowding in national parks.

- *Timeliness.* Do your evidence and warrants represent the most recent or up-to-date information? Statistics about the number of visitors to Terra Nova National Park in the 1960s are not very useful for an argument about overcrowded national parks in the 1990s.

- *Sufficiency.* Do you have enough support to make your claim convincing? Evidence of disoriented grizzlies in Banff is in itself not sufficient to prove a Canada-wide threat to wildlife.

- *Representativeness.* Have you gathered your support from a variety of sources—more than just one or a few? Your support should broadly represent the facts of your case. One writer's comments on overcrowding in national parks will not be as convincing as those of several park officials (past and present), the deputy minister of the environment, and various naturalists.

- *Occam's razor.* Named for a medieval theologian, *Occam's razor* is the principle that the simplest argument is usually the best. What is the simplest case you can make for your claim and still support it convincingly?

- *Utility.* Apply this test to proposal arguments. Is your proposal practical and workable? How confident can you be that it will achieve your aims?

2   Modifying an argument

As you apply the preceding tests, you may find that an argument has fatal flaws of truth or logic. To be reasonable, you'll have to abandon it in favour of a better alternative. But you may find that although an argument is weak, it can be improved. The following modifications will help you clarify or strengthen your case.

- *Citing sources.* If your audience may not accept the truth of your evidence or warrants at face value, citing their sources may improve your credibility. In academic writing especially, cite your sources by name, and document them appropriately. (For MLA citations, see 53; for APA citations, see 56.)

- *Adding qualifiers.* Qualifiers are words that indicate degrees of strength, confidence, or certainty: *may, must, certainly, probably, necessarily, it is unlikely, as far as the evidence goes, it seems, as nearly as I can tell,* and so on. Rarely will you be able to argue with ironclad proof and reach absolute certainty. Add qualifiers to assertions to show the degree of confidence you have in their truth or logic.

         may be
Tourists ~~are~~ responsible for declining wildlife populations in Elk Island

National Park.

[The original version expresses complete confidence in the truth of the assertion; the revision reflects incomplete or inconclusive evidence.]

- *Identifying exceptions.* Rarely will an argument apply to all situations, so explain where it applies and where it doesn't by stating the exceptions. An argument that appears to cover many situations when it really covers only a few will lack credibility.

To protect the natural habitat of our wildlife, Parks Canada should

begin regulating admissions/ at those parks most affected by overcrowding.

[The original seems to apply to all parks without exception. The revision limits the case to parks needing protection; others are exceptions to the claim.]

- *Adding rebuttals.* Most arguments have counterarguments that can be made against them. You will strengthen your case if you summarize opposing arguments and answer them with a rebuttal. Apply the tests in 5c1 to discover their weaknesses and describe what you find.

5d | Identify logical fallacies

You'll improve your ability to test an argument if you can recognize errors in reasoning, known as **logical fallacies.** The following are the most common:

- *Against the person (ad hominem).* Attacking a person rather than rebutting an argument, often by calling people names or pointing fingers: "Susan Hodges is just another tree-loving environmentalist out to take jobs away from hard-working loggers." Attacking a person's character is justified only when self-interest or incapacity may affect the person's ability to argue truthfully or logically.

- *Appeal to the people (ad populum).* Appealing irrelevantly to the attitudes of an audience instead of using logic to do the convincing: "Elect Marla Martin. Born right here in Shelby, she's been a dedicated reformer all her life. You can count on her to finally kill the GST when she gets to Ottawa." Concrete evidence, not an appeal to the audience's likes and dislikes, will support a claim.

- *Bandwagon.* Arguing that one should support a claim because everyone else does. "You need to buy yourself a laptop. You're the only person in residence without one!" The value of a claim does not depend upon how widely it is supported.

- *Begging the question.* Assuming the truth of a statement without proof—circular reasoning: "Surely Margaret Laurence's *Diviners* should be dropped from the curriculum. The novel is bad for growing minds, referring as it does to explicit sexual behaviour." This argument uses as evidence the unproved—"begged"—statement that literature dealing with sexuality is bad for younger readers. Until a statement has been proven true or plausible, it cannot be used to support a claim.

- *Either/or.* Arguing that only two alternatives exist when there may be more—and, often, rejecting one as inappropriate. "Either we pay for a relief mission, or we condemn hundreds of thousands of refugees to death by starvation." In fact, there are many kinds of aid one country can give to another, and sponsoring relief workers is no guarantee that hunger will be alleviated. By the same token, there is no proof that nonintervention will directly lead to starvation. The issues in an argument are rarely only two.

- *Faulty analogy or comparison.* Comparing two subjects that are not really similar in order to force a conclusion. "We must reform schools to make them more like businesses. In business, employees are held accountable for the products they produce. The same should be true of schools, whose product is educated youngsters." Students are more than raw materials to be shaped into products, and so the analogy is false.

- *False cause (post hoc).* The *post hoc* fallacy (which comes from the Latin *post hoc ergo propter hoc,* "after this, therefore because of this") assumes that because one thing precedes another, the first caused the second. But sequence does not always signal a cause/effect relation. "Most people who succeed in business wear suits. If you want to succeed, you'll wear a suit, too." Events may be coincidental, or one may be only an insignificant cause of another.

- *Hasty generalization.* A generalization about a group is hasty when based on insufficient, unrepresentative, or irrelevant evidence. "Walking around campus, I see students with stereo headphones on, students reading comic books or playing computer games, students lying on the grass sunning themselves. Obviously, today's students are illiterates!" A generalization this broad must depend on more evidence than the casual observations of one person.

- *Irrelevant emotional appeals.* Appealing to emotion rather than reason. "Please don't give us a final exam, Professor Moore. It's been a long term. We've worked so hard, and we're tired. Besides, you're such a hard grader." Irrelevant appeals to fear, pleasure, or pity (as in the "sob story") are used to coerce, seduce, or mislead rather than persuade.

- *Irrelevant authorities* (testimonial). Using an opinion that comes from outside that person's area of expertise. Consider ads in which athletes endorse toiletries or celebrities sell automobiles or financial services. This fallacy of irrelevancy attempts to transfer prestige and authority from one area to another.

- *False assumptions (non sequitur).* A "non sequitur," literally "it does not follow," means making false assumptions based on signs or symptoms. "Fred loves to read. I see him in bookstores and the library all the time. With his thick glasses, he even looks like the studious type. He must get straight A's." These traits do not necessarily signal a person's academic success. The support for an argument must lead logically to the claim.

- *Red herring.* Red herring refers to the practice, first recorded in the seventeenth century, of escaped convicts who would drag strong-smelling herring across their trail to disorient bloodhounds that were tracking them. An arguer uses a red herring when he or she purposely introduces irrelevant issues to divert an audience from the real issues. "Of course, you approve of raising admission fees to our national parks. You're wealthy, retired empty-nesters. You have no financial worries." The status of the audience has nothing to do with support for the claim. A red herring is a way of ducking issues.

chapter

6   Arguing Persuasively

If the audience for an argument were all like Mr. Spock, the thoroughly rational Vulcan of *Star Trek* fame, a logical argument would be persuasive by itself. But audiences naturally bring their own interests, understanding, and priorities to an issue, which means that they use more than reason alone to make up their minds. To win your audience's agreement involves adapting an argument to their priorities, building their trust in you, and rousing their desire to accept your position.

6a Adapt your argument to your audience's needs and interests

1 Knowing your audience

Arguments often fail because people make cases that persuade themselves but not necessarily their audiences. As you build an argument, think of your audience and what it will take to persuade them.

- *Audience profile.* Construct a profile of what you know about your audience. (See 1c3.)

- *Audience knowledge.* Decide what your audience knows or believes about your subject. Are your readers opponents or potential allies, skeptical or merely undecided?

- *Interests and priorities.* Identify your audience's interests and priorities. Where your subject is concerned, are your readers interested in fairness, justice, effectiveness, efficiency, health, safety, pleasure, or some other priority? Do they have their own "agenda" about your topic— fears or motives they may be reluctant to acknowledge?

How to . . .

How to Argue Persuasively

1. As you build your argument, construct an audience profile of those you want to persuade. (See 1c3.) Be sure to note their priorities or the "agenda" influencing their response to your case.
2. Write a specific claim tailored to their interests and capacities for action. (See 5a.)
3. From the support for your claim, choose the evidence and warrants most persuasive for this particular audience. Don't distract or alienate them with irrelevant appeals. Arrange your argument for greatest clarity and power. (See 6a3.)
4. Decide what opposing arguments your audience may find appealing. Build a rebuttal of these positions, making concessions or proposing compromise where appropriate.
5. Plan an introduction that will earn your audience's trust. Present your credentials, establish common ground with your audience, create a voice they'll find easy to listen to, and demonstrate your fairness. (See also 8c.)
6. Plan a conclusion that will rouse your audience's feelings in support of your claim. Consider a compelling story that proves your point, a vivid description of something having to do with your subject, or a powerful quotation. (See also 8d.)

2 Building a persuasive argument

As much as possible, make a claim that respects your audience's interests, needs, and capacities. Be clear about what, exactly, you want from them. Avoid claims that may leave them asking, "So? What should be done? By whom? How?" An effective claim answers these questions.

> Because visitor overcrowding
> ~~Overcrowding~~ threatens plant and animal life in our most popular
>
>   parks,
> national ~~parks.~~ environmentally-minded tourists should take their vacations
>
> elsewhere.

[The original claim does not involve the audience. The revision proposes their action in response to the environmental threat.]

As you build your argument, avoid issues that may distract your audience or work against you. For example, if you intended to persuade people concerned with fairness that visits to overcrowded national parks must be reduced, you would probably avoid suggesting a quota system as a solution. This audience may become resentful at the thought of being denied access to a park their tax dollars support.

3 Organizing persuasively

Organize your argument for greatest clarity and logical impact on your readers. You can adapt or combine the following common patterns of argument.

- *Thesis/support.* Putting your claim first, followed by your support, is an effective strategy if your claim is especially strong.

- *Emphatic order.* Generally, the most emphatic arrangement of ideas from a reader's point of view is to place the most important last, the next most important first, the least important in the middle.

- *Warrants first (deductive order).* Begin with the warrants linking your evidence to your claim, follow with the evidence covered by them, and conclude with your claim. This design is effective when readers may not understand how your evidence supports your claim or when they will accept your warrants without question. If they accept these warrants without question and if you can show that your evidence is covered by them, you've made your case.

- *Evidence first (inductive order).* Place your evidence before your claim. Use this pattern when your evidence is dramatic and leads clearly and logically to your claim, or when your audience might reject your claim if you put it first.

- *The pro/con pattern.* Begin by summarizing the arguments for and against a position, and then follow with a claim that chooses between the positions, and conclude by defending your claim as the best choice.

- *The classical argument.* Begin with a summary of the problem and at least a partial statement of the claim. Follow with an argument supporting the claim, a rebuttal answering opponents, and a conclusion that makes new appeals or summarizes your case.

- *The needs/benefits and problem/solution patterns.* First, show that change is necessary. Follow with a claim proposing change or a solution. To conclude, show the benefits of your proposal, explain why it is the best, and, if necessary, explain how to implement it.

- *The narrative pattern.* An argument in story form is most effective when you are offering your own experiences as proof for your claim. But be sure your audience keeps sight of your claim, and remember that anecdotal evidence is the weakest, least convincing kind. If you can add evidence from other sources as you tell your story, you'll strengthen your case.

■ *Concession argument.* This model of argument proposed by psychiatrist Carl Rogers aims at building understanding between opponents when no agreement is currently possible. Begin by summarizing your opponents' position fairly in words they can accept. Then summarize your position in words that won't alienate them while at the same time being fair to your beliefs. Point out key differences dividing you and your opponents as well as the common ground (values, priorities, interests) you share. If possible, conclude by proposing interim activities to foster relations, maintain communication, and lead to eventual resolution.

6b In your introduction, present yourself as trustworthy

An argument may be entirely logical, but if an audience doesn't know or trust the person making it, it will not, by itself, be persuasive. For this reason many persuasions open with what the philosopher Aristotle called *ethos,* an introduction of the person making the case. If you present yourself in the beginning as someone your audience can trust, you'll have an easier time winning people over. Here are ways to build trust in your introduction.

■ *Presenting your credentials.* Present your credentials for writing about your chosen subject. What knowledge, experience, or expertise qualifies you? How can you work these qualifications into your opening without seeming to brag?

■ *Establishing common ground.* If yours is a "friendly persuasion," addressed to people with whom you share values and experiences and who are likely to become your allies, plan an introduction that establishes common ground with them. Identify common experiences or values creating a bond between you. Show that you speak their language; create a voice they will feel comfortable listening to. (See 2c.)

■ *Being fair.* If you're addressing people with whom you have little in common, win their trust by showing fairness to all involved, concern for others instead of yourself, willingness to compromise, and respect for others' opinions.

■ *Building trust in academic audiences.* Most academic writing does not require special efforts to build trust. Your knowledge of your subject, fairness, and documentation of your sources will build academic readers' trust. (For more on introductions, see 8c.)

6c | Conclude with suitable emotional appeals

Most academic writing has little room for emotion; objectivity is the required point of view. But when the occasion permits—in school or out—you can give an argument additional power by including relevant emotional appeals to audience feelings, which Aristotle called *pathos*. Persuasions often conclude with such appeals. Aim to make your position attractive or your opponents' position unattractive. How can you rouse an audience's feelings? Use the following strategies.

- *Anecdotes.* Tell a moving story that illustrates your point.

- *Description.* Describe an emotionally charged scene that helps your audience see things as they were, are, or could be.

- *Quotations.* End with a dramatic quotation, especially a quotation by someone with whom your audience sympathizes.

- *Figurative language.* End with a fresh, vivid metaphor or simile that expresses feeling and understanding. (See 31c.)

How to . . .

How to Revise and Edit Persuasive Writing

Use these questions to guide your revision and editing. Or ask your peers to read your draft with these questions in mind and answer the most important. (For more on revision, see 4b and c.)

1. Does this paper have a clearly identifiable and arguable claim? What revisions would make it clearer or more arguable? (See 5a.)
2. Does the paper support the claim with factual, relevant, timely, representative, and sufficient evidence? Does the paper offer warrants showing the connection between the evidence and claim? What changes will strengthen its argument? (See 5c.)
3. Who is the audience for this paper? Will its argument appeal to their interests and priorities? What changes would strengthen its appeal? (See 6a.)
4. What does this paper do to earn readers' trust? Consider the writer's credentials, voice, establishment of common ground, and fairness. What changes would increase readers' trust? (See 6b.)
5. What does this paper do to make its case emotionally appealing? Look for moving stories, description, and figurative language. Are they relevant to the argument? What changes would improve the appeal of this case? (See 6c.)

Remember to avoid purely emotional appeals. Appealing irrelevantly to your readers' feelings, as in a "sob story" or by name calling, is a logical fallacy. (See 5d.)

6*d* | A sample persuasive essay

The student who wrote the following essay, Heather Sparling, prepared a research project on the same subject: Canada's national parks and the difficulties they face. (See 55.) The challenge was to take her research and present it in an argument attractive to a clearly identifiable audience. In the other paper, she wrote objectively about the threats to wildlife and natural resources within Canada's national park system. Here, she takes a much more personal approach to the same subject—in addressing her appeal to people who share her growing awareness of environmental issues, she is effectively persuasive and convincing. The general subjects of the two papers are similar, but the differing purposes and audiences have led to distinctly different projects. (See 48a for guidelines to the manuscript form for academic writing. See 48c for the Modern Language Association documentation format used in this paper and suitable for post-secondary English classes. See 48d for the American Psychological Association documentation format.)

Protecting Our Parks: Time for Action!
by Heather Sparling

A reminiscence personalizes the problem giving the writer the credibility of an eyewitness	Last summer I had the chance to visit P.E.I. National Park on the Island's north shore. My family and I enjoyed the sunshine and the fresh air, but we were disappointed to learn that we were encroaching on the breeding grounds of the plover, an endangered species of bird which is protected by the park. Only about 2000 breeding pairs remain in North America, with more than a quarter of these in P.E.I. (Sylvester 38). Because of their vulnerability to tides and various predators, the plovers' nesting beaches are cordoned off. But the protected areas are located right beside a popular recreational beach. Although signs and fences warn people away, strollers frequently don't pay attention and boaters often land on what they imagine to be a "deserted" beach. It is not hard to understand why the world plover population is continuing to decline.
MLA in-text citation of sources	
Evidence: Cause/effect	
The writer establishes rapport with the reader by speaking informally	
Emotionally charged language strengthens the contrast	This experience got me quite interested in the role of national parks in protecting wilderness. After the holiday, my mother bought me a coffee-table book as a souvenir. The variety of land revealed in the photographs was incredibly beautiful, but the foreword by David Suzuki was blunt. His dire warning was that Canada's remaining old-growth forests (like the plovers, I guess) are disappearing faster than they can be replaced and that, at the present rate of depletion, they will be gone within a generation!
Note the impact of a well-placed exclamation mark	

The writer's credentials: Research

Evidence: Statistics

Horrified at the prospect, I hit the library. There I learned that Canada has already established 36 national parks protecting around 2% of Canada's land. However, this is nowhere near the 12% that Parks Canada had a mandate to protect by the year 2000. Our national parks are also supposed to represent each of 39 different natural regions in Canada. With only 22 currently represented (Lynch 26), time is running out.

The writer engages the audience with a question/answer format that is not aggressive

The more formal language confirms the writer's seriousness

Evidence: Consequences

So why haven't more parks been established? Understandably, park establishment is a lengthy and difficult process. For each park, a significant, natural area must be identified, then a park area proposed, its feasibility assessed, an agreement negotiated and its establishment finally legislated (Rollins 81). The province containing the park must relinquish the lands to the federal government, often reluctantly, because of the potential for lost development income (Bryan 291). Industry, too, opposes parks in prime resource locations. In fact, even when a park is established, land frequently continues to be exploited to the very borders of the park, adversely affecting animals whose roaming ranges may extend beyond its perimeters.

Citation of authorities with credentials

A warrant (natural law) linking evidence to the claim

Nor is a park necessarily protected just because it is established. As I discovered in P.E.I., humans pose a persistent threat, both as residents and as tourists. Larger communities in parks such as Banff have even greater implications for wildlife. As longtime naturalist and former park warden Sid Marty tells us, with grizzlies as his example, a continuous human presence makes animals alter their normal behaviour either because they lose their natural fear of humans or because roads and people cause them to alter their roaming and range patterns (33).

A rhetorical question

Evidence: Partial solutions

Large numbers of tourists disrupt wildlife in much the same way as urban centres do. Roads, parking lots, campsites, restaurants, hotels and motels are all called for in areas catering to large numbers of people. But what is the point of visiting a national park when the wilderness can't be seen for the tourists?

Citations from authorities

To ease the situation, a number of solutions have been considered or adopted. Parks Canada has a zoning policy that separates highly sensitive areas with strictly controlled human access from urban areas allowing visitor information centres and even commerce (Nelson 710). Park locations that have naturally limited access inevitably restrict visitation (Lynch 33) and require little regulation. When Nature won't help, legislation will. At times, admission charges are levied so that people do not take their right to visit for granted, but the worry here is that such policies discriminate against lower-income families (Bryan 278).

Claim: A call for action by readers (we)

Ultimately, however, it is up to individuals like us to help establish and protect our national parks. Because Parks Canada is required to provide opportunities for public involvement (Eagles 60), we can help by participating whenever such opportunities

Ethos: An emotional appeal to "we," making the writer's suggestions attractive, or at least inoffensive, to the audience

arise. In election years especially, we can remind our government officials that environmental issues make a difference when we are deciding who to vote for. Then again, it is also up to us to set an example when it comes to environmental matters. When we are visiting national parks, all of us need to respect signs and other directives while enjoying the chance to learn about our national treasures. And, finally, we can always do more to make the environment central to our daily lives. We all know we *should* compost and recycle, be more energy conscious and efficient, and support, even promote, companies that are prepared to help Parks Canada achieve its goal to establish eight additional parks in the next ten years ("Mitchell"). Let's do it!

Conclusion: A lesson to be learned

As my encounter with the plovers taught me, all of us need to alter our way of thinking to have an inclusive view of nature. So far, we have been looking at life from the top down, with us at the top. Actions affecting an individual life form may have far-reaching implications that we don't currently understand. Our mindset should not be to determine the minimum amount of space to be set aside for national parks, but to be ready, in the words of environmentalist John Theberge (149), "to consider the whole environment as park and to allow, on a case-by-case basis, only enclaves of disturbed areas within it." Now that might be very unsettling to the tourists who rejoice in what, by contrast to their urban lives, is the peace and quiet afforded by our national parks. To the plovers and other endangered species, as we all must soon appreciate, it could be the only prospect for survival.

Citation from an authority

Ethos: Us vs. them
Connection to the introduction

WORKS CITED

MLA documentation of the writer's sources

Bryan, Rorke. <u>Much Is Taken, Much Remains: Canadian Issues in Environmental Conservation</u>. North Scituate, Mass: Duxbury Press, 1973.

Dearden, Philip, and Rick Rollins, eds. <u>Parks and Protected Areas in Canada: Planning and Management</u>. Toronto: Oxford UP, 1993.

Eagles, Paul F.J. "Parks Legislation in Canada." Dearden and Rollins 57–74.

Lynch, Wayne. "Aulavik." <u>Canadian Geographic</u> Mar.–Apr. 1995: 24–33.

Marty, Sid. "Banff vs. the Bears." <u>Canadian Geographic</u> Jan.–Feb. 1997: 28–39.

Internet source

"Mitchell Announces Major Contribution to Environmental Agenda." *Parks Canada Press Release* 31 Mar. 1999. Parks Canada. 19 Sept. 1999 <http://www.parkscanada.pch.gc.ca/library/news-releases/english/nr1_e.htm>

Nelson, J.G. "Canada's Wildlands." <u>In the Canadian National Parks: Today and Tomorrow: Conference II: 10 Years Later</u> Vol. 2. Ed. J.G. Nelson et al. North Scituate, Mass: Duxbury Press, 1973. 707–23.

Rollins, Rick. "Managing the National Parks." Dearden and Rollins 75–96.

Suzuki, David. Preface. <u>The Last Wilderness: Images of the Canadian Wild</u>. By The Canadian Nature Federation and Freeman Patterson. Toronto: Key Porter Books, 1990.

Sylvester, John. "Privacy Please!" <u>Canadian Geographic</u> Apr.–May 1991: 37–40.

Theberge, John B. "Ecology, Conservation, and Protected Areas in Canada." Dearden and Rollins 137–53.

Paragraphing

Ancient Greek writers drew a mark, called a *parágraphos,* to divide manuscripts into distinct and manageable parts. In the same way, modern **paragraphs** signal changes of subject or purpose and thus make writing and reading easier. Your paragraphs will contribute powerfully to the success of your writing when they unify ideas, develop subjects effectively, and flow coherently from one to the next.

chapter

7 Unifying Your Paragraphs

A good paragraph is like any piece of good writing. It has a purpose, focusses on a single topic, and has an overall design. In a word, it is unified. To create unified paragraphs, you'll need to begin by developing a focus point.

7a Write topic sentences to focus your paragraphs

A **topic sentence** resembles the thesis statement of an essay. It announces a topic or makes a point. Just as everything in an essay supports its thesis, everything in a paragraph supports its topic sentence. Consider this example:

Topic sentence

Sir John Falstaff, a *bon vivant* who is one of Shakespeare's best-loved characters, is first of all a prodigious drinker. This "huge bombard of sack" handily outdrinks everyone in the four plays in which he figures. Interestingly, no amount of drink seems to dull his wits. Shakespeare retains the sympathy of the audience by presenting Falstaff as perennially cheerful—and never as a falling-down drunk. Unfailing gaiety and good humour—even when being insulted, caught in knavery and thievery, or cruelly rejected—these are the qualities that have endeared Falstaff to audiences for ages. Yet, Shakespeare never lets us forget that Falstaff is loaded with faults. He is corrupt; he is a braggart, a liar and a cheat; he is excessive in every appetite; he is a coward on the battlefield. In short, that he is cheerfully and unabashedly human in every respect may well be the secret of Falstaff's universal and ongoing appeal to audiences of all ages.

Falstaff's good points

Falstaff's bad points

A concluding assessment

Topic sentences may appear early in a paragraph, as in the preceding example, or later, to sum up preceding information, as in the following:

Historical context

Until the middle of the twentieth century, everyone simply assumed that there were more economic resources on the Earth than we could ever hope to use up. From cutting trees to killing wildlife to mining minerals to burning fossil fuels, we have only recently begun to recognize the consequences of our having exploited the world around us. Now it is the global syndromes of vanishing rain forests and depleted ozone, recurring famines and spreading pollution that remind us how shortsighted we may have been. Economically, however, it still seems impossible to adopt a system that reflects the reality of "spaceship Earth." Our televisions keep at us to consume more and more, so we suspect the motives of those whose dire predictions would curtail expansion. We especially hate to reduce our fishing and lumber quotas. (Despite the cod moratorium, even our governments preach growth rather than restraint.) Sooner or later, though, we will recognize two things: we can no longer afford to live so indulgently, and the word "afford" refers to "time" and not "money."

Examples of exploitation

Reaction

A topic sentence emphasizing the urgency of action

How to . . .

How to Write Topic Sentences

Follow these tips to write effective topic sentences.

1. As you organize your writing, consider items in outline headings or in lists you have made as potential topic sentences. Compose headings that you can later expand into topic sentences.
2. As you write a first draft and indent for new paragraphs, think of sentences to announce your topics. Where will you put them for best effect? At the beginning, to launch your paragraph? Or at the end, as a destination to aim for?
3. As you revise, decide whether supporting sentences support your topic sentences. If not, decide whether to cut those that don't belong, move them to another paragraph, write new topic sentences, or reorganize to create new paragraphs.
4. As you edit, look for topic sentences in your writing. They should appear regularly, but sometimes a topic sentence in one paragraph will announce a topic for several paragraphs. Sometimes you can imply your point rather than state it explicitly.
5. Reread your writing from your readers' point of view. If you suspect they might ask, "What's the point here?" add topic sentences to answer their question.

One key to successful paragraph design is the placement of the topic sentence. Organize your paragraphs to follow from the topic sentence or lead to it, as in the preceding examples. Another key is emphasis. If you put the most important information early in your paragraph, this is **dramatic order**. If you save it for later, it is called **climactic order.** In the following example, the writer opens with a topic sentence but saves her most important example for the end of her paragraph.

Topic sentence	Neat people are especially vicious with mail. They never go through their mail unless they are standing directly over a trash can. If the trash can is beside the mailbox, even better. All ads,
Clarifying description	catalogs, pleas for charitable contributions, church bulletins and money-saving coupons go straight in the trash can without being opened. All letters from home, postcards from Europe,
Supporting examples	bills and paycheques are opened, immediately responded to, then dropped in the trash can. Neat people keep their receipts only for tax purposes. That's it. No sentimental salvaging of
Most important example	birthday cards or the last letter a dying relative ever wrote. Into the trash it goes.

(Suzanne Britt, "Neat People vs. Sloppy People," from *Show and Tell*)

7b | Adjust paragraph length to express your purpose and suit your audience

1 Paragraph length, purpose, and audience

Paragraphs may be almost any length. Some are necessarily short to set them off or signal changes in topic or purpose: speeches in a dialogue, a paragraph to set off a thesis, transition statements, or emphatic paragraphs. These may be only a sentence or two—even less. Paragraphs that present and develop ideas, such as introductions, body paragraphs, or conclusions, may be much longer.

In any case, you should write paragraphs for your readers' eyes as well as their brains. Too many short paragraphs will make your writing look choppy and disconnected, even when it isn't. Too many long paragraphs may make readers think, "I can't read this; it's too difficult." Paragraphs should look readable.

2 Paragraph length and contents

Paragraphs must not only *look* readable but *be* readable, fully expressing their topic and purpose. Adjusting paragraph length involves more

Computer Tip:

Editing for Paragraph Unity and Length

If you're unsure whether a passage belongs in a particular paragraph, select it, cut it, and paste it temporarily at the end of your paper. Read the paragraph without it. If it belongs, move it back. Otherwise, move it to a suitable spot in another paragraph or delete it.

How to . . .

How to Adjust Paragraph Length

Follow these guidelines to write paragraphs of appropriate length.

1. To divide a paragraph that seems too long, look for break points at shifts in time or place, between subtopics, or before sentences that signal logical shifts.
2. In double-spaced typescript, common in academic writing, break for a new paragraph one to three times per page—every 100–200 words or so. Break more often to increase the pace of your writing or for special purpose paragraphs.
3. In single-spaced typescript, common in business writing, make your paragraphs four to ten lines long. Break more frequently if your information is complex or if your readers may only be skimming your writing for its main ideas.
4. If you are writing in columns, as in technical writing and journalism, break up long paragraphs to make them look readable, usually one to three sentences in length.
5. If you are writing by hand, divide once or twice per page.

than combining short paragraphs and dividing up long ones. As you adjust length, be sure each paragraph connects to the preceding one, that it clearly announces its topic or purpose, and that it is complete. A paragraph may contain six kinds of sentences:

- *Transitional* sentences linking one paragraph to another

- *Introductory* sentences

- *Topic* sentences

- *Supporting* sentences that present a topic or prove a point

- *Clarifying* sentences that explain or restate

- *Concluding* sentences

As you adjust paragraph length, check to see that each paragraph has all the sentences it needs. Not every paragraph contains every kind of sentence, and individual sentences may perform more than one function. But each paragraph has to have the sentences necessary to do its job.

chapter

8 Developing Topics and Paragraphs

8*a* Include details to support your topic sentence

"God is in the details," said architect Mies van der Rohe. As in a well-designed building, the power of a well-designed paragraph lies in its details. If you're writing to readers familiar with your topic, you may not need to say much. However, in most writing, especially in academic writing, readers want enough detail to understand fully the main idea of your topic sentence. That means writing well-developed paragraphs.

How to . . .

How to Write Well-developed Paragraphs

Follow these tips to write well-developed paragraphs.

1. Do exploratory writing or take notes before beginning a first draft. Give yourself material to put in your paragraphs before you write them.

2. As you revise, check that the points in your topic sentences are fully supported by the body of your paragraphs. Add details to prove your points or express your ideas.

3. Read your paragraphs from your readers' viewpoint. Do they answer readers' questions and satisfy their interest in your topic? Add details where necessary.

8b Choose appropriate methods of paragraph development to present a topic

The methods of paragraph development illustrated in this section will enable you to communicate information, experiences, feelings, ideas, and opinions. Sometimes, when an idea needs several kinds of support, you'll combine more than one method in a paragraph, as in the paragraph on wasting resources (see 7a), in which the writer combines narration, description, and example. Sometimes, when subjects are complex or your readers' need for information is great, you may extend one method of development over several paragraphs, all unified by one topic sentence. You may even use one method throughout an entire piece of writing, unified by a thesis statement.

The method you choose will depend on your purpose and your readers' needs. Though each method can serve a variety of purposes, writers customarily use specific methods for specific ends, as the following examples indicate.

1 Narration

Narration organizes events in chronological order to tell a story. Use it to illustrate a point in explanatory writing or argument and to write about personal experience. As in the following example, narrative paragraphs almost always include description to make actions clear and vivid.

Context	During the Great Depression, need sometimes drove people to do foolish things. I'll never forget Grandma's story of a haggard-looking fellow with two sad-eyed kids, who came into
Event 1: Arrival and reaction	Elrose, Saskatchewan, one November. "I'd do most anything," he said, and the sight of the two little ones hanging on to his coat made just about everybody feel bad.
Dramatic description	Now the only thing the stranger had to his name was this dark brown coat, but no one would buy it because that was like stealing from the fellow. Some of the neighbours tried to give the man a couple of dollars "for the children," but he wouldn't accept charity. Suddenly, someone had an idea: the man could
Event 2: The solution	earn the money by taking them up on a dare. Legend had it that anyone hammering a stake into a grave at the local cemetery would never walk out alive. You just had to do the job at midnight—and collect $5 the next morning. What's the power of legend when your little children are starving?
	It seemed harmless enough. Leaving his children with the people at the general store, the man headed off with the stake and a rusty hatchet. He didn't notice the fog, and he didn't care about the damp. Once at the cemetery, he was indiscriminate.

Event 3: The
climax

In no time at all, he found a good spot and bashed at the stake until it was firm in the ground. Then he turned to go—and couldn't move.

Event 4: The
next day

The townspeople found him there the next morning, stone dead on somebody's grave. He had driven the stake through his own billowing coat and had died of fright.

2   Process

Like narrative paragraphs, **process** paragraphs are organized in chronological order. But they emphasize the sequence of events as much as they emphasize the events themselves. Process paragraphs are used frequently to explain steps or stages in informative and how-to writing.

Step 1

Step 2

Step 3

Step 4

Step 5

If you want to write a research paper, you have to invest some time and effort. First, you must decide on a topic, perhaps by discussing the assignment with the teacher or with classmates so that you understand what research to undertake. Then you do this research, either by going to the library or by reviewing class notes and course textbooks. The third step calls for you to classify this information into topics and subtopics in a detailed outline for the paper. Once you have your outline, you can confidently move on to the next, and possibly longest, stage: writing and reviewing and revising. Then, after you have proofread your final draft, the process is over, and you can confidently turn your work in for grading.

3   Description

Description adds sensory details to personal and informative writing—whenever it is important for writers to "see" a subject. Descriptive paragraphs are usually organized in spatial order: left to right, front to back, top to bottom, and so on. The following paragraph is organized to zoom in on the soup pot.

Topic sentence

Visual details

Sensory details

Summary

Nobody could make soup like Grandmaman, probably because no one could ever assemble the ingredients so casually yet so confidently. Her stock pot was always full of leftovers from Sunday dinner or Tuesday lunch: little bits of chicken, a meatball or two, celery leaves, a clove-studded onion. These she would supplement with fragrant dried thyme and laurel leaves from her cupboard and mysterious vegetable-flavoured waters collected in plastic margarine tubs and yogurt containers hidden in the back of her fridge. Nothing was ever wasted in Grandmaman's kitchen. It all went into the soup pot, whether it was a tablespoon or a cup, whether it could be recognized or not.

4 Facts and figures

Factual paragraphs present **facts** or **statistical information** in some clear pattern to provide information or prove a point in an argument. The following paragraph is organized to consider the historical background of champagne and its meaning for the present.

Historical facts

Facts about production

Scientific facts

Wines have been produced in the Champagne district of France since before the Roman occupation. However, a monk named Dom Perignon is credited with bringing world-wide fame to the district in the 1660s by devising methods for producing the delightful celebratory wine known as champagne. It was Dom Perignon who developed methods for inducing and controlling the second fermentation that sometimes occurred naturally in the wine bottle during warm weather. The resulting carbon dioxide trapped in the bottle gives "bubbly" its characteristic effervescence. Generations of champagne makers refined these techniques until methods were standardized in the 1880s. Now, only the product bottled in the Champagne district and made from selected grapes grown there is true champagne.

5 Examples

An **example** uses individual members of a group (people, events, conditions, objects, ideas, and so on) to explain or illustrate the whole group. Explanatory writing and argument frequently depend on examples. Occasionally, they are introduced by signal phrases: *for example, for instance,* or *such as.*

Examples

Topic sentence: Three is significant

Examples

Signal phrase

More examples

When the stock market undergoes a "correction" and a freak snowstorm shuts down the airport, there will always be a pessimist waiting for something else to go wrong. But this gloom-and-doomer is not alone—most people, even those who are decidedly unsuperstitious, agree that things good and bad will happen in threes.

It's common knowledge that if a fairy godmother pops out of the bushes when you're jogging in the park, you get three wishes automatically. If it's Rumplestiltskin instead, you at least have three guesses. Folklore is packed with such examples. Everywhere you look, the good, the bad, and the ugly manifest themselves as three bears or three mice or three mean old step-siblings.

6 Comparison/Contrast

Comparison/contrast presents subjects according to similarities and differences in order to explain a subject or make an evaluation. Comparison/contrast paragraphs may be organized in two ways. In **block comparison,**

as in the first paragraph that follows, one subject is presented and then the other, subject A and then subject B. In **point-by-point comparison,** as in the second paragraph, the comparison moves back and forth, first to one point of comparison, then to a second, and so on, $A_1 B_1$, then $A_2 B_2$, and $A_3 B_3$.

Context | Speaking and writing are two quite different ways of communicating. The contrast has a lot to do with the feedback the speaker or writer expects. A conversation involves two people, both of whom
Communication in conversation | alternate as speakers and listeners. Both are constantly paying attention to non-verbal clues (facial expressions, gestures, and other body language) in addition to what the other is saying. If there is some confusion about the message, it is easy enough for one person
Communication in print | to ask the other to explain what was meant. Writing is much more one-sided: the reader is far away, most often utterly unknown, and the writer has no way of knowing how that person is going to respond or even how much of the message is understood. The words alone must convey all the meaning in writing, for there is no body language to help.

Point-by-point comparison | Because of its personal nature, a conversation is relatively informal. So, good grammar is less important than it is in writing,
Different conventions | where there are many conventions, like accurate spelling, sensible punctuation and complete sentences. Nobody worries about grammar in a conversation, where everyday colloquial expres-
Different dictions | sions are natural and appropriate. Diction is much more important for the writer, who does not want to alienate the reader by seeming overly friendly (with slang) or overly distant (with $50 words). The choice of language should never be haphazard or accidental for a writer, but a speaker can be forgiven for making the
Different responses | odd mistake, if the listener even notices. Mistakes on paper are so much more permanent and, therefore, noticeable. Because of all these differences, there is no guarantee that people who speak confidently and well can write with the same efficiency.

7 Analogy

As a form of comparison, **analogy** uses something simple or familiar to explain something complex or unfamiliar. To help explain the importance of being specific, the following paragraph compares writing and selling.

Topic sentence | Specificity is essential if you want to convince your reader that you know what you are talking about. Comparing writing and sell-
Writing = selling | ing provides a useful analogy. At the store, a customer gains confidence when the salespeople clearly know their products intimately
Readers = customers | and answer questions with concrete details and facts. The customer has no such confidence, however, in the salesclerk who is constantly forced to admit "Gee, I'm not sure about that. I'll have to

Explanation of implications

check." The customer's response is predictable: a frustrated determination to go elsewhere for satisfaction. There is a lesson here. As a writer, you, too, are responsible for making sales. To ensure your success, you must be not only well-informed but also prepared to share your specialized knowledge with your customer (your reader). Whenever possible, then, use concrete details and specific descriptions to add content, colour, and life to what you are writing.

8   Cause/effect

Cause/effect paragraphs divide events into causes and effects in order to explain relationships within a process. They may be organized in two ways: *causes → effects*, as in the following example, or *effects → causes*. Note how the writer arranges causes from most obvious to most serious.

Topic sentence

Cause/effect 1

Cause/effect 2

Cause/effect 3

Summary

Few of us enjoy the challenges of driving in winter weather. Everyone is apprehensive because a number of conditions make driving dangerous. Freezing rain turns roads into ice rinks where there is virtually no traction. If a driver has to stop suddenly, the vehicle can fishtail out of control. Snow-covered roads are no less slippery. Falling snow, of course, creates another problem: reduced visibility. The windshield wipers clear only a small fanlike space for a driver to peer through, and if the car ever frosts over on the inside, the driver has to scrape with one hand while clutching the steering wheel with the other. It is even harder for a driver to see oncoming traffic during blizzards or whiteouts. Strong winds blow the snow not just at the windshield but into drifts across the roadway. A vehicle that smacks into one of these can easily end up in a snow bank or ditch. No matter how much we reduce our speed and increase our caution, winter driving is just something we have to get used to, like it or not.

9   Classification

Classification divides subjects into classes according to characteristics shared by the members of each class. Classification paragraphs are often used in informative and evaluative writing to show how things differ or fit together. They may include examples or description to distinguish the members of one class from another.

Topic sentence

Class one

Class two

There are essentially three kinds of students, all of which may be found in any classroom. The first kind is the bookworm, characterized by a serious expression, ink-stained fingers, an armload of books and a persistent refusal to participate in any activity not involving research. At the opposite end of the scale is the second kind: the social butterfly. This student rarely carries anything but an activities calendar for recording the dates of parties to attend

Class three

and the names of people to go out with. For the social butterfly, the classroom is merely a place to make new friends. Most students, of course, belong to the third category, somewhere in between the extremes of the first two. These people are appropriately studious in class and for a few hours every night, but they also know how to relax by going to an occasional movie or party. Awed by the bookworm and dazzled by the butterfly, they are the ones who are always the easiest for teachers to deal with.

10 Definition

In explanatory writing and argument, **definitions** explain what something is. There are several methods of definition.

- **Formal definition** puts something into a class of related items and then distinguishes it from other words in that class.

- **Functional definition** tells how something works.

- **Etymology** traces the history of a term to its origins.

- **Giving synonym**s compares words with similar or related meanings.

- **Providing examples** defines by illustrating the term.

Definition by origin, by synonym

Functional definition

Our term "jargon" was borrowed from the ancient French word "jargoun," which meant "the twittering of birds," then "gibberish," or "unintelligible language." None of these old definitions is particularly positive, and the twentieth century hasn't helped elevate the word. Its present meaning, occupational dialect, refers to the specialized language professionals use, but we call it "jargon" when we *don't* understand what they are saying.

Examples

In a world packed with "multi-tiered RESP financing," "corporate rightsizing strategies," and "autoexec.bat," we can be forgiven for sometimes feeling quite overwhelmed. For people in the know, however, such language is clear and meaningful. We call it jargon; for them, it saves precious time. Ground water experts, for example, can talk together about "draw-down times" and "cones of influence" for "extraction wells" and be understood. Technical terminology saves a thousand words of explanation—for those in the same field.

Formal definition

But the same language that is so useful to the experts is often just gibberish to the rest of us.

8c Write introductions that attract the reader's interest

Professional writers frequently spend a lot of time on openings. They know that a good lead will take them in the right direction as they begin a draft. They also know they have to arouse interest within the first two or three sentences or risk losing their readers. And they know that effective introductions are sometimes challenging to write because these introductions must do several things at once:

- Identify the writer's topic and, often, the purpose of the writing
- Stimulate the reader's interest
- Create the writer's personality and style
- State the writer's thesis or main idea
- Provide a bridge to carry readers into the body of the writing

The best introductions usually open with something dramatic or intriguing. After that, work-related writing gets down to business. Personal or informative writing, however, often begins more imaginatively and in more detail. Choose the introductory strategy right for the topic and the occasion.

1   Strategies for introductions

The following strategies for introductions are appropriate in many kinds of writing. Choose the one that fits your topic, purpose, and audience expectations.

- Begin with a **dramatic quotation**. Be sure to tell who is speaking and, if necessary, provide explanation to help readers understand how the quotation introduces your topic. (See 4f, the sample essay, or see the sample paragraph in 9a.)

- Open with **dramatic details** or **description**. (See 6d, the sample persuasive essay, or see the sample paragraph in 9b.)

- Open at a **dramatic point** in the middle of things (also referred to as *in medias res*), then flash back to the beginning. (See the introduction to autobiographical and narrative writing in 8c2.)

- Write a **strong statement**: a warning, something that at first seems puzzling or contradictory. (See the introduction to exploratory and informative writing in 8c2.)

- Pose a **problem** to solve or **question** to answer. (See 55, the sample MLA research project, and 63d, the sample report.)

- Open with an **analogy** or **comparison** that describes or illustrates your topic. (See the introductory paragraph in 8b7.)

- Tell an **anecdote**—a brief story—that illustrates your point. Here is an example:

    He was one of the greatest scientists the world has ever known, yet if I had to convey the essence of Albert Einstein in a single word, I would choose *simplicity*. Perhaps an anecdote will help. Once, caught in a downpour, he took off his hat and held it under his coat. Asked why, he explained, with admirable logic, that the rain would damage the hat, but his hair would be none the worse for its wetting. This knack for going instinctively to the heart of the matter was the secret of his major scientific discoveries—this and his extraordinary feeling for beauty.

(Banesh Hoffman, from "Unforgettable Albert Einstein")

2   Introductions, purpose, and audience

Although the introduction guidelines in 8c are suitable for almost any kind of writing, the beginnings of certain kinds of writing usually do certain specific things for their readers.

- **Autobiographical and narrative writing.** Good stories usually begin at a point when something dramatic or important is about to happen. The introduction creates tension or expectation about the events soon to occur. Consider this example:

I think it's important to keep things like this to help you remember how he really was. The stories keep getting told—from this one to that one and back again—but after a while they begin to sound like somebody else. Because nobody knew him very well—except Connie maybe—and I don't claim ever to have talked to him but that once, but I've kept these because they were a part of him, and there doesn't seem to be anything else except the stories.

He only came to the library once. It was after Lydia—about a year, I guess—and before Ophelia started going to school....

(Ken Ledbetter, from *Too Many Blackbirds*)

Readers are keen to find out what souvenirs the narrator has kept of the man whose story she is about to tell.

- **Informative and explanatory writing.** Good introductions to informative and explanatory writing do whatever is necessary to help readers understand the information about to follow. They may put the topic in some larger context, describe the background, define key terms, identify the writer's point of view, present a problem to be solved or questions to be answered, state the purpose of the writing, or review what is already known about the topic. Consider this opening to a formal research report:

Everyone agrees that language is our primary tool, that we achieve our humanity to the degree that we are able to bring form and order to our experiences through the skillful use of language. People who cannot read or write are disabled no matter what area of activity they enter. People who cannot read and write well cannot really think at the level of abstraction that a free and complex society requires of them.

During the past few years, a good deal of public discussion has focussed on the supposition that students in Canadian universities don't write as well as they used to or as well as they should. Universities have tested the language skills of their students and, in some instances, have initiated programs to help those whose skills are considered inadequate. Most universities that have given such tests claim that a high number of students are weak in this area.

In Ontario, the schools have been criticized for failing to provide the degree of education in language that is expected of them. They have replied that, given the increase in the numbers of students, they are doing the best job they can. They, too, are concerned, and they have openly shared this concern with college and university educators across the province. In a series of conferences and seminars, all of these people agreed that a collective effort was needed if the level of language skills on students was to be materially improved. The first step in this collective effort is the following report, representing two days of collaboration on the part of many people in an attempt to determine 1) what level of writing skills constitutes competence for university study, and 2) what steps must be taken to make sure that this level of competence is achieved.

(adapted from "Preface," Writing Skills and the University Student)

In three brief paragraphs, an editorial committee puts the study in a philosophical and historical context, announces the topic and purpose, and poses the question that the report will try to answer. Readers are well-prepared for the information in the report.

- **Argumentative and persuasive writing.** Frequently, writers who intend to change readers' thinking or behaviour begin by establishing a bond with their readers, earning their trust, and presenting their creddentials for making the case that they do. (For persuasive introductions, see 6b.)

8d | Write conclusions that create a feeling of completeness

Conclusions are more than stopping places. For writers and readers alike, they create a sense of unity and completeness. They are not only your final words but your final opportunity to fulfill your purpose for your writing. Consider how this conclusion to an essay describing the scientific approach to innovation leads in the final sentence to a restatement of the writer's main point.

After three years of planning, the advertisers had a new product they knew people would like. They had a name for the product—descriptive, if not inspired—and they were ready for a national introduction. At enormous cost, they retrained their cooks, equipped all their outlets with the necessary utensils and launched their advertising campaign coast to coast. They never once questioned their investment. Because they had used statistical techniques at each step of the product development, they already had a pretty reliable sense of how successful the new pizza would be. How could it have turned out otherwise? In their three years of research and experiment, they had put science at the service of junk food.

Margin notes:
End of story (history)

Analysis

Rhetorical question

Restatement of thesis

How to . . .

How to Revise Introductions and Conclusions

Follow these guidelines for effective introductions.

1. Avoid repeating your title in your opening line; doing so may make your introduction sound monotonous or unimaginative.
2. Cut unnecessary background or warm-up writing that you've used to get yourself started. Advice for movie directors is also good for writers: "Cut to the chase." Open with what will interest your readers.
3. Delete self-conscious statements of purpose: *It is the purpose of this paper to . . .* and so on. Instead of telling your readers what you'll do, just do it.
4. Beware of mysterious openings. It's one thing to stimulate curiosity, quite another to mystify readers or plunge them into the dark. Your introduction should help readers make sound predictions about your topic—even about your design and style.
5. Beware of overworked, unconnected openings such as "The *Oxford English Dictionary* defines...."

Follow these guidelines for effective conclusions.

1. Be sure your conclusion flows smoothly from the body of your writing. If necessary, write transitions or repeat key words.
2. Do more than merely reword the thesis you've already written in your introduction.
3. Avoid stock phrases that tell the obvious: *In conclusion . . . , In closing . . . , In summary . . . ,* and so on.
4. Do not introduce new topics. Refocus attention on your original topic.
5. Be sure your readers will understand a closing quotation. Identify the speaker and, if necessary, explain its point.

1   Strategies for conclusions

As the preceding example illustrates, effective conclusions restate, provide food for thought, and suggest or state outright the implications of the writing. Create a conclusion appropriate to the topic and the occasion.

- Conclude with **your thesis** or another unifying statement. Organize your writing so that it leads naturally and inevitably to your point.

- Ask and respond to a **question** in the way the body of your paper has prepared you to.

- Conclude with a **challenge** to your readers to new thinking or action.

- Conclude with an apt **quotation**. Introduce and explain it if necessary.

- Conclude with an **anecdote** that summarizes your thinking.

- Conclude with a **hook.** Unify your writing by returning to—hooking up with—the subject of your opening and commenting on it in light of what you've written in the body of your paper.

2   Conclusions, purpose, and audience

Like introductory strategies, the preceding conclusion strategies may be adapted to almost any writing situation. But certain kinds of writing tend to do certain things as they close in order to emphasize or achieve the writer's purpose.

- **Autobiographical and narrative writing.** These kinds of writing often end with a discovery the writer has made. The story just completed has brought changes of understanding, outlook, or action, and the conclusion announces or dramatizes them. Consider the following:

Perhaps my situation is exactly like that described by the once popular critic and writer Thomas H. Uzzel, whose 1923 book, *Narrative Technique*, told readers not only what to write about and how to do so but also who should be writing and who shouldn't. In examining the motives of would-be writers, he ridicules one young woman's reasons for wanting to write and tells her to go home and "get married at the earliest possible moment." More unsettling was his response to the man with the "Book Lover Complex," an aspiring author who was very good at reading books but totally incapable of writing them: "He was sent back to his mother and his books."
    How did I react to this attitude?
    "Nonsense!" I retorted haughtily.

(John Vardon, from "A Walk around Writer's Block")

- **Informative and explanatory writing.** These kinds of writing often end by telling readers what can be done with the information they have just received. These conclusions may state the meaning or significance of the information, offer proposals for action, describe the benefits of action, or predict the consequences of action or inaction. (See 4f and 55.)

- **Argumentative and persuasive writing.** These kinds of writing often end with an emotional appeal, an attempt to rouse readers' desire to agree with the writer. (See 6c and d.)

chapter
9 Creating Coherence

Effective writing is **coherent,** meaning that all of its parts fit snugly together. A more descriptive word is **fluent.** Effective writing flows from idea to idea, paragraph to paragraph, sentence to sentence, and so is easy to read. Writing unified by a single topic and overall design already has the essential features of coherence.

To express that coherence while writing a draft, keep going. Write as much as possible at one sitting. If you must stop, stop in the middle of a paragraph that you'll know how to finish when you return. As you rewrite, edit for coherence. If you find a passage that seems choppy or disconnected, try the following strategies.

9*a* | Repeat key words and their synonyms

Some writers believe that repeated words are a sure sign of uninspired, monotonous writing. But key words that name your topics are worth repeating. Readers depend on them just as they depend on highway route markers to tell them they're on the right road. For example, consider the following paragraphs that challenge the concept of democracy. Note how often the word *democracy* and related words are repeated (emphasis added).

> *Democracy* is a superstition of the 20th century. Many indeed find comfort in the thought that our institutions are, in Abe Lincoln's words, "of the *people*, by the *people*, for the *people*." Two operating principles underlie the *democratic* vision: decisions are made by majority rule, and decision makers are elected in contests in which every adult member of society has one equal *vote*.
>
> These principles are *democratic*, however, only when they successfully reflect the *people's voice* rather than the opinions of those in power. Consider elections, for example, as successful representations of the "*voice* of the *people*."

How to ...

How to Edit for Coherence

Follow these editing tips to evaluate your coherence.

1. **Examine your writing.** Be sure you've written topic sentences and necessary transitions. If not, add them.
2. **Mark key words and their synonyms.** If you've written coherently, you'll see key words repeated frequently. If you have marked many different key words, you may have too many topics, and your writing may be disunified or incoherent. Refocus, reorganize, and rewrite to support your thesis and topic sentences.
3. **Reread from the beginning of a paragraph.** When you finish rewriting a paragraph, go back to its beginning and reread. If your rewrite fits coherently, your original and revised sentences will flow together smoothly.
4. **Reread at your readers' pace.** Writers read their writing more slowly than readers, pausing frequently to consider and evaluate. At this slower pace, transitions and repetitions may seem appropriate. But if you reread at your readers' swifter pace, you may discover that momentum will carry you smoothly from one idea to the next without transitions or repetition. Cut unnecessary words.

Computer Tip:

Checking Coherence

As you revise a rough draft, use your word processor's style features (underlining, italics, boldface, even alternative type fonts and sizes) to highlight topic sentences, key words, synonyms, pronouns, and transitions. You can see at a glance whether you've written coherently. Be sure to reformat your final draft before you print it. (See 46a.)

Rarely do more than 50% of eligible *voters* cast ballots in local elections; even in national elections, which often seem more like show business than politics, the participation rate is low. It took the 1995 Québec referendum, with its very real threat to Canadian cohesiveness, to bring more than 90% of the *people* to the polls. Normally, the percentage of total *votes* cast is much, much lower. As one *voter* put it, "What difference will my *vote* make?" The Québec example notwithstanding, our *voter* apathy means that the results do not reflect the will of *all* the *people*. In other words, our decisions are technically not quite *democratic*.

From paragraph to paragraph, sentence to sentence, repeated key words lead readers to a new understanding of democracy. Synonyms and other related words (like "vote" and "voice" and "people") are all used repeatedly to add variety.

9b | Write transitions to connect ideas

Coherent writing not only repeats key words to develop its subject, but also links topics, sentences, and paragraphs with **transitions.** The word *transition* comes from a word that means "going across." Transitional words, phrases, and sentences are like bridges that enable writers and readers to "go across" from one idea to the next. They make the following connections:

- Addition: *again, also, and, as well, besides, furthermore, moreover*

- Comparison: *in the same way, likewise, similarly*

- Concession or agreement: *granted, it is true, of course, to be sure*

- Conclusion: *accordingly, all in all, as a result, consequently, in conclusion, in short, in sum, so, then, therefore, thus*

- Contrast or alternative: *after all, but, conversely, even so, however, in contrast, instead, nevertheless, nonetheless, nor, on the contrary, on the other hand, or, otherwise, rather, still, yet*

- Elaboration: *in other words, in simpler terms, more specifically, that is, to put it differently*

- Emphasis: *in fact, indeed, of course, to be sure*

- Enumeration: *finally, first (second, third), for one thing, last, next*

- Example or illustration: *for example, for instance, specifically, to illustrate*

- Explanation and logical relation: *as a result, because, consequently, for, for this reason, if, since, so, that being the case, then, therefore, thus*

- Place: *above, at this point, below, beyond, close, elsewhere, farther, here, near, next, on the other side, opposite, outside, within, there*

- Summary: *in other words, in summary, on the whole, that is*

- Time: *after, as, at last, at once, at the same time, by degrees, eventually, gradually, immediately, in a short time, in the future, later, meanwhile, promptly, simultaneously, soon, suddenly, then, when, while*

Consider transitions in the following excerpt, in which the writer uses his childhood to make a point about the value of living with risks. Transitions weave action and description into a story, compare the past to the present, and signal conclusions. (Transitions linking paragraphs, sentences, and clauses are emphasized.)

Time transition	**When** I was a boy skating on Brooks Pond, there were no grown-ups around. Once or twice a year, on a weekend day or a holiday, some parents might come by with a thermos of hot chocolate. Maybe they would build a fire (which we were forbidden to do), **and** we would gather around.
Addition	
Contrast	**But for the most part** the pond was the domain of children. In the absence of adults, we made and enforced our own rules. We had hardly any gear—just some borrowed hockey gloves, some hand-me-down skates, maybe an elbow pad or two—**so** we played a clean form of hockey, with no high-sticking, no punching, and almost no checking. A single fight could ruin the whole afternoon. **Indeed,** as I remember it, thirty years later, it was the purest form of hockey I ever saw—until I got to see the Russian national team play the game.
Logical relation	
Emphasis	
Time, contrast	**Yet, before we could play,** we had to check the ice. We became serious junior meteorologists, true connoisseurs of cold. We learned that the best weather for pond skating is plain, clear cold, with starry nights and no snow. (Snow not only mucks up the skating surface but also insulates the ice from the colder air above.) **And** we learned that moving water, even the gently flowing Mystic River, is a lot less likely to freeze than standing water. **So** we skated only on the pond. We learned all the weird whooping and cracking sounds that ice makes as it expands and contracts—**and thus** when to leave the ice.
Addition	
Logical relation	
Logical relation	
Question link	**Do kids learn these things today?** I don't know. How would they? We don't let them. **Instead** we post signs. Ruled by lawyers, cities and towns everywhere try to limit their legal liability. **Try as they might, however,** they cannot eliminate the underlying risk. Liability is a social construct; risk is a natural fact. When it is cold enough, ponds freeze. No sign or fence or ordinance can change that.
Contrast	
Contrast	
Conclusion	**In fact,** by focussing on liability and not teaching our kids how to take risks, we are making their world more dangerous. **When we were children,** we had to learn to evaluate risks and handle them on our own. We had to learn, quite literally, to test the waters. **As a result,** we grew up to be savvier about ice and ponds than any kid could be who has skated only under adult supervision on a rink.
Time	
Logical relation	

(Adapted from Christopher B. Daly, "How the Lawyers Stole Winter," *The Atlantic*, March 1995.)

9c Link sentences with pronouns

Pronouns substitute for nouns and noun phrases—the antecedents of pronouns (see 10b). The result is smoother reading. In the following example, consider how pronouns substitute for key words and, by so doing, link one sentence to another. Also imagine how much choppier the paragraph would seem if the writer had used only nouns. (Pronouns and antecedents are emphasized.)

How to Link with Transitions and Pronouns

Follow these guidelines to use transitions and pronouns effectively.

1. Use transitions sparingly. If you organize effectively, your writing will lead naturally from one topic to the next. You'll need few transitions; more would be distracting.
2. Choose transitions that accurately signal the relationship between ideas and paragraphs—not ones that mean almost what you intend. For example, *and* may mean either "in addition" or "consequently."
3. Choose transitions that suit the formality of your writing. For example, you may use *so* or *but* in informal writing and *therefore* or *nevertheless* in more formal writing.
4. Repeat pronouns frequently to substitute for nouns and noun phrases. As reminders, occasionally repeat the nouns or phrases to which the pronouns refer.

Bicycles are compact. **They** are no trouble at all to store or to park. A **bicycle** takes as much space as a pair of skis and a set of golf clubs, so there's room for **one** in a front hall closet, a rec room, a garage, an attic, a storeroom, just about anywhere in a house. In fact, **it** can even be taken apart and stored in a trunk for the winter. Some **people** have **their** own customized storage racks; **others** have built-ins in **their** hall closets.

Parking a **bicycle** is even easier than storing **it**. Gone is the frustration of the car owner faced with $5–$10 a day in parking fees—the bicycle owner just has to buy a sturdy lock.

9d Write "old/new" sentences: include material from preceding sentences in each new sentence

Fluent sentences repeat "old business" from earlier sentences—words, ideas, or structural patterns—and add "new business" to develop a topic one step further. Read the following paragraph and consider how each sentence is linked to those that precede it. (Sentences are numbered; "old business" in each sentence is emphasized.)

(1) Be willing to make radical changes in your second draft. (2) If your thesis **changed** while you were writing your first draft, you will base your **second draft** on this new subject. (3) **Even if your thesis** has not **changed,** you may need to shift paragraphs around, eliminate paragraphs, or add new ones. (4) Inexperienced writers often suppose that **revising** a paper means **changing** only a word or two or adding a sentence or two. (5) **This kind of editing** is part of the writing process, but it is not the most important part. (6) **The most important part of rewriting** is a willingness to **turn the paper upside down**, to shake out of it those ideas that interest you the most, to set them in a form where they will interest the reader, too.

(Adapted from Richard Marius, "Writing Drafts," from *A Writer's Companion.*)

Sentences 1 and 2	*Changes/changed . . . second draft* are key words used in both sentences.
Sentences 2 and 3	*If . . .* in sentence 2 is grammatically parallel with *Even if . . .* in sentence 3 (parallel structure), and the words *thesis . . . chang*ed are key words used in each sentence.
Sentences 3 and 4	*Revising* in sentence 4 connects with *shift paragraphs around, eliminate paragraphs, and add new ones* in sentence 3 (key words).
Sentences 4 and 5	The key words *This kind of editing* in sentence 5 refer to an activity described in sentence 4.
Sentences 5 and 6	In sentence 6, *The most important part* repeats key words from sentence 5, and a dramatic description of revision reminds readers of the key words *radical changes* in sentence 1.

As you rewrite, examine your sentences to see whether they repeat words, ideas, and patterns from earlier sentences. Without these links, your sentences will seem to jump around, disconnected. With them, your sentences will flow.

A note on needless repetition: If you repeat words or sentence patterns unnecessarily, your writing will sound choppy or wordy. (See 26b and 33a–c.)

Identifying Grammar

Grammar describes how native speakers and writers of a language produce their sentences. It is not so much a list of dos and don'ts as it is a portrait of the way people speak and write. But this description is not what people have in mind when they say, "Watch your grammar!" What they mean is a precise set of language rules known as usage. **Usage** refers to the conventions and language etiquette followed by the members of specific language groups. Grammar says, in effect, "This is what a native speaker or writer does." Usage says, "This is what a speaker or writer ought to do."

The grammar presented in books like this one is actually a combination of the grammar and usage for one version or dialect of English, **Standard Written English**. This is the dialect generally written in schools, the professions, the business world, and the media—and worth knowing because it is so widely shared.

Another reason for learning the grammar presented here is the same one musicians have for learning to read music. Some musicians, unable to read a note, play beautifully, but most have to learn to read music to play well. Like musicians, some writers have an ear for language and write well with seldom a thought for grammar. But most find their writing becomes more accurate, powerful, and expressive the more they know about language. If you're just starting out as a writer, if you doubt you have an "ear" for language, this section will help you develop that ear.

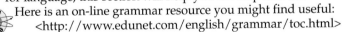 Here is an on-line grammar resource you might find useful:
<http://www.edunet.com/english/grammar/toc.html>

10 Parts of Speech

The term **parts of speech** refers to a system for grouping and labelling English words according to their functions in sentences. Traditionally,

How to . . .

How to Identify Nouns and Verbs

Use the following tips to help you identify nouns and verbs as you edit your sentences.

Nouns

1. Nouns may be preceded by *a, an,* or *the*: *a computer, an apple, the principal.*
2. Most nouns may be singular, plural, or possessive: *horse* [singular], *horses* [plural], *horse's* [possessive], *horses'* [plural possessive].
3. Nouns formed from other words end in *-ance* (*guidance*), *-ation* (*donation*), *-dom* (*freedom*), *-ence* (*reference*), *-hood* (*neighbourhood*), *-ice* (*justice*), *-ion* (*incision*), *-ist* (*tourist*), *-ity* (*generosity*), *-ment* (*establishment*), *-ness* (*business*), *-ship* (*friendship*).

Verbs

1. If you change the time of an action, a verb changes its form (usually known as **tense**): *Aaron opened the book. Aaron is opening the book.* (For more on tense, see 10c3.)
2. Verbs formed from other kinds of words end in *-en, -ize* and *-ify*: *harden, realize, identify.*

A note on adverbs: The adverbs *already, always, never, not, often, only,* and *even* are sometimes placed in the middle of verb phrases to provide additional information: Larry <u>has *already* written</u> the report. Do not mistake adverbs for verbs.

words have been divided into eight parts of speech: nouns, pronouns, verbs, adjectives, adverbs, prepositions, conjunctions, and interjections. But some words change classes as their functions change. Consider the uses of the word *present.*

- A verb that describes action: *A geologist will present the next report.*
- A noun that describes an object: *Larry gave his sister a present.*
- An adjective that describes a feature: *This verb is in the present tense.*

10a Nouns

Nouns name persons, places, or things, including ideas, activities, qualities, conditions, and materials. There are several kinds of nouns.

1   Proper nouns and common nouns

A **proper noun** is capitalized and names a specific person, place, or thing: *Emily Carr, the Saguenay, the Holy Grail*. (See also 42b.) A **common noun** names a general category of person, place, or thing: *pilot, desert, gemstones*.

2   Abstract nouns and concrete nouns

An **abstract noun** refers to an intangible, something that we cannot perceive with our senses: *joy, discipline, democracy*. (See also 31b.) A **concrete noun** refers to a tangible, something we can touch: *glove, computer, book, snow, voter*. (See also 31b.)

3   Count nouns and noncount nouns

A **count noun** refers to something that can be enumerated with numbers: *one apple, three cookies, billions of stars*. (See also 22a.) A **noncount noun** refers to a mass or quantity that cannot be counted: *blood, music, peace, stuff*. (See also 22b.) Be sure to distinguish singular and plural forms, adding the *-s/-es* endings when you mean more than one: *suits, potatoes*.

4   Collective nouns

A **collective noun** names a group acting as a unit: *audience, jury, class, company, community*. (See also 16g and 17c.)

5   Compound nouns

A **compound noun** consists of two or more words and may be written as separate words (*half sister*), as one word (*homemaker, grandfather*), or as a hyphenated word (*brother-in-law*). (For more on hyphens and compounds, see 46b.)

10*b* Pronouns

A **pronoun** refers to a noun, called its **antecedent**, that gives the pronoun its meaning. Pronouns often change form to signal their function in a sentence. (See 19.)

| | personal pronoun | possessive pronoun | reflexive pronoun |
| antecedent | | | |

The little boy boasted that he could tie his shoes for himself.

1   Personal pronouns

Personal pronouns refer to specific persons, places, or things. (See also 19a–d.) Singular: *I, me, you, he, she, him, her, it*. Plural: *we, us, you, they, them*. (Note: *You* is the same whether we address one person or many.)

2   Possessive pronouns

In contrast to possessive nouns, **possessive pronouns** have no apostrophe. Singular: *my, mine, your, yours, his, her, hers, its*. Plural: *our, ours, your, yours, their, theirs*. (See also 19d and 24e.)

3   Demonstrative pronouns

A **demonstrative pronoun** (*this, that, these, those*) points to the noun it replaces.

pronoun   antecedent
These are the grapes that make the best jelly.

4   Indefinite pronouns

An **indefinite pronoun** refers to a nonspecific person or thing. (See also 16f and 17d.)

all	both	everything	neither	several
another	each	few	nobody	some
any	either	little	none	somebody
anybody	enough	many	no one	someone
anyone	everybody	most	nothing	something
anything	everyone	much	one	

5   Interrogative pronouns

An **interrogative pronoun** begins a question: *who(ever), which(ever), whom(ever), whose, what(ever)*: *Who wrote this poem?*

6   Relative pronouns

A **relative pronoun** (*who, which, whom, whose, that*) or **relative adverb** (*where, when*) connects an adjective clause to a noun antecedent. (See also 12b3.)

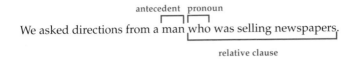

antecedent   pronoun

We asked directions from a man who was selling newspapers.

relative clause

7 Intensive and reflexive pronouns

Intensive and **reflexive pronouns** consist of a personal pronoun + *-self* or *-selves: myself, yourself, himself, herself, itself, ourselves, yourselves, themselves.* (See also 19g.)

- An **intensive pronoun** emphasizes a noun: *Joan designed the house herself.*

- A **reflexive pronoun** identifies the receiver of an action as identical to the doer of the action: *Peter rewarded himself with a day off.*

8 Reciprocal pronouns

A **reciprocal pronoun** (*each other, one another*) refers to an individual part of a compound subject: *Pedro and Jack read each other's essays.*

10c Verbs

Verbs express action, process, or state of being: *run, wish, be, appear, become, taste.*

Carol Grinberg **is campaigning** for a seat in the legislature.

He **seems** content.

1 Helping verbs

Twenty-six **helping verbs** (also called **auxiliary verbs**) help complete the meaning of verbs by introducing either the root form (___ *arrive*) or a participle (___ *arrived,* ___ *arriving*). *Have, do,* and *be* may also be the main verb of a sentence. **Modals** act only as helping verbs. (See also 15d and 23 a–d.)

HAVE, DO, BE	MODALS			
have, has, had	can	could	may	might
do, does, did	shall	should	must	ought to
be, am, is, are, was, were, being, been	will	would	used to	had better

2   Main verb forms

Except for the verb *to be*, the main verb of a sentence has five forms:

- Base or infinitive form: I often (*play, speak*).

- *-s/-es* or third-person form: He often (*plays, speaks*).

- Past tense: Then I (*played, spoke*).

- Past participle: I have (*played, spoken*) before.

- Present participle: I am (*playing, speaking*) now.

A note on participles: When accompanied by helping verbs, participles act as verbs: *They are playing my song.* When they stand without helping verbs, participles act as nouns or adjectives: *Playing is sometimes hard work. Playing softly, the guitarist sang a sad song.* (See 10c5, 12a2, and 23h.)

3   Tense

Helping verbs and main verb forms combine to create **tense**, the time when an action occurs. Standard English has six tense forms, and each one has a **continuous** *-ing* form to indicate action in progress at a given time. (See also 15b and 23a.)

- **Present tense**: for present states and for action that is timeless: *I understand. He speaks often.* Use the **continuous** form for action taking place now: *You/we/they are working.*

- **Past tense**: past action. *I understood. He spoke. You/we/they were working.*

- **Future tense**: action that will take place. *I will understand. He will speak. You/we/they will be working.*

- **Present perfect tense**: past action continuing or completed in the present. *I have understood. He has spoken. You/we/they have been working.*

- **Past perfect tense**: past action completed before another past action. *I had understood. He had spoken. You/we/they had been working.*

- **Future perfect tense**: action that will begin and end before an identified future time. *I will have understood. He will have spoken. You/we/they will have been working.*

4   Transitive, linking, and intransitive verbs

Verbs can be classified by their function in a sentence.

- A **transitive verb** acts upon someone or something called the *direct object*. (See 11c.)

transitive verb   direct object

The player kicked the ball into the net.

- A **linking verb** links a subject usually to a noun, pronoun, or adjective, called the **complement**, that describes the subject. (See also 11d1 and 16c.) Common linking verbs are *appear, be, become, feel, grow, look, remain, seem, smell, sound,* and *taste*.

linking verb   complement

Havana is the capital of Cuba.

- An **intransitive verb** does not require an object or complement to make it grammatically complete, although it may be followed by other words.

  The engine **hummed**. The mechanic **hummed** softly.

5 Verbals

A **verbal** is a verb acting as another part of speech: noun, adverb, or adjective. (See also 12a2 and 23h.)

- Gerunds. A **gerund** is the *-ing* verb form acting as a noun: *Writing is both a craft and an art.* The gerund *writing* is the subject of the sentence.

- Participles. A **participle** is the verb form ending with *-ing, -d, -ed, -en, -n,* or *-t*. When a participle stands alone without a helping verb, it acts as a modifier.

  Writing rapidly, she completed the letter in fifteen minutes.

  Please give me **written** instructions.

- Infinitives. An **infinitive** consists of *to* plus the base form of the verb: *to write*. It may act as a noun, adjective, or adverb.

infinitive as a noun (the subject of the sentence)

To write effortlessly is the goal of every writer.

infinitive as an adjective modifying *assignment*

Here is the assignment to write for next week.

infinitive as an adverb modifying *use*

Use a computer to write your essay.

10d | Adjectives and determiners

1 Adjectives

An **adjective** modifies a noun or pronoun. It answers the questions *Which? What kind?* or *How many?* (See also 20, 22, and 24f.)

which
That rock may contain a fossil.

what kind · · · what kind
The dark clouds warned of a dangerous storm.

how many · · · how many
Lacrosse is played by two teams of ten players each.

A note on adjective series: When two or more adjectives are used together without commas separating them, they must be arranged in a particular order. (See 24f3.)

2 Determiners

This subclass of adjectives includes **quantifiers** (words that answer the question "How many?" or "How much?") and **articles**. *The* is a **definite article** introducing specifically identified nouns: *the dancer, the house. A* and *an* are **indefinite articles** referring to previously unidentified nouns: *a lawyer, an apple.* (See 22.)

10e | Adverbs

An **adverb** modifies verbs, adjectives, or other adverbs. It answers the questions *How? When? Where? Why? Under what circumstances? To what extent?* (See also 20a and c, and 24f.)

an adverb modifying the verb *revise*: when
Revise your paper later.

an adverb modifying the verb *are camping*: where
The scouts are camping nearby.

an adverb modifying an adverb: to what extent
The old man spoke very softly.

10f Prepositions

A **preposition** usually precedes a noun or pronoun called the **object of the preposition**. Together they form a **prepositional phrase** that modifies other words in a sentence. (See also 12a1 and 24g.)

preposition object   preposition object

The children ran into the room and knelt before the fire.

COMMON PREPOSITIONS

about	below	during	opposite	toward
above	beneath	except	out	under
across	beside	for	over	underneath
after	besides	from	past	unlike
against	between	in	regarding	until
along	beyond	into	round	up
among	but	like	since	upon
around	by	near	than	with
as	concerning	next	through	within
at	considering	of	throughout	without
before	despite	off	till	
behind	down	on	to	

A note on phrases as prepositions: Prepositions may also consist of two or more words: *according to, as well as, different from, in addition to, in front of, in spite of, instead of, together with, with respect to,* and so on.

10g Conjunctions

A **conjunction** links words, phrases, or clauses and signals their relationship as grammatically equal or unequal.

1 Co-ordinating conjunctions

Co-ordinating conjunctions (*and, but, for, so, or, nor, yet*) link grammatically equal words and word groups. (See also 13b7, 16d, 17a, 21a, and 24c3.)

Kim **and** Jean played their best tennis of the season, **but** they lost to superior opponents.

2 Correlative conjunctions

Correlative conjunctions are word pairs (*both/and, either/or, neither/nor, not/but, not only/but also, whether/or*) that link grammatically equal words and word groups. (See also 16e, 17b, and 21c.)

Both the Earl of Oxford **and** Ben Jonson have been proposed as the true author of William Shakespeare's plays.

3 Subordinating conjunctions

Subordinating conjunctions begin adverb clauses and link them to independent clauses. (See also 12b2.)

after	even if	provided	until
although	even though	since	when
as	if	so that	whenever
as if	in case	than	whereas
as though	in order that	though	wherever
because	no matter if	till	whether
before	once	unless	while

subordinate clause   independent clause

After they finished breakfast, the campers began loading their gear into the canoes.

4 Conjunctive adverbs

A **conjunctive adverb** is used with a semicolon to link independent clauses. (See also 14b3 and 37b.)

accordingly	furthermore	likewise	otherwise
also	hence	meanwhile	similarly
besides	however	moreover	still
consequently	incidentally	nevertheless	then
finally	indeed	next	therefore
first	instead	nonetheless	thus

It has rained five cm in the last week; **however**, the drought is far from over.

10*h* | Interjections

An **interjection** is a strong expression of feeling or call for attention, followed by a comma or exclamation point: ***Oh**, I'm sorry to hear that. **Ouch!** I've pinched my hand in the door.*

chapter

11 Sentence Parts

A sentence has two parts: a *subject* and a *predicate*. Together they make a complete statement, question, exclamation, or command. (In most commands, the subject *you* is not stated.)

- A statement: subject   predicate
  The sonnet has two forms, the Italian and the Elizabethan.

- A command with an unstated subject (*you* understood):

  predicate
  Be sure to bring the volleyball to the picnic!

11a | Subjects

The **subject** of a sentence names the person, place, or thing that acts, is acted on, or is described. Subjects usually precede the predicate, but may follow it.

She works as a pathologist.

Algae produce their food through photosynthesis.

The batik technique for dyeing fabric was developed in Malaya.

In a box under the porch slept **four tiny kittens**.

1 Simple subjects

The **simple subject** of a sentence is the noun or pronoun by itself, without modifying words, phrases, or clauses: *she, algae, technique, kittens*.

2 Complete subjects

The **complete subject** includes the noun or pronoun and all of its modifiers: *she, algae, the batik technique for dyeing fabric, four tiny kittens*.

3 Compound subjects

A **compound subject** consists of two or more simple subjects linked by a co-ordinating conjunction.

How to . . .

How to Identify the Subjects of Sentences

Use the following tip to help you identify the subjects of sentences and other clauses.

Ask *who* or *what* + verb + remainder of the sentence. *People sometimes find it hard to accept charity.* Who sometimes find it hard to accept charity? *People.* Not all sentences open with the subject, however: *On the doorstep sat a cradle.* What sat on the doorstep? *A cradle.*

subject 1   subject 2

Muscular strength and aerobic efficiency are essential to physical fitness.

11*b* Predicates

1 Simple predicates

The **simple predicate** of a sentence consists of a verb and its helping verbs, if any.

The locksmith **is resetting** the tumblers of the lock.

2 Complete predicates

A **complete predicate** consists of the simple predicate and all words associated with it: modifiers, objects, and complements.

verb   object

The locksmith is resetting the tumblers of the lock.

predicate

3 Compound predicates

A **compound predicate** consists of one or two or more predicates linked by a co-ordinating conjunction.

subject   predicate 1   predicate 2

The locksmith reset the tumblers of the lock and made a new key.

compound predicate

11*c* Objects

1 Direct objects

A **direct object** is the person, place, or thing that receives the action of a transitive verb. (See also 10c4.)

verb   direct object
Mora is growing a new variety of hosta in her garden.

2 Indirect objects

An **indirect object** occurs with certain verbs to identify who or what receives the direct object.

subject   verb   indirect object   direct object
Dr. Watson gave Sherlock Holmes a clue.

11*d* Complements

Complements complete the verb by providing additional information about a subject or object. (See also 16c and 20b.)

1 Subject complements

A **subject complement** is a noun or adjective that describes the subject of a linking verb such as *be, become, feel, taste*. Subject complements are sometimes called *predicate adjectives* or *predicate nouns*. (For more on linking verbs, see 10c4.)

subject complement: an adjective
The sunset is beautiful.

subject complement: a noun
The prince will soon become king.

2 Object complements

An **object complement** follows a direct object and completes it as if there were an implied "to be."

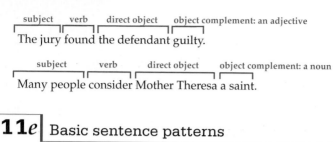

subject   verb   direct object   object complement: an adjective

The jury found the defendant guilty.

subject   verb   direct object   object complement: a noun

Many people consider Mother Theresa a saint.

11*e* | Basic sentence patterns

English sentences can be grouped into five basic patterns according to their parts. Knowing these patterns will help you construct effective sentences. (For more on writing effective sentences, see 25 and 26.)

Pattern 1: Subject + verb

subject   verb

Writers write.

Pattern 2: Subject + verb + object

subject   verb   object

Some writers write books.

Pattern 3: Subject + verb + indirect object + direct object

subject   verb   indirect object   direct object

Many writers write their friends letters.

Pattern 4: Subject + verb + subject complement

subject   verb   subject complement

Writers are creative.

Pattern 5: Subject + verb + direct object + object complement

subject   verb   direct object   object complement

Envious writers call successful writers lucky.

12 Phrases, Clauses, and Sentence Types

To add detail to your writing, you can expand the five basic sentence patterns using single words, phrases, or clauses.

12*a* | Phrases

A **phrase** is a grammatically related group of words with a single main headword. Within a sentence it may act as a noun, verb, adjective, or adverb.

phrase as a noun   phrase as an adjective

In the end, Kevin's decision to sell his bike did not seem very unusual.

phrase as adverb   phrase as verb

1   Prepositional phrases

A **prepositional phrase** consists of a preposition + a noun or pronoun phrase, including modifiers. The noun or pronoun phrase is known as the object of the preposition. (See also 10f and 24g.)

preposition   object: a noun phrase

at the morning roll call

Prepositional phrases may act as adjectives (telling *which* or *what kind*), as adverbs (telling *how, when, why,* or *where*), or as nouns.

prepositional phrase as an adjective: which

The man in the gray suit is my father.

prepositional phrase as an adverb: where

Sally is studying in the biology lab.

prepositional phrase as an noun: subject complement

The best time to see your instructor is before class.

2   Verbal phrases

A **verbal phrase** is a verb and related words acting as a noun, adjective, or adverb. (See 10c5.) There are three kinds of verbal phrases.

■ A **gerund phrase** consists of the *-ing* form of a verb (the present participle) and any related words: *campaigning for office, swimming in the ocean, exercising regularly*. In a sentence, a gerund phrase acts as a noun. (See 23f.)

gerund phrase as a subject
⌐─────────────────────────┐
Campaigning for office requires energy and money.

gerund phrase as a direct object
⌐──────────────────────┐
I enjoy swimming in the ocean.

gerund phrase as a complement
⌐─────────────────────────┐
One key to good health is exercising regularly.

■ A **participial phrase** consists of the present or past participle form of the verb and any related words. A participial phrase always acts as an adjective modifying a noun or pronoun. (See also 10c5 and 13b3.)

participial phrase modifying a subject
⌐────────────────────────────┐
Gazing at the painting, she was reminded of the house where she was born.

participial phrase modifying a direct object
⌐──────────────────────────────┐
The soldier wore a uniform covered with ribbons and medals.

■ An **infinitive phrase** consists of the word *to* followed by the base form of the verb and any related words. It may act as a noun, adjective, or adverb.

infinitive phrase as a noun: direct object
⌐──────────────────────────┐
Paul wanted to learn silk screening.

infinitive phrase as an adjective modifying *place*
⌐──────────────────────────────┐
Unfortunately, the library is no longer a place to find peace and quiet.

infinitive phrase as an adverb modifying *use*
⌐──────────────────────────────┐
Use a spell checker to help you proofread your writing.

3 Appositive phrases

An **appositive phrase** renames or describes a preceding noun or noun phrase. It usually acts like a noun or noun equivalent.

noun　　　　appositive phrase

Shiraz, the ancient capital of Persia, is now a pilgrimage centre for Shiite Muslims.

4　Absolute phrases

An **absolute phrase** consists of a noun or noun phrase and the present or past participle of a verb. As a modifier, it is always preceded or followed by a comma. An absolute phrase modifies an entire sentence or clause.

Hands waving, the children clamoured for the teacher's attention.

The sailors raised the sails eagerly, **their minds filled with dreams of home**.

12*b*　Clauses

A **clause** is a group of words with a subject and a predicate: *roses are red, where the buffalo roam, which essay is best*.

- Independent clauses. An **independent clause** (often called a **main clause**) can stand alone as a complete sentence: *Roses are red*.

- Dependent clauses. A **dependent clause** (often called a **subordinate clause**) cannot stand alone: *where the buffalo roam, which essay is best*. Within a sentence a dependent clause may act as a noun, an adjective, or an adverb: *We were told to decide which essay is best*. The dependent clause *which essay is best* acts as a noun, the object of *decide*.

(To distinguish between independent and dependent clauses, see 13b1, the "yes/no" question test.)

1　Noun clauses

A **noun clause** may act as a subject, object, complement, or appositive, anywhere a noun can work, in fact. Noun clauses usually begin with *how, that, which, who, whoever, whom, whomever, what, whatever, when, where, whether, whose, why*.

subject

Where he went is a mystery to me.

direct object

Researchers have discovered what causes depression.

2 Adverb clauses

An **adverb clause** (often referred to as a **subordinate clause**) begins with a subordinating conjunction such as *after, because, since, when.* (See 10g3 for a list.) Adverb clauses modify entire sentences and tell how, when, where, why, or under what conditions. (See also 13b4.)

adverb clause that tells when

After the hailstorm had ended, the farmers inspected their damaged crops.

3 Adjective clauses

An **adjective clause** (also called a **relative clause**) begins with a relative pronoun (*who, whom, which, that, whose*) or, occasionally, with a relative adverb (*when, where*). Relative clauses act as adjectives and tell which or what kind. (See also 13b5.)

We plan to hire someone **who can do technical writing**.

The park **where we used to jog** has an expensive new fountain.

12c | Sentence types

Sentences can be identified by the clauses they contain or by their purpose. Knowing these sentence types will help you create sentences that are emphatic, varied, and interesting to read. (For more on emphasis and variety, see 25 and 26.)

1 Classifying sentences by their clauses

- A **simple sentence** has one independent clause and no dependent clauses. It may also have compound subjects or predicates, as well as one-word or one-phrase modifiers.

independent clause

The Roman poet Virgil is the author of the *Aeneid*.

independent clause

Adam and Eve left the Garden of Eden and entered a hard new world.

- A **compound sentence** has two or more independent clauses and no dependent clauses. Its clauses may be linked by the co-ordinating conjunctions *and, or, but, yet, so, for, nor* or by a semicolon. (See also 36a and 37a.)

independent clause | independent clause

A penny saved is a penny earned, but the earnings don't come to much.

- A **complex sentence** has an independent clause and at least one dependent clause.

dependent clause | independent clause

When the wind changed direction, the temperature began to drop.

- A **compound-complex sentence** has at least two independent clauses and at least one dependent clause.

independent clause | independent clause
dependent clause | dependent clause

Imran knew that he should help, but he wasn't sure what he should do.

2 Classifying sentences by their purpose

- A **declarative sentence** makes a statement: *Bumblebees hummed in the doorway of the abandoned house.*

- An **interrogative sentence** asks a question: *Where is Lake Agassiz located?*

- An **imperative sentence** issues a command, makes a direct request, or gives advice: *When you come to the meeting, bring your copy of the annual report.*

- An **exclamatory sentence** makes an exclamation of excitement or emotion: *That's the best performance of* Othello *I've seen!*

Editing Grammar and Usage

13 Editing Sentence Fragments

13a | Connect fragments to complete sentences or rewrite them as complete sentences

A **sentence fragment** is an incomplete sentence, often added as an afterthought. To be complete, a sentence must have an independent clause—a subject and verb that can stand alone. (See 11a and b, 12b.) In the following examples, fragments are italicized.

> Despite its characterization as the "Frozen North," Canada has areas of dense rainforest. *For example, Glacier National Park in British Columbia.*

[The italicized word group is a noun phrase introduced by a prepositional phrase.]

> Last night I opened my window to enjoy the autumn air. *Which unfortunately was filled with ragweed pollen from the vacant lot next door.*

[The italicized word group has a subject and verb, *which . . . was filled,* but the relative pronoun *which* cannot be the subject of an independent clause.]

If you sometimes write fragments, you can teach yourself to recognize these and rewrite them as complete sentences. Most can be revised in one of two ways.

1 Connecting fragments

Connect the fragment to a nearby complete sentence. Repunctuate as necessary. Follow this method if your main idea is expressed in the sentence rather than the fragment.

> Despite its characterization as the "Frozen North," Canada has areas of dense rainforest/ ,~for~ ~For~ example, Glacier National Park in British Columbia.

13*a* frag

How to Edit Sentence Fragments

To identify fragments, follow these tips as you reread your writing:

1. Beginning at the end of your paper, read each sentence aloud. Isolating each sentence in this way will help you hear the incomplete thoughts that signal fragments.
2. Look for words that sometimes signal sentence fragments: (a) *-ing* verbs without accompanying helping verbs (see 13b3); (b) opening subordinating conjunctions such as *although, because, when, after, if,* and so on (see 13b4); (c) relative pronouns—*who, which, whom, that*—at the beginning of statements that are not questions. (See 13b5.)
3. Use the "yes/no" question test. (See 13b1.) If a word group is not already a question, turn it into one answerable by *yes* or *no*. If it makes sense and sounds complete, the original is a complete sentence; if not, it is a fragment.

Fix fragments by connecting them to nearby complete sentences or by rewriting them as complete sentences, with subjects, verbs, and, if necessary, helping verbs. (See 13a.)

2 Rewriting fragments

Rewrite the fragment as a complete sentence. Add words or change word forms. If necessary, rearrange for clarity or emphasis. Use this method to emphasize an idea in the fragment or to create two sentences where one would be too long.

Last night I opened my window to enjoy the autumn air. ~~Which~~ Unfortunately, it

~~unfortunately~~ was filled with ragweed pollen from the vacant lot next

door.

[The relative pronoun *which* cannot be the subject of a sentence. The revision substitutes the personal pronoun *it*, which can be a subject, and rearranges for emphasis.]

13*b* | Learn the clues that signal sentence fragments

1 The "yes/no" question test

If you're unsure whether a construction is a complete sentence, try the "yes/no" question test. If it is not already a question, turn the word group into one that can be answered by "yes" or "no." The first word will always be an auxiliary verb like *have* or *do* or *be*. If your question makes sense, you probably have an independent clause, which can be punctuated as a complete sentence. If not, you likely have a fragment to revise.

English has borrowed many words from indigenous languages.

[A "yes/no" question: *Has English borrowed many words from indigenous languages?* The question makes sense and sounds complete. The original is, therefore, an independent clause and may be punctuated as a sentence.]

Because English has borrowed many words from indigenous languages.

[*Has because English borrowed many words from indigenous languages?* The question doesn't make sense; the original is, therefore, a fragment.]

Another aspect of this test focusses on whether the answer itself sounds complete. Accordingly, a construction can be considered a complete sentence if it fits naturally into the following pattern: **It is true that** ___. Of the previous examples, only the first works: *It is true that English has borrowed many words from indigenous languages.*

Certain word groups are often inappropriately written and punctuated as sentences. Below you will learn to recognize them as sentence fragments.

2 Appositive phrases without verbs

Look for noun phrases—appositive phrases—that describe a word at the end of the preceding sentence. An appositive phrase standing alone, without a verb, is a fragment. Usually you can connect these fragments to the preceding sentence with a comma. (See also 12a3.)

The first Canadian to be awarded the Booker Prize for fiction was Michael Ondaatje/Author ~~, author~~ of *The English Patient* and *Running in the Family.*

[A "yes/no" question: *Is author of* <u>The English Patient</u> *and* <u>Running in the Family</u>? It sounds odd, as does the answer: *It is true that author of* <u>The English Patient</u> *and* <u>Running in the Family</u>. This fragment needs revising.]

3 Phrases with present participles and no helping verbs

Phrases with *-ing* verbs—present participles—and no helping verbs are participial phrases, which cannot be punctuated as complete sentences. They lack subjects and complete verbs. (See 12a2.) Usually you can connect these fragments to the preceding sentence. If necessary for clarity or emphasis, put the *-ing* phrase first, as in the following example.

, the
~~The~~ English language has always proven itself accommodating.
Borrowing many words from indigenous languages.

[A "yes/no" question: *Is borrowing many words from indigenous languages?* It sounds incomplete, and the original is, therefore, a fragment.]

4 Word groups beginning with subordinating conjunctions

Subordinating conjunctions such as *after, because*, and *when* link dependent to independent clauses. (See 10g3 for a list.) A dependent clause has a subject and verb, but its subordinating conjunction prevents it from being a complete sentence. A dependent clause standing by itself is a fragment. Connect it to a sentence nearby. If necessary, move it next to the words it modifies, as in this example.

Because his paintings celebrate the loneliness of the Canadian landscape,
Tom Thomson is admired by many. ~~Because his paintings celebrate the loneliness of the Canadian landscape.~~

[A "yes/no" question: *Is because his paintings celebrate the loneliness of the Canadian landscape?* The question doesn't make sense, and the original is, therefore, a fragment.]

A reminder about punctuation: Introductory phrases and clauses are usually set off from the main part of the sentence with a comma. (See 36b.)

5 Word groups beginning with relative pronouns

Relative pronouns (*who, whom, whose, which, that*) link a group of words—an adjective clause—to an independent clause. (See 12b3.) Although it has a subject and verb, a relative clause is not a complete sentence. If you find a capitalized relative pronoun at the beginning of a word group that is not a question, you may have found a fragment.

Each judge gave a long speech praising the contestants_∧,␣who ~~Who~~ stood near

the podium, smiling nervously, waiting for the winner to be announced.

[A "yes/no" question: *Is who stood near the podium smiling nervously, waiting for the winner to be announced?* The result is a nonsense question, and the original is, therefore, a fragment.]

6   Lists punctuated as sentences

Connect fragmentary lists to the clause that introduces them. Use a colon, a dash, or an introductory phrase such as *for example, such as,* or *including.* (See 38a and 41a.)

Plans for rehearsing the play should be precise_∧: two ~~Two~~ weeks for

memorizing the script, two weeks for learning the music, one month for

practising the dance routines.

[To hear the fragment, apply the "yes/no" question test to the list.]

7   Disconnected compound predicates

One part of a compound predicate (see 11b3) separated from the other part and punctuated as a complete sentence is a fragment. Connect it to the preceding sentence.

Critics raved about Jessica Tandy's performance as Blanche Dubois in
A Streetcar Named Desire in the '40s_∧,␣and ~~And,~~ about fifty years later, applauded

her portrayal of Iggy Threadgood in *Fried Green Tomatoes.*

Their engines groaning, several cars slowly climbed the steep mountain
road_∧,␣then ~~Then~~ disappeared over the summit.

[To hear the fragments in these examples, apply the "yes/no" question test to each statement punctuated as a sentence. You'll be able to distinguish complete sentences from fragments.]

8   Long prepositional phrases

Look for phrases beginning with *during, concerning, except, in addition to, instead of.* (See 10f for a list of prepositions.) A phrase that is not connected to an independent clause is a fragment. Attach it to the preceding sentence.

Some of the most stunning vistas in Canada belong to mountain lakes. ~~Like~~ like Lake Louise and, further north, Lake Maligne.

[To hear the fragment, apply the "yes/no" question test to each statement punctuated as a sentence.]

13c | Occasionally add fragments for special effect

Most writing for school, business, and the professions requires complete sentences. But occasionally, in personal, informal, or emotionally charged writing, you may write fragments to emphasize an idea, avoid repetition, or create speech rhythms. To decide whether a fragment is appropriate, consider whether the situation permits informal or emotionally charged writing. Use fragments sparingly. (Fragments are italicized in the following examples.)

1 Fragments for emphasis and economy

The Grad House. What passionate literary afternoons we were to spend there with our creative writing class. *Not to mention evenings. And sometimes even mornings, as we cranked away on the poetry mag we thought a fair rival for* Fiddlehead *or* Tamarack.

2 Fragments for emphasis, feeling, and speech rhythms

Canadians by and large tend to think of Canada as a land of immense potential. *Not just as a big land, which it unquestionably is. Or a privileged land, as many others enviously regard us. But as a land of limitless promise. A land, perhaps, on the threshold of greatness.*

(Pierre Elliott Trudeau)

14 Fixing Comma Splices and Fused Sentences

14*a* | Fix comma splices by repunctuating or rewriting

A **comma splice** results when two or more independent clauses (grammatically complete word groups) are linked by a comma. They are "spliced" together as if they were parts of one sentence instead of being punctuated as the separate statements they actually are. Consider the examples below. Independent clauses are italicized.

> *Raphael performed well* on the first test, *he expected to do even better* on the second.
>
> [*Raphael performed well* is one independent clause with its own subject and predicate; *he expected to do even better* is another.]

In Standard Written English, independent clauses are separated by something other than a comma. Learn to identify and fix comma splices. Choose the solution that helps you emphasize the point you want to make.

Some languages and English dialects permit comma splices. Standard Written English does not.

1 Repunctuating

- Use a **period** to turn each clause into a separate sentence.

  Raphael performed well on the first test/ ~~he~~ **. He** expected to do even better on the second.

- Use a **semicolon** (;) to join related independent clauses when they are nearly equal in importance. (See 37a.)

  Raphael performed well on the first test**;** he expected to do even better on the second.

- Use a **colon** (:) to join independent clauses when one introduces or explains the other. (See 38a.)

  Professor Li is the best instructor I've had**:** he knows his subject and presents it in an imaginative way.

How to Edit Comma Splices

To identify possible comma splices, ask yourself the following questions whenever you use commas to signal a pause.

1. Are word groups before and after a comma independent clauses? (Apply the "yes/no" question test in 13b1 to see.)
2. Is there a linking word after the comma other than *and, but, or, for, so, yet, nor*? (See 14b3.)
3. Can you replace the comma with a period and make a complete sentence of each word group? (See 14b1.)

Fix comma splices by repunctuating with a period, semicolon, colon, or dash. Or rewrite, turning one independent clause into a dependent clause or a phrase. (See 14a.)

■ Use a **dash** to join independent clauses when the second makes a surprising or abrupt response to the first. (See 41a.)

Murray asked Betsy if she knew where the car keys were, she didn't.

2 Adding a co-ordinating conjunction

Add a co-ordinating conjunction (*and, but, or, nor, so, yet, for*) following the comma that joins two independent clauses. The result is a compound sentence. (See 12c1.)

and
Raphael performed well on the first test, he expected to do even better on

the second.

3 Rewriting to create one complete sentence

■ Add a subordinating conjunction (*because, although, when*, and so on) to connect one clause grammatically to the other. (See 10g3.) The result is a complex sentence that emphasizes one clause and de-emphasizes the other. (See 12c1.)

Because
Raphael performed well on the first test, he expected to do even better on

the second.

■ Turn one clause into a phrase that modifies the remaining independent clause. The result is a simple sentence. (See 12c1.)

~~Raphael performed~~ _{After performing} well on the first test, ~~he~~ _{Raphael} expected to do even better on

the second.

14*b* | Learn the clues that signal comma splices

1 Independent clauses on both sides of a comma

Examine the words on both sides of a comma. If you can put a period after both passages, you've found two independent clauses and a comma splice. Fix the comma splice by repunctuating or rewriting.

I'm not going to university just because my parents told me to/there are

specific subjects I want to study.

[To the left of the comma, *I'm not going to university* is an independent clause; to the right, *there are specific subjects* is an independent clause.]

To identify independent clauses, use the "yes/no" question test. (See 13b1.) The first word group in the preceding example becomes *Am I going to university just because my parents told me to*? The second becomes *Are there specific subjects I want to study*? Both questions sound complete and make sense; they are, therefore, independent clauses joined by a comma—a comma splice.

2 A second clause that begins with a pronoun

In some comma splices the subject of the second independent clause is a pronoun referring to the subject of the first.

Julian refused the award for heroism/_{. He} said he had only done what

anyone would.

[The *he* following the comma is the subject of the second independent clause; it also refers to the subject of the first clause, *Julian*.]

3 Independent clauses joined by a comma and a transition or conjunctive adverb

Transitions and conjunctive adverbs link words and word groups (see 9b and 10g4).

COMMON TRANSITIONS AND CONJUNCTIVE ADVERBS

accordingly	at the same time	for instance	in fact
after all	besides	furthermore	in other words
also	certainly	hence	in the first place
anyhow	consequently	however	likewise
anyway	conversely	indeed	meanwhile
as a matter of fact	even so	instead	moreover
as a result	finally	in addition	nevertheless
at any rate	for example	in conclusion	next
now	otherwise	still	therefore
of course	similarly	subsequently	thus
on the contrary	specifically	then	that is
on the other hand			

These words look similar to the co-ordinating conjunctions (*and, but, for, nor, or, so,* and *yet*) but are grammatically different. Joining independent clauses with a comma + a transition or conjunctive adverb produces a comma splice. Use a semicolon instead.

Mass transit offers many environmental benefits/for example, the

nitrogen emissions responsible for smog are greatly reduced.

[Two independent clauses linked by a comma and the transition *for example* produce a comma splice. To join independent clauses, use a semicolon before a transition.]

John did not enjoy mathematics/however, if he was going to study

economics, he had to understand statistics.

[Two independent clauses linked by a comma and the conjunctive adverb *however* produce a comma splice. To join independent clauses, use a semicolon before a conjunctive adverb.]

A note on other uses of conjunctive adverbs. A comma + a transition or conjunctive adverb does not always signal a comma splice: *Both parents may work part-time, however, to share the care of their children*. The group of words before *however* is an independent clause that can stand alone. But the second is a phrase. The commas before and after *however* signal pauses in a single independent clause. (See also 36f.)

14c | Fix fused sentences by punctuating or rewriting

A **fused sentence,** sometimes called a **run-on**, results when two or more grammatically complete sentences are joined with no punctuation between them. They are joined ("fused") so tightly that, at a glance, they appear to be a single sentence, not two sentences. Consider this example:

How to Edit Fused Sentences

You can identify fused, run-on sentences in two steps.

1. Reread your writing aloud at a slow and steady pace. If you've written a fused sentence, you may stumble where two separate thoughts blur together. Pause and study your words. Divide them into two separate groups.

   The film jammed in the camera none of their holiday pictures turned out. [1] *the film jammed in the camera* [2] *none of their holiday pictures turned out.*

2. Apply the "yes/no" question test to each word group.

   Did the film jam in the camera? Did none of their holiday pictures turn out? [The "yes/no" question test reveals two word groups that sound complete and make sense. They are independent clauses that should be punctuated as two sentences.]

To fix fused sentences, insert a period, semicolon, colon, or dash between the independent clauses. Or rewrite to create one complete sentence.

   The film jammed in the camera. None of their holiday pictures turned out.

Soon the holidays will be here once more many will miss an opportunity to share themselves and their possessions with the less fortunate.

Did you stumble as you read this example? If so, you experienced the effect of fused sentences. Learn to identify and rewrite fused sentences, usually by adding punctuation or making one sentence subordinate to the other.

1   Adding punctuation

■ Use a **period** to separate one independent clause, which can stand alone as a complete sentence, from another.

   . Once
Soon the holidays will be here ~~once~~ more many will miss an opportunity

to share themselves and their possessions with the less fortunate.

[In this example, *the holidays will be here* is one independent clause; *many will miss an opportunity* is the second.]

- Use a **semicolon** to link related independent clauses roughly equal in importance. (See 37a.) Use a **colon** to link independent clauses when one clause introduces or explains the other. (See 38a.).

The Grand Canyon is not the first choice of travellers familiar with

canyon scenery ; that honour goes to Zion National Park or Bryce Canyon.

It all began like this : I had a new computer and needed help installing the

software.

- Insert a comma before a **co-ordinating conjunction** (*and, but, or, nor, so, yet, for*) to link related independent clauses.

I enjoy cooking , but cleaning up afterward is another matter.

- Insert a semicolon before a **transition** or **conjunctive adverb** linking independent clauses. (For a list of transitions and conjunctive adverbs, see 14b3.)

The Jensens knew that starting a business would not be easy ; however ,

they did not imagine how difficult it would be.

[The semicolon links two independent clauses; the comma is added following *however* to signal a pause. For more on punctuating transitional words and phrases, see 36f.]

2   Rewriting to make one clause subordinate to the other

Add a subordinating conjunction (*because, although, when, since,* and so on) to an independent clause to make it a dependent clause. Connect the dependent clause to the remaining independent clause to make one complete sentence. (For a list of subordinating conjunctions, see 10g3.)

The witness did not understand the lawyer's question about Cape
            because   *there*
Breton ^ he had never been ~~to Cape Breton~~.

[The second independent clause, beginning with *he had*, has been turned into a dependent clause by adding the subordinating conjunction *because*.]

3   Compressing two independent clauses into one sentence

Omit words or change word forms to make one shorter sentence out of two independent clauses.

Travellers

~~The Grand Canyon is not the first choice of travellers~~ familiar with

canyon scenery ~~that honour goes to~~ *prefer* Zion National Park or Bryce

to the Grand Canyon
Canyon.

The Jensens ~~knew that starting a business would not be easy however~~

~~they~~ did not imagine how difficult it would be. *to start a business*

chapter

15 Choosing Verb Forms

15*a* Use the standard forms of irregular verbs

1 Identifying main verb forms

Except for the verb *be*, the main verb of a sentence has five forms:

- Base or infinitive form. *I often* (*play, speak*).
- *-s/-es,* or third person singular form. *He often* (*plays, speaks*).
- Past tense. *Then I* (*played, spoke*).
- Past participle. *I have* (*played, spoken*) *before.*
- Present participle. *I am* (*playing, speaking*) *now.*

How to Edit Troublesome Verbs

Follow these tips to identify and edit verbs:

1. To find the verbs in a sentence, change the time of the action, from present to past, past to present, and so on. The verbs will change form and reveal themselves. *The neighbours played cards. The neighbours are playing cards.* (See 10c3.)
2. To find the correct forms of irregular verbs like *blow, lay,* and *lead,* see the lists in 15a3.
3. To choose the right tense when writing about literature, quoting, or arranging events in sequence, see 15b.

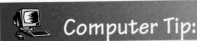

Computer Tip:

Using Your Spell Checker to Edit Verbs

Use your spell checker to check for verbs with incorrect endings. These often show up as misspellings.

2 Identifying regular and irregular verbs

Regular verbs form the past tense and past participle in predictable ways, by adding *-d* or *-ed*. **Irregular verbs** are "irregular" because they form the past tense and past participle in various unpredictable ways.

	PRESENT TENSE	PAST TENSE	PAST PARTICIPLE
Regular verbs	play believe	played believed	played believed
Irregular verbs	begin eat	began ate	begun eaten

All past tense verbs stand alone as single words: *The pianist played softly. The pianist began her solo.* When they act as the main verb of a sentence, both regular and irregular past participles require a helping verb like *be* or *have* to complete them: *The song was played repeatedly. The concert has begun.*

3 Identifying irregular verbs

If you're unsure about the form of an irregular verb, consult your dictionary or this list of common irregular verbs:

ROOT FORM	PAST TENSE	PAST PARTICIPLE
arise	arose	arisen
awake	awoke, awakened	awoken, awakened
be	was, were	been
beat	beat	beaten
begin	began	begun
bend	bent	bent
bet	bet	bet
bite	bit	bitten
blow	blew	blown
break	broke	broken
bring	brought	brought

ROOT FORM	PAST TENSE	PAST PARTICIPLE
broadcast	broadcast	broadcast
build	built	built
burst	burst	burst
buy	bought	bought
catch	caught	caught
choose	chose	chosen
come	came	come
cost	cost	cost
cut	cut	cut
do	did	done
draw	drew	drawn
drink	drank	drunk
drive	drove	driven
eat	ate	eaten
fall	fell	fallen
find	found	found
flee	fled	fled
fly	flew	flown
forget	forgot	forgotten
freeze	froze	frozen
get	got	gotten
give	gave	given
go	went	gone
grow	grew	grown
hang (suspend)	hung	hung
hang (execute)	hanged	hanged
hear	heard	heard
hide	hid	hidden
hit	hit	hit
hold	held	held
hurt	hurt	hurt
keep	kept	kept
know	knew	known
lay (place, set)	laid	laid
lead	led	led
leave	left	left
lend	lent	lent
let	let	let
lie (recline)	lay	lain
light	lit	lit
lose	lost	lost
make	made	made
meet	met	met
pay	paid	paid
put	put	put
quit	quit	quit
ride	rode	ridden
ring	rang	rung

ROOT FORM	PAST TENSE	PAST PARTICIPLE
rise	rose	risen
run	ran	run
say	said	said
see	saw	seen
send	sent	sent
set (lay, place)	set	set
shake	shook	shaken
shine	shone	shone
shoot	shot	shot
shrink	shrank	shrunk
shut	shut	shut
sing	sang	sung
sink	sank	sunk
sit	sat	sat
sleep	slept	slept
slide	slid	slid
speak	spoke	spoken
speed	sped	sped
spend	spent	spent
spit	spat	spat
spring	sprang	sprung
stand	stood	stood
steal	stole	stolen
strike	struck	struck
swim	swam	swum
swing	swung	swung
take	took	taken
teach	taught	taught
tear	tore	torn
tell	told	told
throw	threw	thrown
understand	understood	understood
wake	woke, waked	woken
wear	wore	worn
weave	wove	woven
win	won	won
wring	wrung	wrung
write	wrote	written

4 Avoiding nonstandard verb forms

Some speakers of English use verb forms different from those of Standard English. They add regular endings to irregular verbs (*blowed* instead of *blown*), treat regular verbs as if they were irregular (*drug* instead of *dragged*), or use the past participle in place of the past tense (*seen* instead of *saw*).

NONSTANDARD ENGLISH	STANDARD ENGLISH	NONSTANDARD ENGLISH	STANDARD ENGLISH
bended	bent	drived	drove
binded	bound	growed	grew
blowed	blew	shaked	shook
boughten	bought	shooken	shaken
brang	brought	snuck	sneaked
brung	brought	swang	swung
creeped	crept	sweared	sworn
drawed	drew	wrang	wrung

In your writing, use the appropriate standard forms for the past tense and past participle of regular and irregular verbs.

They asked where she had ~~boughten~~ the soapstone carving.
bought

[*Buy* is an irregular verb that forms its past participle without *-en*.]

The sports car ~~weaved~~ through the traffic recklessly.
wove

[*Weave* forms the past tense irregularly.]

We ~~seen~~ him working in the basement last night.
saw

[The past form of *see* is *saw*, not *seen*, which is the past participle.]

Once they had ~~shook~~ hands, the debaters took their places.
shaken

[The past participle is required after the auxiliary verb *have*.]

5   Spelling irregular verbs correctly

Because of their similarity to other words, the following are sometimes misspelled.

- *Laid/layed.* The past tense of *lay* is *laid*, not "layed."

  He ~~layed~~ the book on the table.
  laid

- *Led/lead.* The past tense of the verb *to lead* is *led*, not "lead."

  The leader ~~lead~~ the soldiers into battle.
  led

  [When *lead* is pronounced like "led," it refers to the soft gray metal, or to pencil lead.]

- *Lose/loose. Lose* is a verb; *loose* is an adjective.

  If he doesn't improve his grades, he may ~~loose~~ his scholarship.
  (lose)

- *Paid/payed.* The past tense of *pay* is *paid*, not "payed."

  The workers were ~~payed~~ weekly.
  (paid)

15*b*   Choose verb tenses that put events in sequence

Tense refers to the form a verb takes to indicate the time of an action: present (*she is studying*), past (*she studied*), and so on. Sometimes it is difficult to know which tense to choose to describe an action, especially if more than one action is involved. The following guidelines will help you decide. (To review the six tenses of English verbs and the way to create them using helping verbs and main verb forms, see 10c3 and 23a.)

1   Using the present tense in special situations

- *Writing about literature.* Authors of fiction, poetry, and nonfiction usually write in the past tense, for example: *The eight scouts left their horses and advanced on foot, stealthily, as though stalking a Blackfeet camp, and vanished among the trees* [Rudy Wiebe]. But to summarize action in a literary paper, use the present tense. (See 60f2.)

  The scouts ~~left~~ their horses and ~~advanced~~ on foot, before they ~~vanished~~
  (leave)   *(advance)*   *(vanish)*

  into the forest.

- *Introducing quotations, summaries, and paraphrases.* In research writing, use present tense verbs such as *reports*, *suggests*, and *argues* in signal phrases that introduce quotations, summaries, and paraphrases. Follow this convention whether the writer you cite is living or dead. (See also 52c1 for a list of verbs.)

  In the essay "Violent Crime," Bruce Shapiro ~~argued~~ that current
  (argues)

  anticrime legislation is based on a "delusion, a myth" about criminals.

  A note on APA style: If you include a date in the text of your writing, as the American Psychological Association style requires, use the past tense to introduce your borrowing: *In the essay "Violent Crime," Shapiro*

(1995) *argued that current anticrime legislation is based on a "delusion, a myth" about criminals.* (See also 56a1.)

- *Describing scientific principles and general truths.* Use the present tense to describe accepted scientific principles or general truths.

Ohm's law ~~described~~ *describes* the amount of resistance in an electrical circuit.

Canada's 1982 Charter of Rights and Freedoms ~~guaranteed~~ *guarantees* Canadians four fundamental freedoms, which ~~included~~ *include* freedom of peaceful assembly and freedom of conscience and religion.

2 Using the present perfect for past action still valid in the present

Use the present perfect tense (*has/have* + the past participle: *has laughed, have eaten*) when actions begin in the past and continue to the present or occur at no specific time.

I ~~never forgot~~ *have never forgotten* my mother's words of wisdom.

[Because the writer still remembers these words, the present perfect tense is appropriate.]

3 Using the past perfect for past action completed before other past action

Use the past perfect tense (*had* + the past participle: *had laughed, had eaten*) when a past action begins and is completed before another past action.

The police officer stated that my brother ~~was~~ *had been* in an accident.

[The accident occurred before the officer informed the writer.]

When the hikers reached the lake, they found that someone *had* camped there recently.

[Others had camped there before the hikers arrived.]

4 **Using infinitives and participles in a sequence of events**

Use infinitives and participles to refer to actions related in some way to the action expressed by the main verb.

- *Simultaneous actions: the present infinitive.* Use the present infinitive (*to* + the base verb form: *to laugh, to eat*) for actions occurring at the same time or immediately after the action of the main verb.

  Park officials try to ~~have sprayed~~ spray for mosquitoes after every rain.
  [The action of the infinitive *to spray* occurs at the same time as the action of the main verb *try*.]

- *One action and then another: the present perfect infinitive.* Use the present perfect infinitive (*to have* + the past participle: *to have laughed, to have eaten*) for actions occurring before the action of the main verb.

  The Mayor would like to ~~give~~ have given a speech before the council made its

  decision.
  [The speech would have occurred in the past before the Mayor's wish. Therefore, the present perfect infinitive (*to have given*) is required.]

- *Simultaneous actions: the present participle.* Use the present participle (-*ing*) for an action occurring simultaneously with that of the main verb: *Pulling into the parking lot, he saw a thief smashing a car window.*

- *One action and then another: the past participle or present perfect participle.* Use the past participle (*laughed, eaten*) or the present perfect participle (*having* + the past participle: *having laughed, having eaten*) for an action occurring before that of the main verb.

  Having finished
  ~~Finishing~~ his exam before time was up, Kim asked to be excused.

15c Beware of dropped or confused verb endings in words like *used, supposed, asked,* and *would have*

Influenced by the sound of spoken English, writers occasionally omit or confuse verb endings. Follow these guidelines to Standard English verb endings:

1   *Used to* and *supposed to*

"Use to" and "suppose to" are nonstandard. Write *used to* and *supposed to*.

Polly was ~~suppose~~ to fly to Goose Bay at the beginning of the month.
^{supposed}

Scientists ~~use~~ to believe that outer space was filled with ether.
^{used}

2   **Past and past perfect endings**

Signal the past and past perfect tenses of regular verbs with *-d* and *-ed* endings.

The little boy ~~frighten~~ the ducklings.
^{frightened}

My mother has ~~ask~~ me to call her every week.
^{asked}

3   *Would, could, should*

"Would of," "could of," and "should of" are nonstandard. Write *would've* or *would have*, *could've* or *could have*, *should've* or *should have*.

We would ~~of~~ won the tournament if we ~~could of~~ practised harder.
^{have}   ^{could have}

15*d* | Use the subjunctive mood for wishes and other nonfactual statements

The **mood** of a verb is a characteristic that indicates how the writer or speaker views the action expressed by the verb. The **indicative mood** is the most common form. It expresses facts or opinions, makes assertions, and asks questions: *She looked happy. We have not eaten yet. Are you sad?* The **imperative mood** is used for commands or direct requests (with *you* as the implied subject): *Come home. Try again.*

The **subjunctive mood** of verbs is used for statements contrary to fact: wishes, speculations, assumptions, recommendations, indirect requests, and hypothetical situations.

- Present subjunctive. To form the present tense subjunctive, use the base form of the verb (*be, give, arrive*): *It is necessary that everyone arrive by nine o'clock.*

- Past subjunctive. To form the past tense subjunctive of *be*, use *were*, not *was*: *If he were better organized, he would do more.* For all other past subjunctives, use the plain past tense.

Although slowly disappearing from English, the subjunctive still remains in certain phrases and situations, especially in writing.

1 Wishes and desires

Use the subjunctive to express wishes and to follow verbs expressing wishes or desires: *ask, demand, insist, prefer, recommend, request, require, suggest, urge.*

We recommend that the college ~~extends~~ [extend] an honorary fellowship to Sheila

Rogers.
[present subjunctive]

Gena wished that the instructor ~~was~~ [were] finished with his lecture.
[past subjunctive]

2 Nonfactual statements

Use the subjunctive after *if* or *as if* to express hypothetical or nonfactual situations.

If I ~~was~~ [were] you, I would study harder for tomorrow's quiz.

3 Indirect requests

Use the subjunctive to express indirect requests.

It is important that you ~~are~~ [be] in your seat before the concert begins.
[present subjunctive]

4 Speculation

Use the subjunctive to make a speculation.

James looked as though he ~~was~~ [were] enjoying the movie.
[past subjunctive]

129

chapter

16 Making Subjects and Verbs Agree

Agreement refers to the forms that words take to represent consistent number, person, case, and gender. When subjects and verbs *agree*, they match in number (singular or plural) and person (first, second, and third), as in the following examples.

	SINGULAR	PLURAL
First person	I run	we run
Second person	you run	you run
Third person	he/she/it runs, Pauline runs	they run

third person singular agreement

On weekends Penny volunteers at a homeless shelter.

third person plural agreement

Two homeless shelters were opened during last January.

How to . . .

How to Edit for Subject-Verb Agreement

Follow these tips to identify and correct errors in subject-verb agreement:

1. Look for long sentences.
2. Look for clue words that may accompany agreement errors: the sentence openers *There is/are, Here is/are* (16b); the conjunctions *and, or, nor* (16d and e); indefinite pronouns, such as *each, anyone, everybody* (16f); collective nouns, such as *team, committee, group, number* (16g); plural nouns considered as a single unit, such as *economics* and *measles* (16h); and the relative pronouns *who, which, that* (16i).
3. To decide whether subjects and verbs agree, first identify the subject and verb. (See 10c and 11a for guidelines.) Then read the subject and verb, omitting the words that come between. Rewrite if they do not have the same number (singular or plural) and person (first, second, or third person).

16*a*   Make separated subjects and verbs agree

Subjects and verbs are sometimes separated by other words. But no matter how far apart the two are, subjects determine the person and number of their verbs.

plural subject   plural verb
The tapestries on the walls of the palace were woven by children.

believes
Not one of the scientists investigating AIDS ~~believe~~ a cure will soon be

found.

[The subject of the sentence is *one*. *Scientists* is the object of the preposition *of* and cannot be the subject of the sentence.]

are
The beneficial effects of her enthusiastic work is apparent everywhere.

[The subject is the plural *effects*. *Work* is the object of the preposition *of* and cannot be the subject of the sentence.]

A note on prepositional phrases: Prepositional phrases that begin *accompanied by, along with, as well as, except, in addition to, including, no less than, together with,* or *with* do not add to a subject to make it plural. Identify the noun, pronoun, or noun phrase that is the true subject.

was
The valedictorian, together with her classmates, ~~were~~ asked to stand for

the audience's applause.

[The subject, *valedictorian*, is singular; *her classmates* is the object of the preposition *together with* and is not part of the subject. To form a plural subject, use a conjunction: *the valedictorian and her classmates*.]

16*b*   Make the subject and verb agree when the subject follows the verb

Normal English word order is subject + verb: *The geese were flying*. Occasionally, however, normal word order is inverted, and the subject follows the verb (verb + subject): *On the pine branch sat two large bluejays*. Whatever its position, the subject determines the number of the verb. Compare these two examples:

plural verb   plural subject
Seated in the front row were the parents of the bride and groom.

are
In his backpack ~~is~~ enough food and clothing for two weeks of camping.

[*Backpack* is the object of the preposition *in*; it is not the subject of the sentence. The subject is a compound, *food and clothing*, so the verb must be plural.]

A note on there *and* here: In sentences beginning *there is, there are, here is,* and *here are,* the subject follows the verb. Compare these two examples:

plural verb   plural subject

There are three reasons to elect Boris Brown to the Student Council.

The last time I looked there ~~was~~ a dictionary and a thesaurus on my desk.

were

[The compound subject, *a dictionary and a thesaurus,* is plural, so the verb must be plural.]

16*c* | Make a linking verb agree with its subject, not with a subject complement

Linking verbs (*am, is, are, was, were, seem, become, appear, feel, smell, sound, taste*) link a subject to an adjective or a noun—a *subject complement*—that explains the subject: *Becky Martin is a social worker.* Do not confuse the subject with the subject complement. In most sentences, the subject precedes a linking verb. (See 10c4 and 11d1.)

are

A loving family, loyal friends, and interesting work ~~is~~ my definition of

happiness.

[The three-part subject is plural and so the verb must be plural, even though the subject complement, *definition,* is singular.]

is

The most attractive feature of the house ~~are~~ the large, arched windows.

[The subject, *feature,* is singular, so the verb must be singular.]

If a grammatically correct sentence seems awkward, rewrite to turn the subject complement into the subject: *My definition of happiness is a loving family, loyal friends, and interesting work. The large, arched windows are the most attractive feature of the house.*

16*d* | With most compound subjects, use a plural verb

Most compound subjects are linked by the co-ordinating conjunction *and.*

plural subject   plural verb

Cairo and Alexandria are the two largest cities in Egypt.

are

The dress and equipment for racquetball ~~is~~ similar to those for tennis.

A note on unit compounds and compounds headed by each *or* every: If a compound subject is thought of as a unit, refers to one person, or is headed by *each* or *every*, use a singular verb.

The **horse and buggy is** the primary mode of transportation among the Old Order Mennonites.

The **company's president and chief operating officer has announced** her retirement.

Fortunately, **every man, woman, and child was rescued** from the sinking ship.

16*e* | With compound subjects linked by *or* or *nor*, make the verb agree with the closer subject

When both parts of a compound subject joined by *or* or *nor* are singular or plural, agreement is an easy match of subject and verb forms.

singular subject *nor* singular subject = singular verb

Neither Anna nor Gary plays chess well enough to be on the chess team.

plural subject *or* plural subject = plural verb

Either tulips or daffodils are a good choice for early spring flowers.

But when one subject is singular and the other is plural, the subject closer to the verb determines its number as singular or plural. When the closer subject is singular, the verb is singular. When the closer subject is plural, the verb is plural.

Neither the children nor their mother ~~were~~ was happy when the parade

ended.

[The singular *mother* is closer to the verb, so the verb must be singular.]

Either the lawyer or her clients ~~has~~ have been available each day for

interviews.

[The plural *clients* is closer to the verb, so the verb must be plural.]

To avoid awkwardness, rewrite using *and*: *The children and their mother were unhappy when the parade ended.* But note that *or* may be necessary to signal alternatives, either one subject or the other: *The children or their mother carries an umbrella to every parade.*

$16f$ | Treat indefinite pronouns as singular

Indefinite pronouns refer to indefinite, unspecified persons or things. (See 10b4.) The following indefinite pronouns usually take singular verbs.

another	each	everything	nothing
anybody	either	neither	somebody
anyone	everybody	nobody	someone
anything	everyone	no one	something

These words may seem to be plural and are often treated as such in speech. *Everybody* seems to refer to more than one person. But because their form is singular—there is only one *body* in *everybody*—indefinite pronouns take singular verbs. (See also 17d.) Compare these examples:

Each of the flowers is blooming.
Anyone who wants to be a good writer also has to be a good editor.

Neither of Joe's roommates ~~have~~ *has* signed up for intermural sports.
[*Neither* means not one, so the verb must be singular.]

Either of the mechanics ~~are~~ *is* able to repair the car.
[*Either* means one or the other, so the verb must be singular.]

A note on all, any, most, none, *and* some: These indefinite pronouns may be singular or plural, depending on the sense of the sentence or the words to which they refer.

All of the volunteers **have** arrived.
[*All* refers to more than one volunteer; the sense is plural.]

All that she has left **is** twenty-five dollars.
[*All* refers to the twenty-five dollars as a unit; the sense is singular.]

Most of the speakers **have** supported the proposal.
[The sense of *most* is plural.]

Most of the snow **has** melted.
[*Most* refers to snow, which is usually singular.]

$16g$ | Treat collective nouns as singular unless their individual members act separately

Collective nouns are words like *class, committee, couple, dozen, family, group, herd, jury, number, public, remainder,* and *team*. If their members act collectively, as a unit, collective nouns take a singular verb. If their members act separately, they take a plural verb. Compare these examples:

My daughter's **class is** going to Stratford to see *Hamlet*.

The class ~~is~~ *are* in their seats.

[In the first example, the class attends together as one, and the verb is singular. In the second, the individual members of the class take their own seats, the sense of the subject is plural, and the verb must be plural.]

The **jury is deliberating**.

The jury ~~is~~ *are* divided over the verdict.

[In the first example, the jury deliberates together as one, and the subject is singular. In the second, the individual members of the jury hold separate opinions, the sense of the subject is plural, and the verb must be plural.]

A note on noncount nouns: Noncount nouns referring to things as a whole (*advice, equipment, furniture, homework, luggage,* and so on) may seem like collective nouns. But noncount nouns are almost always singular and require singular verbs: *Our luggage is in the trunk of the car.*

A note on the difference between the number of *and* a number of: *The number* is a singular noun and takes a singular verb, unlike *a number of*, which is actually a quantifier meaning *some*. *A number of* is therefore plural and calls for a plural verb.

The number of students who prepare writing portfolios **is** increasing.

A number of these students **have** prepared portfolios.

16*h* With plural nouns singular in meaning, use singular verbs

Some plural nouns are singular in meaning or understood as a unit: *athletics, economics, mathematics, measles, news, physics, statistics.* These words take singular verbs. Compare these examples:

After last night's dinner, **three dollars was** all he had in his wallet.

Fifteen kilometres is a long way to hike through mountainous terrain.

Mathematics sometimes ~~cause~~ *causes* a disturbance known as "math anxiety."

Now that there is a vaccine, mumps ~~are~~ *is* no longer commonplace.

A note on units of measure: If units of measure refer to separate persons or things, use a plural verb. Otherwise, the verb is singular.

Three-fourths of the students **are** doing a work report.

Three-fourths of the school year **has** passed.

[In the first example, the students work individually, the sense of the subject is plural, and the verb is plural. In the second, *three-fourths* refers to one part of the year, and the verb is singular.]

A note on unit plurals: Some plural words thought of as a unit take a plural verb: *glasses, scissors, tweezers, jeans, groceries, headquarters, clothes.*

The **scissors were** lying on the table.

16*i* | With *who*, *which*, and *that*, use verbs that agree with their antecedents

To decide whether a relative pronoun is singular or plural, identify its **antecedent**, the noun or pronoun it refers to. (To learn to recognize nouns and pronouns, see 10a and b.)

noun   pronoun verb

The Atlas Mountains, which extend from Morocco to Tunisia, are among the highest in western Africa.

[The relative pronoun *which* refers to the Atlas Mountains, a plural noun, so the verb *extend* must be plural.]

1   *One of the . . . who/which/that*

The construction *one of the . . . who/which/that* usually precedes a plural verb. Compare these examples:

plural   plural plural

Leslie is one of the few members of this class who understand quadratic equations.

[*Who* refers to members, not *Leslie* or *one*; therefore, *who* is plural and the verb *understand* is plural.]

have

Rondeau is one of many provincial parks that ~~has~~ scenery worth a

second visit.

[*That* refers to *parks*; therefore, the verb must be plural.]

2   *Only one of the . . . who/which/that*

The construction *only one of the . . . who/which/that* usually precedes a singular verb. Compare these examples:

singular   singular   singular   singular

Leslie is the only one of these students who understands quadratic equations.

lives

The manatee is the only one of the elephant's relatives that ~~live~~
under water.

[*That* refers to *one*, not *relatives*. Only one relative lives under water.]

Note another version of the same construction: *I am the only person I know who actually enjoys airports.*

16*j* | With titles and words mentioned as words, use singular verbs

Whether the words in titles are singular or plural, individual works are considered one by one. The same is true for words used as examples. Use singular verbs for these.

When I was a child, *Alice's Adventures in Wonderland* **was** one of my favourite books.

[One book, singular, takes a singular verb.]

Wharves is the plural of *wharf*.

[A word used as a word takes a singular verb.]

was

Sunshine Sketches of a Little Town ~~were~~ written by Stephen Leacock.

[*Sunshine Sketches* is the title, not a description. It calls for a singular verb.]

---

chapter

17 Making Pronouns and Antecedents Agree

A pronoun refers to a noun or another pronoun, called the **antecedent**. (See 10b.) Whether appearing in the same sentence or different sentences, pronouns and antecedents must match (agree) in person (first, second, or third), number (singular or plural), and gender (masculine, feminine, or neuter).

third person singular feminine agreement

The **mother** cradled **her** child in **her** arms.

third person plural agreement

The **students** exchanged **their** essays to read and discuss.

third person singular neuter agreement

The **cat** pounced. Soon, **it** reappeared with a mouse in **its** mouth.

17*a* | With compound antecedents linked by *and*, use plural pronouns

David and **Darrell** congratulated **themselves** on their good luck.

17*b* | With compound antecedents linked by *or* or *nor*, make the pronoun agree with the appropriate antecedent

Neither **Tiffany** nor **Louise** uses a computer to write **her** papers.

[*Neither* means not one or the other; the pronoun must be singular.]

Either the **Cardinals** or the **Cubs** have a chance to win the World Series if **they** improve **their** pitching.

[Both antecedents are plural; the pronoun must be plural.]

Neither **Mrs. Newton** nor **her daughters** visit as often as they would like.

Neither **Mrs. Newton** nor **her daughters** visit as often as she would like.

Neither **Mrs. Newton** nor **her daughters** visit as often as any of them would like.

[The antecedent is *daughters* in the first sentence, *Mrs. Newton* in the second, and *Mrs. Newton and her daughters* in the third.]

If one antecedent is male and the other female, rewrite to avoid awkwardness or ambiguity. *Either Paul or Jill will share her notes* is unclear. An alternative: *Either Paul will share his notes, or Jill will share hers.*

17c | With collective nouns, use singular pronouns unless individual members act separately

Collective nouns are words like *audience, class, committee, couple, crowd, dozen, group, herd, jury, number, public, remainder,* and *team*. Compare these examples:

The **audience** gave **its** approval.

[The audience acted together, as a unit, and so the pronoun is singular.]

The **jury** refused to discuss **their** opinions of the defendant.

[Each member of the jury had a separate opinion, and so the pronoun that refers to *jury* is plural. An even better solution is to add the phrase *members of the* to make the plural agreement clear: *Members of the jury refused to discuss **their** opinions of the defendant.*]

its
The **jury** delivered ~~their~~ verdict.

[The members of the jury function together, as a unit, and so the pronoun that refers to *jury* must be singular.]

Remember that noncount nouns (see 10a6, 22b) are not plural and that any pronoun with a noncount antecedent will be singular: *Here is my luggage. Can you manage it?*

How to Edit Noun-Pronoun Agreement

Follow these tips to find pronouns and antecedents that may need editing for agreement:

1. Look for long sentences or passages in which your ideas are complex.
2. Look for the antecedents that may cause noun-pronoun disagreement: nouns linked by *and, or, nor* (17a and b); nouns referring to groups, such as *committee* or *audience* (17c); words referring to individuals without regard to gender, such as *student* or *everyone* (17d); names of organizations (17e).
3. To hear noun-pronoun disagreement, read a pronoun and its antecedent aloud, omitting any words between them.
4. Use singular pronouns to refer to singular antecedents; use plural pronouns to refer to plural antecedents.

Computer Tip:

Using Search and Replace to Find Antecedents That May Cause Pronoun Error

Use the Find or Search and Replace commands to locate *and, or, nor* and pronouns containing *-body, every-, -one.* (See item 2 in the "How To" box above.)

17d | With generic nouns and indefinite pronouns, avoid disagreement and stereotyping

Generic nouns and **indefinite pronouns** refer to individuals without regard to gender.

SAMPLE GENERIC NOUNS
person, student, professor, lawyer, chemist, secretary, doctor, athlete, bicyclist, firefighter, flight attendant

SAMPLE INDEFINITE PRONOUNS
anyone, each, everybody, nobody, none, someone, something, and so on (For a complete list, see 10b4.)

Using a singular pronoun (*he, she, his, her,* and so on) to refer to a generic noun or to an indefinite pronoun can create gender stereotyping. Consider this example: *A doctor owes his primary loyalty to his patients.* The pronouns in this sentence may imply that all doctors are male. In casual speech generally we avoid such stereotyping by using plural pronouns: *A person who goes out of their way to help others is a good Samaritan. Did everybody remember to bring their skis?* In this way, *person* and *everybody* may refer to male or female. But in your writing, pronouns and antecedents should agree in number. To make pronouns agree with generic nouns and indefinite pronouns—and to avoid gender stereotyping—follow these guidelines:

■ When possible, use plural nouns and pronouns.

Good Samaritans are people ~~A good Samaritan is a person~~ who ~~goes~~ *go* out of their way to help others.

[The plural generic noun *people* takes a plural pronoun, *their.*]

When ~~everyone~~ *the students* had finished studying, they picked up their books and left.

[Replacing the indefinite pronoun *everyone* with a plural generic noun *students* makes the plural personal pronoun *they* agree.]

- When possible, omit the generic noun or the pronoun.

  Good Samaritans make sacrifices to help others.

  ~~A good Samaritan is a person who goes out of their way to help others.~~
  ^

                                                    a
  Someone had walked off and left ~~their~~ backpack under a tree.
                                          ^

  [With rewording, these sentences omit the pronoun *their*.]

- When the sense of a sentence must be singular, use *he or she, his or her, him or her* to refer to a singular generic noun or an indefinite pronoun.

                                           his or her
  A good Samaritan is a person who goes out of ~~their~~ way to help others.
                                                    ^

                            his or her
  Someone had walked off and left ~~their~~ backpack under a tree.
                                       ^

  Avoid awkward chains of paired pronouns: *Everyone in the building was angry when he or she received his or her latest rent increase.* In formal writing do not use the slash to link pronouns, as in *he/she, his/her,* and so on. (See 41e2.)

17e | With nouns that name organizations, use singular pronouns

It may be logical to think of an organization in terms of its members and to refer to it with a plural pronoun. But use *it* and *its* to refer to a single organization.

                                                        It   has
  A good library contains more than books and periodicals. ~~They~~ also ~~have~~
                                                        ^   ^

  audiovisual materials of all kinds.

  [The pronoun *it* refers to the organization *library*.]

                            its
  St. Mary's Hospital cares for ~~their~~ patients' emotional as well as physical
                                    ^

  health.

  [*Its* refers to the organization *St. Mary's Hospital*.]

chapter

18 Making Pronoun Reference Clear

A pronoun refers to a noun or other pronoun, its **antecedent**, which gives the pronoun its meaning.

As *Stephanie* watched quietly, **she** saw a red *fox* emerge from **its** den.

Writers use pronouns to link one part of their writing to another and to avoid the monotony of repeated nouns. But when they use pronouns without specific antecedents or use too many pronouns, the result is faulty pronoun reference and writing that is vague and hard to understand. To help make your writing clear and coherent, follow these guidelines.

How to . . .

How to Clarify Pronoun Reference

Use the following tips to identify and correct unclear pronoun reference:

1. Locate your pronouns, and see whether each refers to a specific noun or pronoun. (See 18a.)
2. Look for nouns that refer to organizations and for possessive nouns (ending -'s or -s'). Then look for nearby pronouns and decide whether they can logically refer to these nouns. (See 18a1 and 2.)

   When my brother's car broke down near Wawa, he had to hitchhike over two hundred kilometres.

   [The antecedent of *he* cannot be the possessive noun *brother's*, which functions here as an adjective. Rearrange the sentence to include a noun antecedent: *When his car broke down near Wawa, my brother had to hitchhike over two hundred kilometres.*]
3. Look for the pronouns *you, it, this, who, which,* and *that,* especially at the beginning of sentences or clauses.
4. To decide whether pronoun reference is faulty, substitute the antecedent for the pronoun and reread. You'll hear the problem. (See 18a and b.)
5. Add a specific noun, indefinite pronoun, or noun phrase to be the antecedent for a pronoun.
6. Rewrite to replace an unclear pronoun with a clarifying word or phrase.

18*a* | Make pronouns refer to specific antecedents

You should be able to point to the antecedent that a pronoun refers to. If you can't identify the specific word or phrase, rewrite to supply the missing antecedent or to omit the pronoun.

My grandfather may have been seriously ill, but he declared that he
wasn't dead yet and wasn't afraid of ~~it~~.
                                  dying

[The pronoun *it* cannot refer to the adjective *dead*. To hear the faulty reference, try rereading the sentence using *dead* in place of *it*. The revision substitutes the noun *dying*, which completes the meaning of the sentence.]

Unemployment in Canada in the '30s was so severe that ~~they~~ had to
                                               homeless civilians
~~shelter them~~ in relief camps.
be sheltered

[In this sentence, *they* and *them* have no antecedents. The revision omits *they*, replaces *them* with *homeless civilians*, and changes the verb form.]

1   Not using *they, them,* and *their* to refer to organizations

A pronoun that takes the place of an organization should refer to the organization (*it, its*), not to its members (*they, them, their*).

In 1999, Eaton's announced that **it** was closing all **its** stores.

To revise faulty references to organizations, you can omit the faulty pronoun, substitute the appropriate pronoun, or add the name of the organization.

                                          its
Everyone likes the University Club because ~~their~~ menu is very exotic.

[The revision omits a pronoun that refers to people and replaces it with a pronoun referring to the restaurant itself.]

                    the Mint
On April 20, 1989, ~~they~~ printed the last $1 bill in Canada.

[The revision replaces a pronoun with an identifying noun.]

2   Not using pronouns to refer to possessive nouns

Nouns that end in *-'s* or *-s'* act as adjectives, not nouns, and so cannot be the antecedents for pronouns. Rewrite to supply a noun antecedent for each pronoun or to correct faulty pronoun reference.

                 its
As Lucy admired ~~the motorcycle's~~ sleek design, she knew she wanted to
the motorcycle.
own ~~it~~.

[*Motorcycle's* cannot be the antecedent of *it*. To hear the faulty reference, reread the sentence replacing *it* with *motorcycle's*.]

Jill bent to hear the old ~~woman's voice, who was~~ ^{woman}mumbling of old friends long dead.

[*Woman's* cannot be the antecedent of *who*. To hear the problem, try replacing *who* with *woman's*. The revision allows for the ownership of the mumbling.]

3 Not using *you* as an indefinite pronoun

You is a personal pronoun, used as an indefinite pronoun only in speech. In public writing, use *you* only to address readers directly. To refer to people in general, use *people* or *one*. If these words make your writing sound stuffy, rewrite to omit the pronoun.

Even in remote wilderness, ^{one can find}~~you can find~~ pollution, litter, and environmental damage.

Even in remote wilderness, ^{it is easy to}~~you can~~ find pollution, litter, and environmental damage.

4 Not using *it* to refer to authors or their writing

In summarizing, do not use the pronoun *it* to refer to authors or their works in phrases like *it says that*.

~~In~~ Margaret Atwood's *Survival*, ^{points out}~~it says~~ that feeling victimized is a Canadian trait.

[Logically, the author does the saying, not the book. The revision above emphasizes the book's message. Another revision emphasizes the author: *In* Survival, *Margaret Atwood points out that it is a Canadian trait to feel victimized.*]

18*b* Avoid ambiguous reference

Pronoun reference is ambiguous when a pronoun seems to refer to more than one antecedent. Rearrange or rewrite so that each pronoun has one clear antecedent.

^{When abusive}~~Abusive~~ parents often hit their children ^{are angry, they}~~when they are angry.~~

[In the original sentence, it is unclear who is angry. The revision clarifies the antecedent for *they*.]

To polish the watches, the ~~them~~
~~The~~ jeweller removed ~~the watches~~ from the display cases ~~to polish them~~.

[In the original, it is unclear whether the jeweller intended to polish the watches or the display cases. The revision clarifies the antecedent of *them*.]

18*c* | Generally avoid using *it*, *this*, *that*, and *which* to refer to whole sentences

If you use *it*, *this*, *that*, and *which* to refer broadly to whole sentences, you may confuse readers. Replace these pronouns with their antecedents or rewrite to clarify meaning.

When prices rise, consumers purchase less and production decreases.
pattern
This leads to higher unemployment.

[In the original, the antecedent for *this*, the cause of higher unemployment, is unclear.]

That most
~~Most~~ communities now offer door-to-door pickup of recyclables/ ~~which~~

has dramatically reduced the amount of garbage in local landfills.

[In the original, the pronoun *which* refers to the offering of door-to-door services, not to the pickup of the recyclables.]

18*d* | Use *who*, *whose*, or *whom* to refer to people and to animals with names

whom
Many early blues musicians, few of ~~which~~ could read or write music,

who
are remembered today only because of the historians ~~which~~ recorded

them.

Use *that*, *which*, and *whose* to refer to objects and unnamed animals.

The planets **that** orbit farthest from the sun are Neptune and Pluto.

The deer, **whose** food was threatened by drought, began foraging in suburban backyards.

19 Choosing Pronoun Case Forms

Nouns and pronouns change what is known as **case form** to signal their functions as subjects, objects, and possessives. Deciding the appropriate case form of nouns is rarely a problem because nouns change form only in the possessive (with the addition of an apostrophe).

- Subject and object forms: *That little <u>dog</u> just bit your <u>dog</u> on the tail.*

- Possessive forms: *My <u>dog's</u> bark is louder than your <u>dog's</u>.*

Personal pronouns and the relative pronouns *who* and *whoever* change form to signal each function.

| | | POSSESSIVE FORMS | |
SUBJECT FORMS	OBJECT FORMS	ADJECTIVE FORMS	NOUN FORMS
I	me	my	mine
you	you	your	yours
he/she/it	him/her/it	his/her/its	his/hers/its
we	us	our	ours
they	them	their	theirs
who/whoever	whom/whomever	whose	whose

To choose the pronoun form that matches its function in a sentence, use the following guidelines.

19*a* Use the subject form for subject pronouns and for pronouns that identify subjects

Singular pronoun subjects seldom cause a problem.

When **she** saw her nephew playing with the puppy, **she** laughed so hard that **she** almost cried.

1 Using pronouns in compound subjects

To determine the correct pronoun in a compound subject, use the "drop" test. Drop everything from the compound except the pronoun in question, say the sentence, and trust your ear to guide you.

Kim and ~~me~~ spent spring vacation in Vancouver.

[Drop *Kim* to hear the problem in *me spent*. The first person pronoun *I* is appropriate.]

> ### How to Edit Pronoun Case Forms
>
> To identify and revise pronouns that may not fit their roles in a sentence, follow these tips:
>
> 1. The "drop" test. When a pronoun is part of a compound or identifies a nearby noun, use the "drop" test. Drop everything from the compound except the pronoun in question, or drop the nearby noun. Reread the sentence, and trust your ear to tell you the correct form. (See 19a–c.)
>
>   The limousine brought Alice and I to our hotel.
>   The limousine brought … I to our hotel.
>
>   [The "drop" test reveals that *I* should be *me*, the direct object of the verb *brought*. *The limousine brought Alice and me to our hotel.*]
>
> 2. Pronouns before gerunds (-*ing* verb forms used as nouns). Use the possessive forms (*my, your, her, our,* and so on) for nouns and pronouns preceding gerunds: *I appreciate his loaning us his car.* (See 19d.)
>
> 3. *Who* or *whom.* When you're trying to decide between *who/whom* or *whoever/whomever,* follow the four-step formula in 19e.
>
> 4. Pronouns in comparisons. When a pronoun follows *than* or *as* in a comparison, mentally complete the thought to hear the correct form: *She's a much better tennis player than he [is].* (See 19f.)
>
> 5. Reflexive pronouns. Use reflexive pronouns (*myself, yourself,* and so on) only when the receiver of an action or the object of a preposition is identical to the doer of the action: *I did it myself.* (See 19g.)

We took the path because ~~me and him~~ *he and I* had been told it was open to bicyclists.

[Drop one half of the compound at a time to hear the problems: *me [. . .] had been told* and *him had been told.* In a compound construction, put the other person before yourself.]

2 Using pronouns as subject complements

Use the subject case form for pronouns that identify the subject or subject complement of a linking verb like *am, is, are, was,* or *were.* (See also 11d1.)

The only one to read the complete report was ~~me~~ *I*.

[*One* is the subject of the verb *was*. *I* complements—identifies—the subject and takes the subject form.]

In Standard Written English, subject complements are always in the subject form, but if this sounds stuffy, try another version of the sentence: *I was the only one to read the complete report.*

3 Using pronoun appositives that identify subjects

An **appositive** renames or describes a preceding noun. (See 12a3.) Use the subject case form for pronoun appositives that describe subjects.

At the end, only two spectators, Aftab and ~~me,~~ remained to mourn our
                                           ^I

team's loss.

[Use the "drop" test to remove everything from the subject phrase except the pronoun: *only [. . .] me remained. I* is the appropriate form.]

4 Using *we* or *us* before subjects

Use the subject form *we*, not the object form *us*, to precede and identify a subject.

                                    we
Does Professor Desai know that ~~us~~ students want to postpone the exam?

[Use the "drop" test to omit the subject and hear the problem in *that us [. . .] want to postpone the exam. We* is appropriate.]

19*b* | Use the object form for pronouns that are objects

Single direct objects, indirect objects, or objects of prepositions seldom cause a problem.

Lisa's parents saw **her** sitting on the porch.

To choose the correct pronouns for compound objects, use the "drop" test. Drop everything from the object except the pronoun, read the sentence, and trust your ear to guide you.

1 Using pronouns in compound direct and indirect objects

When pronouns act as direct or indirect objects to complete the meaning of a verb, use the object case form. (See 11c.)

                                  me
Please help my friend and ~~I~~ with this calculus problem.

[Drop *my friend and* to hear the problem in *help [. . .] I. Me* is appropriate.]

2 Using pronouns as objects of prepositions

Use the object form for pronouns following prepositions. (See 12a1.)

I wish someone would settle a friendly debate between my father and ~~I~~. *me*

[*Between* is a preposition. Drop *my father and* to hear the error in *between [. . .] I*. *Me* is correct.]

3 Using pronoun appositives that describe direct or indirect objects

Appositives follow a noun and identify it. (See 12a3.) Use the object form for pronouns in an appositive that follows a direct or indirect object.

Professor Konewski chose two new research assistants, John Park and ~~I~~. *me*

[Drop *two new research assistants, John Park and* to hear the problem in *chose [. . .] I*. *Me* is appropriate.]

19*c* | Use the object form in the compound subjects and objects of infinitives

An **infinitive** consists of *to* plus the base form of the verb: *She asked me to bake a chocolate cake.* But the *to* is sometimes omitted: *She helped me bake a cake.* (See 12a2.) To hear the correct pronoun form with infinitives, use the "drop" test. Drop everything from the compound except the pronoun in question, reread the sentence, and trust your ear.

Our English instructor has asked Oscar and ~~I~~ to critique each other's *me*

essays.

[Drop *Oscar and* to hear the problem in *has asked [. . .] I to critique*. The object form in *has asked [. . .] me* is appropriate.]

Penny volunteered to tutor John and ~~I~~. *me*

[Drop *John and* to hear the problem in *to tutor [. . .] I*. The object form in *to tutor [. . .] me* is appropriate.]

19*d* | Use the possessive form for nouns and pronouns before gerunds

A **gerund** is an *-ing* verb used as a noun: *Flying is safer than driving.* (See 12a2.) Use the possessive case form for nouns and pronouns that precede gerunds: *the pilot's flying, his flying.*

Roger appreciated ~~Celeste~~ ^{Celeste's} helping him learn Spanish.

Dorothy received the credit for ~~him~~ ^{his} being elected to the council.

A note on participles and gerunds: Do not confuse participles with gerunds. A participle is an *-ing* or *-ed* verb used as an adjective: *Flying low, the hawk searched for prey.* Here *flying* is an adjective describing *hawk.* Do not use the possessive form before participles.

- No possessive before a participle: *Kevin observed a hawk [that was] flying above the field.*

- A possessive before a gerund: *Amelia Earhart's flying made her a hero.*

A note on possessive pronouns and the apostrophe: Possessive pronouns do not contain apostrophes: *yours, hers, its, ours, theirs,* and *whose.* (See 39a.)

19e Use *who* and *whoever* for subjects and subject complements, *whom* and *whomever* for objects

Follow these four steps to help you decide when to use *who, whoever, whom,* and *whomever.**

- Step 1: Consider the words following *who/whom.* In the sentence *The reporter was uncertain who/whom she should interview,* look at the words *who/whom she should interview.*

- Step 2: Rearrange these words to make a complete sentence. Leave a blank where the pronoun should go: *She should interview _____ .*

- Step 3: In the blank put *he, she, him, her, they,* or *them,* whichever is correct: *She should interview him.*

- Step 4: Go back to your original sentence, and use the subject form *who* or *whoever* when Step 3 calls for *he, she,* or *they,* or use the object form *whom* or *whomever* when Step 3 calls for *him, her,* or *them: The reporter was uncertain whom she should interview.*

Another example:

Who/whom do you think should receive the award?

[Step 1: Consider the words following the pronoun. Step 2: Rearrange them to make a sentence, with a blank where the pronoun should be: *Do you think ____ should*

---

*For the formula to discover pronoun case, we are grateful to Maxwell Nurnberg, *Everything You Always Wanted to Know about English* (New York: Pocket Books, 1972).

receive the award? Step 3: In the blank, put *he, she, him, her, they,* or *them,* whichever is correct: *Do you think they should receive the award?* Step 4: Replace *he, she, they* with *who* or *whoever;* replace *him, her, them* with *whom* or *whomever: Who do you think should receive the award?*]

19*f* For the correct form in comparisons using *than* or *as*, mentally complete the sentence

Informal spoken English often uses an object pronoun after *than* and *as*: *Brenda likes jazz more than me.* But this construction is ambiguous. Does it mean Brenda likes jazz more than I like jazz, or Brenda likes jazz more than she likes me? In your writing, use the subject or object forms following *than* or *as* to make your meaning clear. To choose the correct form, complete the thought: *Brenda likes jazz more than I do.*

Fran may be younger than her supervisor, but she is as qualified as ~~him~~. *he [is qualified]*

[*He* is the subject of the unstated verb *is qualified.* If it sounds stuffy to end a sentence with *he,* add the verb: *she is as qualified as he is.*]

Our next-door neighbour gets along better with his pets than us. *he does with*

[To remove ambiguity in writing, spell out the full comparison: either *gets along better with his pets than we do* or *than he does with us.*]

19*g* Use reflexive (-*self*) pronouns only to refer to an identical preceding noun or pronoun

Reflexive pronouns are formed by adding -*self* to pronouns: *myself, yourself, itself, himself, herself, ourselves, themselves.* They identify objects that are the same as the subject: *The baby scratched itself. We are going for a walk by ourselves.* (See also 10b7.) When dealing with a compound, use the "drop" test to hear the correct form. Drop everything from the compound except the pronoun in question, reread, and trust your ear.

Howard and ~~myself~~ have operated our antique store for only a year.

[Drop *Howard and* to hear *myself have operated. I have operated* is appropriate.]

Marta has invited your parents and ~~yourselves~~ to the concert. *you*

[Drop *your parents and* to hear *invited yourselves. Invited you* is appropriate.]

Please contact Mr. Edwin or ~~myself~~ if you have questions. *me*

[Drop *Mr. Edwin or* to hear *contact myself. Contact me* is appropriate.]

A note on nonstandard forms: Hisself, themself, theirself, or *theirselves* are not Standard English. Use *himself, herself,* or *themselves.*

chapter

20 Choosing Adjectives and Adverbs

20a | Use adjectives to modify nouns and pronouns; use adverbs to modify verbs, adjectives, and other adverbs

1 Using adjectives

Adjectives modify—provide information about—nouns and pronouns by indicating which, what kind, or how many. (See 10d.)

          which   what kind

That tall, heavyset man is an excellent dancer.

A note on adjectives in sequence: When two or more adjectives are used without commas separating them, they must be arranged in a specific order. (See 24f3 and 36d.)

2 Using adverbs

Adverbs modify verbs, adjectives, or other adverbs to indicate time, place, manner, frequency or degree: *She spoke enthusiastically.* (See 10e.) Many adverbs, as in this example, end in *-ly,* but not all: *always, here, nearby, then, there,* and *very.* And some *-ly* words are adjectives: *friendly* and *lovely.*

In casual speech, adjectives are sometimes substituted for adverbs, usually by dropping the *-ly.* In writing, however, be sure to use adverbs when called for.

                    certainly
Stock market investors in 1929 ~~sure~~ did not expect the market to crash.

[An adverb is necessary to modify the verb *expect.*]

                    rapidly
Second parent adoption is a ~~rapid~~ growing practice.

[*Rapidly* is necessary to modify the verbal adjective *growing.*]

How to . . .

How to Edit Adjectives and Adverbs

Follow these tips to identify and edit adjectives and adverbs:

1. Adjectives answer the questions *Which? What kind? How many?* They modify (provide information about) nouns and pronouns. Adverbs answer the questions *How? When? Where? Why?* They modify verbs, adjectives, and other adverbs. (See 20a.)
2. Look for linking verbs (*appear, be, become, feel, grow, look, prove, remain, seem, smell, sound, taste, turn*) that are often followed by complements, words describing the subject of the sentence. Be sure that these complements are adjectives or nouns, not adverbs. (See 20b1.)
3. Look for the verbs *call, consider, create, elect, find, keep*, and *make*. Use adjectives, not adverbs, to complement their direct objects. (See 20b2.)
4. Look for *good, bad, well, badly*. Use *good* and *bad* as adjectives, especially after linking verbs like *be, look, smell*, and so on. Use *well* as an adjective to refer to health; otherwise, use *well* as an adverb. Use *badly* as an adverb.
5. Look for comparative statements. Use comparative forms (*-er, more, less*) to compare two subjects; use superlative forms (*-est, most, least*) to consider three or more. Use one comparative form at a time, *-er* or *more, -est* or *most*. (See 20d.)
6. Look for absolutes, words like *unique, perfect*, or *priceless* that cannot be compared. Omit the comparative or superlative, or rewrite to make your meaning clear. (See 20d4.)
7. Look for negative words. Use one negative word at a time. (See 20e.)

Everybody needs to drive ~~slow~~ slowly in residential areas.

[An adverb is necessary to modify the verb *drive*.]

It was a ~~right~~ very fine morning, perhaps the best of the summer.

[In casual speech, words like *real* and *right* and *way* are often used to modify adjectives like *fine*. Standard writing calls for *very*.]

20b | Use adjectives as complements

Adjectives usually appear before nouns. But they may also follow certain verbs as complements, words that complete the meaning of a noun or pronoun. Sometimes it is difficult to decide whether to use an adjective complement modifying a noun or an adverb modifying a verb.

1   Using subject complements

Subject complements describe or rename the subjects of the linking verbs *appear, be, become, feel, grow, look, prove, remain, seem, smell, sound, taste, turn*. (See 11d1). Use an adjective as a subject complement following a linking verb. Compare these examples:

She *appears* angry.

Does anything smell as ~~sweetly~~ ^{*sweet*} as a freshly mowed lawn?

[*Sweet*, an adjective, modifies the subject *anything*, not the verb *smell*. It describes a thing, not an action.]

2   Using object complements

Object complements give information about the direct objects of the verbs *call, consider, create, elect, find, keep,* and *make*. (See 11c1 and 11d2.) Use adjectives to modify noun and pronoun direct objects.

A safety deposit box will keep valuable papers ~~safely~~ ^{*safe*}.

[Because the papers will be secure, use the adjective *safe* to describe the direct object *papers*, rather than the adverb *safely*, which tells how the action of keeping is done.]

20*c* | Use *good/well* and *bad/badly* correctly

Some writers find these words troublesome because of the influence of casual speech; others may try too hard to use them correctly. Follow these guidelines to the correct use of *good, well, bad,* and *badly*.

1   Use *good* and *bad* as adjectives

Use *good* and *bad* as adjectives after linking verbs (see the list in 20b1): *The fresh bread smelled good. The music from those speakers sounds bad.*

As the coach studied her players, she thought how ~~well~~ ^{*good*} everyone

looked.

[*Good* is a subject complement accompanying the linking verb *looked* and describing the appearance, not the health, of the subject *everyone*.]

Bill felt ~~badly~~ ^{*bad*} about his behaviour.

[Following the linking verb *felt*, *bad* is an adjective, a subject complement describing the subject *Bill*. Compare with *Bill felt sad* (not *sadly*) *about it*.]

2 Using *well* as an adjective or an adverb

Use *well* as an adjective to refer to health or well-being. Otherwise, use it as an adverb modifying verbs, adjectives, and other adverbs.

After three weeks' rest, I feel ~~good~~ again. [*well*]

[Here *well* is an adjective following a linking verb and completing the subject *I*.]

After a tuneup, the car runs ~~good~~. [*well*]

[Here *well* is an adverb modifying the verb *runs*.]

3 Using *badly* as an adverb

Use *badly* only as an adverb: *The team played badly.*

20d Use the comparative and superlative forms appropriately

1 Forming comparatives and superlatives

Adjectives and adverbs have three forms to indicate degree or intensity: **positive**, **comparative**, and **superlative**.

POSITIVE	COMPARATIVE	SUPERLATIVE
good	better	best
bad	worse	worst
far	farther, further	farthest, furthest
little	less	least
much, many	more	most
old	older, elder	oldest, eldest
expensive	more expensive, less expensive	most expensive, least expensive

To form comparatives and superlatives, follow these guidelines:

- One-syllable adjectives and adverbs generally use *-er* and *-est* (*taller, tallest; faster, fastest*).

- Two-syllable adjectives accented on the first syllable use *-er* and *-est* (*happier, happiest; lovelier, loveliest*).

- Three-syllable adjectives use *more/most, less/least* (*more beautiful, most beautiful; less beneficial, least beneficial*).

- Two- and three-syllable adverbs, especially those ending in *-ly*, use *more/most, less/least* (*more slowly, most slowly; less happily, least happily*).

2 Choosing between comparative and superlative forms

Use the comparative form to compare two things, the superlative to compare three or more.

Although Ernest Hemingway and Morley Callaghan are considered

major novelists, Hemingway has been ~~most~~ *more* influential.

[Two writers are compared; the comparative is necessary.]

My chores were weeding, planting, and, ~~worse,~~ *worst of all* emptying garbage.

[Three activities are compared; the superlative is necessary.]

3 Avoiding repetition of comparative or superlative forms

Use either *-er/-est* or *more/most*, not both.

Decreasing the number of pollutants will lead to a ~~more~~ healthier

environment.

That was the most ~~unkindest~~ *unkind* remark I have ever heard.

4 Avoiding comparison of absolutes

Absolutes are words describing characteristics that cannot be compared. When *unique* means one of a kind, something cannot be more "unique" or "most unique." If an object is *priceless*, it is without price. It cannot be "more priceless" or "most priceless." Other absolutes: *absolute, boundless, circular, complete, definite, empty, even, eternal, favourite, final, full, inevitable, mutual, perfect, perpendicular, round, square, sufficient, supreme, total, triangular, universal, vacant.* Avoid the comparison of absolutes.

Your story will be ~~more~~ complete when you add an exciting ending.

Of all the modern jazz artists, Peter Appleyard is my ~~most~~ favourite.

20*e* | Avoid double negatives

A **double negative** says no twice and seems to contradict itself: *Eighteen-year-olds don't have nothing to lose by staying in school.* A logical person might say that if these young people do *not* have *nothing* to lose, then they must have *something* to lose. One negative cancels the other and turns a negative statement into a positive. Of course, no one misunderstands double negatives in this way. In many dialects of English, the double negative is a way of saying no emphatically.

But Standard English tends to be logical. Therefore, avoid double negatives in writing. Avoid using *not, never,* or *no* with other negative words, such as *no one, nobody, neither, none, nothing, barely, hardly,* and *scarcely.*

Eighteen-year-olds ~~don't~~ have nothing to lose by staying in school.

She ~~can't hardly~~ swim a stroke.
    can barely

Despite what some advertisers promise, it is impossible to lose weight without doing ~~no~~ exercise.
    any

An exception: You may use a double negative to soften the intensity of a positive statement or to suggest irony: *Karen was not unhappy to learn she would graduate with honours.*

chapter

21 Putting Linked Words in Parallel Form

Parallel form (also known as *parallelism* or *parallel structure*) refers to the pairing of grammatical structures with two or more words, phrases or clauses, particularly those linked by co-ordinating conjunctions.

In the phrase *Newfoundland and Labrador, Newfoundland* and *Labrador* are parallel nouns linked by a co-ordinator. Similarly, *stay or go* is a pair of linked, parallel verbs. The popular definition of democracy as government *of the people, by the people* and *for the people* is a series of parallel prepositional phrases. And from the American president John F. Kennedy's inaugural address, *ask not what your country can do for you—ask what you can do for your country* is a pair of parallel clauses. Parallelism is a way to join and emphasize equally important ideas.

Faulty parallelism occurs when linked words do not have the same grammatical form. To put something *orally and in writing* links an adverb with an adverb phrase. *To like hiking* and *to ski* links a verbal noun with an infinitive. *Tall, handsome, and with a sly smile* links two adjectives to a prepositional phrase. To make your sentences emphatic and grammatical, put linked words in parallel form. (See also 25c.)

21a Make words linked by co-ordinating conjunctions parallel in form

Co-ordinating conjunctions (*and, but, yet, or, nor*) link grammatically equal words. (See 10g1.) Use parallel forms before and after these conjunctions.

> *jogging*
> Among her favourite sports, Lucy likes ~~to jog~~ and racquetball the most.

[In the original, the verb *to jog* is linked to a noun, *racquetball*. The revision links a noun to a noun.]

> *having*
> Nearing thirty-five and ~~with~~ only a high school diploma, Alan is
>
> pessimistic about his future.

[In the original, an adjective phrase *nearing thirty-five* is linked to a prepositional phrase, *with only a high school diploma*. The revision links two adjective phrases, *nearing thirty-five* and *having only a high school diploma*.]

> *for running*
> We enjoyed everything about the trip except ~~when we ran~~ out of gas in
> *getting caught in*
> Lethbridge and a violent rainstorm in Medicine Hat.

[In the original, the clause *when we ran out of gas in Lethbridge* is linked to the noun phrase *a violent rainstorm in Medicine Hat*. The revision links two gerund phrases as objects of the preposition *for*.]

21b Put words in a series or a list in parallel form

Words in series may be linked by a conjunction, or they may be a list. In either case, make each item in the series grammatically parallel to the others.

How to Edit for Parallel Form

Follow these tips to identify and fix faulty parallelism:

1. Look for the conjunctions *and, but, or, yet, nor*, alone and in pairs with *both, either, neither*, and *not only*.
2. Look for comparisons. Be sure that the items being compared have the same grammatical form. (See 21d.)

How to ...

As I plan this term, I am dividing my life into three areas: ~~academic,~~ ^school^

work, and leisure.

[In the original, the adjective *academic* is linked with two nouns. The revision links three nouns.]

The last comedian to appear was loud, rude, and ~~had a~~ belligerent ~~way~~

~~of talking~~.

[The original links two adjectives (*loud* and *rude*) to a verb phrase (*had a belligerent way of talking*). The revision links three adjectives.]

21*c* | Make words linked by correlative conjunctions (*either . . . or*) parallel in form

Correlative conjunctions are linking phrases that come in two parts: *either . . . or, neither . . . nor, not only . . . but also, both . . . and, whether . . . or.* (See 10g2.) Make words linked by correlative conjunctions grammatically parallel. Do not use a comma after the first part unless you join two complete sentences.

When it comes to fast food, I love not only old favourites like

hamburgers ~~,~~ but ~~I~~ also ~~like~~ ethnic foods like felafel.

[The original links a noun phrase *old favourites like hamburgers* to a clause *I also like ethnic foods like felafel*. The revision links two noun phrases: *old favourites like hamburgers* and *ethnic foods like felafel*.]

Cassie was undecided about going either white water rafting or ~~to camp~~. ^camping^

[The original links a gerund *rafting* to the infinitive phrase *to camp*. The revision links two gerunds, *rafting* and *camping*.]

21*d* | Make comparisons using *than* or *as* parallel in form

Many students find it easier to write a research paper than ~~composing~~ a ^to compose^

poem.

[The original links the infinitive *to write* and the gerund *composing*. The revision links two infinitives, *to write . . . than to compose*.]

You can prepare meals in a microwave oven twice as fast as ~~using~~ ^{on} a

conventional stove.

[The original links the prepositional phrase *in a microwave oven* to a gerund phrase *using a conventional stove*. The revision links two prepositional phrases.]

21e Repeat function words to achieve parallel form

Readers depend on function words to signal grammatical forms and relations. Function words are prepositions (*to, by, in,* and so on), articles (*a, an, the*), the infinitive *to,* and introductory words at the beginning of clauses (*that, who, which, because, when, if,* and so on). If readers may misunderstand you, repeat function words before parallel statements. To see the effect of repetition, read the following examples in their original versions and then in revision.

The climbers deserved praise for risking their lives to save their injured friend but not *for* the recklessness that led to his fall.

The keys to academic success, Jana decided, were to attend class as if she were going to work and *to* study as if she were playing a sport.

The waiter was fired not only because he was incompetent but also *because* he had twice taken money from the cash register.

Roughly speaking, an **idiom** is a construction that "sounds right" to a native speaker of a language. There is no simple explanation for it, it occurs unpredictably, and it defies logic. As you can imagine, idiomatic usage is very frustrating for someone who is just learning the language, for it calls for memorization and constant practice.

If English is not your first language, the chapters in this section will provide immediate answers to your questions about idiomatic structures and constructions. Use them as a review of grammar rules, a quick reference while writing, a checklist for revising, and an index to other sections that contain important information for all writers.

If you are a native speaker of English, some of the material in this section may surprise you. You can put it to use in two situations: (1) to clear up your own occasional problems with idioms, and (2) to provide a solid introduction to constructions you need to know if you want to tutor or teach someone who is learning English as another language. Given the ever-growing number of international opportunities, it is certainly to your advantage to have a knowledge of English that goes beyond saying "it just sounds right."

Whether English is your native language or not, you will find detailed answers to questions about usage in the following widely available references:

- Dictionaries: *Cambridge International Dictionary of English, Collins Cobuild Essential Dictionary,* or *Oxford Advanced Learner's Dictionary.*

- Phrasebooks and idiomatic dictionaries: *The Penguin Dictionary of English Idioms* or the *Oxford Dictionary of Current Idiomatic English.*

- Practice for advanced speakers and writers of English: Betty Schrampfer Azar, *Understanding and Using English Grammar* (Prentice Hall) or Michael Swan, *Practical English Usage* (Oxford).

chapter

22 Determiners

Articles (*a, an, the*) and quantifiers (*a few, many, some, much,* and so on) introduce nouns, which may or may not be preceded by other words. We call them **determiners** because they often determine the kind of noun that will follow (singular, plural, noncount, specific, nonspecific).

article + noun

The cloth was unusually expensive.

article + adjective + noun

An exquisite cloth covered the table.

quantifier + noun

Some cloth was needed to finish the curtains.

How to Edit Sentences When English Is Not Your First Language

How to . . .

Once you have written your first draft, take time to look at the structure of your sentences. Use this checklist to help focus on typical problem areas:

1. *Determiners.* Do they suit the nouns they introduce? Be sure to include required articles and quantifiers, especially with singular count nouns (See 22.)
2. *Subjects and verbs.* Agreement rules apply here. Singular subjects take singular verbs; plural subjects take plural verbs. Do your subjects and verbs match? (See 16 and 23b.)
3. *Verb forms.* All the verbs in a verb phrase have to match in time, number, aspect, and voice. Make sure that your verbs match their context. Check also that you've used the right auxiliaries with your main verbs. (See 23.)
4. *Idioms.* When you aren't sure that the expression is just right, check a dictionary or ask a native speaker of English. Be especially careful of idiomatic verb combinations and the prepositions that go with certain verbs. (See 23h and i.)
5. *Completeness.* Does each sentence contain all its essential parts? (See 24b.)
6. *Word order.* Look at your base sentence; then consider the modifiers. Is your subject/verb order appropriate for statements or questions? (See 24d.) Are modifiers in the right place? (See 28a and b, 24f3 and 4.)
7. *Word endings.* Check word endings twice. First of all, are they right for their roles as nouns (for example, *safety*), verbs (*save*), adjectives (*safe*), or adverbs (*safely*)? Use a dictionary to help you make decisions. Second, do they agree in number (singular or plural), tense and participle form (past or present), case (subject, object, or possessive), and so on?
8. *Prepositions.* Keep a master list of idiomatic pairs. Use your dictionary or a phrase book to confirm their use. (For phrases of place and time, see 24g.)

22*a* | Use *a/an* with nonspecific singular count nouns

Count nouns name persons, places, or things that can be counted numerically. They may be singular or plural: *student/students, city/cities, computer/computers*. **Nonspecific count nouns** are nouns that have not yet been specifically identified:

A computer does calculations.   Computers do calculations.

As this example illustrates, nonspecific singular count nouns can be introduced by *a* or *an*.

1 Matching *a* with consonant sounds, *an* with vowel sounds

- Use *a* before words beginning with a consonant sound: *a book, a happy man, a pen*.

- Use *an* before words beginning with a vowel sound (*a, e, i, o, u*, or silent *h*, as in *hour*): *an apple, an episode, an impossible task, an operator, an understanding, an honour*.

2 Knowing when to use *a* or *an*

With singular countable nouns, use *a* or *an* in the following situations:

- To mean "one of a certain type": *A banana will give you more energy than an apple*.

  Most moral issues have ᵃ⌃ grey area where right and wrong become cloudy.

- To refer to "one out of many choices": *Choose an apple from this bowl*.

  I have just received ᵃⁿ⌃ exciting job offer.

- To mention something for the first time: *A dish* [first mention] *fell off the counter and broke. The dish* [second mention] *belonged to my grandmother*.

  Exceptions: *The* is used generically with certain nonspecific singular count nouns to mean "one representative of a certain type or class."

- Classes of humans, plants, or animals: *The woolly mammoth lived in Siberia 6 000 years ago*.

- Parts of the body: *The funny bone is very sensitive.*

- Inventions and devices, including musical instruments: *The koto, a stringed instrument similar to the zither, is important to Japanese sacred music.*

22b | Never use *a/an* with noncount nouns

Noncount nouns refer to things that must be measured, not counted, and things that cannot be made plural. They are never introduced by *a* or *an*.

- **Whole groups of similar items:** *baggage, clothing, equipment, food, fruit, furniture, garbage, hardware, jewellery, junk, luggage, machinery, mail, make-up, money/cash/change, postage, scenery, traffic,* and so on.

                                    one piece of
  When I return home next time, I will take only ~~a~~ luggage.

  [To refer to countable units of noncount nouns, use measures like *one piece of* or *a little.* See 22e3.]

- **Abstractions:** *advice, beauty, courage, education, grammar, happiness, health, homework, honesty, importance, information, knowledge, laughter, music, news, peace, progress, sleep, time, violence, vocabulary, wealth, work,* and so on.

  On television, /\ violence is often presented as attractive and exciting.

- **Liquids:** *water, coffee, tea, milk, oil, soup, gasoline, blood, . . .*
- **Solids:** *ice, bread, butter, cheese, meat, gold, iron, silver, glass, paper, wood, cotton, wool, . . .*
- **Gases:** *steam, air, oxygen, hydrogen, smoke, smog, pollution, . . .*
- **Particles and powders:** *rice, chalk, corn, dirt, dust, flour, grass, hair, pepper, salt, sand, sugar, wheat, . . .*
- **Languages:** *Arabic, Chinese, English, Polish, Sanskrit, Spanish, Urdu, . . .*
- **Fields of study:** *chemistry, engineering, history, mathematics, . . .*
- **Recreation:** *baseball, bridge, chess, soccer, tennis, . . .*
- **General activities:** *driving, studying, travelling, . . .*
- **Natural phenomena:** *darkness, dew, electricity, fire, fog, gravity, hail, heat, humidity, lightning, rain, sleet, snow, thunder, weather, wind, . . .*

Note: Many nouns have both count and noncount uses: *Please bring us two coffees* [count noun]. *The caffeine in coffee* [noncount noun] *keeps me awake.* Your dictionary may help you distinguish between units and masses with dual nouns like these.

22c | Use *the* with nouns whose specific identity your readers know

The definite article *the,* indicating "this" or "that," introduces a specific person, place, or thing singled out from others. Use *the* in the following situations:

- When readers know exactly what the noun represents: *I have to go to the bank to get some money.*

  the
  Many societies have abandoned ˄ death penalty.

- When the noun refers to a unique person, place, or thing: *Last year we visited the Vatican, but we didn't see the Pope.*

  the   the
  A full eclipse of ˄ sun or ˄ moon is quite impressive to see.

- When the noun is mentioned for the second time: *Last night I went to a new restaurant* [first mention]. *They call the restaurant* [second mention] *Le Cochon Dingue.*

- When the words following the noun make its identity clear: *The student who won the chess championship was Clara Vaz.*

  the
  In this poem, ˄ speaker reminds us that flowers, too, are mortal.

- When the noun is modified by a superlative adjective.

  The tallest player on the team is Nestor Wozny.

  When I finally got married, **the most relieved person in the room** was my mother.

22d | Do not use *the* with most proper nouns and statements meaning "all" or "in general"

1 Proper nouns

Do not use *the* before most singular proper nouns, including languages (*French, English*), people (*Brian Tobin*), organizations (*Greenpeace*), special days (*Valentine's Day*), continents (*South America*), countries (*Scotland*), provinces (*Manitoba*), cities and towns (*St. John's*), streets and roads (*Bank Street, University Avenue*), squares (*Place Ville-Marie*), parks (*Victoria Park*), individual lakes (*Canoe Lake*), bays (*James Bay*), islands (*Prince Edward Island*), and specific mountains (*Mount Robson*).

In ~~the~~ Japanese, the saying "Look up into the sky" means "Stop and smell the roses."

Some singular proper nouns are exceptions and require *the*:

- Use *the* before phrases identifying a specific language: *the Russian language, the Portuguese language,* and so on.

- Use *the* before the names of certain countries: *the United States, the Netherlands, the Philippines, the People's Republic of China.*

- Use *the* before the names of regions (*the East Coast*), deserts (*the Sahara*), peninsulas (*the Malay Peninsula*), and bodies of water other than lakes (*the Pacific Ocean, the Mediterranean Sea, the Davis Strait*).

- Use *the* before names with *of* in the title (*the Bank of Montreal, the University of New Brunswick*) and for organizational subdivisions (*the Faculty of Music, the Department of Fisheries*).

- Use *the* before plural proper nouns, such as *the United Nations, the Himalayan Mountains, the Great Lakes, the Thousand Islands.*

2   General statements

Do not use *the* before plural or noncount nouns used in a general sense.

~~The~~ Students today are drinking less but smoking more.

In dangerous situations, ~~the~~ courage may not be as important as ~~the~~ patience.

3   Certain place expressions

Do not use *the* before general uses of the words *school, class, work, church, town,* and *bed.*

This term I am at ~~the~~ school only three days each week.

4   Games

Do not use *the* before the names of games: *chess* [not *the chess*], *baseball, soccer.*

5   Subjects of study

Do not use *the* before subjects of study: *economics* [not *the economics*], *history, mathematics, political science, sociology,* and so on.

When I took ~~the~~ art history, I studied both Western and Asian painters.

22e Match quantifiers with appropriate count or noncount nouns

Quantifiers are words or phrases that tell how much or how many: *two millimetres of rain, a few students.* Be sure the quantifiers match the kinds of nouns used with them.

1 Using quantifiers with singular count nouns

Use *one, each, every, either, neither,* and *another* with singular count nouns: *one apple, each student, every computer, either one, neither friend, another movie.*

2 Using quantifiers with plural nouns

Use the following quantifiers with plural nouns to tell "how many": numbers greater than one, *both, a couple of, few/a few, many, a number of, several.* For example: *seven apples, many oranges, a number of computers.*

3 Using quantifiers with noncount nouns

Use *little/a little, much, an amount of,* and *a great deal of* with noncount nouns to tell "how much": *little news, not much snow, a great deal of progress.*

4 Using quantifiers with plural and noncount nouns

Use the following quantifiers with either plural or noncount nouns to tell "how many" or "how much" according to their countability: *all, almost all, almost no, a lot of, enough, hardly any, lots of, a majority/minority of (the), most, not any/no, plenty of, some.* For example: *all the apples, all the snow, hardly any students, hardly any progress, some computers, some fog.* When count nouns follow such quantifiers, be sure to make them plural.

Some ~~university~~ universities make an extra effort to help international students feel

at home.

5 Using articles and quantifiers together

Generally, one determiner alone will do the job of introducing a noun. If you are using a quantifier, you will probably not include an article as well:

There was ~~a~~ plenty of food at the picnic.

The umpire explained the ruling to ~~the~~ both teams.

At the same time, remember that many quantifiers contain articles: *a few, a little, a number of, a lot of,* and so on. It would be a mistake to leave the articles out here:

We went skiing in the Laurentians _^*a* few years ago.

_{chapter}

23 Verbs

This chapter focusses on features of English verbs frequently troublesome to nonnative speakers. Features that may be troublesome to native and nonnative speakers alike are treated elsewhere in this book.

- Irregular verbs: See 15a.
- Specific uses of verb tenses: See 15b.
- Subject-verb agreement: See 16 and 23b.
- Dropped or confused verb endings: See 15c.
- The subjunctive mood for wishes and nonfactual statements: See 15d and 29d1.
- Active and passive voice: See 25a, 29d2, 33c4.

23*a* | To express tense correctly, match appropriate helping and main verb forms

1 Forming tenses

Tense literally means "time": past, present, or future. English verbs have a simple form to represent actions or states occurring at these three times and a perfect form for those occurring *prior to* another time or action. Each of these six tense forms also has a continuous form (a form of *be* + *ing*) to indicate ongoing or lasting action. To form verb tenses correctly, use the following combinations of helping verbs and main verbs:

- Present: For action that takes place regularly or at any time, use the base or *-s/-es* form of the main verb: I *write* often. He *speaks*. Use the present continuous to indicate action in progress at the present time: I *am studying* now. She *is speaking*. You/we/they *are working*.

- Past: To represent what happened in the past, use the past tense form (regular or irregular) of the main verb: I *wrote* yesterday. He *spoke*. Use the past continuous for actions in progress at a specific past time: I/he/she/it *was working* then. You/we/they *were working*.

- Future: To show what will take place, use *will* + the base form of the main verb: I *will write*. She *will speak*. Use the future continuous for actions in progress at a specific future time: They *will be working* then.

- Present perfect: To emphasize past action with a connection to the present, use *has/have* + the past participle form of the main verb: I *have written* already. He *has spoken*. For past action continuing to the present and on to the future, use the present perfect continuous: We *have been working* all day. See 15a for information on the past participles of irregular verbs.

- Past perfect: To emphasize the earlier of two actions occurring in the past, use *had* + the past participle form of the main verb: She *had spoken* before he did. For lasting past perfect action, use the past perfect continuous: We *had been working* for an hour by the time he finally spoke. (See 15a.)

- Future perfect: To emphasize the earlier of two actions occurring in the future, use *will have* + the past participle form (regular or irregular) of the main verb: She *will have spoken* before he does. For lasting future perfect action, use the future perfect continuous: We *will have been working* for an hour by the time he finally speaks. (See 15a.)

As you revise, be sure that you have used the correct combination of helping and main verbs to express tense.

She is ~~change~~ changing her major from biology to botany.

[The *-ing* verb form is necessary to form the present continuous, indicating present ongoing action.]

Scientists ~~had~~ have now demonstrated that some animals are capable of reason.

[*Has* or *have* is necessary to form the present perfect, indicating past action completed prior to the present as indicated by *are*.]

A note on tense consistency: Two or more verbs that refer to the same action must be in the same tense. (See 29c.)

2   Avoiding inappropriate omissions

Always include verbs even when the meaning or verb tense seems clear without them.

So far, they are the friendliest students in my residence.

[The helping verbs *be, have,* and *do* may stand alone as main verbs. Here *are* is necessary to connect the subject *they* to its complement, *the friendliest students.*]

has
She been a member of Amnesty International for five years.

[*Has* is necessary to create the present perfect tense.]

3   Identifying verbs that lack continuous forms

The following verbs do not generally appear in the continuous *-ing* forms.

- Verbs referring to mental states: *believe, doubt, feel, forget, imagine, intend, know, mean, need, prefer, realize, recognize, remember, suppose, understand, wish.*

  have known
  I ~~am knowing~~ the Patel family for seven years.

- Verbs referring to emotional states: *appreciate, care, dislike, envy, fear, hate, like, love, mind, want.*

- Verbs referring to the act of possessing: *belong, contain, have, own, possess. Have* is sometimes used to show duration instead of ownership: *She is having a baby. She is having lunch. She is having a party.*

- Verbs referring to sense perceptions: *feel, hear, see, smell, taste.* Exceptions: These verbs may appear in continuous forms with a change of meaning. For example, in *I feel the soft ground beneath my sleeping bag, feel* refers to tactile experience. But in *I'm feeling good this morning, feeling* refers to the speaker's mood.

23*b*   Use *-s/-es* on present-tense verbs that have third-person singular subjects

English adds *-s* or *-es* to third-person singular verbs in the present tense: *he works.* In your writing, take care to add *-s* or *-es* when called for—and especially following the words listed on the next page. (See also 23c.)

- Singular nouns: *Joan hikes. The baby cries.*

- Singular personal pronouns: *She hikes. He sings. It falls.*

- Indefinite pronouns, which are usually singular: *Everyone hikes. Each sings.*

  tries   keeps
  He ~~try~~ to come home early, but his job often ~~keep~~ him out late.

23c | Use the Standard English forms of *be, have,* and *do*

Use Standard English verb forms in your writing.

1 *Be*

The eight forms of *be* (*be, am, is, are, were, was, been, being*) make it the most complex English verb.

	SINGULAR	**PLURAL**
First person	I am/am being/ was/have been	we are/are being/ were/have been
Second person	you are/are being/ were/have been	you are/are being/ were/have been
Third person	she is/is being/ was/has been	they are/are being/ were/have been

To use *be* in its Standard English forms, follow these guidelines:

- Use *am, is,* and *was* with first-person and third-person singular verbs; use *are* and *were* with all others.

She ~~were~~ trying to get her essay published in the campus magazine. ^{was}

[*She* takes a third-person singular verb, *was*.]

- Use *am, is,* and *are* + the present participle (*-ing*) to indicate events currently in progress as well as continuous events: *she is laughing, they are studying.*

He going to school. ^{has}

[He is on his way to school.]

He ~~be~~ going to school. ^{has}

[He is currently attending school.]

- Informally, verbs are sometimes contracted with their subjects: *I'm, you're, she's, we're, they're.* But these verbs may not be omitted entirely. (See also 23a2.)

I working forty hours a week. ^{'m}

That bus better be on time. ^{had}

2 *Have*

Use the *-s* form *has* for the third-person singular (*John has*); use *have* for all other present tense and present perfect forms (*we have*). Do not omit *has* or *have* when these forms are used as helping verbs: *John has worked, we have lived.* (See also 23a2.)

She ~~have~~ come to every meeting of the drama club.
   has

He been a successful businessperson for twenty years.
 has

They been going to the Gaspé every summer for five years.
  have

3 *Do*

Use the *-es* form *does* for the third-person singular (*she does*); use *do* for all other present tense forms. (See also 23d.)

Merrilee ~~don't~~ want to go to the party this weekend.
    doesn't

~~Do~~ he ever consider other people's feelings?
Does

23d After the helping verbs *do*, *does*, and *did*, use only the base form of the verb

The helping verb *do* appears in questions, in negatives with *not* or *never*, and in emphatic statements. Use the appropriate form to signal tense and number (singular or plural): *do* = the base form, *does* = -s form (third-person singular), *did* = past tense. Following *do, does,* or *did*, use the base form of the main verb. Do not omit *do, does,* or *did* even if the meaning seems clear without them. (See the exception in summarized quotations, 24d1.)

- A question: *Do you have the videotape I requested?*

- A negative statement: *He doesn't* [present tense: *does not*] *know what he wants for dinner.*

- An emphatic statement: *We did* [past tense] *offer to help whenever we could.*

23e | Use modal verbs to indicate your attitude toward the action of a main verb

The modal helping verbs *can, could, may, might, must, shall, should, will,* and *would* express the writer's attitude toward an action. Auxiliary verbs like *ought to, had better,* and *have to* do the same.

- Capability: *I can help you with your calculus.*
- Intention: *I will finish by tomorrow.*
- Possibility: *They might go to the party.*
- Probability: *She must have gone home already.*
- Permission: *You may leave when you finish the exam.*
- Advisability: *He should edit his writing more carefully.*
- Necessity: *We must finish the book by this weekend.*

Use only one modal before a main verb.

> They might ~~could~~ take a Spanish class next semester.

1 Using present/future forms

For action in the present or future, use *can, may, might, must, should, had better, ought to, will* + the base form of the main verb. Do not add an *-s,* even when the subject is *he, she,* or *it: Next semester I will take fewer classes.*

> will
> Nadia says she come to the party this evening.
>   ^

[The modal verb *will* expresses future action and the closing phrase, *this evening,* indicates future time.]

> can
> Tamiko assured her supervisor that she ~~cans~~ finish the project by
>   ^

> Tuesday.

[Modal verbs never take the *-s* verb ending.]

> volunteer
> With a little encouragement, Henry may ~~volunteers~~.
>   ^

[The modal *may* must be followed by the base form *volunteer.*]

> play
> Lucia might ~~to play~~ a Chopin sonata at her next recital.
>   ^

[Following the modal *might,* the base form of the main verb *play* is required. (For uses of the infinitive, see 23h.)]

2 Using past forms

For past action, use *would, could, might, used to, had to* + the base form of the main verb. Do not use any other form of the main verb: *Ernie used to smoke* [not *smoked*] *cigars.*

As she listened to their explanation, she ~~can~~ ^could^ understand their motives.

When I saw how pale she was, I thought she might ~~been~~ ^be^ sick.

3 Using past perfect forms for potential past action

For past action that did not actually occur, use *could (not) have, should (not) have, would (not) have* + the past participle of the main verb: *Sven should have covered his roses to protect them from frost.* (See also 23g.)

With regular feeding, the fish would not have ~~die~~ ^died^.

They should ^have^ waited a week or two before planting the flowers.

$23f$ | Use the passive voice when a subject receives the action of a transitive verb

In passive voice expressions, a passive subject receives the action of a transitive verb. The subject is acted on instead of performing an action.

a subject receiving action

In ancient Ethiopia, coffee was consumed as a food rather than a beverage.

1 Confusing voice and tense

Do not confuse the passive voice with the past tense. A passive voice verb may appear in the past, present, or future. To form the passive, use the appropriate form of *be* to signal number and tense followed by the past participle of the main verb. Note that *be, being,* and *been* must be preceded by another helping verb.

Present passive: *The music is played.*
Present continuous passive: *The music is being played.*
Present perfect passive: *The music has been played.*
Past passive: *The music was played.*
Past continuous passive: *The music was being played.*

Past perfect passive: *The music had been played.*
Future passive: *The music will be played.*
Future perfect passive: *The music will have been played.*

2 Misusing the passive

- To form the passive voice, use the past participle form of main verbs, not the base or past tense forms.

  The movie will be ~~release~~ _^released in China early next year.

  The emigrants who left Ireland in the 1840s were ~~drove~~ _^driven by famine.

- Include the appropriate form of *be* in all passive voice expressions.

  In our culture today, too much emphasis _^is placed on material goals.

- Make sure you use a verb that can be made passive.

  The accident ~~was~~ happened downtown.

23g Use appropriate verb tenses in conditional (*if . . .*) sentences

Conditional sentences usually consist of two parts: (1) an *if* dependent clause stating conditions and (2) a main clause stating results.

conditions · results
If we have time, we'll go bicycling this weekend.

results · conditions
We used to go bicycling when we had the time.

results · conditions
We would go bicycling this weekend if we had enough time.

conditions · results
If we had had enough time, we would have gone bicycling last weekend.

These examples illustrate three features of conditional sentences: (1) the *if* clause may appear before or after the main clause stating results; (2) not every conditional sentence contains *if*; and, most important, (3) the kind of conditional statement determines the tenses of the verbs.

1 Determining habitual past and present conditions

For conditions that occur again and again in the past or present, use the same tense in the *if* clause and the "results" main clause.

present tense (*if* clause)   present tense (*results* clause)

If we have enough time, we go bicycling on weekends.

past tense (*if* clause)   past tense (*results* clause)

When we had enough time, we went bicycling on weekends.

2   Describing possible future conditions

To predict future conditions and results:

- In the *if* clause, use *if* or *unless* + the present tense (not the future tense).
- In the "results" clause, use *can, may, might, should,* or *will* + the base form of the verb.

present tense (*if* clause)   *may* + base form (*results* clause)

If we have enough time, we may go bicycling this weekend.

will + base form (*results* clause)   present tense (*if* clause)

We will go bicycling this weekend unless it rains.

3   Speculating about present or future conditions

To speculate about imagined conditions in the present or future:

- In the *if* clause, use *if* + the past tense (not the present tense) unless you use a form of the verb *be*. In this case use *were* instead of *was*, whether the subject is singular or plural. (See also 15d.)
- In the "results" clause, use *could, might,* or *would* + the base form of the verb.

past tense (*if* clause)   *would* + base form (*results* clause)

If the weather were better today, we would go bicycling.

might + base form (*results* clause)   past tense (*if* clause)

We might go bicycling if it stopped raining.

4   Speculating about past conditions

To speculate about what might, could, or should have happened in the past:

- In the *if* clause, use *if* + the past perfect tense (*had* + past participle).
- In the "results" clause, use *could have, might have,* or *would have* + the past participle.

past perfect tense (*if* clause)   *would have* + past participle (*results* clause)

If it had stopped raining, we would have gone bicycling.

23*h* vb/id

We could have gone bicycling if the weather had been better.

23*h* | Learn which verbs may be followed by infinitives, gerunds, or either verb form

An **infinitive** is the base form of a verb preceded by *to*: *to study*. A **gerund** is the *-ing* form of a verb used as a noun: *Studying is difficult after a full day's work.* Following certain verbs, infinitives or gerunds may appear as objects.

1 Verb + infinitive

- Some verbs are followed by an infinitive (*to* + base form), not a gerund:

agree	come	happen	offer	seem
appear	decide	hope	plan	swear
arrange	deserve	live	pretend	threaten
claim	fail	long	refuse	yearn

  The group agreed **to study** [not *studying*] in the library after dinner.

- When used in the active voice, a related group of verbs takes an object (noun or pronoun) before the infinitive. These verbs fit in the following pattern: *We _____ her to do something.*

advise	convince	force	permit	schedule	urge
allow	enable	instruct	persuade	teach	warn
cause	encourage	invite	remind	tell	
command	forbid	order	require		

  verb + noun + infinitive

  We have invited Gary to join us for dinner.

  verb + pronoun + infinitive

  Kayla advised me to apply for a scholarship.

- A small group of verbs may be followed by either the infinitive or an object (noun or pronoun) + infinitive:

ask	dare	help	mean	prepare	want
beg	expect	intend	need	promise	wish
choose	get	like	prefer		

  verb + infinitive

  The lawyer asked to address the court.

  verb + noun object + infinitive

  The lawyer asked the plaintiff to address the court.

■ When the verbs *have* ("cause"), *let* ("allow"), and *make* ("force") are followed by a noun or pronoun + infinitive, the *to* is omitted, as it is with the "sense" verbs *watch*, *see*, *hear*, and *feel*:

Please have the carpenters **finish** [not *to finish*] their work by Thursday. With *help*, the *to* is optional: *We helped them finish it.*

2 Verb + gerund

■ These verbs may be followed by a gerund [*-ing*] but not an infinitive:

admit	deny	imagine	postpone	resent
anticipate	discuss	involve	practise	resist
appreciate	dread	keep	put off	resume
avoid	enjoy	mention	quit	risk
consider	escape	mind	recall	suggest
delay	finish	miss	recommend	tolerate

Keiko recalled **leaving** [not *to leave*] her gloves in the car.

■ The following expressions with prepositions may be followed by a gerund or a possessive + gerund:

account for	be used to	have an influence on
accuse someone of	believe in	help in
apologize for	care about	insist on
approve of	complain about	keep someone from
be accustomed to	concentrate on	look forward to
be capable of	consent to	object to
be excited about	consist of	prevent someone from
be famous for	delight in	
be fond of	depend on	recover from
be interested in	disapprove of	stop someone from
be jealous of	dream of	succeed in
be known for	feel like	talk about
be responsible for	forgive someone for	think about
be tired of	get around to	

                                  verb + preposition + gerund

For more than a year Annette and I have dreamed of travelling to Italy.

        verb + preposition + pronoun + gerund

Our success depends on his arriving on time.

3 Verb + infinitive or gerund

■ Certain verbs may be followed by infinitives or gerunds with little or no change of meaning: *begin, cease, continue, hate, like, love, prefer, start.*

Ali **loves playing** the guitar.

Ali **loves to play** the guitar.

- After the verbs *forget, remember, stop,* and *try,* the infinitive and gerund have different meanings:

    A good Samaritan is someone who **stops to help** those in need. [provides assistance]

    Concerned with his own problems, Felix **has stopped helping** those in need. [no longer provides assistance]

23i | Use two-word verbs correctly

A **two-word verb** (also called a *phrasal verb*) consists of a verb and a preposition-like word called a **particle**. The meaning of a two-word verb differs from the meaning of its individual words, as the following examples with *call* show:

    I promised to **call up** my parents this weekend. [to telephone]

    When I get the information, I'll **call** you **back.** [to return a telephone call]

    Her soufflé recipe **calls for** half a dozen eggs. [to require]

    The instructor **called** the student **in** for a conference. [to ask to come to a specific place for a specific purpose]

    I'm going to **call on** you tomorrow. [to ask to speak, to visit]

    The umpire **called off** the game because of rain. [to cancel]

1 Using a dictionary or phrase book

Because English two-word verbs are so numerous and their meanings are almost always idiomatic, use a dictionary or phrase book of idioms as you write and edit. Check to see that you've used the correct verb + particle combination for the meaning you intend.

2 Placing objects and particles following the verb

The **particle** in a two-word verb is either inseparable or separable from the verb.

- An **inseparable particle** follows the verb immediately.

    The instructor **called on** Sergei to answer the question.

    Today's students often **drop out** of school for a few years and then return.

    Winston eventually **got over** his disappointment.

■ A **separable particle** may be separated from a transitive verb accord-ing to two patterns:

Noun objects. If the object of a separable two-word verb is a noun, place it either after the particle or between the verb and particle: *The umpire called off the game* (verb + particle + noun). *The umpire called the game off* (verb + noun + particle).

Pronoun objects. If the object of a separable two-word verb is a pronoun, it must go between the verb and particle: *The umpire called it off* (verb + pronoun + particle).

chapter
24
More Idioms

24a | Use words idiomatically

The term **idiom** applies to words and phrases given special meaning by native speakers of a language. Idiomatic usage has to be learned, not guessed at. For example, "Good evening" and "Good night" might look synonymous, but the first is a greeting and the second a farewell—they are not at all interchangeable. To keep things sounding idiomatic, watch for three main trouble spots.

1 Misusing individual words

Individual words are frequently used in some situations but not in others that may appear similar:

The murderer massacred his victim and buried her remains in the flowerbed.

[*To massacre* may mean to kill pitilessly; at the same time, it refers to mass slaughter as in *The early Jesuits were massacred by the Iroquois*. In idiomatic English, a single vic-tim cannot be "massacred," but is slain, killed, or even butchered.]

2 Using stock phrases

Stock phrases are verbal formulas such as *stand pat, come in handy, be on the ball, see red, travel light, make do, move heaven and earth, take stock, cut corners,* and so on. Such expressions are often overused. (See 31d1.)

3   Misusing prepositions

Prepositions (*in, by, on, with,* and so on) and preposition-like words called **particles,** which follow verbs (*agree with/to, prevent from, fight against/for, abide by,* and so on), are especially idiomatic, appearing only in certain situations and after particular words.

about
Parents who really care ~~for~~ their children's education provide their sons

with
and daughters many learning opportunities outside school.

[Idiomatic English calls for *care "about"* when concern is the issue instead of *care "for,"* which means "love." With *provide,* the preposition *with* is called for when the recipients are referred to in the sentence: *They provided the opportunity,* although *we provided her <u>with</u> that opportunity*.]

Native speakers of a language generally use words idiomatically, but nonnative speakers and writers who choose words outside their everyday vocabularies may have difficulties.

- If you're uncertain of a word or phrase, check usage notes in dictionaries. See also 34.

- For stock phrases unlisted in dictionaries, refer to special dictionaries and collections of idioms in libraries or bookstores.

- For prepositions, look up the word preceding the preposition (*care* and *provide* in the above example) in a dictionary. (See also 23i and 24g.)

24*b* Include all necessary words

1   Including subjects

Except for imperatives, all English sentences require a subject. Be especially careful to include personal pronoun subjects that refer to antecedents in preceding clauses or sentences. Compare these examples:

The Hindu god Brahma is considered equal to Vishnu and Siva. However, **he** has had only one temple dedicated to him, at Pushkar in India.

he
Because Ray practises speaking into a tape recorder, has excellent

pronunciation.

She says
Tina is such an optimist. ~~Says~~ that problems are only clouds hiding the

sun.

2 Including the expletives *it*, *here*, and *there*

Expletives are words used primarily for grammatical purposes. They provide a subject for a sentence that doesn't logically have one, or they introduce a subject following the verb. An expletive is usually followed by a form of *be*.

It *is* raining again.

delayed subject

There *are* many Andean mountains higher than 6 700 metres.

Do not omit *it*, *here,* and *there* even though they contribute little meaning to your sentences, and be sure the verb agrees with its actual subject. (See also 16b.)

It is
~~Is~~ necessary to take health precautions before travelling in tropical

countries.

[*It* is required to introduce the subject of the sentence, *to take health precautions.*]

, there
Ten years ago was a severe drought in Arkansas.

[The subject of the sentence is not *ten years ago* but *a severe drought* following the verb *was*. *There* is required to introduce it.]

There are
~~Is~~ two solutions to the problem of illegal immigration.

[The subject of the sentence, *two solutions*, requires the plural verb *are* to follow *There*.]

24c Avoid unnecessary repetition

1 Avoiding unnecessary repetition of a subject

Do not repeat a subject within its own clause, even when the subject and verb are separated.

American soft drink manufacturers ~~they~~ advertise heavily throughout

Asia.

The
~~In the~~ essay/it discusses the effects of acid rain on sugar maples.

2 Avoiding unnecessary object and adverb repetition

Do not repeat an object or adverb in an adjective clause beginning with a relative pronoun (*who, which, whom, whose, that*) or relative adverb (*where, when*).

Kevin is the one person whom I can always trust ~~him~~ to tell the truth.

[The relative pronoun *whom* is also the object of the verb *trust*; the objective pronoun *him* is unnecessary. Even if *whom* were omitted, *him* would be unnecessary: *Kevin is the one person I can always trust to tell the truth.*]

Marrakech sits on a high plain where the air is thin and the sun is

brilliant ~~there~~.

[*There* repeats the meaning of the relative adverb *where* and is, therefore, unnecessary.]

3 Avoiding duplicate conjunctions

Co-ordinating conjunctions (*and, or, but, nor, so, yet, for*) link main clauses. Subordinating conjunctions (*although, because, if, when*, and so on) link dependent clauses to main clauses. Use only one conjunction to link clauses in writing. (See also 10g.)

Although credit cards are very convenient, ~~but~~ they can lead to

overspending.

[The subordinating conjunction *although* links the first clause, *credit cards are very convenient,* to the following main clause, so *but* is unnecessary. To put equal emphasis on both clauses, the writer omits *although* and retains *but*: *Credit cards are very convenient, but they can lead to overspending.*

24d Follow these guidelines to summarize questions and speech

---

1 Summarizing questions

Summarized questions (also called indirect questions) are usually part of a longer statement of fact; therefore, they follow the word order and punctuation of declarative sentences. (See 12c2.)

■ After the question word (*who, which, when, why, where, what, whom, how,* and so on) that introduces the summarized question, make sure the verb follows the subject.

The panel considered where ~~is~~ air pollution is the most severe.

- Use *whether* to introduce summarized "yes/no" questions and "or" questions that pose alternatives.

  I have not decided <del>will I</del> go home for the summer or attend summer

  whether I will

  school.

- Omit *do, does, did* from summarized questions; signal tense (the time of the action) with the appropriate form of the main verb.

  whether *needed*

  He asked me <del>did</del> I <del>need</del> help with my experiment.

  [*Needed* matches the past tense form of the main verb *asked.*]

- Punctuate summarized questions in a way appropriate to the complete sentence.

  The judge asked the jury whether it had reached a verdict.

2 Summarizing speech

In **summarized speech** (also called **reported speech** or **indirect quotation**), a writer restates a direct quotation in his or her own words, without quotation marks.

- Write the summarized speech as a noun clause within your own sentence.

DIRECT QUOTATION	SUMMARIZED SPEECH
She said, "A monsoon is a strong seasonal wind."	She said that a monsoon is a strong seasonal wind.

[*That* may be omitted from certain noun clauses. (See 27d2.)]

- Change the present tense or present continuous of direct quotations to the past tense or past continuous in summarized speech. An exception: Use the present tense if the summarized speech is a general truth or habitual action, as in the preceding example.

DIRECT QUOTATION	SUMMARIZED SPEECH
She said, "My report is finished."	She said that her report was finished.
She said, "I am finishing my report."	She said that she was finishing her report.

- Change the past tense or present perfect of direct quotations to the past perfect of summarized speech.

DIRECT QUOTATION	SUMMARIZED SPEECH
She said, "They arrived an hour ago."	She said that they had arrived an hour before.
She said, "I have tried to help him."	She said that she had tried to help him.

- With modal verbs in summarized speech, change *can* to *could, will* to *would, may* to *might, must* to *had to.*

DIRECT QUOTATION	SUMMARIZED SPEECH
She said, "I will call him next week."	She said that she would call him next week.

- To summarize commands, use *to* + the base form of the verb (the infinitive).

DIRECT QUOTATION	SUMMARIZED SPEECH
She told her students, "Go to the lab."	She told her students to go to the lab.

24e | Show possession with an apostrophe or an *of* phrase

English signals a possessive noun with an apostrophe or a phrase using *of*: *India's president, the president of India.* In some cases, as in the preceding examples, the forms are interchangeable; often they are not.

1 Indicating possession with an apostrophe

To make a singular noun or indefinite pronoun possessive, usually add -'s: *the student's book, someone's book.* To make a plural noun ending in -s possessive, usually add only an apostrophe: *the students' request.* An apostrophe is generally used with nouns referring to persons and other living beings: *the editor's opinion, the lions' roar.* (For more on the possessive form and the apostrophe, see 19d and 39a.)

2 Indicating possession with *of*

To signal possession by things, you would typically use an *of* phrase: *the body of the car, the soles of my feet.* An *of* phrase may also be used to emphasize a source rather than a possessor: *the novels of Chinua Achebe.* Do not use possessive *of* phrases with personal pronouns: *her book,* not *the book of her.*

Many parents do not consider the TV violence ~~effect~~ on their children.
_{effect of}

Without ~~the~~ help ~~of him,~~ we could not have afforded the trip.
_{his}

Exceptions: The apostrophe form of the possessive appears frequently in references to time (*an hour's drive, a month's time*), natural phenomena (*the sun's rays, Earth's atmosphere*), political organizations (*the city's parks, the government's transfer payments*), and groups of people working together (*the ship's crew, the company's employees*).

24*f* Use adjectives and adverbs with care

1 Forming adjectives

Adjectives modify nouns by telling which, what kind, how many: *the tall man, a new student, four flowers.* (See 10d and 20a.) Some languages add endings to adjectives so that they match the nouns they modify; however, in English, adjectives do not change form. Indeed, even when they look as if they should be plural because they contain a number, do not add an *-s*: *Dianne bought three two-dollar stamps to mail her parcel.*

Jordan wore a three-piece~~s~~ suit to his interview.

2 Using participles (*-ing* and *-ed* verb forms) as adjectives

To form some adjectives, English uses the present participle (*-ing*) and past participle of verbs: *a terrifying story, a crowded street.* Both kinds of participles may appear before a noun or following a linking verb: *The terrifying story is true. The story is terrifying. The terrified child could not speak. The child was terrified.* But present and past participles may not be used interchangeably.

- Use **present participle adjectives** (ending in *-ing*) to describe something going on or stimulating an experience: *The survivors told a terrifying story to their fearful listeners* [the story caused terror in the listeners].

They jumped in surprise at the sound of ~~broken~~ glass.
_{breaking}

- Use **past participle adjectives** (ending in *-ed, -d, -en, -t*) to describe a person or thing undergoing an experience: *The listeners were terrified by the survivors' story* [the listeners experienced terror].

I felt ~~embarrassing~~ when my instructor read my paper aloud.
_{embarrassed}

3 Arranging cumulative adjectives

Cumulative adjectives are two or more adjectives that are not separated by commas and that modify the whole phrase following them: *the large round Persian rug.* To use cumulative adjectives correctly, arrange them in this order:

1. Article, possessive, or quantifier: *the, my, Teresa's, some, four …*
2. Comparative and superlative: *younger, older, best, worst, least …*
3. Evaluator (a word that can be preceded by *very*): *beautiful, courageous, responsible …*
4. Size: *large, small, gigantic, tall …*
5. Length or shape: *long, round, oval, square, triangular …*
6. Age: *young, old, new, antique, modern, twentieth-century …*
7. Colour: *green, yellow, violet …*
8. Nationality: *Peruvian, Iranian, Polish, American …*
9. Religion: *Baptist, Buddhist, Christian, Hindu, Muslim, Protestant …*
10. Material: *wood, walnut, metal, gold, wool …*
11. Noun used as an adjective: *guest* (as in *guest room*), *history* (as in *history class*) …
12. Noun modified: *room, class, truck, table …*

Compare these examples:

Four old wooden clocks will be sold at the auction.

The baby was being entertained by her older ~~two~~ sisters. _(two inserted above)_

A note on adjective series: Avoid long series of adjectives. Generally use no more than two or three between an article, possessive, or quantifier and the noun it modifies: *an old Hindu temple, Alan's famous buttermilk pancakes, several well-known European scientists.*

4 Placing adverbs

Adverbs used to modify verbs may appear at the beginning, at the end, or in the middle of a sentence. However, do not place an adverb between a verb and a direct object. (See also 28a.) Compare these examples:

Carefully, she took her daughter's hand.

He turned the dial **carefully.**

He walked **carefully** along the ledge.

carefully
To complete my art history project, I examined ~~carefully~~ Mayan
architecture.

24g | Choose the appropriate preposition for expressions of place and time

English expressions of place and time using *at*, *in*, and *on* can be trouble-some. Here are some guidelines to their use. Note, however, that exceptions do exist. Consult a dictionary, such as the *Collins Cobuild Essential Dictionary* or the *Oxford Advanced Learner's Dictionary*.

1 Indicating place

- Use **at** before a specific location, meeting place, the edge of some-thing, the corner of something, or a target: *arriving at school, seated at the table, turning at the corner, living at 73 Queen Street, aiming at the bull's eye.*

- Use **in** before an enclosed space or geographic location: *growing in the garden, standing in the phone booth, hiking in the mountains, living in Mexico City.*

- Use **on** before a surface or street: *lying on the table, hanging on the wall, walking on Dalhousie Street.*

2 Indicating time

- Use **at** before specific expressions of time: *She arrived at 2:30. They left at dawn.*

- Use **in** before a month, year, century, period of time, or part of a twenty-four-hour period: *in May, in 1865, in the twentieth century, in the morning.*

- Use **on** before a day or date: *on July 20, on Thursday.*

3 Arranging place and time phrases

In most English expressions, *place* comes before *time*: *My relatives arrived at my house in the early morning.* However, a prepositional phrase of time often appears at the beginning of a sentence: *In the early morning, my relatives arrived at my house.*

Crafting Sentences

How to ...

How to Edit for Emphasis and Variety

To make your sentences clear, emphatic, and interesting to read, follow these guidelines.

1. Place important ideas at the end of a main clause or at the end of a sentence. (See 25a and e.)
2. De-emphasize less important ideas in subordinate phrases or clauses. (See 25b.)
3. Link related important ideas in a co-ordinate structure. (See 25c.)
4. Repeat important words for emphasis. (See 25d.)
5. Count the number of words in your sentences. If you find passages in which sentences repeatedly have nearly the same structure, you may have found a choppy or monotonous passage to rewrite. Vary the length and structure of your sentences. (See 26a–c.)
6. Look for words to cut, such as needless repetition or forms of the verb *be*. Look for sentences in which you can compress a wordy phrase to fewer words and still say the same thing. (See 33a–c.)

Divide long, rambling sentences. The most readable sentences usually have one main idea, or set of related ideas, and one purpose. (See 26c.)

chapter

25 Writing Emphatically

In emphatic sentences, important ideas stand out. Not only do they appear where readers expect them, but they are arranged to attract attention. The following guidelines will help you give your sentences this kind of impact.

25a | Use the active voice when possible

Voice refers to verb forms that show whether a subject performs an action or is acted on. In the **active voice,** an active subject—an actor—performs the action of a transitive verb.

   subject verb   direct object
   Jane mailed the letter.

In the **passive voice,** a passive subject receives the action of the verb.

subject   verb
The letter was mailed.

1 Using the active voice for emphasis

In the active voice, a sentence becomes a little story. *Jane heaved a sigh and mailed the letter.* Someone or something does something. This kind of sentence is usually the simplest to write, the shortest and the easiest to read. And simplicity and brevity usually make main ideas stand out.

As you edit your writing, look for forms of the verb *be* (*be, am, is, are, was, were, being, been*) and passive voice sentences. If a sentence lacks action or fails to emphasize what's most important, rewrite it. Choose an action verb, make the actor the subject of the sentence, or, if necessary, identify the actor.

This award ~~is in recognition of~~ recognizes your months of hard work.

[The revision moves the action of the sentence to the verb, reducing the length of the sentence by three words.]

Many doctors oppose children's
~~Children's~~ sports leagues ~~are opposed by many doctors.~~

[The phrase *many doctors,* referring to the actors, has become the subject of the verb *oppose.*]

The Board of Governors is considering tuition
~~Tuition~~ increases of ten percent ~~are being considered~~ for next year.

[The revision adds the actors who perform the action of the sentence.]

2 Using the passive voice effectively

Two situations call for the passive voice:

■ When actors are unknown or unimportant, use the passive voice.

Nearly half of the world's fresh water **is locked** in the Antarctic ice sheet.

■ When actors are the most important, use the passive voice to feature them at the end of the sentence, where they receive the greatest emphasis.

During the last Ice Age, the Great Lakes **were scooped** out and **shaped** by gigantic moving sheets of ice.

To put a verb in the passive voice, use a form of the helping verb *be* + the past participle of the main verb: *is mailed, was loved, will be chosen.* Don't confuse "passive" with "past"; as these examples illustrate, the passive voice may appear in any tense. (See also 23f.)

25b | Subordinate less important ideas

To emphasize important ideas, put them in an independent clause, the main part of a sentence. To de-emphasize less important ideas, subordinate them in dependent clauses or phrases connected to the independent clause. What you choose to emphasize will depend not only on what is most important about your topic but also on the way one sentence fits with those that precede and follow. (For more on subordination, see 26b and 33c.)

1 Subordinating with dependent clauses

You can de-emphasize an idea by expressing it in a **dependent clause**, a group of words with a subject and verb that cannot stand by itself as a complete sentence.

- Add a **subordinating conjunction** such as *after, although, because, when,* and so on to create a dependent clause. Connect it to a related independent clause. (For a list of subordinating conjunctions, see 10g3.)

Although
Grey Owl was originally an Englishman named Archie Belaney, ~~but~~ he is

better remembered as a conservationist than as an imposter.

[By subordinating the first half of the sentence as a dependent clause, the revision emphasizes Grey Owl's place in history and minimizes his masquerade.]

- Add a **relative pronoun** such as *who, which,* and *that* to act as the subject of a dependent clause. Use it to modify a word in the main clause or to act as part of the main clause. (See also 12b1 and 12b3.)

, who
Grey Owl was originally an Englishman named Archie Belaney, ~~but he~~ is

better remembered as a conservationist than as an imposter.

[The dependent clause de-emphasizes Belaney's origins. The independent clause emphasizes the conservationism.]

191

2 Subordinating with phrases

You can reduce the importance of an idea further by putting it into a **phrase,** a word group lacking a subject, a verb, or both.

- Put a less important idea in an **appositive phrase**, a nounlike word or phrase that describes a nearby noun.

Grey Owl, ~~who was~~ originally an Englishman named Archie Belaney, is

better remembered as a conservationist than as an imposter.

- Put a less important idea in a phrase headed by the *-ing* or *-ed* participial forms of the verb. Put the phrase near the noun or pronoun it modifies.

Better remembered as a conservationist than as an imposter,
Grey Owl was actually an Englishman named Archie Belaney/~~but he is~~

~~better remembered as a conservationist than as an imposter.~~

[By de-emphasizing the second half of the sentence in a participial phrase, this revision emphasizes Grey Owl's origins, now in an independent clause.]

25c | Use co-ordination to emphasize equal ideas

Co-ordination (also called **parallel form**) refers to linked words having the same grammatical form. (See 21.) It is a way to emphasize the equality of related words and ideas.

1 Co-ordinating with a conjunction

Use a co-ordinating conjunction (*and, but, or, yet, nor*) to link and emphasize equally important words and phrases.

> linked words
> Horns and sirens announced the ship's arrival.

> linked phrases
> The violin evolved from ancient Asian fiddles and medieval stringed instruments.

2 Co-ordinating with a comma and co-ordinating conjunction

Use a comma and co-ordinating conjunction to link equally important independent clauses. (See also 36a.)

The old cabin looked warm and cozy̶/̶I̶t̶s̶ , but its roof leaked, even in a gentle rain.

3 Co-ordinating with a semicolon and a transition or conjunctive adverb

Use a semicolon and a transition or conjunctive adverb such as *however* or *therefore* to link related and equally important independent clauses. (For a list of transitions and conjunctive adverbs, see 14b3; see also 37b.)

Toller Cranston's innovative manoeuvres won him many medals/H̶e̶ ; however, he never won gold at the Olympics or the World Figure Skating Championships.

4 Co-ordinating with a semicolon alone

Use a semicolon standing alone to balance equally important clauses that are similar in structure. (See 37a.)

Natural air pollutants include dust, gases, spores, and pollens/A̶r̶t̶i̶f̶i̶c̶i̶a̶l̶ ; artificial air pollutants include smoke and gases from industries, vehicles, and households.

A note on faulty co-ordination: Avoid stringing co-ordinate word groups together into loose, rambling, unemphatic sentences. (See 26c.) Also avoid the faulty parallelism that occurs when grammatically unequal words are linked. (See 21a–c.)

25*d* | Repeat key words to emphasize ideas

To affirm your beliefs, express feelings, or give special emphasis, repeat key words in grammatically equal (parallel) structures. Parallel structures are italicized in the following passages.

> There must be *tolerance* in any work situation: *tolerance that allows* each person to accept others for *what they are*, not *what someone thinks they should be*; *tolerance that permits* one to notice *others' strengths* rather than *their shortcomings*; *tolerance that will respect differences* rather than *make them a source of tension and conflict*.

In this extended sentence, the parallelism not only makes the sentence easy to read but also adds emotion and power. Memorable speeches feature many similar examples. Remember, however, that excessive parallelism and repetition may make your writing sound choppy or overly emotional. (See 26b and d.)

25e Place important ideas in emphatic positions

Beginnings and endings—especially endings—are emphatic positions. Consider:

> Stars, like people, do not live forever. But the lifetime of a person is measured in decades; the lifetime of a star in billions of years.
>
> (Carl Sagan, from *The Cosmic Connection: An Extraterrestrial Perspective*)

The writer might have begun *Like people, stars do not live forever.* But because he is more interested in the age of stars than of people, he begins and ends with stars and their lifetime.

1 Putting emphasis at the beginning

To emphasize a topic at the beginning of a sentence, make it the subject and open with the main clause. Consider these examples:

> *Lamb's quarters clump along the fence-lines* which form a straggled delineation of the groomed fields beyond and the wilderness that bursts up from the ditches, encroaching on the road with weedy patches of purslane and wild aster.
>
> (Sandra Birdsell, "Disappearances," *Saturday Night*, emphasis added)

[In the main clause that opens the sentence, the topic—the greenery (*lamb's quarters*)—is the subject, and the verb *clump* provides the main image, which is described in the series of modifying phrases at the end.]

~~The truck swerved and hit~~ the ancient elm standing ^was hit by a swerving truck.^ in front of my house.

[The revision makes the direct object of the original sentence—*the ancient elm*—into the subject.]

2 Putting emphasis at the ending

Design your sentences so that the main idea comes in the final phrase or word. Compare these examples:

Nothing can prepare you for the experience of **being laid off.**

The transformation of American horror movies began with
Alfred Hitchcock's *Psycho* ~~began the transformation of American horror~~
~~movies~~.

You can create an especially emphatic ending by writing a **periodic sentence.** Open with modifying phrases or clauses that lead to a closing main clause and, often, to an important idea that comes in the last phrase.

> Surrounded by the incessant song of crickets, the dry perfume of sun-bleached grasses, or the rubberband chorus of frogs, *the swimming hole has a delicious magic all its own.*
>
> (Mark Fawcett, "To Dig a Swimming Hole,"
> *Harrowsmith Country Life*, emphasis added)

> When managers sit down to analyze the many problems that add up to downtime in production or when they pore over files full of customer complaints, *the accusing finger almost always ends up pointed at ineffectual communication.*

When you occasionally add a periodic sentence to your writing, you delay your readers' understanding momentarily, heighten suspense, and emphasize the main clause at the end.

3 Ordering items in series from least to most important

To develop suspense in a series, place the most important item or most impressive image last. To protest boxing's brutality, the writer of the following example builds to a final italicized description of a boxer punishing his injured opponent.

> It is nonsense to talk about prize fighting as a test of boxing skills. No crowd was ever brought to its feet screaming and cheering at the sight of two men beautifully dodging and weaving out of each other's jabs. The time the crowd comes alive is *when a man is hit hard over the heart or the head, when his mouthpiece flies out, when blood squirts out of his nose or eyes, when he wobbles under the attack and his pursuer continues to smash at him with poleax impact.*
>
> (Norman Cousins, "Who Killed Benny Paret?"
> *Saturday Review*, emphasis added)

chapter

26 Adding Variety

26*a* | Vary the length of your sentences

Effective writing is like music. Repeated words and sentence patterns create an emphatic rhythm, and varied patterns make a melody that adds surprise, moves readers ahead, and prevents monotony. One of the most important creators of this musical style is variety in sentence length. Long sentences, short sentences, sentences in between—like musical notes, they give writing a varied tempo, a pace that makes reading easier and more interesting.

Consider the following example. The numbers to the left indicate the number of words per sentence:

12 A textbook, no matter how good, can never utterly replace the teacher. It is,
25 after all, the teacher who ends up in class rephrasing, interpreting, explaining, and analyzing most of what there is in the assigned readings.
7 The problem may even be the author. One writer forgets that students do
32 not know very much about the subject and offers highly technical information, while another, who appreciates the need for brevity, ends up
17 offering too few illustrations. Students who are confused by unfamiliar terms and abstract explanations are actually lucky to be in school. They are
15 lucky, that is, if they have a teacher prepared to translate for them.

As you write and revise, use short sentences to emphasize important ideas. The topic sentences of paragraphs are often shorter than those that follow; so are emotionally charged sentences and climactic sentences that make a closing point. Use longer sentences to explain, describe, and restate. The following guidelines will show you how to create this variety.

26*b* | Combine short, choppy sentences

One or two short sentences will emphasize important ideas, but several choppy ones may create a monotonous, singsong effect. To combine choppy sentences, do the following: eliminate unnecessary words, reword, rearrange, and repunctuate.

1 Subordinating less important ideas

Combine choppy sentences by reducing one sentence to a subordinate phrase or clause. (See 25b.)

Although many

~~Many~~ people try to avoid jury duty. ~~But~~ those who serve often praise

for the

their experience. ~~They speak of~~ new insights into human nature they

have gained.

[The revision combines three sentences into one, subordinating the first sentence as a dependent clause and the third as a phrase.]

2 Co-ordinating equal ideas

Use parallel forms to co-ordinate related, equally important ideas. (See 25c.)

too much

Some people are concerned that high school students watch television,

~~several hours a day. They~~ spend little time on homework, ~~They~~ seldom

read and never write for pleasure.

[The revision eliminates pronouns and repunctuates to link the uses of high school students' time into an emphatic series.]

3 Rearranging and combining sentences

To emphasize what is most important, you may have to rearrange ideas.

Because they

~~Jurors~~ often come from vastly different backgrounds, ~~jurors~~ ~~Before beginning~~

~~their deliberations, they~~ must spend time learning one another's values

before beginning their deliberations.

and attitudes.

[To emphasize the time jurors spend becoming acquainted, the revision subordinates the first sentence as a dependent clause, combines sentences, and moves the opening phrase of the second sentence to the end.]

26c Divide loose, rambling sentences into two or more separate sentences

Carefully crafted long sentences can be as clear, emphatic, and easy to read as shorter sentences. But long, rambling sentences may obscure important ideas and be tiresome to read.

1 Dividing loose sentences at conjunctions or transitions

Omit conjunctions or transitions if possible. Then check to see that your revised sentences are varied and emphatic.

Some exceptional children have severe emotional, social, and
psychological problems; ~~and~~ others have attention deficiency
. Therefore,
disorders, ~~so~~ it is rarely possible for them to join regular summer camp
especially when
programs; ~~besides,~~ the staff generally lack training in how to deal with
the exceptional child.

2 Dividing sentences at subordinating conjunctions or relative pronouns

Too many dependent clauses in a sentence make reading difficult, especially when they come at opposite ends of the sentence. Rewrite dependent clauses to make them complete sentences.

As the soil of forests in the North becomes less fertile, lumber companies
. Once
turn to federal lands and their prime stands of old-growth timber/
however,
~~although, once~~ logging begins, these forests will last less than a decade.

[To create two sentences, the revision omits a subordinating conjunction, *although,* and adds a conjunctive adverb, *however,* as a transition.]

At the upper edge of earth's atmosphere, chlorine atoms attack the
. This
ozone layer/ ~~which is a~~ form of oxygen (O_3) ~~that~~ collects in a thin band
above the stratosphere/ and ~~which~~ protects the earth from ultraviolet
radiation.

[To make two sentences, this revision turns a clause, *which is a form of oxygen,* into a phrase, *this form of oxygen,* that becomes the subject of a second sentence and then omits two relative pronouns, *that* and *which,* to create the main verbs.]

26*d* | Vary your sentence types

Sentences can be classified according to the clauses they contain: simple, compound, complex and compound-complex. (See 12c1.)

Using several sentence types will help you emphasize important ideas and vary sentence length and rhythm. Consider the varied sentences in the following example.

Complex	For people who firmly believe that "there is nothing to fear but fear itself" or that "murderers and con-artists don't prey
Compound	on ordinary people," the tales told around the office water-cooler offer an opportunity to reconsider. After all, urban legends are supposed to be disturbing, so they are carefully designed to prick a hole in one's urban security. A good story
Complex	introduces a sinister array of characters, from innocent-looking passers-by with bizarre, blood-thirsty agendas to monstrous animals that are mistaken for household pets. The
Simple	thrill of these stories lies in their closeness to home. With
Compound-	chilling predictability, the twisted and macabre invade
Complex	ordinary life, and when real-life situations begin to echo these "friend of a friend" stories, the media take on the role of national storyteller—graphically reminding everyone how EVIL is never really very far away.

26e | Vary the structure of your sentences

1 Varying sentence openers

Most sentences, like this one, open with their subjects. But too many of these sentences in a row can be monotonous. Vary your sentence openers occasionally to create new rhythms and to direct readers to the ideas you want to emphasize.

- **Adverbs** can appear almost anywhere in a sentence.

The bicyclist pedalled ~~slowly~~ up the steep hill. *[Slowly, the]*

~~Runners~~ and bicyclists should not wear portable stereos ~~when they exercise.~~ *[When runners]* *[exercise, they]*

- Open with a **participial phrase** beginning with the *-ing* or *-ed* form of the verb. Follow it with the noun or pronoun that it modifies.

The paddle-wheel steamer/~~churning the brown river~~/pulled from the dock. *[Churning the brown river, the]*

- Open with a **prepositional phrase**, often a modifier of the main verb of the sentence.

The Seagram Museum closed its doors forever ~~at the end of March 1997.~~ *[At the end of March 1997, the]*

- Open with an **introductory series** in order to move important ideas to the end of a sentence. Use a dash to connect the series to the main clause. (See also 41a3.)

Flipping burgers, stocking shelves, tearing ticket stubs—these are the ways many
~~Many~~ high school students spend valuable homework time ~~flipping~~

~~burgers, stocking shelves, and tearing ticket stubs.~~

- Open with an **appositive**, a noun or noun phrase that modifies a nearby noun.

A   Karen Kain
~~Karen Kain, who was a~~ silver medallist in Moscow in 1973, went on to

become Canada's prima ballerina for over twenty years.

- Open with an **absolute phrase**, a modifier containing a subject and part of a verb.

Lip   the small boy
~~The small boy, lip~~ trembling and knees knocking, confessed to having

broken the window.

- Open with an **infinitive phrase**, a *to* verb and its related words.

To buy food or drink or to pay for their rooms, many
~~Many~~ of the Impressionist painters had to sell their works ~~to buy food or~~

~~drink or to pay for their rooms.~~

2 Inverting sentence order

The most common English word order is subject + verb + object, complement, or verbal modifier. If you invert this order, putting the verb or other later words before the subject, you will change the rhythm of a sentence and create variety.

Among the first settlers of New France was
Hélène Boullé, the wife of Samuel de Champlain, ~~was among the first~~

~~settlers of New France.~~

[This revision moves a prepositional phrase to the beginning and reverses the subject and verb.]

Use inverted sentences like these sparingly; writing with too many of them can sound awkward or pretentious.

26f | Ask an occasional question

Most sentences are declarative sentences that provide information. (See 12c2.) You can increase your sentence variety and attract readers if you alternate declarative sentences with questions. (This strategy is italicized in the following examples.)

1   Using questions that begin paragraphs

Placed at the beginning of a paragraph, questions can give direction to your writing and involve readers in a search for answers.

> *What do we do when time is tight?* Naturally, we look for shortcuts. We scan our newspapers for "news-in-brief" digests at the front of each section. We look at the contents pages of magazines to discover which article to read while we wait for our turn at the dentist's office. We check the TV listings to determine what show sounds interesting enough to watch. If there is a summary available, it makes sense to read it before deciding what to spend our time on.

2   Using rhetorical questions

Rhetorical questions, assertions rephrased as questions, vary the expression of your ideas and opinions.

> *Isn't it really the public's fault that athletes take performance drugs?* Not only do we reward winners with instant celebrity and millions of dollars, but we damn with token bonuses and anonymity those who come in second. We idolize heroes and scorn the also-rans. *What choice is there for the junior star with average talent? With such relentless public pressure to succeed, is it any wonder that so many young athletes ignore the long-term health risks in favour of drug-enhanced glory?*

chapter

27   Avoiding Mixed and Incomplete Messages

No matter how vivid, insightful, or stylish your writing, if your sentences don't make sense or say what you intend, the virtues of your writing will be lost on readers. The following guidelines will help you express your meaning accurately.

27*a* | Write subjects and predicates that make sense together

Subjects must fit logically with their predicates, consisting of the main verb and any associated words. When they do not, the error is known as **faulty predication.** Subjects must be able to do what their verbs say they are doing. Subjects and subject complements must fit together naturally and appropriately.

The ideal of public service ~~has dwindled among~~ *has been neglected by* many young people.

[Logically, an ideal cannot dwindle, which means to become smaller. The problem is not the size of the ideal but people's awareness of or opposition to it.]

1 Avoiding subjects that fit only part of a compound predicate

A subject must make sense with all of its verbs.

Hot air ballooning experienced a renaissance
~~The renaissance of hot air ballooning came~~ in the early 1960s and has since then grown increasingly popular.

[The original version says that a *renaissance* [. . .] *came* [. . .] *and has grown*[. . .] *popular.* But the renaissance did not grow popular. The writer means to say that hot air ballooning has grown popular.]

2 Avoiding illogical subject complements

An adjective or noun that follows a verb must logically describe or rename the subject of the sentence.

~~Secretaries, filing clerks, and customer service representatives are only a~~
Some ~~few~~ of the part-time positions the company wants to fill *are for secretaries, filing clerks, and customer service representatives.*

[The original says that people are positions. By turning the sentence around, the writer avoids making this illogical parallel.]

3 Avoiding *is when, is where*

These phrases are common in casual speech, but often, especially in definitions, they create statements that are not grammatical or logical.

How to Edit to Say What You Mean

As you reread your sentences, ask "What's happening here?" Rewrite so that actions and events make sense.

1. Identify actors and their actions, subjects and their verbs. Do they go together logically? As you rewrite, try to keep your subjects and verbs as close together as possible. Your meaning will be clearer. (See 27a and b. To learn to identify subjects and verbs, see 10c and 11a.)
2. Study your sentences, asking "What goes with what?" Rewrite to create logical relationships.
3. Be sure comparisons are logical and complete. (See 27c.)
4. Study your sentences to see whether they have all the words necessary to express your meaning accurately. (See 27d.)
5. Consider words that precede and follow commas. If one word group modifies the other, be sure the relation is logical. (See 28a and b.)
6. Check to see that pronouns are consistent in their reference and verbs are consistent in their forms. (See 29a–e.)

the
Algophobia is ~~when a person has~~ excessive fear of pain.

[*When* is an adverb of time, but *algophobia* is a condition. The revision connects the term to its definition.]

in which
Cubism was an early twentieth-century artistic style ~~where~~ painters

presented multiple perspectives of three-dimensional objects.

[*Where* is an adverb of place, but Cubism was an artistic movement.]

27*b* | Avoid mixed constructions that say one thing in two ways

Many ideas can be expressed in more than one way. A **mixed construction** occurs when two ways of saying the same thing are combined in one sentence. To rewrite a mixed construction, identify the two patterns of expression and choose the one that best fits the surrounding sentences and most clearly expresses your ideas.

Figures

~~According to the figures~~ released by Statistics Canada point to the

changing composition of the typical Canadian family.

[In the original, a prepositional phrase, *according to the figures released by Statistics Canada*, seems to be the subject of the sentence—a grammatical impossibility. The revision uses a noun phrase, *figures released by Statistics Canada*, as the subject. Another revision might follow the pattern begun by the original opening: *According to the figures released by Statistics Canada, the composition of the typical Canadian family is changing.*]

27c | Make comparisons logical and complete

1 Comparing comparable items

To make a logical comparison, make sure that both subjectcs are genuinely comparable.

drive   rented

To get from Edmonton to Vancouver, it is cheaper to fly than to ~~rent~~ a car.

[The original sentence compares flying to renting, only one of which is a method of travelling. The revision compares two methods of travelling.]

2 Using complete formulas

Comparisons are made with certain verbal formulas that establish the comparative relationship. To be logical, supply all words necessary to complete the formula. (See also 21d.)

those of

Imports often have warranties longer than domestic cars.

[The original seems to compare a warranty to a car: *warranties longer than domestic cars. Those of*, supplied in the revision, completes the comparison between two kinds of warranties.]

they spend with

Alcoholics often spend more time drinking with friends than their

families.

[The original seems to say that alcoholics drink more with their friends than their families do. Inserting *they spend with* distinguishes time spent with friends from time spent with families.]

3 Making complete comparisons

To be complete, comparisons must include all items being compared.

than the Hamilton Tigercats

The Calgary Stampeders are not just a bigger and faster football team.

Man for man, they are also more experienced.

4   Making comparisons with *any* and *any other*

Use the comparative *-er/more* form to compare two separate items, the superlative *-est/most* form to consider one item's highest or lowest position within a group. Use *any other* with comparatives to keep the items separate, and use *any* with superlatives to include the item within the group.

other

The United States has a higher divorce rate than any country.

The United States has the highest divorce rate of any ~~other~~ country.

[The first sentence needs *any other* to keep the United States separate from all the others in the comparison. In the second sentence, the United States must be included in the group with *any*.]

27*d* Include all necessary key words and function words

1   Checking for omitted key words

Omitting key words may produce illogical statements. As you rewrite, be sure your sentences have all the words necessary to express your ideas completely.

for teachers

High school homeroom periods last just long enough to take attendance
for students to
and hear announcements.

[The original says, illogically, that the homeroom periods take attendance and hear announcements. The revision adds the subjects for these actions, *teachers* and *students*.]

When we reached a clearing in the forest, we found ourselves knee-deep
lost in metre-high ,   *blinded by*
in green slime, weeds ~~six feet tall~~ and clouds of flying insects.

[In the original, the hikers improbably appear to be knee-deep in metre-high weeds and clouds of insects, as well as slime. The added verb phrases describe their situation in an accurate and parallel fashion.]

2 Checking for omitted function words

Function words help to identify the grammatical functions performed by the key words of sentences. Include all the function words necessary to signal the direction your sentences are taking.

- Include articles (*a*, *an*, and *the*) before nouns to make series or compounds grammatically complete.

  Onto the stage walked a doctor, _^*an* astronaut, and _^*the* president of the

  university.

  [It is necessary to add the articles (*an* before a word beginning with a vowel and the definite article *the* before the title of a specific person) to prevent the reader from wondering if all three aren't one and the same.]

- You may often omit the subordinating conjunction *that* from your sentences: *Leslie stuffed her backpack with all [that] she would need for two weeks*. But include *that* if readers may not see that a clause follows a verb instead of a direct object.

  Kevin found _^*that* the historic house he wanted to photograph had been

  demolished.

  [Adding *that* indicates that the historic house is the subject of a clause, not the direct object of *found*.]

- Even though a verb may be common to both parts of a compound structure, you must repeat the verb to keep things parallel. (See 21e.)

  The centenarian told her new doctor that she liked to _^*have* and intended to

  keep having a glass of sherry before bedtime.

  [Without the addition of *have*, the sentence produces the ungrammatical *liked to [. . .] having*.]

- If the relative pronoun *who* changes case from one part of a compound structure to another, use both case forms. (See 19e.)

  Arthur Ashe was a man _^*whom* many thought the greatest tennis player of his

  generation but who should be remembered more for his social activism.

  [*Whom* must be added to the first half of the compound to signal that it is in the object case as the direct object of the verb *thought*. In the second half, *who* is in the subject case as the subject of the verb *should be remembered*.]

chapter

28 Placing Modifiers

| **28***a* | Move misplaced modifiers near the words they modify |

A **misplaced modifier** is a word or phrase that is located incorrectly in relation to the words it modifies. The result may be an illogical sentence that is difficult to follow. If you spot a misplaced modifier, rearrange the sentence to make sense and to make reading easier.

> The antique chair looked as if it needed *badly* to be repaired ~~badly~~.

[The original seems to call for some bad repairs. The revision moves the modifier next to the word it describes, *needed*.]

> The secretary asked us to report *to her* every long distance call we had made ~~to her~~.

[In the original, the secretary seems to be asking only for calls that have been made personally to her. Moving the modifier means all long distance calls must be reported.]

1   Using limiting modifiers correctly

Limiting modifiers restrict or limit the meaning of the words they modify: *almost, even, exactly, hardly, just, merely, nearly, only, scarcely, simply*. To make your meaning clear and unambiguous, place these modifiers before the words they modify.

> Barry ~~only~~ *only* chose the chocolate-covered caramels.

> The personnel manager ~~nearly~~ *nearly* interviewed a dozen applicants this morning.

2   Avoiding squinting modifiers

Squinting modifiers appear to modify both preceding and following words, creating ambiguous meaning. Move the modifier before the word it modifies or rewrite to eliminate ambiguity.

Because she wanted to work for the federal government, Nancy

seriously

‸considered ~~seriously~~ studying for a degree in political science.

[The original seems to say that Nancy considered doing some serious studying. The revision says that the way she considered was serious.]

often

Students who do not study ~~often~~ have trouble on exams.
‸

[It is impossible to tell whether *often* refers to *study* or *have trouble* until the word is moved. Another revision is possible: *Students who do not often study have trouble on exams.*]

3   Avoiding split infinitives

An infinitive is the *to* form of the verb *to go*. **Split infinitives** occur when a modifier comes between *to* and the verb: *to boldly go*. Avoid split infinitives when they sound awkward or when readers may be confused.

politely

Gavin's mother told him to ~~politely~~ apologize for his behaviour.
‸

without much preparation

Sheri hoped to ~~without much preparation,~~ pass her French final exam.
‸

Split infinitives are, however, appropriate in some circumstances:

- To avoid ambiguity. Consider the difference between these two sentences, the first containing a split infinitive: *The Minister refused to further delay antismoking legislation. The Minister refused to delay further antismoking legislation.* In the first sentence, the Minister refused to increase the delay. In the second, he refused to delay more legislation.

- To avoid awkwardness. Consider this sentence containing a split infinitive: *Before Emma took drama lessons, she used to just whisper her lines.* This version is clearer and more natural than *Before Emma took drama lessons, she used just to whisper her lines.*

28*b* | To connect dangling modifiers, rewrite or add missing words

A **dangling modifier** has no words to modify. It "dangles" disconnected or appears to make an illogical connection.

1   Rewriting dangling participles

A participle is the *-ing* or *-ed* verb form acting as an adjective. A **dangling participle** "dangles" because there is no subject to go along with the action that it names. Rewrite to identify this subject. Either introduce it right after the participle phrase, or rewrite the phrase as a clause which includes the subject.

> Driving his Jaguar recklessly, ~~the light turned red before~~ Dan had *not* cleared
> the intersection *before the light turned red.*/
>
> [In the original, the light seems to be driving the car. The revision turns the clauses around so that Dan is the actual driver.]

> *I was*
> While shaving one morning, an idea for a new play occurred to me.
>
> [In the original, the idea itself seems to be shaving. Adding a subject, *I*, to turn the opening phrase into a dependent clause, clarifies the meaning.]

2   Rewriting dangling infinitives

When an infinitive phrase (*to* + verb and related words) introduces a sentence, its logical subject must appear as the subject of the main clause. Otherwise, the infinitive will appear to "dangle." As a revision, either add the subject to the sentence, or include it in the infinitive phrase, often in a prepositional phrase introduced by *for*.

> *you must return goods*
> To apply for a refund, ~~goods must be returned~~ in the original packaging.
>
> [The original suggests that the *goods* will be applying for a refund. The revision makes the sentence active, with *you* as the subject of both verbs.]

> *for writers*
> Careful proofreading is essential to avoid embarrassing errors.
>
> [In the original, there is no one to do the action expressed by the verb *avoid*. The revision adds a prepositional phrase to include the missing actor.]

3   Rewriting a modifier that appears to modify a possessive

Modifiers that provide information about nouns or pronouns cannot modify possessive -'*s* words, which act as adjectives rather than nouns. Rewrite to omit the possessive or to supply a noun or pronoun.

> *her ankle*
> Falling heavily on the ice, the skater~~'s ankle~~ broke in three places.
>
> [In the original, the ankle itself seems to have done the falling. The revision makes the skater, not the ankle, the subject.]

chapter

29 Avoiding Faulty Shifts

29a | Maintain a consistent point of view

Point of view is the perspective of a piece of writing: **first person** point of view (*I* or *we*), **second person** (*you*), or **third person** (*he, she, it, one,* or *they*). A faulty shift in point of view frequently involves a shift from first or third person to second person, for example, from *I* or *they* to *you*. As you write, settle on a point of view appropriate to the subject and occasion. For informal writing, first person point of view is acceptable, but for more formal writing, third person is more appropriate. Once you've decided on your point of view, maintain it consistently.

> My job washing dishes may be damp and dirty, but at least no one ever
> bothers ~~you~~ me while ~~you are~~ I am working.

> Pedestrians stared suspiciously at the Jeffreys as they searched for the right
> address. Wherever ~~you~~ they turned, ~~you~~ they were inspected from head to foot.

A note on direct address: Write *you* only when you mean to address readers directly, as in instructions or advice: *When you finish a rough draft, let it sit for a while before you begin revising.* (See 18a3.)

29b | Avoid inconsistent shifts in number

If you begin writing about a subject using the plural, stick to the plural; if you begin in the singular, stick to the singular.

> Street crime has made many people afraid to leave their ~~home~~ homes at night.

29*c* | Stay in one tense unless the time of the action changes

When you use more than one verb to describe an action, put all the verbs in the same tense. A faulty tense shift between past and present sometimes occurs in narratives about past events.

> On the first day of school, my kindergarten teacher welcomed me
>
> warmly and showed me where my seat ~~is~~ *was*.

[The original shifts from the past tense *welcomed* and *showed* to the present *is*. The revision makes all the verbs past tense.]

> At the beginning of Shirley Jackson's short story, Mr. Johnson leaves his
>
> house in love with the world. He ~~wanted~~ *wants* to make others feel as good as
>
> he ~~did~~ *does*.

[The original, from a student paper about a short story, shifts from present to past tense. The revision makes all the verbs present tense, the appropriate tense for writing about literature and the events that take place in individual stories, novels, and plays. (See also 15b1.)]

29*d* | Maintain a consistent mood and voice

1 Avoiding shifts in mood

Mood identifies the kind of statement a verb makes: an expression of fact (**the indicative mood**), a command or advice (**the imperative**), and wishes or speculation (**the subjunctive**). Stick to one mood unless you have reason to change. (See also 15d.)

> For best growth and colour, ~~it is important that marigolds be planted~~ *plant marigolds* in
>
> full sun. Water them often and pinch back the blooms to encourage
>
> further growth.

[The original shifts from the subjunctive mood in the first sentence, *be planted*, to the imperative mood in the second, *water . . . and pinch back*. The revision puts both sentences in the imperative mood appropriate for instructions.]

2   Avoiding shifts in voice

Voice refers to the relationship between a subject and verb. (See 25a.) In active voice expressions, an active subject performs the action of the verb: *The child hit the ball.* In passive voice expressions, a passive subject is acted on: *The ball was hit.* Maintain a consistent voice unless you have reason to change. (See also 25a.)

>   *she had achieved*
> Amanda congratulated herself because all of her goals ~~had been~~
> ^   ^
> ~~achieved.~~

[The original shifts from the active voice, *congratulated*, to the passive, *had been achieved.* The revision maintains the active voice throughout.]

29e | Avoid inconsistent shifts from indirect to direct discourse

Direct discourse consists of word-for-word quotations and questions addressed directly to listeners or readers. **Indirect discourse** summarizes quotations and questions. Be consistent in the form of discourse you use. (See 24d.)

> Last week Dr. Lambert told us that we were behind schedule ~~and said,~~
>   *and that we would*   *our*
> ~~"You'll~~ have to finish ~~your~~ report by the end of the month.~~"~~
>   ^   ^

[The original shifts from summary to direct quotation. The revision maintains indirect discourse throughout. An alternative revision would quote all of Dr. Lambert's remarks: *Last week Dr. Lambert told us, "You're behind schedule. You'll have to finish your report by the end of the month."*]

> During the nineteenth century, doctors were uncertain whether the
>   *whether they should*
> causes of mental illness differed for men and women and ~~if so, should~~
>   ^
> ~~they~~ be treated differently~~?~~
>   ^

[The original opens with an indirect question and shifts to a direct question. The revision maintains indirect discourse throughout.]

Choosing Words

How to . . .

How to Choose the Right Words

Follow these guidelines as you write and edit.

1. Experiment as your write. When you come to a word that doesn't seem exact, try several alternatives. If you don't find the exact word, put a ? in the margin as a reminder to reconsider your choice as you revise. (See 30.)
2. Whenever possible, choose words you know well. Look up words outside your everyday vocabulary. To decide which word best fits the context of your writing, use the list of synonyms after many dictionary entries, consult a thesaurus, or see the guide to troublesome words and phrases in 34.
3. Whenever possible, use concrete and specific pictorial words. (See 31a and b.)
4. Create metaphors and similes to describe your subject, make judgments, or express your feelings. (See 31c and d.)
5. Choose words that fit the seriousness of your subject. The more serious the subject, the more formal your vocabulary should be. (See 32.)

chapter

30 Choosing Exact Words

30*a* Denotation: Choose words that say exactly what you mean

The **denotation** of a word is, literally, its dictionary definition. Although writers don't plan to use the wrong word, even the best occasionally choose a word that is not quite right. As you write and revise, look for mismatches between what you mean to say and what your words actually mean.

1 Checking for ambiguous words

Writers sometimes choose words that, in the context of their writing, may have multiple, or **ambiguous**, meanings. To write unambiguously, choose specific words that express only the meaning you intend. (See 31a.)

Although many were dissatisfied with Judge Tanaka's decision, they did

agree that it was ~~fair~~.
     impartial

[*Fair* may mean that the judge ruled without favouritism, the meaning of *impartial*. But *fair* may also mean in the best interests of each person involved or without self-interest. The exact meaning of *fair* is unclear in the original sentence.]

2   Checking for approximate words

Some words are near synonyms of other words. But, as Mark Twain once observed, the difference between the right word and the almost-right word is the difference between lightning and a lightning bug. To distinguish between words with similar meanings, use the synonym section of dictionary entries or a thesaurus. (See 30c and d.)

                                ~~quietly weakly~~ *faintly*

At dawn, the cardinal's song echoed ~~feebly~~ over the roof tops.

30*b* | Connotation: Choose words that convey appropriate feelings and attitudes

The **connotation** of a word is the emotional associations and attitudes that the word calls up. Words similar in dictionary definition often differ widely in connotative meaning. Consider the connotations of the word pairs in the following sentences. The words in each pair are similar in denotation but differ in connotation. Is the connotation of each word positive, negative, or neutral?

> On the dining room table was a vase filled with *artificial/fake* flowers.
>
> The old *cabin/shack* stood near the edge of a forest.
>
> Political parties aim to *educate/indoctrinate* voters.

1   Matching connotation and the writer's attitude

Choose words whose positive, neutral, or negative connotation matches your attitude toward your subject. Find the right word in the synonym section of a dictionary entry or in a thesaurus. (See 30c and d.)

    aroma

The ~~odour~~ of holiday baking always reminds me of my childhood.

[*Odour* generally has negative, unpleasant associations. If the writer's memories are positive, *aroma*, associated as it is with savoury smells, is the better choice.]

2 Expressing connotation in public writing

Decide whether words with strong connotations are suitable. Not all situations permit such expressions of feeling or attitude, either positive or negative. Informative writing in school and on the job usually requires neutral or subdued words.

> A ~~mob~~ ^{crowd} of reporters ~~stormed~~ ^{rushed to} the hotel where Celine Dion was making her
>
> announcement.
>
> [The strong negative connotations of the original words are inappropriate for writing from an objective perspective.]

30c Learn to use all parts of a dictionary entry

A good desk dictionary—such as the *Gage Canadian Dictionary, Funk & Wagnalls Canadian College Dictionary, ITP Nelson Canadian Dictionary,* or the *Penguin Canadian Dictionary,* not to mention *Webster's Tenth New Collegiate Dictionary* and the *Oxford English Dictionary*—does more than give spelling and basic definitions. To choose the exact word for your context, you need to know—and take advantage of—all that a dictionary entry contains. Here is an example from the *Gage Canadian Dictionary.*

Pronunciation   Grammatical labels

ef·fect (i fekt') *n., v.—n.* **1** whatever is produced by a cause; something made to happen by a person or thing; result. **2** the power to produce results; force; validity. **3** influence: *The medicine had an immediate effect.* **4** the impression produced. **5** the combination of color or form in a picture, etc.: *Sunshine coming through leaves creates a lovely effect.* **6** purport; intent; meaning. **7 effects,** *pl.* personal property; belongings; goods.   **Definitions**

for effect, for show; to impress or influence others.
give effect to, put in operation, make active.
in effect, a in result; in fact; really. **b** in operation; active: *The new rules are now in effect.*
into effect, in operation; in action; in force.
of no effect, with no results; useless.
take effect, begin to operate; become active: *The new prices will take effect on January 1st.*
to the effect, with the meaning or purpose.   **Grammatical labels**

Idioms

—*v.* **1** produce as an effect; make happen; get done; bring about. **2** *Rare.* make; construct. [ME < L *effectus < efficere < ex-* out + *facere* make]   **Etymologies (word origins)**

Usage label

✏ *Syn. n.* **1. Effect, consequence, result** = something produced by a cause. **Effect** applies to whatever is produced by a cause, particularly what happens or occurs directly and immediately: *The effect of raising the speed limit was a number of bad accidents.* **Consequence** applies to something that follows, but is not always closely or directly connected with the cause: *As a consequence, there was a provincial investigation of highway conditions.* **Result** applies to what happens as a final effect or   **Examples**

Synonyms (related words)

consequence: *The result was a new set of traffic regulations.* **7.** See note at **property**.

☛ *Usage.* **Effect, affect.** Because these words sound similar, they are often confused in writing. Most commonly, **effect** is a noun, meaning "result", and **affect** is a verb, meaning "to influence": *We don't know what effect the new rule will have. The new rule will affect everybody.* However, in formal English **effect** is also used as a verb meaning "get done, bring about": *He effected an improvement in the working conditions.* Thus *to affect a proposal* means to influence it or make a change in it, while *to effect a proposal* means to get it done or bring it to completion.

You can have online access to two major dictionaries with these URLs:

<http://c.gp.cs.cmu.edu:5103/prog/webster>
<http://www.oed/com/oetc.html>

1 Locating spelling, word division, and pronunciation

Words are divided by syllables: **ef·fect.** Two words with the same spelling but different meanings are numbered to signal their difference. Compounds are written as one word (*handbook*), with a hyphen (*hand-me-down*), or as two words (*hand grenade*). When two or more spellings or pronunciations are correct, the preferred appears first. The phonetic alphabet (as in i fekt') is explained in the dictionary's introduction and in the pronunciation key usually found at the bottom of the page. Accent marks (') indicate the most heavily stressed character or syllable.

2 Locating grammatical labels and word endings

Labels indicate the grammatical function (part of speech) of a word and its various endings: *tr.v.* **-fect·ed, -fect·ing, -fects** (and, if it has unusual endings, these are included in boldface).

adj. adjective	*interj.* interjection	*prep.* preposition
adv. adverb	*n.* noun	*pron.* pronoun
aux. auxiliary	*pl.* plural	*sing.* singular
conj. conjunction	*pl. n.* plural noun	*tr.* transitive
def. art. definite article	*pref.* prefix	*intr.* intransitive
indef. art. indefinite article	*suff.* suffix	*v.* verb

Whenever a word changes grammatical function, alternatives are listed in boldface accompanied by a grammatical label:—**effects**, *pl.* All abbreviations are defined in the dictionary's introduction (see the table of contents after the title page).

3 Locating definitions and etymologies

Definitions are numbered and arranged by frequency of use or according to meaning clusters. Letters following numbers identify closely related definitions. Examples occasionally illustrate a word's use. The **etymology** of a word (its origin or history) is often an important guide to its meanings and associations. **Effect,** for example, comes from Middle English (ME) via Latin this way: **L** *effectus* < *efficere* < *ex-* out + *facere* make.

4   Locating usage labels

Labels preceding a definition tell under what conditions that definition is appropriate: *Informal, Slang, Nonstandard, Offensive, Archaic, Obsolete, Chiefly British.* Field labels identify special areas such as music, art, computer science, and medicine where specific definitions apply.

5   Locating synonyms and usage

Following the main entries of many words are notes that distinguish among related words (see the synonyms of *effect*) or that compare actual uses of words with what experts consider correct uses (see the Usage Note on *effect* and *affect* in 34).

30*d* | Use a thesaurus to find the exact word, not necessarily the biggest or fanciest

A **thesaurus** (from the Latin word for "treasure") lists words together with their synonyms, antonyms, and related words. A thesaurus may be a printed reference work, such as *Bartlett's Roget's Thesaurus,* or *Webster's Collegiate Thesaurus,* or a data file accompanying a computer word processor. Here is an entry from *Webster's Collegiate Thesaurus.**

Headword   Grammatical label   ┌Numbers identifying different senses of the headword

believe *vb* **1** to have a firm conviction in the reality of something   Illustration

Synonyms   < *believes* in ghosts > ─────────────────   of the core
listed   *syn* accept, || buy, swallow   meaning of
                                                              the headword

Related words ─ *rel* accredit, credit, trust; admit
that are not
synonyms   ┌ *idiom* have no doubts about, hold the belief that, take
               (or accept) as gospel, take at one's word, take one's word for

Idiomatic   ┌ *con* discredit, distrust, doubt, mistrust, question, suspect;   ┌ Cross refer-
equivalents   challenge, dispute; reject, turn down   ence number

Contrasting   ┌ *ant* disbelieve, misbelieve   A signal to
words that are **2** *syn* FEEL **3.** consider, credit, deem, hold, sense, think check usage
not antonyms   labels in a
              3 *syn* UNDERSTAND **3.** assume, expect, gather, imagine,   dictionary
Antonyms ─ || reckon, suppose, suspect, take, think

 Roget's Thesaurus is available on-line at this URL:
        <http://humanities.uchicago.edu/forms_unrest/ROGET.html>

---

*By permission. From Merriam-Webster's Collegiate® Thesaurus ©1988 by Merriam-Webster, Incorporated.

1   Matching words to contexts

Although a thesaurus groups words having related meanings, it cannot identify the specific contexts in which each word is appropriate. As you decide between synonyms or related words, consider the denotation and connotation of each word, your readers' vocabulary, and the formality of the occasion. (See 32a and b.) In most contexts, synonyms are not interchangeable with one another.

>   ~~anxious~~ ~~desirous~~ eager
> We were ~~dying~~ to share our experiences from our trip to Hong Kong.
>
> [*Dying* is too casual for academic and most public writing. *Desirous* sounds too stuffy. And *anxious* suggests apprehension. *Eager* combines the senses of keen anticipation and desire in a word appropriate for writing.]

2   Choosing exact words instead of impressive words

Many writers use a thesaurus because they doubt that their words sound polished or impressive enough. But consider how you respond to people who try to impress you with their vocabularies. Use a thesaurus to help you find exact but familiar words. (See 32a and 32d1.)

>   begun   avoid   high-sounding words
> I have recently ~~commenced~~ to ~~eschew~~ ~~orofundity.~~

30*e* | Distinguish between frequently confused words

Writers confuse one word with another for several reasons.

- **Homophones** sound alike but are spelled differently and have different meanings: *there, their, they're; affect, effect; complement, compliment.*

- **Near homophones** sound enough alike to be confused with each other: *adapt, adopt; allusion, illusion, delusion; ambiguous, ambivalent; lie, lay.*

- **False synonyms** are related but different words often used in similar contexts: *imply, infer; fewer, less; contagious, infectious; number, amount.*

- Some words have similar roots but different prefixes or suffixes: *disinterested, uninterested; empathize, sympathize; incredulous, incredible; assume, presume; nauseous, nauseated; sensuous, sensual.*

To avoid confusion, look up words outside your everyday vocabulary and memorize differences between words that you have confused. (For a listing of many frequently confused words, see the Guide to Usage in 34.)

31a exact/d

integral

Movies have become an ~~intricate~~ part of North American culture.
∧

[*Intricate,* meaning complex or elaborate, and *integral,* meaning essential or necessary, are near homophones differing greatly in their denotations.]

chapter

31 Choosing Vivid Words

As a writer, you want words that say what you mean, and you want powerful words that will make readers pay attention to your ideas. Such words transform writing into what the English poet Sir Philip Sidney called "a speaking picture." They are vivid, descriptive words that bring ideas to life.

31a When possible, choose specific rather than general words

Words can be classified as specific, general, or somewhere in between. **General words** are umbrella terms that refer to many things. **Specific words** refer to individual persons, places, things, actions, or qualities.

GENERAL WORDS ⟵				SPECIFIC WORDS ⟶
artist		painter		Mary Cassatt
urban area		city		Calcutta
vegetation	tree	evergreen	fir	spruce
observe		look		stare
textured	uneven	rough	coarse	scratchy

Because they are precise in meaning and feeling, specific words tend to be more pictorial than general words and to make a subject clearer and easier to grasp. Choose them for these reasons.

Consider the italicized specific words in this passage from a memoir of childhood.

> The bodies of the men I knew were twisted and maimed in ways visible and invisible. The *nails* of their *hands* were *black* and *split,* the *hands tattooed* with *scars.* Some had lost *fingers.* Heavy lifting had given many of them *finicky backs* and *guts* weak from *hernias.* Racing against *conveyor belts* had given them *ulcers.* Their *ankles* and *knees* ached from years of *standing on concrete.* Anyone who had worked for long around machines was *hard of hearing.* They *squinted,* and the *skin of their faces* was *creased like the leather of old work gloves.* There were times, studying them, when I dreaded growing up.
>
> (Scott Russell Sanders, from *The Paradise of Bombs*)

As you write, create the rhythm of general and specific language illustrated by the preceding passage. Use general words to identify a subject, make assertions, and provide background. Use specific words to support assertions and bring ideas to life.

> Drivers are becoming increasingly ~~dangerous~~: hostile. They tailgate at ninety
>
> kilometres an hour, drag race from stop signs, curse, and honk at whatever they
>
> think threatens their sacred right to the road.

[*Dangerous* is a general word that may refer to unskilled drivers or, as the writer intended, to driver hostility. The added specific examples prove the point and dramatize it.]

>   by developers and commercialization   is now a protected historical site.
> Once threatened, Castle Kilbride in Baden, Ontario, ~~now appears to be~~
> ~~safe.~~

[The additions specify both the threats to the mansion and its current status.]

31*b* | When possible, choose concrete rather than abstract words

Concrete words refer to things you see, hear, taste, touch, and smell: *rock, trumpet, tomato, fur, rose*. **Abstract words** refer to conditions, qualities, and ideas: *democracy, honour, equality, misery, hope*. Use concrete words to bring abstractions to life. In the following passage, the emphasized concrete words explain and illustrate *entropy*, the principle of disorder.

> Because of its unnerving irreversibility, entropy has been called the *arrow* of time. We all understand this instinctively. *Children's rooms*, left on their own, tend to get messy, not neat. *Wood rots, metal rusts, people wrinkle* and *flowers wither*. Even *mountains wear down;* even the *nuclei of atoms decay*. In the *city* we see entropy in the *rundown subways* and *worn-out sidewalks* and *torn-down buildings*, in the increasing disorder of our lives. We know, without asking, what is old.
>
> (K. C. Cole, "Entropy," *The New York Times*)

1   Using concrete words for description

As you write and revise, think of concrete nouns to describe your subject and concrete verbs to dramatize its actions.

An autumn bicycle tour in southeastern Manitoba ~~is a wondrous sensory journey~~ ^offers a sensory feast:^ the intense red and yellow of maples, musty aromas of just-harvested corn and beans, sounds of cattle and roosters, and the texture and taste of apples mounded in baskets at roadside stands.

2 Avoiding the seven deadly nouns

When possible avoid *area, experience, factor, field, situation, thing,* and *type,* words so abstract and vague that they deaden almost any idea.

Attending a stamp fair is ~~a quality-type experience~~ ^an education^ for ~~anyone interested in getting involved in the area of philately.~~ ^budding philatelists.^

Chantal would improve her golf game if she ~~changed a few things in her swing~~ ^planted her feet before her swing and followed through after her shot.^

3 Choosing alternatives to weak verbs

Whenever you can find alternatives to weak verbs like *have* or *be,* your writing will become more vivid and imaginative.

~~The~~ average taxpayer ~~is concerned~~ when ~~government cutbacks have the effect that~~ ^Government cutbacks exasperate the^ hospitals ~~are closed or amalgamated, that~~ ^they shut down,^ tuition fees ~~are higher~~ ^inflate,^ and ~~that~~ support for the arts ~~is reduced~~ ^slash.^

31c | Use figurative language to dramatize ideas, opinions, and feelings

Figurative language (also called **figures of speech**) uses words imaginatively and nonliterally to describe, evaluate, and express feelings. The most frequently used figure of speech is **figurative comparison,** which reveals hidden similarities between dissimilar subjects by transferring the features of one subject, called the **vehicle,** to the writer's true subject, called the **tenor.** Consider these lines from Robert Burn's famous love poem:

O, My Luve's [love's] like a red, red rose

That's newly sprung in June.

| My luve | is like | a red, red rose |
| [tenor] | | [vehicle] |

The features of the rose: its beauty, soft petals, freshness, and the feelings associated with its colour and fragrance

In two short lines, the poet describes his beloved, praises her beauty, and expresses his feelings for her. Because figurative comparisons say so much in so few words, they are an especially vivid use of language, one that can make your writing colourful and powerful, a pleasure for you and your readers.

1 Using similes

A **simile** is a **figure of speech** that explicitly compares two dissimilar subjects using *like, as, as if,* or *as though.* Describing an early morning walk on an ocean beach, essayist David Black tells how "the waves, as they slid up the sand, foamed and hissed like butter sizzling in a frying pan" (waves = sizzling butter). Along the way, he fills his pockets with water-polished rocks "shaped as perfectly as eggs" (rocks = eggs) and pauses to watch seagulls that "stood in crowds, each gazing over the heads of the others, like guests at a chic party on the lookout for celebrities" (gulls = guests). Here similes describe concrete subjects by adding details of sound, shape, texture, appearance, and action. But they may also describe less tangible subjects, as in this description of communication:

> Since, like teletype machines that won't shut off, we are always sending messages, it is certainly to our advantage (and to the benefit of those around us) to understand as much as we possibly can about the physics of the whole communication process. Then, we can effectively harness and purposefully direct the constant pulsing energy of our language to get the results we want—as individuals, as department heads, as company leaders.

[Comparing our own communication (tenor) to machinery (vehicle) not only dramatizes the mechanics of our language but also suggests something of its nonstop power.]

2 Using metaphors

A **metaphor** compares implicitly: not *X is like Y,* but *X is Y.* Tenor and vehicle are fused; one becomes the other.

How to . . .

How to Create Similes and Metaphors

If you're unsure how to create a metaphor or simile, use the following figurative language formula. Try several alternatives until you find one that is accurate, original, and appropriate. Then, as you write and revise, omit the formula and work the figure of speech into the context of your sentences.

If ___(my subject)___ were ___(choose from one of the following categories)___ , it would/would not be ___(make up a term to complete the formula)___ .

a movement	a food	a musical instrument
a place	a road	a piece of furniture
a toy	a shape	an article of clothing
a person	a sound	a means of transportation
a smell	a work of art	an animal
a colour	music	the weather
an object	a building	vegetation

If *grammar* were *a musical instrument*, it would be *a piano played by ear*.

Grammar is a piano I play by ear, since I seem to have been out of school the year the rules were mentioned. All I know about grammar is its infinite power. [a metaphor]

(Joan Didion, "Why I Write," *New York Times Book Review*)

As you edit figurative language, avoid clichés (unoriginal figures of speech) and mixed metaphors (two or more figures of speech about the same subject that clash with each other). (See 31d.)

Superstition seems to run, a submerged river of crude religion, below the surface of human consciousness.

(Robertson Davies, "A Few Kind Words for Superstition," *Newsweek*)

[*Superstition* (tenor) becomes *a submerged river* (vehicle) and acquires the river's traits: depth, darkness, cold, and power.]

Art is not a mirror, but a hammer.

(John Grierson, as quoted in *Colombo's Canadian Quotations*)

[Art (tenor) acquires all the power and potential of a hammer (vehicle), which itself could break the reflecting mirror that art is not.]

$31d$ | Avoid clichés and mixed metaphors

1 Avoiding clichés

You recognize clichés because you can fill in the spaces once you get started, something like this: *Watch out! Grandpa got up on the wrong . . . .* Here are some other clichés to watch out for (in addition to *getting up on the wrong side of the bed*, that is.)

avoid something like the plague	last but not least	take a step in the right direction
beat around the bush	life is a bowl of cherries	wake up and smell the coffee
beyond the shadow of a doubt	light as a feather	water under the bridge
blind as a bat	on the brink of disaster	window of opportunity
crystal clear	play with fire	without a word of a lie
climb the ladder of success	sadder but wiser	
dead as a doornail	since the dawn of time	
easy as pie	snatch victory from the jaws of defeat	
have a sneaking suspicion	stubborn as a mule	

The simile *stubborn as a mule* and the metaphor *life is a bowl of cherries* were once lively expressions of stubbornness and life's sweetness. But after decades—centuries, even—of popularity, the mule has died and cherries come packed in freezer cartons. Dead, frozen, drained of colour and flavour, clichés may not convey your exact thoughts and feelings, and readers may dismiss them the way they do an old story heard too many times.

If you write a catchy metaphor or simile you've heard others use, chances are it is already a cliché. Create your own fresh, original figurative language. The figurative language formula on p. 223 will help.

2 Avoiding mixed metaphors

A **mixed metaphor** combines two or more comparisons that don't make sense together and often cause unintended humour. To write effective metaphors and similes, make a single figurative comparison.

The *Abbey Road* album ~~was the springboard that~~ reignited the Beatles' musical career.

[According to the original, the album is compared to a springboard and, through the verb *reignited,* to something that could start a fire. But a springboard cannot start a fire. The revision omits the illogical metaphor.]

chapter
32 Choosing Appropriate Words

32a | Choose words that fit the occasion

Choose an informal or a formal vocabulary appropriate for your subject and the occasion. An **informal vocabulary** will make your writing personal and give it a conversational style. A **formal vocabulary** will convey a serious and more objective attitude. Once you decide what vocabulary is appropriate, use the following to guide your writing and editing.

FEATURES OF INFORMAL VOCABULARIES

Contractions: *can't, it's, 'til, won't,* and so on

Slang and casual expressions: *broke, strapped, dirt poor, wrack your brains, bone up on, brainer,* and so on

Frequent use of *I, we, us,* and *you* to bring the writer closer to the reader

Familiar words used in conversation: *out of money, poor, think, smart,* and so on

Words with obvious connotative meaning: *ruined, homeless, picture it, bright,* and so on

FEATURES OF FORMAL VOCABULARIES

No contractions

No slang, few casual expressions: *poor, destitute, concentrate, study, intelligent,* and so on

I, we, us, and *you* rarely used; subject rather than writer or audience receives emphasis

Words that appear more often in writing, words with Latin roots: *insolvent, impoverished, speculate, intelligent,* and so on

Words with subtle connotations: *destitute, poverty-stricken, contemplate, clever,* and so on

1 Choosing words in academic writing

Generally use a formal vocabulary for informative or persuasive writing about serious subjects. You shouldn't sound stuffy or use words you're uncomfortable with, but choose words that convey the importance of the occasion. Refer to yourself as *I* if you are involved with your subject, but focus on your subject rather than yourself. Avoid slang and most contractions. Use an informal vocabulary only for personal narratives, nonserious informative writing, and humorous writing.

2 Choosing words in job-related writing

For business letters, memos, and reports addressed to strangers or superiors, write with some formality. Choose familiar words to avoid sounding stuffy or pretentious, but consider words subdued in connotation that fit the seriousness of the occasion. For memos and reports addressed to co-workers, less formal words will express your close professional relationship. Aim to sound as if you're talking to them about a subject of mutual concern. (See also 63a–d.)

3 Maintaining consistent formality

Maintain a consistent attitude toward your subject and a consistent relationship with readers. As you edit, look for shifts from one vocabulary to another. Because you talk more than you write, take special care in serious writing to look for shifts from formal to informal words.

> *severely criticized*
> Contemporary religious philosophers have ~~come down hard on~~ society
> as selfish and materialistic.

[*Come down hard on* is slang. Its conversational tone makes this expression inappropriate for academic writing on serious subjects.]

> *Currently, however,*
> ~~Right now, though,~~ compressed natural gas has several ~~bugs~~ *problems* in its
> storage that prevent its wide use as an alternative to gasoline.

[*Right now, though,* is too conversational and imprecise for serious academic writing. *Bugs* is slang and a cliché, inappropriate in objective writing.]

32*b* | In most academic and public writing, avoid slang, regionalisms, and nonstandard words

The larger or more diverse your audience, the more careful you should be to choose words that all your readers will understand and feel comfortable with. You may speak a social or regional dialect of English rich with its own vocabulary, but, for diverse readers, such words are inappropriate. Use a widely understood vocabulary instead.

1 Avoiding slang

Slang is the informal vocabulary of a group or subculture. It is colourful, rapidly changing, strong in feeling, and often not understood by outsiders. Consider examples of slang popular among young people just since World War II: *hot, cool, bad, groovy, hip, awesome, rad, wicked, raging,* *super dooper, funky, heavy, bummer, razzle-dazzle, outasight, shaka zula.* Note how dated most of these words sound.

Some slang becomes widely accepted and proves so durable that it becomes part of our vocabulary: *movie, handout,* and *hydro* were once slang.

More usually, slang is incomprehensible to outsiders, has a shelf-life of only a few months or years, and is more often spoken than written. For these reasons, it is appropriate only for very informal writing to readers you know well.

2 Avoiding regionalisms

Regionalisms are a kind of slang typical of a geographic area. Canada has made its own colourful contributions to English vocabulary—from *cow chip* to *chimo,* from *rink rat* to *the whole shebang.* Such language may be colourful and energetic, but, like slang, it rarely suits the context in writing.

3 Avoiding nonstandard words

Some regions have their own grammatical variants, too. For example, many people say *youse* as a plural form of address, and others add an -*s* to say *anywheres, somewheres,* and *nowheres.* In some parts of the country, people say it is *real cold;* elsewhere it is *right cold, some cold* or even *right some cold.* In writing, consistency and conventions are essential, so avoid spoken expressions that are considered **nonstandard.** (See 34. See also 15c–d, 19g, 20e and 23b–c.)

32c | Use jargon and neologisms only with specialized audiences

 In its technical sense, **jargon** is the technical language of a profession, craft, trade, or activity. Computer operators, for example, use acronyms like *VGA;* metaphors like *motherboard* and *parking a hard drive;* words derived from people's names, like *baud;* compounds like *online* and *log in;* shortened words like *e-mail* and *modem;* and old words with new meaning, like *server.*

A **neologism** is a newly invented word. Often neologisms begin their lives as jargon, slang, or media expressions: *vaporware, cyberspace, CAT scan, morphing, disco.* Many neologisms, such as *radar* and *scuba,* prove useful and eventually become part of standard English; the rest disappear.

Jargon and neologisms enable members of special interest groups to communicate with one another clearly, economically, and efficiently. They cause problems, however, when addressed to outsiders. Therefore, follow these guidelines:

1 Writing for nontechnical audiences

When writing for nontechnical audiences, avoid jargon and neologisms. Choose accurate, widely understood words. If no other words will say what you mean, provide definitions.

With new computer-imaging technology, movie makers are now able to ~~morph~~ *transform* one image into another, for example, fading the head of a man into that of a lion.

2 Academic writing

In academic writing for readers who understand your subject, choose words appropriate to the field or discipline. Demonstrate your knowledge of technical language, but avoid technical words used merely to impress. If in doubt about the proper vocabulary, check with your instructor.

3 Technical writing

In technical writing for knowledgeable readers—for example, in on-the-job memos and reports—a technical vocabulary is appropriate. But carefully consider your audience's knowledge. (See also 63.)

Jargon is sometimes used broadly to refer to flowery words used to impress readers. These words are never appropriate. See the following section.

32d | Avoid pretentious words, "doublespeak," and most euphemisms

1 Avoiding pretentious words

Pretentious writing aims to impress more than communicate. Most readers are annoyed by it. Therefore, avoid the following kinds of words:

- Unfamiliar "big" words, often with Latin roots.

Some ~~educators in the~~ *teachers* humanities have been ~~dilatory in their cognizance~~ *slow to recognize how* ~~of the pedagogical ramifications of~~ new instructional technologies *can improve their teaching*.

■ Flowery words.

The warm sunrise promised

~~Rising into azure heavens flecked with billowy clouds, the warm sun~~

                                              a fine autumn

~~foretold a wondrous autumnal~~ day.

■ Scientific-sounding words that aren't really scientific.

       communication   *enable them*

Increasing ~~the interface~~ between technicians and supervisors will ~~permit~~

       decide what changes will improve

~~the input necessary~~ to ~~determine the parameters affecting inefficient~~

production.

2   Avoiding doublespeak

Doublespeak, a term invented by George Orwell in his novel *1984*, refers to words and expressions that deliberately mislead. Doublespeak aims to create a favourable impression opposite that of the truth. It is an essential feature of political propaganda, but you can find it wherever writers disguise the truth: in advertisements; in government, military, and business writing; even, occasionally, in academic writing. Here are some examples of doublespeak:

downsizing or rightsizing = laying off	revenue enhancements = tax increases
final solution = kill	sanitize = censor
pre-owned = used, second hand	substandard housing = slum
	tanker accident = oil spill
resource recovery facility = incinerator	terminated = fired

Although doublespeak may mislead readers momentarily, its ultimate effect is almost always their cynicism and mistrust. Avoid misleading language.

3   Avoiding euphemisms

Like doublespeak, euphemisms hide the truth. But a **euphemism,** from Greek words meaning "good speech," is a pleasant-sounding word or expression that aims to soften a topic some people may consider distasteful, ugly, or difficult to speak of. Euphemisms usually concern emotionally charged subjects like death (*to pass away, expire*), economic status (*disadvantaged* for *poor, affluent* for *rich*), the body (*rear end, chest*), bodily functions (*go to the bathroom*), and sex (*X-rated, make love, sleep together*).

Most readers expect you to avoid vulgarity but to write clearly and directly. Unless your audience will be offended or hurt by direct language, avoid euphemisms. They make you seem prudish or mealy-mouthed, rather than objective and direct.

32e | Avoid offensive words

Across Canada, human rights codes remind us of the importance of equal and ethical treatment of all people, regardless of race, colour, origin, creed, gender, sexual orientation, disability, age, family status, and so on. Your readers will expect you to use language that is responsible, objective, and fair. It makes good sense to avoid words that others may consider discriminatory and offensive.

1 Avoiding stereotypes

Stereotyping lumps all members of a particular group together and defines them in broad generalizations. Much comedy depends on this kind of oversimplification, but for every one who laughs there is another who finds the humour questionable. Nobody likes to be the butt of a joke. Stereotyping is, of course, inappropriate in any situation where you expect to be taken seriously, even if the label seems complimentary. It's as much a mistake to describe all Canadians as polite as it is to characterize all Americans as gun-happy.

All overgeneralizations are potentially offensive. Here are some general categories to avoid: occupational stereotypes (*dishonest lawyers, sadistic dentists, pedantic English teachers, gay fashion designers*, etc.), ethnic stereotypes (*stuffy Britishers, dour Scots, beer-loving Germans, inscrutable Asians*, etc.), religious or philosophical stereotypes (*placid Mennonites, misanthropic animal activists, militant Islamics, money-grubbing capitalists, Catholics with large families*, etc.), and personal stereotypes (*impossible mothers-in-law, dumb blondes, tomboys, jocks, preppies*, and so on).

2 Avoiding demeaning language

It would seem a matter of common courtesy, if not plain common sense, to avoid using offensive language. Words that belittle, abuse, or disparage are often crude as well. Such language puts its user in a particularly bad light, suggesting that the person is narrow-minded, even bigotted.

Avoid any language that does not respect the dignity and individuality of all people. Be wary of **sexist words** that describe men or women, typically women, in demeaning language (*chick, broad, babe, hunk*) or deny men and women equal status (*the girls in the office, lady doctor, woman writer, male secretary*). Avoid **racist words** and **ethnic slurs**, even if commonly heard, because they belittle or denigrate (*Frog, Newfie, Yankee, Canuck,*

Polack, Paki). And never use slang descriptions that cheapen people (*butch, nerd, geek, geezer, kid, punk, old fogey, fag, workie*).

Even if the words are not obviously colloquial or slang, they may not be words that members of those groups would use. Make yourself aware of, and use, preferred terms.

Inuit, Inuk, not Eskimo

disabled, challenged, not handicapped, crippled

First Nations, Aboriginal people, native Canadians, not Indians

gay, lesbian, not homosexual

Black, person of colour, not Negro, coloured

people with diseases, not victims of diseases

3 Avoiding gratuitous descriptions

Sometimes the demands for specificity seem to contradict expectations of fairness. Before adding details about a person's age, marital status, religion, origin, physical attributes, and so on, verify that these are relevant additions. Make sure, too, that by adding such descriptions you are not subconsciously stereotyping.

Margaret Smythe, a ~~forty-something single mother from Aylmer~~, will be [machinist with twenty years' seniority]

representing the union in the next round of negotiations.

[Ms. Smythe's age, origin, and family status have nothing to do with her selection; the revision appropriately identifies her qualifications instead.]

Winning gold at the Summer Games was another coup for the ~~handsome blond~~ 14-year-old from Rimouski.

[This swimming champion's looks did not contribute to his victory, though his age and origin may be important distinguishing features.]

4 Avoiding non-inclusive language

Be sure to use occupational titles, generic terms, or common expressions that apply to all people regardless of gender or other distinguishing characteristics. By choosing language that includes everyone, you show yourself to be objective and fair-minded, qualities that add immeasurably to your own credibility.

NON-INCLUSIVE LANGUAGE	INCLUSIVE LANGUAGE
actor/actress	actor
alderman	councillor
anchorman/anchorwoman	anchor
businessman/businesswoman	businessperson, executive

NON-INCLUSIVE LANGUAGE	INCLUSIVE LANGUAGE
chairman/chairwoman	chair, chairperson, head, moderator
Christmas party	holiday party, year-end party
cleaning lady	cleaner, janitor, custodian
draftsman	draftsperson
fireman	firefighter
fisherman	fisher
forefathers	forebears, ancestors
foreman	supervisor
freshman	first-year student
gentleman's agreement	unwritten agreement
hero/heroine	hero
host/hostess	host
landlord, landlady	owner
maiden name	birth name
mailman	letter carrier, postal worker
the average man, man on the street	the ordinary person, ordinary people
mankind	humanity, human beings, people
man-made	synthetic, hand-crafted, manufactured
manned	staffed
manpower	staff, personnel, workers, workforce, labour force
man-sized	big, large, hearty, jumbo-sized
man-to-man	person-to-person, heart-to-heart
night watchman	security guard
office boy/office girl	office assistant
one-man show	solo show
repairman	repairer
right-hand man	chief assistant
salesman/saleslady	salesclerk, salesperson, sales representative
spokesman/spokeswoman	spokesperson, representative
sportsmanlike	sporting
sportsmanship	fair play
steward/stewardess	flight attendant
waiter/waitress	server
workman	worker
workmanlike	professional, efficient

Using inclusive language involves watching out for situations where you may unintentionally exclude people.

Employees are invited to bring ~~their wives~~ *a guest* to the ~~Christmas~~ *year-end* banquet.

[Not all employees may be men; not all may be married; not all may be heterosexual; not all may celebrate Christmas. The revision recognizes the diversity of the audience.]

In your writing, do not use *he, him,* and *his* to refer collectively to men and women. If you would rather not overuse pairs of pronouns (*he or she, hers and his, him- or herself*), you should revise your sentence to make everything plural. (See also 17d.)

Each candidate must write an essay explaining ~~his~~ *his or her* qualifications.

When ~~a teenager~~ *teenagers* first ~~gets his~~ *get their* driver's ~~licence~~ *licences*, ~~he wants~~ *they want* to drive everywhere.

The principle of parallel language calls for consistency when referring to pairs of people. Use parallel terms, rather than terms that seem to place the people on two different levels:

husband and wife, not man and wife
women and men, gentlemen and ladies, not men and ladies
Joseph and Rita Alvarez, not Joseph Alvarez and his wife Rita or Mr. and Mrs. Joseph Alvarez
Carmen Green and Harry Redfern, her assistant, not Ms. Green and her assistant Harry

chapter

33 Editing Wordiness

Except for those who like to hear themselves talk, most people aren't wordy on purpose. But for writers, finding what to say and choosing the best words are often roundabout, messy processes of trial and error. They often end up with more words than readers need to get the message. And so they have to rewrite, cutting words that in a final draft might cloud meaning or waste readers' time. To make your writing clear, forceful, and direct—and to earn readers' gratitude—say all that you have to say in as few words as possible.

33*a* Eliminate redundancy

Redundancy is unnecessary repetition, as in *close proximity, first and foremost,* or *crisis situation.* One word in each of these examples implies the meaning of the other. Eliminate redundant words from your writing, but remember that sometimes you need to repeat for emphasis or clarity. (See 25d and 27d.) Here are repetitions to avoid:

1 Needlessly repeated words

As I watched her skate, ~~the impression that was most impressed on~~ me ^{what most impressed}

was her athletic grace.

The man turned the pages of the magazine for a moment or two, then

laid ~~the magazine~~ on the end table. ^{it}

[Use pronouns to avoid unnecessary repetition of nouns and to create variety.]

2 Needlessly repeated ideas

Cut unemphatic words that merely repeat the meaning implied by other, more important words.

The roots of the ancient elm had grown entangled ~~together~~

[If the roots are entangled, they twist together; *together* is redundant.]

~~The reason why airline~~ hijackings seldom occur in North America ~~is~~ ^{Airline}

because the airlines have improved passenger screening ~~procedures~~

[*Reason, why,* and *because* mean the same thing in this sentence; two of the three words can be cut. *Passenger screening* implies *procedures;* this word can be omitted.]

3 Redundant pairs

Writers sometimes pair words with the same meaning: *each and every, full and complete, wishes and desires, goals and objectives, honest and open,* and so on. If you have a redundant pair, cut one of the words.

Elaine ~~had hopes and aspirations of graduating~~ in three years. ^{hoped to graduate}

The ~~basic and~~ fundamental right to freedom of expression ~~in Canada~~ is

guaranteed by the Canadian Charter of Rights and Freedoms.

How to Edit Wordiness

Follow these guidelines.

1. Don't be concerned about wordiness as you plan and write a first draft. But if you're having trouble saying what you mean, look for words that get in the way of your message. Cutting extra words often clarifies meaning.

2. As you edit, look for these clues to wordiness and begin cutting where they occur.

- Needless words, sentences, or extra paragraphs at the beginning or end of your writing.
- Needlessly repeated words or ideas (the reason why is because). (See 33a.)
- Empty sentence openers (In my opinion . . .), needless intensifiers (really, very) or qualifiers (somewhat, seems), and unnecessary impersonal constructions (there is, there are, it is). (See 33b.)
- Padded transitions that link sentences or sentence parts (because of the fact that), unnecessary clause openers (which is/are, who is/are), and nouns ending in -ence, -ance, -ment, and -tion that could be reworked into the main verb of the sentence. (See 33c.)

If a wordy passage contains essential words, replace inflated expressions with concise synonyms, rewrite indirect expressions to make them direct, or combine two wordy passages into one. (See 33c3.)

---

4 Redundant modifiers

Some modifiers are unnecessary because their meaning is contained in the words they modify: *basic fundamentals, the colour blue, sudden crisis, end result, past memories, period of time, personal opinion, shiny appearance, square in shape, true facts,* and so on.

According to statistics, a ~~new~~ baby is born in Canada every two minutes. [When born, all babies are new; the modifier is unnecessary.]

If the supplier expedites our order ~~as quickly as possible~~, we will

~~completely~~ finish the project before the deadline.

[*To expedite* means to speed a process, and to finish something is to complete it; *as quickly as possible* and *completely* are redundant.]

33b | Cut empty words and phrases

1 Cutting empty sentence openers

The meaning of an opening phrase may be implied by the rest of the sentence. Generally cut openers such as *I think that, in some ways, needless to say, in some respects, for the most part, as everyone knows, the fact is, obviously,* and *as we see.* See the following examples:

~~In my opinion, murders~~ Murders are often committed by people too enraged to

consider the consequences of their actions.

[In making an assertion, writers give their opinion. They do not need to state that their opinion is their opinion.]

~~The purpose of the meeting is to~~ The meeting will inform employees about changes in

their benefits.

[Information about the subject of the meeting identifies its purpose.]

2 Cutting empty qualifiers and intensifiers

Intensifiers and **qualifiers** are modifiers that express degree: *very, definitely, really, truly, uniquely, wonderfully, apparently, perhaps, probably, somewhat, quite,* and so on. You may need them to indicate the strength of a statement or shade your meaning. More often, they suggest that writers doubt the force of their ideas. Prefer the plain truth.

To a Maritimer like me, the Rocky Mountains are ~~truly~~ breathtaking.

After two terms at university, ~~it seems~~ I now feel like ~~something of~~ a

survivor.

3 Cutting unnecessary impersonal constructions

Impersonal constructions begin *there is/are* or *it is.* They enable writers to move ideas to the end of a sentence or to emphasize actions that lack actors: *There are three good reasons to put money into an RRSP every year,* or *It is raining.* But when impersonal constructions are unnecessary, cut them and rewrite.

~~There is some~~ Some urban land ~~that~~ is set aside each year for new parks but

not enough to equal the hectares buried under new subdivisions and

shopping malls.

> *Businesses*
> ~~It seems clear that businesses~~ have a social obligation to support
>
> nonprofit organizations in their communities.

33c | Compress padded writing

Wordiness sometimes results not only from extra words but from **padding**, the addition of inflated or indirect expressions. Look for and eliminate the following wordy expressions in your writing.

1 Cutting padded phrases

Compress inflated phrases to one or two words.

INFLATED	CONCISE	INFLATED	CONCISE
as a matter of fact	in fact	for the reason that	because
at the present time	now, currently	have the ability to	be able to
at this/that point in time	now, then	in order to	to
at the same time as	while	in spite of the fact that	although, even though
be in a position to	can	in the event that	if
by means of	by	in light of the fact that	because
due to the fact that	because	in the near future	soon
for the purpose of	for, to	in today's modern world	now, today
		prior to	before
		with regard to	about

We were impressed ~~by the fact~~ that the courthouse had been renovated

so quickly.

to paint
The stagehands erected the scaffold ~~for the purpose of painting~~ the set.

2 Cutting padded clauses

Compress padded dependent clauses to a phrase or word. (To learn to recognize clauses, see 12b.)

In front of the peacekeepers stood their duffle bags, ~~which had been~~ packed with their gear for the next twelve months.

~~Because they don't know how~~ *Unable* to handle their new freedom, some recent high school graduates have difficulty adjusting to university life.

3 Cutting padded sentences

Look for two padded sentences to combine. (For sentence-combining strategies, see 26b.)

The most scenic tour of Mammoth Cave is a six-kilometre *, four-hour* walk that ~~lasts about four hours. This tour~~ includes lunch in the Snowball Room and ends at Frozen Niagara.

Home fires have three common ~~causes. The first cause is the~~ *causes:* careless ~~use of~~ smoking *,* ~~materials. The second and third are~~ faulty wiring, and defective furnaces.

4 Avoiding indirect use of the passive voice

The passive voice often requires more words than the active. Use the active voice to make your writing concise and direct. (To learn when the passive voice is appropriate, see 25a2.)

~~First prize was~~ *The judges* awarded ~~by the judges~~ *first prize* to a poem called "Violet Voices."

5 Avoiding indirect use of nominals

A **nominal** is a noun derived from a verb, often ending *-ence, -ance, -ment, -tion:* dependence (depend), guidance (guide), argument (argue), adaptation (adapt). Nominals often appear in wordy, indirect writing. When you can do so, transform a nominal into its verb form, eliminate empty words or phrases (like *of the*) and rewrite.

The personnel manager selects

~~Selection of~~ appropriate candidates ~~is the responsibility of the personnel~~
^

~~manager.~~
[Removing two nominals, *selection* and *responsibility*, eliminates the empty verb *is* and reduces the sentence to six words from eleven.]

chapter

34 A Guide to Usage: Troublesome Words and Phrases

This glossary contains commonly confused words (such as *less* and *fewer*); words frequently misused (such as *aggravate*); nonstandard words (such as *ain't*); and colloquialisms inappropriate for formal writing (such as *okay*). Strunk and White's classic *Elements of Style* is a handy reference, now available on-line at this URL:

<http://www.columbia.edu/acis/bartleby/strunk>

a, an. Use *a* before words beginning with a consonant sound or an *h* that is pronounced: *a student, a sparrow, a happy man, a hospital*. Use *an* before words beginning with a vowel sound (*a, e, i, o, u*) or a silent *h*: *an apple, an investment, an hour, an honour*.

accept, except. *Accept*, a verb, means "to receive, agree, or believe": *The singer accepted the bouquet from an admirer*. As a preposition, *except* means "but" or "other than": *Everyone is here except James*. As a verb, *except* means "to leave out, exclude": *The last three names were excepted from the list*.

adapt, adopt, adept. *Adapt*, a verb, means "to adjust or to become accustomed": *Some wild animals have adapted to urban environments*. *Adopt*, also a verb, means "to take up and make one's own": *Many childless couples wish to adopt children*. *Adept*, an adjective (or a noun), means "very skilled": *He was adept at the violin*.

advice, advise. *Advice* is a noun, *advise*, a verb: *The lawyer advised her client to accept the advice*.

affect, effect. *Affect* is usually a verb meaning "to influence or act on." *Effect* is usually a noun meaning "a result"; occasionally it is a verb meaning "to bring about." *Smoking affects the body in many ways. Smoking has many harmful effects. Negative advertising may effect a decrease in tobacco use.*

aggravate. *Aggravate* means "to make worse or more troublesome": *High sugar diets often aggravate childhood misbehaviour*. In formal writing, avoid the colloquial use of *aggravate,* "to annoy or irritate." *The traffic was irritating* [not *aggravating*].

agree to, agree with. *Agree to* means "to consent": *The lawyers agreed to the proposed settlement. Agree with* means "to be in accord or to match": *She didn't agree with him about the causes of the problem.*

ain't. *Ain't* is nonstandard. Use *am not, is not, has not, have not,* and so on: *They have not* [not *ain't*] *repaired the motor yet.*

aisle, isle. *Aisle* refers to a passageway, usually between seats: *The bride walked down the aisle. Isle* refers to an island: *He dreamed of retiring to a tropical isle.*

all ready, already. *All ready* means "fully prepared." *Already* means "before or by this time." *By the time everyone was all ready to leave, it was already too late.*

all right (not alright). *All right* is two words; *alright* is nonstandard.

all together, altogether. *All together* means "in a group": *They stood all together near the doorway. Altogether* means "entirely, completely, totally": *They were altogether drenched by the sudden rain.*

allusion, illusion, delusion. An *allusion* is an indirect reference: *Writers and speakers make frequent allusions to Shakespeare.* An *illusion* is a false perception of reality: *A mirage is an optical illusion created by alternate layers of hot and cool air.* A *delusion* is a false belief or opinion, especially as a symptom of mental illness: *People who are paranoid suffer the delusion that others are persecuting them.*

a lot (not alot). *A lot* is two words, not one. *We have had a lot of rain this spring.*

among, between. Use *among* to refer to three or more things, *between* to refer to two: *There was little agreement among the members of the jury. It is so difficult to choose between strawberry and butter pecan ice cream.* When pronouns follow *between,* they must be in the objective case: *Between you and me* [not *between you and I*], *that is the worst show on television.* (See 19b2.)

amount, number. Use *amount* with things that cannot be counted; use *number* with things that can: *The amount of happiness people enjoy is often related to the number of friends they have.*

and/or. Avoid *and/or* except in technical writing, where it may be necessary for precision.

angry at, angry with. *Angry at* is nonstandard; use *angry with. I was angry with* [not *at*] *him because he had cheated.*

ante-, anti-. *Ante-* means "prior to, earlier, before, in front of": *antecedent, anteroom. Anti-* means "opposed to, against": *antihero, antisocial.*

anxious, eager. *Anxious* means "uneasy or worried." In formal writing, avoid using *anxious* to mean "eager." *We are eager* [not *anxious*] *to meet our new director.*

anymore. *Anymore* means "at the present, any longer, or from now on." Use *anymore* only in negative statements: *We will not listen to them any-*

more. In formal writing, avoid the colloquial use of *anymore* to mean "nowadays." *People spend so much time working nowadays* [not *anymore*] *that they have little time to consider the value of their labour.*

any one, anybody, anyone. *Any one* refers to a choice of *one* specific person or thing in a group: *Any one of our staff will help you.* *Anybody* and *anyone* mean "any person at all": *I have not found anyone who knows the answer.* *Anybody* and *anyone* are singular.

anyplace. *Anyplace* is appropriate for informal writing. For formal writing, use *anywhere*.

any way, anyway. *Any way* means "by whatever means or manner." *Any way you choose to travel will bring you unimagined adventures.* *Anyway* means "nevertheless, at least": *We asked them not to bother us, but they did anyway.*

anyways, anywheres. *Anyways* and *anywheres* are nonstandard forms of *anyway* and *anywhere*.

as, as if, like. *As if* is a subordinating conjunction that joins a subordinate clause to a main clause: *The last runners to finish looked as if they were in a trance.* *Like* is a preposition that should be followed only by a noun or noun phrase: *The last runner looked like a zombie.* In informal speech, *like* is often substituted for *as* or *as if*, but in formal writing, use *as*: *As* [not *like*] *Shakespeare put it, "Lord, what fools these mortals be!"*

ascent, assent. *Ascent* refers to the act or process of rising or going upward: *The climbers began their ascent to the summit.* *Assent* means "agreement or consent": *The crowd cheered its assent.*

aspect, respect. When *aspect* means "the look of something" and *respect* means "reverence," the two nouns are rarely confused. Be careful, however, when *aspect* means "angle" and *respect* means "point": *This aspect of the issue is interesting in a couple of respects.*

awesome, awful, awfully. *Awesome* and *awful* are essentially synonymous when they mean "awe inspiring," but *awesome* has the colloquial meaning of "wonderful," where *awful* means "horrible": *Technology has increased the awesome/awful power of weapons. John's English mark was awesome, while Joseph's was awful.* *Awfully* has the colloquial meaning of "very": *The mark was awfully low.* Avoid all the colloquial uses in writing.

awhile, a while. *Awhile* is an adverb meaning "a short time": *He visited awhile, then left.* The two-word phrase *a while* combines an article and a noun to refer more generally to "a period of time": *He stayed a [short] while.* Use the two-word form after a preposition like *after, for,* or *in,* as well as before *ago*.

bad, badly. *Bad* is an adjective that often follows linking verbs: *A bad storm is approaching. I feel bad today.* *Badly* is an adverb that modifies verbs, adjectives, and other adverbs: *He played badly.* (See 20c.)

bare, bear. As a noun, *bare* means "naked," and as a verb, "to uncover, to reveal": *I want to bare my soul to someone.* As a verb, *bear* means "to hold up, support, carry, endure, or exhibit": *I can't bear to listen to his complaints.*

basis, bases. *Basis* is singular, *bases,* plural.

being as, being that. *Being as* and *being that* are nonstandard; use *because* or *since:* *Because* [not *being that*] *I work overtime every day, I have almost no social life.*

beside, besides. *Beside* is a preposition meaning "at the side of or next to": *They walked beside the river. Besides* is a preposition meaning "in addition to or except for": *Besides jazz, I also enjoy bluegrass and gospel music. Besides* is also an adverb meaning "also or furthermore": *My pen has run out of ink; besides, my mind has run out of ideas.*

better, had better. *Had better* is a modal helping verb; be sure to include *had: They had better* [not *they better*] *finish their project this week.* (See 10c1 and 23c.)

between, among. See **among**.

brake, break. As a verb, *brake* means "to reduce speed or to apply a brake": *Brake lightly on slippery streets.* Among its many meanings as a verb, *break* means "to divide, fracture, vary, force one's way out of, to smash into pieces, to reduce in rank, to violate, and to give up": *I have tried for a year to break my smoking habit.*

breath, breathe. *Breath* is a noun, *breathe* a verb: *Relax, and take a breath; now breathe again.*

bring, take. Use *bring* when the action is toward the speaker: *Please bring me a cup of coffee.* Use *take* when the action moves away from the speaker: *Be sure to take some identification when you travel to the States.*

burst, bust, busted. *Burst* is an irregular verb meaning "to open, fly apart, or express suddenly." Its past and past participle forms are the same as its base. Even when they are used to refer to drug crackdowns, rather than confused with *burst,* the forms *bust* and *busted* are colloquial, to be avoided in formal writing: *When he lost, he burst* [not *busted*] *into tears.*

but. You may begin a sentence correctly using *but* to dramatize a contrast.

but what, but that. *But what* and *but that* are colloquial phrases following expressions of doubt; use *that* instead: *I do not doubt that* [not *but what*] *they intend to do the right thing.*

can, may. *Can* expresses ability, knowledge, or capacity: *I can speak. May* expresses possibility or permission: *It may snow tomorrow. You may borrow my calculator.* In formal writing, avoid using *can* to mean permission: *May* [not *can*] *we send you a brochure?*

capital, capitol. *Capital* refers to a city, *capitol* to a building.

censor, censure. As a verb, *censor* means "to remove or eliminate something objectionable": *Some people want to censor the news.* As a verb, *censure* means "to criticize severely, to blame: *The Speaker of the House censured the MP for calling her colleague a liar.*

centre around. Nonstandard; use *centre on: The dispute centred on* [not *centred around*] *issues of wages and benefits.*

cite, site. The verb *cite* means "to mention as proof or to quote as an authority": *If you wish to be believed, cite your sources.* As a noun, *site* means "a place or setting for something": *They visited famous battlefield sites.* Be careful of the homophone *sight*, referring to vision or things to see, as in *sightseeing* [not *siteseeing*].

climactic, climatic. *Climactic* means "relating to or constituting a climax": *The climactic scene of the play was incredibly violent.* *Climatic* means "of or pertaining to climate": *Climatic conditions can change suddenly on the Prairies.*

cloth, clothe. *Cloth* is a noun, *clothe,* a verb: *The best cloth for sportswear pulls perspiration away from the skin. A compassionate government will feed, clothe, and house citizens who cannot care for themselves.*

coarse, course. *Coarse* means "rough in texture or unrefined": *The coarse fabric of his jacket scratched his skin.* *Course* usually refers to a unit of study, a direction of movement, a playing field, or part of a meal. *Of course* means "naturally or certainly." *Next semester I plan to take a course in Asian art. Of course, we are coming to the party.*

come, go. Like *bring* and *take,* these verbs are chosen according to the location of the speaker with respect to the destination. *Come* means "approach the speaker"; *go* means "head in the opposite direction": *Many tourists come to Canada, and many Canadians go abroad.*

compare to, compare with. Use *compare to* when showing that two things are similar or belong in the same category: *In height, the Alps compare to the Rocky Mountains.* Use *compare with* when you intend to examine things side by side to discover similarities and differences: *Compared with their defence budget, the Americans' foreign aid budget is quite small.*

complement, compliment, complementary, complimentary. *Complement* means "to go with or complete" or "something that makes up a whole": *His artistic skill complements his creativity. She took a full complement of courses. Compliment* means "to praise or flatter": *She complimented him on his tact. Complementary* means "completing or offsetting": *She chose complementary colours for the design. Complimentary* means "expressing a compliment or given freely, as an act of courtesy": *He received complimentary software with his new computer.*

conscience, conscious. *Conscience* refers to "moral awareness or the source of moral judgment": *Lying gave him a guilty conscience. Conscious* means "mentally aware or alert": *Before my morning coffee, I am barely conscious.*

contact. Some readers object to the informal use of *contact* as a verb meaning "to get in touch with." (Formally, *contact* is a noun meaning "the touching of two objects.") Business writing, however, now accepts the verb *contact* because there are so many ways to do this: *Please contact me* [call, fax, e-mail, visit] *when you return.* In formal writing, define the action instead: *The MLA called* [not *contacted*] *his press agent.*

continual, continuous. *Continual* means "recurring regularly or frequently": *The dog's continual barking kept Joe awake. Continuous* means "uninterrupted in time or sequence": *The siren rose and fell in a continuous wail.*

could care less. Some people generally use *could care less* to mean *couldn't care less.* The latter expression is logical: *She couldn't care less* [not *could care less*] *about the lives and loves of Hollywood celebrities.* Neither belongs in formal writing, however.

could of. Nonstandard for *could have* or *could've*: *With his talent, John could have* [not *could of*] *been very successful.*

council, counsel. *Council* is a noun referring to an assembly of people or their discussion: *The city council voted to support the mayor.* As a noun, *counsel* refers to a lawyer: *The counsel for the defence rose to speak.* As a verb, *counsel* means "to advise": *His art teacher counselled him to take a CAD/CAM course, against the recommendation of the guidance counsellor.*

criteria. *Criteria* is the plural of criterion, which refers to the standard or rule for a decision or judgment. *One criterion for success is hard work. Two other important criteria are preparation and imagination.*

data. *Data* is the plural of *datum,* meaning "a fact or piece of information used to make a decision." In scientific contexts, and in formal writing, use *data* as a plural: *These* [not *this*] *data show* [not *shows*] *that soil erosion is increasing.* Informally, *data* is used as a noncount noun, like *information.*

different from, different than. *Different from* is always correct: *Is a man's thinking process different from a woman's?* Informally, you may use *different than* when it is followed by a clause: *Television has made our thinking process different than it was fifty years ago.*

differ with, differ from. To *differ with* is to disagree with someone: *The student differed with her professor about the meaning of the poem.* To *differ from* is to contrast or be unlike: *The student's interpretation differed from her professor's.*

disinterested, uninterested. *Disinterested* means "unbiased, impartial, objective": *An umpire is supposed to be a disinterested observer. Uninterested* means "without interest": *He was uninterested in their opinion.*

dominant, dominate. *Dominant,* an adjective, means "exercising the most influence or control, most prominent": *Human beings are the dominant species on earth. Dominate,* a verb, means "to control, govern, or rule": *A miser is dominated by greed.*

done. In formal writing, avoid the imprecise use of *done* to mean "finished or complete": *By 1914, work on the Panama Canal was nearly complete* [not *done*].

don't. *Don't* is the contraction for *do not.* Avoid using *don't* as a contraction for *does not,* which is *doesn't*: *She doesn't* [not *don't*] *waste any time.*

dual, duel. *Dual* means "double or composed of two usually equal parts": *She performed dual roles as teacher and counsellor. Duel* means "a prearranged combat or to oppose actively": *In 1851, the premier of P.E.I.*

and the leader of the opposition fought a duel, which neither of them won or lost.

due to. *Due to* means "because of." It is correct when used to introduce a subject complement following a linking verb: *The airplane's crash was due to icy weather.* However, some readers dislike its use, preferring *because of: The airplane crashed because of* [not *due to*] *icy weather.*

effect, affect. See **affect**.

elicit, illicit. *Elicit* means "to draw out or bring out": *With a little coaxing, she was able to elicit the right answer. Illicit* means "unlawful": *He was convicted of the illicit use of drugs.*

emigrate from, immigrate to. It is important to distinguish "here" and "there" with these verbs. To *emigrate from* means "to leave one country or area for another" [leave there]: *During the 1840s, many people emigrated from Ireland because of famine.* To *immigrate to* means "to enter and settle [come here]": *During the 1840s, many Irish immigrated to North America.*

eminent, imminent. *Eminent* means "prominent or standing above others": *She was an eminent biologist. Imminent* means "impending, about to occur": *They left quickly because a hurricane was imminent.*

etc. Avoid *etc.* (*et cetera*) in formal writing. End a list with a specific example or, occasionally, *and so on.*

eventually, ultimately. *Eventually* means "occurring at an unspecified time in the future": *Something worth doing will get done eventually. Ultimately* means "at last, in the end": *Ultimately, most battles are won by the largest army.*

every body, everybody. See **every one**.

every day, everyday. *Every day* is the noun *day* preceded by the adjective *every: I try to exercise every day. Everyday* is an adjective meaning "appropriate for ordinary days or routine occasions": *Wear your everyday clothes to the party.*

every one, everyone. *Every one* is the pronoun *one* preceded by the adjective *every,* meaning "each individual or thing in a particular group": *Every one of the students was prepared for the exam. Everyone* is an indefinite pronoun meaning "every person": *Everyone was prepared for the exam.* Both are singular. (See 16f and 17d.)

except, accept. See **accept**.

explicit, implicit. *Explicit* means "fully and clearly expressed, with nothing implied": *I was given explicit instructions. Implicit* means "not directly expressed but understood": *We made an implicit agreement to avoid the issue.*

farther, further. *Farther* refers to physical distance: *I can run farther now than I could six weeks ago. Further* refers to quantities or degree and means "more or to a greater extent": *When we inquired further, we found he had changed jobs twice within a year.*

female, male. Many people prefer to use *female* and *male* exclusively as adjectives, considering their use as nouns impersonal, even dehumanizing. Use *woman* and *man* for nouns instead: *Scholarships have been awarded equally to female and male athletes. A man and two women stood patiently in line.*

fewer, less. Disregard the supermarket signs that say "Ten items or less." Use *fewer* with items that can be counted, *less* with things that are not counted: *Fewer* [not *less*] *students now major in business. We had less snow this winter than last.*

firstly. *Firstly* sounds pretentious, as do *secondly, thirdly,* and so on; use *first, second, third.*

folks. Informal for "parents, family, or people in general." In formal writing, use a more precise alternative: *My parents* [not *folks*] *plan to retire to Victoria.*

fun. Many readers object to the use of *fun* as an adjective meaning "enjoyable or amusing": *We spent an enjoyable* [not *a fun*] *week in Mexico City.*

further, farther. See **farther.**

get. Because *get* has so many colloquial uses (meaning "become" or "have" or "receive," among others), it can be vague or ambiguous. Whenever possible, especially in formal writing, find a more precise word: *Perhaps we can persuade* [not *get*] *her to help.*

go, say. *Go, goes, went* are colloquial synonyms of *say, says, said.* Don't use them in writing. *When he says* [not *goes*] *"I'm not making this up," you know he is making it up.*

good, well. *Good* is an adjective: *This salsa tastes good. Well* is an adverb: *This old watch still runs well.* Use *well* to refer to someone's health: *After a long rest, he is well again.* (See 20c.)

got, have. *Got* is the past tense of *get.* Do not use the colloquial *got* in place of *have: They have* [not *got*] *the best reputation for reliability.* Do not use *got, got to, has got to,* or *have got to* in place of *must: They must* [not *have got to*] *change their priorities.*

hanged, hung. Use *hanged* to refer to executions, *hung* to refer to what is attached or suspended: *The criminal was hanged at dawn. The coat was hung in the closet.*

hardly, scarcely. Avoid the colloquial double negatives *can't hardly, not hardly, can't scarcely, not scarcely: I can hardly* [not *can't hardly*] *explain what it felt like.* (See 20e.)

has got, have got. Redundant; write *has* or *have* instead: *We have* [not *have got*] *to find more information.*

have, got. See **got.**

have, of. Use *have* following the modal verbs *could, should, may, might, must,* and *would: They should have* [not *of*] *received an invitation.* (See 15e3.)

he/she, his/her. Many readers object to the awkward abbreviations *he/she, his/her;* use *he or she* or one of the alternatives in 17d. Do not use *he* by itself to mean *he or she.* (See 32e4.)

hopefully. *Hopefully* is best used to mean "in a hopeful manner": *He looked hopefully at the clock.* Many readers object to its use to mean "it is to be hoped": *Hopefully, job opportunities for graduates will soon improve.* Avoid the problem in writing by pointing out who is doing the hoping: *We hope job opportunities for graduates will soon improve.*

if, whether. Use *if* to introduce statements of condition and *whether* to introduce alternatives: *If we have enough volunteers, we can finish; it makes no difference whether they are young or old.*

imminent, eminent. See **eminent**.

impact. Many readers object to the use of *impact* as a verb: *The recent election will have an impact on* [not *will impact*] *proposed antipollution laws.*

implement. Often a pretentious way to say "do," "carry out," or "achieve," *implement* has a simpler alternative: *We carried out* [not *implemented*] *his instructions promptly.*

implicit, explicit. See **explicit**.

imply, infer. *Imply* means "to express indirectly": *She glanced at her watch to imply that it was time to leave. Infer* means "to draw a conclusion": *After studying the evidence, we inferred that the fire was caused by lightning.*

incredible, incredulous. *Incredible* means "unbelievable or astonishing"; *incredulous* means "skeptical, disbelieving": *As he told his incredible tale, she gave him an incredulous look.*

individual. Use as an adjective, not a noun: *Her tastes are very individual. The police questioned several people* [not *individuals*].

infer, imply. See **imply**.

ingenious, ingenuous. *Ingenious* means "creatively skillful or imaginative": *His solution to the puzzle was the most ingenious. Ingenuous* means "without sophistication, artless, frank": *To win their trust, he tried to appear ingenuous.*

irregardless. Nonstandard for *regardless*.

isle, aisle. See **aisle**.

is when, is where, is why, is because. Avoid these imprecise and illogical expressions in writing definitions and explanations: *A paceline is a line of cyclists tightly grouped* [not *A paceline is when cyclists group together tightly*] *to reduce wind resistance.* (See 27a.)

its, it's. *Its* is the possessive pronoun: *The dog twitched its tail. It's* is the contraction of *it is* or *it has*: *It's good to hear that they arrived safely. It's been years since we saw them last.* There is no such form as *its'*.

kind(s), sort(s), type(s). *Kind, sort,* and *type* are singular: *This kind of word is* [not *these kind of words are*] *easy to spell. Kinds, sorts,* and *types* are plural, referring to more than one kind or sort: *These kinds of flowers grow well in the shade.*

kind of, sort of. In writing, avoid using *kind of* and *sort of* to mean "somewhat": *I was somewhat* [not *kind of*] *disappointed by the novel's conclusion.*

lay, lie. *Lay,* a transitive verb meaning "to put or set down," always takes a direct object: *Lay the pencil on the table.* Its other forms are *laying, laid,*

laid. Lie, an intransitive verb meaning "to rest on a surface or occupy a position," does not take a direct object: *The pencil lies on the table.* Its other forms are *lying, lay, lain.*

lead, led. *Lead* (the metal) sounds like *led* (the past tense of the verb *to lead*); do not confuse them: *Laura Secord led* [not *lead*] *her cow through enemy lines.*

leave, let. *Leave* means "to go away"; *let* means "to give permission or allow." Do not use *leave* when you mean *let*: *Let* [not *leave*] *him clean up the mess he has made.*

less, fewer. See **fewer**.

like, as. See **as**.

loose, lose, losing. *Loose* is an adjective meaning "not fastened or contained"; *lose* is a verb meaning "to misplace." Do not use one word when you mean the other, and do not write "loosing" when you mean *losing.* (See 15a6.)

lots, lots of. In formal writing, avoid the colloquial expressions *lots* and *lots of,* meaning "many, much, or a lot": *Many* [not *lots of*] *medicines are produced from rain forest plants.*

male, female. See **female**.

mankind. Many readers consider that the generic term *mankind* excludes women. Use *humanity, humans, the human race,* or *people* instead.

may be, maybe. *May be* is a verb phrase: *The computer may be unplugged. Maybe* is an adverb meaning "possibly" or "perhaps": *Maybe the computer is unplugged.*

may, can. See **can**.

may of, might of. Nonstandard for *may have* and *might have.* See **have, of**.

media, medium. *Media* is the plural of *medium: Among the news media, television is the most popular medium but the least informative.*

most. In formal writing, avoid using *most* as a substitute for *almost: Almost* [not *Most*] *everyone arrived on time.*

must of. See **have, of**.

myself, himself, herself, yourself. Do not use the intensive or reflexive pronouns *myself, himself, herself,* or *yourself* where personal pronouns are appropriate: *Cynthia and I* [not *myself*] *will announce the awards, and then Janna and you* [not *yourself*] *will escort the winners to the stage.* (See 19g.)

nauseous, nauseated. *Nauseous* means "sickening": *A nauseous gas filled the room. Nauseated* means "to feel nausea, loathing, or disgust": *I felt nauseated as soon as I smelled the gas.*

neither. When used as an indefinite pronoun, *neither* is singular. (See 16f and 17d.)

nowhere near. *Nowhere near* is informal. In formal writing, use *not nearly: I was not nearly* [not *nowhere near*] *ready to leave when they arrived.*

nowheres. *Nowheres* is nonstandard.

number, amount. See **amount**.

of, have. See **have, of**.

off of, off from. *Off of* and *off from* are redundant; write *off: The cat jumped off* [not *off of*] *the table.*

ok, O.K., okay. All three spellings are acceptable, but avoid these colloquial expressions in formal writing. Use the adjectives *acceptable, satisfactory,* or *all right* or the verbs *approve of, agree to,* or *authorize: If my application is satisfactory* [not *okay*], *will you authorize* [not *okay*] *my loan?*

passed, past. *Passed* is the past tense of the verb *pass: The sports car passed the truck. Past* refers to a time before the present or a place farther than another: *The old man spoke nostalgically of his past. He lives two houses past the grocery store.*

percent, per cent, percentage. *Percent/per cent* is always used with numbers written as words: *By 1991, almost thirty-three percent of Canadians were over 45 years of age. Percentage* means "a proportion or amount" and is used with descriptive words like "large," "small," and "greater" rather than a number: *A large percentage of students take more than four years to earn a BA.*

phenomena. *Phenomena* is the plural of *phenomenon,* "a perceptible event, happening, or occurrence": *Many supposedly supernatural phenomena are easily explained natural occurrences. One such phenomenon is the aurora borealis, or northern lights.*

plus. In formal writing, avoid using *plus* to mean "and," "in addition," or "as well as": *Culture consists of the shared knowledge and beliefs of a human community, as well as* [not *plus*] *the tools that use and express culture.*

precede, proceed. *Precede* means "to come before"; proceed means "to go forward": *Preceded by her parents, the bride proceeded down the aisle.*

principal, principle. As a noun, *principal* means "the head of a school or organization" or "a sum of money"; as an adjective it means "first or most important." *Principle* is a noun meaning "a basic truth or law": *My principal taught me the principle known as the Golden Rule.*

proceed, precede. See **precede**.

quote, quotation. *Quote* is a verb, *quotation* a noun. Do not use *quote* as a substitute for *quotation: I have several good quotations* [not *quotes*] *supporting my argument.*

rarely ever. Redundant; write *rarely* or *hardly ever: They rarely* [or *hardly ever,* not *rarely ever*] *come to visit anymore.*

real, really. *Real* is an adjective, *really* an adverb. In formal writing, do not use *real* as a substitute for *really: He was really* [not *real*] *pleased to receive the award.*

reason is because, reason why. *Reason is because* is illogical; use *that* instead of *because: The reason they lost was that* [not *because*] *they hardly ever practised. Reason why* is redundant: *The reason that* [not *why*] *the economy has improved is technological advance.*

relation, relationship. *Relation* refers to a connection between two or more things: *The relation between drunk driving and auto accidents is clear. Relationship* refers more specifically to a relation between people: *Their relationship grew from friendship into love.*

revolve around. In formal writing, avoid using *revolve around* as a substitute for "concern," "involve," or "associated with": *The causes of the war involved* [not *revolved around*] *ethnic hatreds.*

scarcely, hardly. See **hardly.**

sensual, sensuous. *Sensual* means "gratifying physical appetites, erotic, lustful": *Many religions condemn the pursuit of sensual pleasure. Sensuous* means "pleasing to the senses": *Reading poetry aloud is a sensuous experience.*

set, sit. *Set,* meaning "to put or place," has the principal parts *set, set, set.* It is a transitive verb that takes a direct object: *Set the computer on this desk. Sit,* an intransitive verb meaning "to be seated or to rest," has the principal parts *sit, sat, sat: Sit here next to me.*

shall, will. *Shall* has nearly disappeared as a helping verb used with *I* or *we* to signal action in the future. It now appears mainly in polite requests, legal documents, and emphatic statements: *Shall we go? Both parties shall agree. I shall return. Will* is appropriate for most future statements.

should of. See **have, of.**

since. If you use *since* as a substitute for *because,* be sure there is no ambiguity. Use *since* to mean "from then until now" or "between then and now": *Because* [not *since*] *it rained so hard last night, the game has been postponed. We have been waiting since six o'clock.*

sit, set. See **set.**

site, cite. See **cite.**

so. In formal writing, avoid using *so* as a substitute for the intensifier *very,* unless you plan to finish the comparison with a *that* clause: *It rained very* [not *so*] *hard last night. It rained so hard that the sewers backed up.*

some. In formal writing, avoid *some* as a substitute for words like *remarkable, memorable,* and *impressive:* Schindler's List *is a remarkable* [not *some*] *movie.*

someone, somebody, something. *Someone, somebody,* and *something* are singular. (See 16f and 17d.)

some time, sometime, sometimes. *Some time* is the determiner *some* modifying the noun *time: She wants to spend some time with her grandparents. Sometime* is an adverb meaning "at an indefinite or unstated time": *We'll be there sometime soon. Sometimes* is an adverb meaning "at times, now and then": *Sometimes we don't understand each other.*

sort, kind. See **kind(s), sort(s), types(s).**

suppose to, use to. Write *supposed to* and *used to.* (See 15e1.)

sure and. *Sure and* is nonstandard for *sure to: Be sure to* [not *sure and*] *bring the blueprints to our next meeting.*

take, bring. See **bring.**

than, then. *Than* is a conjunction that links unequal comparisons: *Harry types faster than Kevin. Then* is an adverb meaning "at that time or next in time": *She turned first one way and then another.*

that. See **who, which, that.**

that, which. Many writers use *that* to introduce essential or restrictive clauses, *which* to introduce nonessential or nonrestrictive clauses. (See 36e.) *Which*, like *who*, can introduce either kind of clause. Now that grammar checkers point out an error when there is no comma before *which*, it seems safer to follow the trend and include the comma.

that there, this here, these here, those there. *That there, this here, these here,* and *those there* are nonstandard for *that, this, these,* and *those.*

their, they're, there. *Their* is a possessive pronoun: *They received their diplomas. They're* is the contraction of *they are: They're good dancers. There* means "at, in, to, or toward that place": *We saw them standing there by the fountain.*

theirself, theirselves, themself. *Theirself, theirselves,* and *themself* are nonstandard for *themselves: They decided to go by themselves* [not *theirselves*].

them. Do not use *them* as a substitute for *these* or *those: How do you like those* [not *them*] *new hiking boots?*

then, than. See **than.**

tinge, twinge. *Tinge* means "a tint or a trace": *The morning sky was tinged with red. Twinge* is a sharp, sudden physical or mental pain: *He felt a twinge of remorse.*

to, too, two. *To* is a preposition or the infinitive marker; *too* means "very" or "also"; *two* is the number: *At twenty-two, she was still too young to leave home.*

try and. *Try and* is nonstandard for *try to: Try to* [not *try and*] *remember where you last saw your keys.*

ultimately, eventually. See **eventually.**

unique. *Unique* is an absolute meaning "one of a kind"; avoid using *unique* with qualifiers such as *more* and *most: She is a unique* [not *the most unique*] *writer.* (See also 20d4.)

usage. Often a pretentious substitute for *use* and therefore worth avoiding: *The use* [not *usage*] *of computer networks has enabled many people to work at home.*

use to, suppose to. See **suppose to.**

utilize. Often a pretentious substitute for *use: Tools were widely used* [not *utilized*] *during the Bronze Age.*

way. In writing, avoid the colloquial use of *way* as an intensifier of comparisons: *The deficit was much* [not *way*] *larger than they had expected.*

ways. In formal writing, avoid the use of *ways* to mean "distance": *They have come a long way* [not *ways*] *to get where they are today.*

weather, whether. *Weather* refers to climate; *whether* is a conjunction that introduces alternatives: *Football is played whether the weather is fair or foul.*

well, good. See **good**.

where. In formal writing, avoid using *where* to substitute for *that* or *when*: *I recently read that* [not *where*] *the news is more balanced than critics claim. Surprisingly, Christmas is a time when* [not *where*] *many people are the most unhappy.*

which. See **that, which**, and **who, which, that**.

who, which, that. Use *who* to refer to people, *which* to things, and *that* to groups of people or to things: *The man who just left carried a suitcase, which he shifted from hand to hand. I want a book that tells me something new.* (See 18d; see also **that, which**.)

who, whom. *Who* is used with subjects and subject complements, *whom* with objects. (See 19e.)

whose, who's. *Whose* is a possessive pronoun; *who's* is a contraction of *who is*: *Whose essay is this? Who's ready for dessert?*

will, shall. See **shall**.

would of. See **have, of**.

your, you're. *Your* is a possessive pronoun: *Your time is up. You're* is a contraction of *you are*: *You're our first choice.*

How to Edit Common Punctuation Errors

Read your writing aloud to hear punctuation errors. Then follow these guidelines:

Periods. Remove unnecessary periods following (1) the titles and subtitles of your papers, (2) abbreviations that end a sentence, (3) question marks and exclamation points, (4) all-capital abbreviations. (See 35a4.)

Commas. Add required commas (1) before a coordinating conjunction like *and* or *but* joining independent clauses, (2) after introductory words, (3) between items in a series, (4) between coordinate adjectives, (5) before and after word groups that interrupt the flow of a sentence. (See 36a–g.)

Omit unnecessary commas (1) between subjects and predicates, (2) between verbs and the remainder of the predicate, (3) before indirect quotations, (4) before the comparative *than*, (5) after subordinating conjunctions like *although* and phrases like *such as* to introduce a list, (6) before and after essential modifiers, (7) before parentheses or brackets, (8) after question marks or exclamation points. (See 36k.)

Look for comma splices—the error that results when independent clauses are joined only by a comma (see 14b). Add a coordinating conjunction like *and* or *but*, or replace the comma with a period or semicolon.

Semicolons. Use a semicolon instead of a comma before a transition or conjunctive adverb (such as *for example* or *however*) that links independent clauses (see 14b3). To identify independent clauses, use the "yes/no" question test (see 13b1). If items in series contain internal commas, use semicolons between items (see 37c).

Do not use semicolons between (1) dependent and independent clauses, (2) modifiers and the words they modify, or (3) lists and the words that introduce them. (See 37d.)

Colons. After an independent clause, use colons to introduce lists, quotations, and explanations (see 38a). To identify independent clauses, use the "yes/no" question test (see 13b1).

Omit colons (1) after words like *such as, like,* or *including,* (2) between verbs and the remainder of the predicates, (3) between subordinating conjunctions and the clauses that follow, or (4) between prepositions and their objects (see 38c).

Apostrophes. Add an apostrophe before the *s* if the word is singular, after the *s* if the word is plural. (See 39a.)

(continued)

How to...

How to Identify and Correct
Common Punctuation Errors *(continued)*

To decide whether a noun is possessive and requires an apostrophe, try to create an *of* phrase (the paper *of the student*? or the paper *of the students*?) or see whether you can insert own (*his* or *their own paper*). If you can do these, make sure the original word takes an apostrophe. (See 39a.) Possessive pronouns (*his, hers, its, ours, yours, theirs,* or *whose*) never take an apostrophe, however.

Quotation marks. Use double quotation marks around quotations, no matter how brief. Use single quotation marks only for quotations within quotations. (See 40 a and d.)

Place periods and commas inside double and single quotation marks. Place semicolons and colons outside quotation marks. Place question marks and exclamation points inside if they are part of the quotation, otherwise outside. (See 40b.)

Use quotation marks around the titles of short works. (See 40e.) Use underlining or italics for the titles of long works. (See 43a.)

Omit unnecessary quotation marks around indented quotations, the titles of your own writing, slang, and indirect or summarized quotations. (See 52d1 and 40f.)

chapter

35 End Punctuation

35a Use a period to mark sentences and abbreviations

1 Marking sentences

Use a period to end all sentences except direct questions and genuine exclamations. Use a period to end sentences that summarize questions, make polite requests not phrased as questions, and give commands that are not exclamations.

Megan called the ticket office to ask whether the concert had been cancelled.

Please respond to the memo as soon as possible.

Return the rental car by Friday at noon.

2 Marking abbreviations

The punctuation of abbreviations varies. When in doubt, consult a dictionary, style manual, or publication guide appropriate to your subject or audience. The Modern Language Association provides these guidelines.

- Use a period after most abbreviations ending in lower-case letters. Do not put a space between lower-case letters that represent separate words.

Mr.	Inc.	Capt.	a.m.
Mrs.	Jan.	Maj.	p.m.
Ms.	Feb.	etc.	e.g.
Dr.	Sept.	intro.	i.e.

- Do not use a period after acronyms, in all-capital abbreviations or after Canada Post's abbreviations of provinces (or those of American states).

ALL-CAPITAL ABBREVIATIONS				CANADA POST ABBREVIATIONS			
CBC	NATO	BA	IOU	NF	NB	MB	BC
CRTC	RCMP	CAT scan	IQ	PE	PQ	SK	NT
EEC	UNESCO	HIV	MSW	NS	ON	AB	YT

3 Writing about literature

- When citing a passage from a literary work, use a period with no intervening spaces between the divisions of the work.

    Hamlet 3.2.16–23 or *Hamlet* III.ii.16–23 [act, scene, lines]

    Paradise Lost 10.55–57 or *Paradise Lost* X.55–57 [book, lines]

4 Avoiding unnecessary periods

- Do not use a period after the titles of your papers, even if they are complete sentences. Except for headings running into the text of your writing, do not use periods after section headings in your papers. (See 48b1.) Use question marks and exclamation marks in headings where appropriate.

- When an abbreviation ends a sentence, do not add a second period.

    The shipment will be delivered by 9 a.m./

- Do not use a period after a sentence within a sentence.

    "The concert is dead" is a comment attributed to Glenn Gould but never actually confirmed.

    Constructive criticism (now there's an oxymoron for you) tells "off" more than it tells "how."

■ Do not use a period following items in a vertical list unless all the items are complete sentences.

35b | Use a question mark to signal questions, requests, and doubts

1 Signalling questions

Use a question mark after direct questions.

How long did Susanna Moodie live in Cobourg?

Do not use a question mark after indirect or summarized questions. (See 40a1 and 24d.)

She asked when the order would be delivered?

You may use question marks following questions in a series even when they are not complete sentences.

Will reducing income taxes stimulate savings? Encourage investment? Weaken social programs? Enlarge the federal budget deficit?

2 Signalling expressions of doubt

Use a question mark in parentheses to signal uncertainty.

In 1001 (?), Leif Erikson discovered Baffin Island and Labrador.

3 Signalling polite requests

Use a question mark following a polite request phrased as a question.

Could you please send me an admissions application?

4 Punctuating a question within a sentence

Place question marks inside quotation marks when the quotation is a question; otherwise, put them outside.

The ticket agent asked, "Is this your suitcase?"

What famous philosopher said, "I think; therefore, I am"?

When a question within a sentence is followed by other words, put a question mark after the question and a period at the end of the sentence.

"What time does the play begin?" he asked.

35*c* | Use an exclamation point for an outcry, emphasis, and irony

1   An outcry

"A horse! A horse! My kingdom for a horse!" cried Richard III desperately.

2   An expression of emphasis

Charles de Gaulle will never be forgotten for his 1967 exhortation, "Vive le Québec libre!"

3   An expression of irony

Standing in the mud, shivering in the rain, she muttered, "I keep reminding myself that this is the vacation of a lifetime!"

Avoid overusing exclamation points. They rarely appear in academic writing, especially in serious informative writing. Even in personal or narrative writing, too many will create a melodramatic or false tone.

chapter

36   The Comma

36*a* | Use a comma before a co-ordinating conjunction (*and*, *but*) that links independent clauses

When the co-ordinating conjunctions *and, but, or, nor, so, for,* and *yet* link independent clauses—word groups that can be punctuated as complete sentences—they are preceded by a comma. (To identify independent clauses, use the "yes/no" question test, 13b1; also see 14c.)

Groups of sharks attack their prey ferociously, but they never bite one another.

Lana loves animals, so it's natural that she's majoring in veterinary medicine.

If the meaning of a compound sentence is clear and the independent clauses are short, you may omit the comma before the conjunction.

The horn sounded once and the boat left the dock.

Do not use a comma before conjunctions that link phrases or dependent clauses. (To learn to identify phrases and dependent clauses, see 12a and b.)

The musicians played sad songs on the way to the funeral/but joyful

songs on their return.

[The *but* in this sentence joins two phrases, *sad songs [. . .] but joyful songs [. . . ,]* so the comma is unnecessary.]

Good writers seek to convince the reader that they know what they are

talking about/and that their ideas are sound.

[The *and* in this sentence joins two dependent clauses opening with the subordinating conjunction *that: that they know what they are talking about* and *that their ideas are sound.* Neither clause can be punctuated as a complete sentence, so the comma is inappropriate.]

36*b* Use a comma after introductory words

Use a comma to set off an introductory word, phrase, or dependent clause from the rest of the sentence. (To learn to identify phrases and clauses, see 12a and b.)

Unfortunately, exotic species introduced to new habitats often threaten native species.

Growing up in India, David had been entertained by storytellers of all kinds.

After Harriet Tubman escaped the South, she became a "conductor" on the Underground Railroad that carried slaves north.

You may omit the comma following a short introductory phrase, but you are never wrong to leave it in.

By noon (,) the storm had passed.

Be sure, however, to use commas to prevent misreading.

> When Denis left his girlfriend, Elsa, promised to write every day.

36c | Use a comma between items in a series

Use a comma to separate three or more words, phrases, or clauses written as a series. The Modern Language Association and the American Psychological Association require a comma before the conjunction preceding the last item in a series.

> Winter drivers should carry a scraper, shovel, sand, flares, extra washer fluid, and a blanket.

36d | Use a comma between co-ordinate adjectives but not between cumulative adjectives

1 Using a comma between co-ordinate adjectives

Two or more adjectives are **co-ordinate** if each modifies the noun by itself. Use a comma after each adjective to signal its separate function.

> Those leather armchairs are striking, exotic, imaginative pieces.
>
> [Each adjective—*striking, exotic, imaginative*—modifies *pieces* by itself.]

2 Avoiding a comma between cumulative adjectives

Two or more adjectives are **cumulative** if each modifies all the words that follow it, adjectives and noun together. Because meaning accumulates as the phrase unfolds, do not separate the adjectives by commas.

> *Canadian Homes* features some striking contemporary furniture designs.
>
> [*Furniture* modifies *designs*, *contemporary* modifies *furniture designs*, and *striking* modifies *contemporary furniture designs*. Meaning accumulates as the phrase unfolds.]

3 Identifying co-ordinate and cumulative adjectives

Two tests will help you distinguish between co-ordinate adjectives and cumulative adjectives.

- **The *and* test.** If you can put *and* between the adjectives, they are co-ordinate and require a comma between them to signal their separate functions. Consider the two preceding examples: *Striking and exotic and imaginative pieces* reveals co-ordinate adjectives that require commas to separate them. But you would not write *striking and contemporary and furniture designs*, so these are cumulative adjectives not separated by commas.

- **The reversal test.** If you can reverse the order of the adjectives, they are co-ordinate and require a comma between them (*striking, exotic, imaginative pieces* may become *imaginative, exotic, striking pieces*). But you would not write *furniture contemporary striking designs*.

36*e* | Use commas to set off nonessential modifiers; do not use commas to set off essential modifiers

1 Using commas with nonessential modifiers

Nonessential modifiers (also called **nonrestrictive modifiers**) are words, phrases, or clauses that add extra information but are not essential to the basic meaning of a sentence. Omitting these modifiers does not drastically alter the meaning. Use commas to signal their nonessential nature.

> Alfred Burr, **our Chief of Police**, has volunteered to head the Heart Fund drive.
>
> [Because it is nonessential, *our Chief of Police* is set off with commas.]

> Winnie-the-Pooh, **the honey-loving bear who became Christopher Robin's best friend**, is featured on a commemorative stamp.
>
> [Details about Winnie-the-Pooh provide extra information only, so they are set off with commas.]

> In 1989, Samuel Beckett died in Paris, **where he had written *Waiting for Godot* forty years before.**
>
> [Information about Beckett's biography is interesting but not essential to the sentence, so it is set off with a comma.]

2 Avoiding commas with essential modifiers

Essential modifiers (also called **restrictive modifiers**) restrict the meaning of the words they modify to a special sense. If they are omitted, the meaning of the sentence changes. To signal their essential nature, do not set off essential modifiers with commas. Consider how a comma changes the meaning of these sentences:

> The lawyer has passed the file on to her assistant **who specializes in real estate** [essential modifier].
>
> [The modifier *who specializes in real estate* identifies which one of a number of assistants received the file. Because it is basic to the meaning of the sentence, it is not set off with commas.]

The lawyer has passed the file on to her assistant, **who specializes in real estate** [nonessential modifier].

[The lawyer has only one assistant, and this assistant just happens to specialize in real estate. The assistant's specialty does not distinguish him or her from any colleagues, so the modifier is set off with commas.]

3 Identifying nonessential and essential modifiers

Sometimes it is difficult to tell whether a modifier is nonessential or essential. Try reading the sentence without the modifier. If the basic meaning is unchanged, the modifier is nonessential and set off by commas. If the sentence changes or loses meaning, the modifier is essential and should not be set off. Compare:

Ernest Hemingway's story "Hills Like White Elephants" portrays a couple debating the consequences of an abortion.

Ernest Hemingway's story [. . .] portrays a couple [. . .].

[Without the title of the story and *debating the consequences of an abortion,* the sentence has no meaning. These are both essential modifiers not set off by commas.]

If after rereading you're still not sure whether a modifier is nonessential or essential, use these clues.

- Modifiers of proper nouns (see 10 a) are usually nonessential and set off by commas.

  Nimi speaks Hindi, **which is the official language of India.**

- Clauses beginning with *although, even though,* and *whereas* are usually nonessential and set off by commas.

  The burglar was captured within hours, **even though he was sure he had left no clues.**

- Modifiers of indefinite pronouns such as *anyone* and *something* are usually essential and are not set off by commas.

  Anyone **who studies the textbook** can pass this course.
  [The clause *who studies the textbook* is essential to identify *anyone* and is therefore not set off by commas.]

- Relative clauses beginning with *that* are essential modifiers and are not set off by commas.

  Cars **that require the fewest repairs** have the highest resale value.

- If you can substitute *that* for *who, whom,* or *which,* the clause is an essential modifer and is not set off by commas. (For guidelines about when to use *that,* see 18d.)

  The painter **whom/that** I admire most is Lawren Harris.

- If you can omit *who, whom,* or *that,* do not punctuate.

  The painter [**whom**] I admire most is Lawren Harris.

- Concluding adverb clauses beginning with *as soon as, before, because, if, since, unless, until,* and *when* are essential to the basic meaning of a sentence and are not set off by commas.

  Because spaces are limited, students should sign up for the Writing Clinic **as soon as they can.**

36*f* Use commas to set off transitions, parenthetical expressions, and contrast statements

1 Using commas with transitions

Set off conjunctive adverbs such as *however* and transitional phrases such as *for example* with commas. (For a complete list of conjunctive adverbs and transitional phrases, see 14b3.)

Most people refuse to think about pain. Some kinds of pain, **however,** are important to recognize and understand.

Some common pain killers have harmful side effects. **For example,** aspirin may cause internal bleeding.

When you connect independent clauses with a transition, use a semicolon before the transition and, usually, a comma following it. (See 37b.)

If you want to bring your spouse to the conference, let the organizers know immediately; **otherwise,** we will book you a single room.

If little or no pause follows a transition, you may omit the comma.

We have never planned a long bicycle trip; **therefore** we're asking for your suggestions.

2 Using commas with parenthetical expressions not enclosed in parentheses

Use commas to set off parenthetical expressions that add supplemental or explanatory information.

Habits learned early, **as we've all discovered**, are the hardest to break.

Bernie was the last to leave, **as usual.**

When the word *too,* meaning "also," appears in the middle or at the end of a sentence, it is usually set off with commas.

Muslims, too, believe that Jesus was born of the Virgin Mary.

3   Using commas with contrast statements

Use a comma to set off statements of contrast or contradiction, usually beginning *not, nor, never, but,* or *unlike.*

People, **like roses**, become prickly when mishandled.

Aunt Rita gave the last piece of pie to Jerry, **never one to refuse an extra dessert.**

36g | Use commas to set off signal statements, direct address, and mild interjections

1   Using commas with signal statements

Use a comma to set off a signal statement at the beginning or end of a sentence.

As Pierre Berton said, **"A Canadian is somebody who knows how to make love in a canoe."**

"I'll do it tomorrow," Michele said lazily.

Do not use a comma if the quotation is the subject or complement of the sentence.

"The medium is the message/" is Marshall McLuhan's best remembered

comment on communications.

2   Using commas in direct address

Use commas to set off words that signal you are addressing readers directly: names or titles, question tags, the words *yes* or *no.*

Thank you, **Professor Jevons,** for writing a recommendation for me.

The book is better than the movie, **don't you think?**

No, the midterm exam has not been postponed.

3 Using commas with mild interjections

Use commas to set off mild expressions of feeling.

Well, no one was surprised to see Shelley get that promotion.

36*h* Use commas with titles and degrees, dates, addresses, place names, and numbers

1 Titles and degrees

Use commas to set off titles or degrees that follow a person's name.

Martin Luther King, **Jr.,** campaigned for peace as well as for civil rights.

The keynote address will be given by Jean Payne, **president of Marion Ross Investments.**

2 Dates

In dates, use a pair of commas to set off the year from the rest of the sentence. Do not use commas if the date is inverted or only the month and year are given.

On January 22, **1901,** Queen Victoria died, ending the longest reign by any British monarch.

On 1 January **2000,** everyone was relived that the Y2K scare was over.

In **May 1953,** a claim staked near Elliot Lake turned out to be the biggest uranium find in Canadian history.

3 Addresses and place names

Use commas following addresses and place names. Do not use a comma before a postal code.

Back orders will be filled by Mission Press, now located at 1521 Dundas St. West, Vancouver, B.C. V7N 4P8.

Canada's worst coal mining disaster was not the one at Springhill, Nova Scotia, in 1891, but the coal dust explosion in Hillcrest, Alberta, in 1914.

4 Numbers

In numbers of four digits or more, use commas to divide numerals into groups of three (in numbers of four digits, the comma or space is optional). Note: If you need to be consistent with international standards, use spaces rather than commas.

1,466	or	1 466
186,000	or	186 000
6,286,837	or	6 286 837

Exceptions: Do not use commas within street numbers, postal codes, telephone numbers, or years: 6206 Main Street, 1-800-495-7662, 1997.

A note on units of measure: With the Imperial System, use figures for measurements, and do not use commas to separate feet and inches, for example, or pounds and ounces.

My Newfoundland puppy already stands **1 foot 9 inches** tall and weighs **24 pounds 4 ounces.**

36*i* Use commas to signal omissions and prevent misreading

The hikers took the right fork in the path; their rescuers, the left.

To Franklin, Carlos remained a puzzle.

36*j* Follow these guidelines to use commas with quotation marks, parentheses, and brackets

1 Using commas with quotation marks

Place commas inside closing quotation marks, single and double, whether the quotation is a word, phrase, complete sentence, or several sentences. (See 40b.)

It is "time to stop thinking of wild animals as 'resources' and 'game,' " claims Joy Williams in her argument against hunting.

2 Using commas with parentheses and brackets

Place commas outside closing parentheses and brackets.

Caused by an extra number 21 chromosome (three instead of the usual two), Down's syndrome is characterized by developmental delays and a flattened facial profile.

36k | Avoid unnecessary commas

1 Avoiding unnecessary comma dividers

- Do not use a comma between a subject and its predicate.

  Revenues that communities receive from legalized gambling/are often

  offset by the losses of local gamblers.

- Do not use a comma between a verb and the object or complement that follows.

  Men and women in their thirties often protest/their increasingly limited

  career choices.

- Do not use a comma before conjunctions joining phrases or dependent clauses. (To learn to identify phrases and dependent clauses, see 12a and b.)

  The coach warned her team that their next opponents were not only tall

  and fast/but also very experienced.

- Do not use a comma before the conjunction *than* in comparison statements.

  I'd rather visit the ancient ruins of Egypt and Greece/than go to Disney

  World.

- Do not use commas between cumulative adjectives or between adjectives and nouns.

  Dylan fished all day but caught only one/small/red snapper.

  [*One* and *small* are cumulative adjectives and do not take commas.]

  One wrong turn after another led him into difficult, nearly impassable/

  terrain.

  [*Impassable* is an adjective modifying the noun *terrain,* so no comma separates them.]

- Do not use a comma before a summarized or indirect quotation.

  A famous philosopher once wrote/ that anything worth saying can be

  said clearly.

2   Avoiding unnecessary introductory commas

- Do not use a comma after *such as* or *like* to introduce a list.

    Morris liked many things about his new job, such as/the flexible hours,

    the generous benefits, and the clear possibility of promotion.

- Do not use a comma after a subordinating conjunction that introduces
  an adverb clause.

    The mayor continued the sprinkler ban, although/rain had fallen weekly

    for a month.

- Do not use a comma after a phrase that opens an inverted sentence.

    In the shadow of the CN Tower/stands Toronto's Skydome, which was

    completed in 1989.

- Do not use commas before the first or after the last item in a series
  (but do use commas to separate the other items).

    Laura's favourite flowers are/hollyhocks, day lilies, and irises.

    Someone who enjoys camping, hiking, and cycling/shouldn't mind a

    little rain.

3   Avoiding commas with essential modifiers

Do not use commas to set off modifiers essential to the basic meaning
of a sentence.

Children/who no longer believe in Santa Claus or the Tooth Fairy/are

definitely growing up.

[Readers need the modifier *who no longer believe in Santa Claus or the Tooth Fairy* to
know which children are being referred to. Because not all children are being
described, the modifier is essential and cannot be set off with commas.]

Sam's mother loved to visit places/where she had never been before.

[Readers need the modifier *where she had never been before* to know which places
Sam's mother likes to go. It is therefore necessary and not to be set off with commas.]

4   Avoiding commas with other punctuation

- Do not use a comma before parentheses. Include one only if (once you
  ignore what's in parentheses) it is called for by the construction of the
  sentence.

Although critics of rock and roll often quote Plato/(who favoured the

strict regulation of music), few have examined his argument carefully.

- Do not use a comma after a question mark or exclamation point.

"What's a thousand dollars?"/asked Groucho Marx. "Mere chicken feed.

A poultry matter."

chapter

37 The Semicolon

37a Use a semicolon to join closely related independent clauses

A semicolon usually links grammatically equal word groups. Use it in place of a comma and co-ordinating conjunction (*and, but, so, or, nor, for, yet*) to link independent clauses closely related in subject or structure. To identify independent clauses, use the "yes/no" question test. (See 13b1.)

> Some etiquette rules, like using a dessert fork rather than a spoon, may seem arbitrary; others make good sense, like not talking with food in your mouth for fear of choking.

Joining independent clauses with a comma instead of a semicolon creates an error known as a comma splice. (See 14a.)

> Students of the 1960s were activists and dreamers;/students of the 1990s
>
> were less idealistic and more practical.

37b Use a semicolon before a conjunctive adverb or transition joining independent clauses

Conjunctive adverbs and transitional phrases such as *however* and *for example* are linking words. (For a complete list, see 14b3.) Although they often mean the same as co-ordinating conjunctions, such linking words must be punctuated differently. Use a semicolon before conjunctive adverbs or transitions that link independent clauses. To use a comma instead is to make a comma splice. (See 14a.)

The runner slid into second base certain she was safe; however, the umpire called her out with a swift jerk of his thumb.

There is still no treatment for smallpox; even so, a vaccination against the disease has been in use since 1796.

Note: If the conjunctive adverb or transitional phrase does not come at the beginning of the second independent clause, use a semicolon between clauses and enclose the conjunctive adverb or transitional phrase in commas, as you would with any nonessential modifier.

The runner slid into second base certain she was safe; the umpire, however, called her out with a swift jerk of his thumb.

37*c* Use a semicolon between items in a series if one or more items contain internal punctuation

Use semicolons to separate internally punctuated items in a series.

Exotic species posing severe threats to native North American wildlife are the ruffe, which may drive the Great Lakes perch to extinction; the Muscovy duck, which has ousted the Florida mallard; Mute Swans, which kill related species' goslings and ducklings; and the starling, which has displaced flickers, wrens, swallows, and bluebirds.

37*d* Avoid unnecessary semicolons

Do not use semicolons between grammatically unequal word groups.

1 Avoiding semicolons between dependent and independent clauses

Do not use a semicolon between a dependent clause and the rest of the sentence even if there is an added transition. Use a comma instead. To identify dependent and independent clauses, use the "yes/no" question test (see 13b1).

Once her cooks were allowed to experiment; however, they created spectacular gourmet dishes.

If a nonessential dependent clause ends a sentence, precede it with a comma, not a semicolon. (See 36e1.)

The smallpox vaccine was developed by Edward Jenner / after he

discovered that a mild infection acquired from cows would provide

immunity from the contagious disease.

2 Avoiding semicolons between independent clauses linked by a co-ordinating conjunction

Do not use a semicolon between independent clauses linked by a co-ordinating conjunction such as *and* or *so*. Use a comma instead. (See 36a.)

The applicant has an excellent educational background and work record /

but he lacks on-the-job experience.

3 Avoiding semicolons between a list and the words that introduce it

Do not use a semicolon to introduce a list. Use a colon instead. (See 38a.)

Only three of the rides at the fall fair were suitable for children / the ferris

wheel, the merry-go-round, and the bumper cars.

chapter

38 The Colon

38*a* | Use a colon following an independent clause to introduce a list, quotation, appositive, or explanation

A colon functions almost like an equal sign to introduce a list or any elaboration. Technically, it comes at the end of a sentence to direct the reader's attention to the particulars that follow. A colon is thus a compressed way of saying "namely" or "that is."

1 Using a colon with a list

Use a colon to introduce a list or series.

TV program listings feature only information that is relevant to the viewer: the shows, the stars, the times, the channels, as well as the occasional plot synopsis.

2 Using a colon with a quotation

Use a colon to introduce a quotation.

Animal trainer Vickie Hearne describes the brutal brevity of life in the wild: "In Africa, 75 percent of the lions cubbed do not survive to the age of two. For those who make it to two, the average age at death is ten years."

Note: If the quotation is a complete sentence or more, begin with an upper-case letter.

3 Using a colon with an appositive

Use a colon to emphasize an appositive that explains a preceding noun.

Many hyperactive children eat only one thing: junk food.

4 Using a colon with an explanation

Use a colon to introduce an explanation of what has come before.

Conversation is reciprocal: there is always give and take.

Note: If an independent clause follows the colon, begin with a lower-case letter, as in the preceding example. If two or more complete sentences follow, begin each with a capital letter and set them off with bullets. (See 48b2.)

If your dishwasher does not start, take the following steps:
• Check to see whether it is plugged in.
• Check to see whether a fuse has blown.
• Check the position of the On/Off switch.

38b Use a colon to separate related formal elements

1 Using colons in business letters

Use a colon to separate the salutation from the body of a business letter.

Dear Director of Admissions:

2 Using colons in bibliographic citations

In bibliographic citations, use a colon to separate the title from the subtitle, the city of publication from the publisher.

McLean, Stuart. *Welcome Home: Travels in Smalltown Canada*. Toronto: Penguin, 1993.

3 Using colons with numbers

Use a colon to separate hours and minutes (9:36 a.m.), ratios (15:1), volume and page numbers (4: 98–115), and biblical chapter and verse (John 3:16).

Note: The Modern Language Association requires a period instead of a colon in Bible verses (John 3.16).

38c Avoid unnecessary colons

A colon is generally appropriate if you can place a period where you intend to use a colon, as with the colon preceding this sentence. Do not use a colon where no punctuation should be used.

1 Avoiding colons after *such as, like,* or *including*

Do not use a colon after words that introduce items in a series.

The children took whatever food they could eat while they played, such as/candy bars, carrots, and sandwiches.

[Because the sentence cannot be ended with *such as,* a colon is inappropriate. Do not separate a list from an introductory phrase.]

2 Avoiding colons between a verb and its object
or complement

Do not use a colon to separate a verb from its object or complement.
(To identify objects and complements, see 11c and d.)

Good managers are⁄energetic, diplomatic, and versatile.

Most research reports indicate⁄that capital punishment is no deterrent to

murder.

3 Avoiding colons between a preposition and its object

Do not use a colon to separate a preposition and its object. (For a list of
prepositions, see 10f.)

Computerized checkouts at supermarkets effortlessly keep track of⁄

quantities, prices, and types of food or merchandise purchased.

c h a p t e r

39 The Apostrophe

39*a* | Use an apostrophe to signal possession by
nouns and indefinite pronouns

As a grammatical term, **possession** refers not only to actual possession or
ownership, as in *the student's book*, but also to relationships, associations,
amounts, and duration: *the flower's fragrance, Peggy's Cove, your money's
worth,* and *two days' journey.* To decide whether a noun should be written as
a possessive, try three tests.

- **The *of* phrase test.** Try to turn the words into an *of* phrase: *the
  fragrance of the flower, the worth of your money, a journey of two days.* (To
  learn when to use an apostrophe for the possessive and when to use
  an *of* phrase, see 24e.)
- **The noun-plus-noun test.** In may cases, if two nouns appear together
  and the first noun ends in *-s*, add an apostrophe to this first noun to
  show possession: students (noun) + council (noun) = students'

council; library (noun) + acquisitions (noun) = library's acquisitions. (See below for distinctions between singular and plural possessors.)

■ **The *own* test.** If two nouns appear together and possession could be involved, check to see whether the addition of *own* makes sense between them: the student's(?) book = the student's *own* book; the flower's(?) fragrance = the flower's *own* fragrance; the library's (?) acquisitions = the library's *own* acquisitions. (To learn to identify nouns, see 10a.)

1   Forming possessives of singular nouns

To form the possessive of singular nouns, add an apostrophe + s (-'s).

the sun's rays	television's influence	Dr. Benton's lecture
the girl's bicycle	Aesop's fables	Governor General's awards
an hour's work	John Keats's poems	IBM's new computer

Exceptions:

■ Awkward pronunciation. Add an apostrophe but no s to singular possessive nouns if pronunciation would be awkward: *Moses' commandments, Aristophanes' plays, Achilles' tendon.*

■ Institutional and place names. Some institutional and place names have traditionally omitted the apostrophe: *Deadmans Bight (Nfld.), Rogers Pass (B.C.), James Bay, the Human Rights Commission, Northlands College (Sask.).* Check a dictionary, an atlas, or an encyclopedia.

2   Forming possessives of plural nouns

To form the possessive of plural nouns ending in s, add an apostrophe.

the planets' orbits	the players' coach	the banks' prime lending rates
the machines' noise	the Johnsons' car	the provinces' assent

A note on irregular plurals: To form the possessive of irregular plural nouns, add an apostrophe + s (-'s): *children's games, The Women's Health Network, the news media's accuracy.*

3   Forming possessives of indefinite pronouns

Most indefinite pronouns (*everyone, everybody, no one, something*) are singular. To form the possessive, add -'s. (For a complete list of indefinite pronouns, see 10b4.)

To **no one's** surprise, the Bears won the championship game.

A democratic government must represent **everyone's** interest.

4 Indicating joint and individual possession

To signal joint possession, make only the last noun possessive. To signal individual possession, make each noun possessive.

■ Joint possession.

Don and Angie's new baby

Tricia, Tony, Kirsten, and Erik's science project

■ Individual possession.

Betty's and **James's** skis

Plato's and **Gandhi's** philosophies

5 Forming possessives of compound nouns

To form the possessive of compound nouns, add -*'s* to the last word if it is singular, -s' to the last word if it is plural.

my **father-in-law's** birthday

the **Board of Governors'** approval

39b Use an apostrophe to signal contractions

Use an apostrophe to signal omissions of letters or numbers.

It's [it is] not easy to read by candlelight.

Rock **'n'** [and] roll sounds best when the volume is turned way up.

The blizzard of **'93** [1993] was hardly as dramatic as the blizzard of **'77** [1977].

Remember that contractions are inappropriate in most serious academic writing.

39c Use an apostrophe and an -*s* with plural letters and words used as words

Conventions vary regarding the use of the apostrophe to form the plural of letters and words used as words. The Modern Language Association guideline is to use -*'s*.

The *A***'s** and *B***'s** on this assignment outnumber the *C***'s** and *D***'s**.

Let's finish this project without any more *if*'s, *and*'s, or *but*'s.

Individual letters and words used as words are italicized or underlined, but the apostrophe and *s* are typed without italics or underlining, as in the preceding examples.

39d Avoid unnecessary apostrophes

1 Avoiding apostrophes with plural numbers and abbreviations

Conventions vary on the use of apostrophes with plural numbers and abbreviations. The Modern Language Association guideline is to omit the apostrophe.

The winning hand was a pair of **8s** and three **3s.**

This season Berenson has a batting average in the high **280s.**

In the **1990s,** not even people with **MAs, PhDs,** and high **IQs** could be sure of finding jobs.

Two **IDs** are required for customers who want to pay by personal cheque.

2 Avoiding possessives that sound like contractions

Do not confuse contractions with similar-sounding pronouns that do not take an apostrophe: *you're (you are)* with *your, it's (it is)* with *its, they're (they are)* with *their, who's (who is)* with *whose.*

You're
~~Your~~ going to thank me for this advice.

3 Avoiding apostrophes with possessive pronouns

Possessive pronouns (*hers, his, its, ours, theirs, whose, yours*) do not take an apostrophe.

its
The tree was losing ~~it's~~ leaves because of a fungus.

[*It's* is the contraction of *it is.*]

Whose
~~Who's~~ backpack is sitting under the desk?

[*Who's* is the contraction of *who is.*]

4 Avoiding apostrophes with nouns that are not possessive

Not all nouns that end in -s take an apostrophe. Use the apostrophe only when it is required to signal possession.

The Bates' family is away on vacation.

[The *Bates* do not possess the family; *Bates* is their name.]

The decision of the judges' will be final.

[Possession is already signalled by the *of*, so the apostrophe is redundant.]

The hungry roommates ordered three pizza's.

[This is a plural, not a possessive. Do not use an apostrophe.]

chapter

40 Quotation Marks

40a | Enclose direct quotations in double quotation marks (" ")

Use double quotation marks at the beginning and end of all word-for-word quotations of speech or writing.

Kim Campbell lived to regret the comment she made the night of her first political defeat: "Charisma without substance is a dangerous thing."

Real estate agents emphasize one principle when they are assessing properties: "Location! Location! Location!"

1 Avoiding quotation marks in indirect quotations

Do not use quotation marks around indirect (summarized) quotations.

Kim Campbell's 1986 comment about the dangers of charisma with no substance to it came back to haunt her in 1993.

2 Using quotation marks in paragraphing

In writing dialogue, begin a new paragraph to signal a change in speaker, no matter how brief each person's speech.

"Girl number twenty," said Mr. Gradgrind, squarely pointing with his square forefinger, "I don't know that girl. Who is that girl?"

"Sissy Jupe, sir," explained number twenty, blushing, standing up, and curtseying.

"Sissy is not a name," said Mr. Gradgrind. "Don't call yourself Sissy. Call yourself Cecilia."

(Charles Dickens, from *Hard Times*)

A note on multiparagraph speeches: If one person's speech runs for two or more paragraphs, open each paragraph with quotation marks, but do not use closing quotation marks until the end of the speech.

40b | Punctuate quotations correctly

1 Periods and commas

Put periods and commas inside quotation marks, even when the quotation is less than a sentence.

"Writing is a very painful process," says essayist and novelist Tom Wolfe. "I never understand writers who say it's enjoyable."

E. J. Pratt's shark is described as having a fin "like a piece of sheet iron."

A note on MLA in-text documentation: When you use the Modern Language Association's in-text documentation format, place the period after the quotation marks and parenthetical documentation. (See 53a.)

The metaphor of anatomy appeals to Frye because of "its intellectual exuberance" (Hamilton 179).

2 Colons and semicolons

Put colons and semicolons outside quotation marks.

Murphy's Law ought to be called "Murphy's Threat": If something can go wrong, it will.

Shakespeare wrote, "All the world's a stage"; if he were a member of today's music video generation, he'd write, "All the world's a sound stage."

3 Question marks and exclamation points

Put question marks and exclamation points inside quotation marks if they are part of the quotation. Otherwise, put them outside.

Joe Clark spent his first years as leader of the Progressive Conservatives nicknamed "Joe Who?"

What famous mystery writer said, "Where there is no imagination there is no horror"**?**

A note on MLA in-text documentation: When you use the Modern Language Association's in-text documentation format, punctuate quoted questions and exclamations according to the preceding guidelines, followed by the parenthetical documentation and a period.

> When the Commander challenges the protagonist of Margaret Atwood's *The Handmaid's Tale* to a game of scrabble, he asks an ambiguous question, "You know how to play?" (131).

4 Introducing quotations

To introduce a quotation, use a colon, comma, or no punctuation, whichever is appropriate to the context. (See also 52c and d.)

- Use a colon after an introductory independent clause.

> Sue Hubbell explains that bees communicate by dancing**:** "Bees tell other bees about good things such as food or the location of a new home by patterned motions."

- After opening quotation signals like *he said* or *she observes*, use a comma.

> Futurist Frank Ogden **warns,** "As this bulldozer of change rolls over our planet, we all have to learn that if we don't become part of the bulldozer, we'll become part of the road."

- When a signal statement closes a quotation, use a comma after the quotation unless it ends with a question mark or exclamation point.

> "The other America, the America of poverty, is hidden today in a way that it never was before**,"** **argues** social critic Michael Harrington.

> "Dr. Livingstone, I presume**?"** **asked** explorer H. M. Stanley when he found the doctor on the shores of Lake Tanganyika in 1871.

- Use no punctuation before a quotation that is the object or complement of a verb, a clause following a subordinating conjunction, a modifying phrase, or the object of a preposition.

> The British Council **notes that** "80% of the world's electronically stored information is in English."

> Describing Nose Park Hill in Calgary, Aritha van Herk is enthralled **by** "its soft wedges and coulee clefts as subtle and erotic as a Scottish heath."

5 Interrupted quotations

If you interrupt a quotation with a signal statement in the middle of a sentence, set off the tag with commas.

"God is subtle," **quipped Einstein,** "but he is not malicious."

If you interrupt a quotation at the end of a complete sentence, use a comma before the signal statement and a period following. Then resume the quotation.

"Linguistically Canada had a confused and difficult upbringing," points out Mark Orkin. "The early British and American settlers filled the towns and clearings with their dialects, ruling out all possibility of a standard speech for many generations."

6   **Long quotations**

Guidelines for presenting long quotations vary. For MLA guidelines, see 52d; for APA guidelines, see 48d4.

40c | Use single quotation marks (' ') only to enclose quotations within quotations

As Phillip walked into class, he muttered, "Someone should post a sign outside this room that quotes Dante: 'Abandon hope, all ye who enter here.' "

Some writers assume that quotations of single words or brief phrases should be enclosed with single quotation marks. Not so. Use single quotation marks only for quotations within quotations.

A note on quoting nested quotations: If you must quote a passage that contains a quotation, alternate quotation marks: double, single, double (" ' "..." ' "). Be sure to use as many closing as opening quotation marks.

Kerry continued, "Then Lisa whispered, 'Don't forget the old saying, "If at first you don't succeed, try, try again." ' "

40d | Use quotation marks to enclose titles of short works

Use quotation marks around the titles of magazine and newspaper articles, essays and book chapters, short stories, poems, songs, and episodes of radio and television programs.

Margaret Laurence's "The Loons" tells the story of what we stand to lose when we grow up or, by extension, when we become civilized.

Every Remembrance Day, schoolchildren recite John McCrae's "In Flanders Fields."

A note on titles of long or complete works: Italicize or underline the titles of books, plays, long poems, films, television and radio series, and the names of magazines and newspapers. (See 43a.)

40*e* | Occasionally use quotation marks to signal words used in a special sense

Although italics or underlining is the preferred method to signal a word used as a word or in a special sense, you may use quotation marks. Be consistent throughout your writing.

> A French Canadian pronunciation of the word *cheval* (*horse* in English) lent itself to the name for the dialect—*joual.*

> A French Canadian pronunciation of the word "cheval" ("horse" in English) lent itself to the name for the dialect—"joual."

Note: Foreign words are underlined or italicized. (See 43c.)

40*f* | Avoid unnecessary quotation marks

1 Avoiding quotation marks around titles of your own papers

On the title page or first page of the papers you write, do not put quotation marks around your title unless it is an actual quotation.

2 Avoiding quotation marks for emphasis or slang

Do not use quotation marks for emphasis or to set off slang.

> Store owners who sell cigarettes to teenagers often receive only a ⁓slap on the wrist.⁓

3 Avoiding quotation marks with indirect quotations

Do not use quotation marks with indirect (summarized) quotations.

> Doctors everywhere are warning their patients that ⁓they must cut down on their cholesterol.⁓

chapter

41 Other Punctuation Marks

41a | Use a dash for a change of thought, parenthetical remarks, or faltering speech

 Computer Tip:

Typing Em Dashes

Many word processing programs automatically turn a pair of hyphens with no spacing (--) into a dash (—), called an **em dash**. Others feature the em dash as an insertable symbol.

Type a dash as two hyphens, with no space before or after (*word--word*). Use the dash to send the following signals.

1 Indicating an emphatic change in thought or feeling

Use a dash to signal an emphatic change in thought or feeling.

Think about how technology has changed in your lifetime—or even in just the last five years.

2 Setting off parenthetical material

Use a pair of dashes to set off and emphasize parenthetical material.

Whatever you are writing—a memo, a letter, a report, an e-mail message—you want to be both concise and precise.

Note: As the preceding example illustrates, a dash is the strongest mark of parenthetical punctuation. Dashes emphasize what they enclose; parentheses and commas de-emphasize. (See 41b.)

41*a* —

3 Displaying lists

Use a dash to introduce a list or to connect a list to the main part of the sentence.

Florence's room is packed with evidence of her passion for rock collecting—hammers and chisels, rock fragments, geological survey maps, fossil specimens, chunks of minerals, display cases, petrie dishes, and spelunker's gear.

Appreciated, took pleasure in, enjoyed, welcomed, was delighted by, pleased with, grateful for—all express gratitude in terms that are undeniably positive.

Note: A colon may also introduce a list; a dash is less formal but more emphatic.

4 Setting off parenthetical modifiers containing punctuation

Modifiers rename, explain, or add information to nearby words. Often they are set off by commas, but if they contain internal punctuation, commas may be confusing. Use dashes to set off modifiers that contain internal punctuation.

These days the volume of business communications—from customers and suppliers, from supervisors, colleagues and staff—has mushroomed.

5 Indicating faltering speech

Use a dash to signal faltering speech.

"I—I—don't know how it could have happened," he said, astonished by the accident.

6 Avoiding unnecessary dashes

Consider the dash to be as dramatic as a pointing finger. In serious academic writing, prefer the comma, colon, or parentheses, saving the dash for a compelling, perhaps concluding point. Too many dashes will make your writing sound emotional or chaotic, rather than objective.

A majority of students surveyed ~~71 percent~~ (71 percent) favoured the elimination

of 8:30 a.m. classes.

41*b* Use parentheses to enclose parenthetical remarks and numbers that mark items in a series

1 Using parentheses for parenthetical remarks

Use parentheses to set off supplemental or explanatory information.

Manuals and textbooks can't replace instructors, but they can do some things more efficiently (besides being easier to keep in a desk!).

Note: Of all the punctuation used to enclose, parentheses signal the greatest separation between the supplemental or explanatory material inside and the material that precedes or follows it. Dashes emphasize what they enclose; parentheses seem to hide it. (See 41a2.)

2 Using parentheses for numbers or letters to mark a series

Use parentheses to enclose numbers or letters that identify items in a series.

Touring bicyclists should carry what they need to cope with unpleasant surprises: **(1)** a ground sheet for their tent, **(2)** waterproof matches, **(3)** water purification tablets, **(4)** twine and tape, **(5)** extra flashlight batteries, **(6)** a folding tire, **(7)** extra inner tubes.

3 Using parentheses correctly and effectively

- Put commas and semicolons, when called for, only after parentheses, not before them. (See 36k4.)

  The text of government documents is intended for many, many readers, (corporate chiefs, as well as politicians), but a surprising number read only the executive summary.

- If one sentence contains a second sentence enclosed by parentheses, do not open the parenthetical sentence with a capital or end it with a period.

  The police officer was delighted that the witness could describe the getaway car (it was a black 1999 Acura Integra with New York plates).

- When a parenthetical sentence stands by itself, open with a capital letter and close with appropriate end punctuation.

41c [ ]

The nursery rhyme about Little Jack Horner pulling a plum from his Christmas pie has historical sources. **(**The real Jack Horner was a cunning sixteenth century Englishman who helped King Henry VIII seize land from the Catholic Church.**)**

■ Avoid unnecessary parentheses. Readers tend to skip parenthetical remarks. Parentheses may also make your sentences overly complex and difficult to read.

To test the effects of overpopulation, researchers (in 1999) released a herd of fifteen (15) deer in a forest preserve (it was 300 hectares in size and surrounded by subdivisions).

[handwritten: 300-hectare]

41c | Use brackets for insertions

Use square brackets, typed or hand drawn, to insert explanations, clarifications, or corrections within direct quotations and to enclose parentheses within parentheses.

1 Using brackets for explanations

Use brackets to insert information necessary for readers to understand a quotation.

According to the latest medical predictions, "More than 33 000 cases [of skin cancer] leading to nearly 7 000 deaths are expected this year alone."

2 Using brackets for clarifications

Use brackets to insert the antecedent nouns referred to by quoted pronouns or to take the place of omitted words.

"Citizens' groups have labelled this [distortion of test results] a coverup."

"First tested in 1981 aboard the second space shuttle mission [the Canadarm] has exceeded its initial design goals."

[The original of this quotation is *First tested in 1981 aboard the second space shuttle mission it has exceeded its initial design goals.* For clarity *it* has been replaced by the understood antecedent, *the Canadarm*.]

3 Using brackets for corrections

Always quote accurately. If a quotation contains an error, insert *sic* (Latin for "so," "thus," "in this manner") in brackets immediately following the error. The alternative is to paraphrase the original, avoiding the error altogether.

Banting's few scribbles in a notebook—"Diabetus [sic]. Ligate pancreatic ducts of dog."—herald the discovery of insulin as a treatment for diabetes.

4 Using brackets for parentheses within parentheses

In research papers that follow the Modern Language Association format for in-text documentation, use brackets to enclose documentation within parenthetical remarks.

The years after World War II saw the British influence on Standard English decline in favour of American English (see review in *English Today* [Graddol 41]).

5 Using brackets with ellipsis points

The Modern Languages Association requires brackets to enclose ellipsis points that signal an omission from a direct quotation. (See 41d.)

41*d* | Use ellipsis points to signal omissions

Ellipsis is the omission of words, phrases, or sentences from quoted material. Use ellipsis points to signal omissions from direct quotations.

A note on the use of brackets with ellipsis points: In the *MLA Style Manual*, 2nd edition (1998), the Modern Language Association requires that ellipsis points be enclosed between square brackets to signal that the ellipsis points have been added and do not appear in the original quotation. Other manuscript styles, such as those of the American Psychological Association and the *Chicago Manual of Style*, do not require brackets. Unless otherwise indicated, *The Ready Reference Handbook* follows MLA guidelines.

- *Spacing.* Type three equally spaced periods enclosed by brackets. Leave no space between the brackets and the periods. When an ellipsis appears within a sentence, leave a space before and after the brackets.

"The flock of geese turned [. . .] in a large circle above the lake."

[The original sentence reads, *The flock of geese turned slowly, sweeping in a large circle above the lake.*]

- *End punctuation.* If an ellipsis comes at the end of a quoted sentence, leave a space before the opening bracket and immediately follow the closing bracket with a period or other end punctuation and closing quotation marks.

"The flock of geese turned slowly [. . .]."

- *Internal punctuation.* When ellipsis points precede or follow internal punctuation, reproduce the internal punctuation exactly as it appears in the original. Do not leave a space between the closing bracket and any punctuation.

"The flock of geese turned [. . .], sweeping in a large circle above the lake."

1 Using ellipsis points with prose quotations

Use ellipsis points to signal the omission of a word, phrase, sentence, or longer passage from a quotation.

> According to essayist Lewis Thomas, "It begins to look [. . .] as if the gift of language is the single human trait that marks us all genetically, setting us apart from all the rest of life. [. . .] Language is, like nest-building or hive-making, the universal and biologically specific activity of human beings."
> [The first ellipsis signals the omission of a phrase; the second, signals the omission of a complete sentence.]

To use ellipsis points effectively, follow these guidelines:

- A quotation containing an ellipsis must be grammatically correct. You would not write *According to essayist Lewis Thomas, "the gift of language [. . .] setting us apart from the rest of life."* The quotation is not grammatical. Use additional brackets to insert words that make elliptical quotations grammatically correct: *"the gift of language [. . .] [sets] us apart from the rest of life."* (See 41c.)

- Do not use ellipsis points at the beginning of a quotation. Use ellipsis points at the end only if you have omitted words from the last sentence quoted.

  According to essayist Lewis Thomas, "language is the single human trait that marks us all genetically[. . .] ."

- Do not use ellipsis points if the quotation is an obviously incomplete sentence.

  Essayist Lewis Thomas calls language the "biologically specific activity of human beings."

- To use the Modern Language Association in-text format to document a quotation that ends in an ellipsis, follow this pattern: space + three ellipsis points enclosed in brackets + quotation marks + space + parenthetical documentation + a final period.

  According to essayist Lewis Thomas, "language is the single human trait that marks us all genetically [. . .]" ("Social Talk" 105).

- Do not put one or two ellipsis points at the end of one line and the rest on the next. Put the ellipsis points in brackets and any auxiliary punctuation all on one line.

2   Using ellipsis points with poetry quotations

When quoting poetry, use three ellipsis points within brackets to signal the omission of less than a line. To omit a line or more, use a line of spaced periods with brackets equal to the length of a complete line.

[. . .] Flying deeper into the century,

my hands are prayers, hooks, streamers.

[. . . .]

The end of the century is a bedspread up to the eyes.

I want to be there [. . .] .

(Pier Giorgio Di Cicco)

3   Using ellipsis points to indicate pauses, interruptions, or incomplete thoughts

Use ellipsis points—without brackets—in narratives or dialogue to signal pauses, interruptions, or incomplete thoughts. At the end of a sentence left intentionally incomplete, use the three ellipsis points and omit the final period.

"It has to be . . . ," he worried, shuffling the papers on his desk. "I'm sure I saw it sitting on top of . . . "

41e | Use the slash with poetry and paired words

1   Using slashes with run-in quotations of poetry

Use a slash to separate two or three lines of poetry run into your text. Add a space before and after the slash.

Flaunting his poetic powers, Shakespeare opens one of his most famous sonnets with "Not marble, nor the gilded monuments / Of princes, shall outlive this powerful rhyme."

When quoting more than three lines of poetry, use the indented quotation format. (See 52d.)

2   Using slashes with paired words

Use the slash to separate paired words or abbreviations: *AC/DC, CAD/CAM, true/false, introvert/extrovert.* Do not use a space before or after the slash. Overuse of the slash in this way will make your writing seem finicky or choppy. Especially avoid *and/or, he/she, his/her.*

Mechanics

chapter

42 Capital Letters

42*a* | Capitalize the first word of sentences, deliberate fragments, and lines of poetry

1 Sentences

The wind blew the snow in swirling circles.

A note on quotations: Do not capitalize the first word of a quoted sentence you have incorporated into your own sentence.

Wilfrid Laurier's prediction that ~~"The~~ "the twentieth century belongs to

Canada" represents the height of Canadian optimism.

A note on parenthetical sentences: Do not capitalize the first word of a parenthetical sentence contained within another sentence.

It is as foolish to believe in superstitions as it is to build a house of straw ~~(Both~~ (both will collapse one day).

2 Deliberate fragments

Capitalize the first words of deliberately written sentence fragments.

What's the natural response of anyone who suspects you of having a hidden agenda? Suspicion. Wariness. Mistrust.

3 Poetry

When you quote poetry, capitalize and punctuate everything exactly as it appears in the original. (If the first words in lines are lowercased, do not change them.)

Some people are a country
and their deaths displace you.
Everything you shared with them
reminds you of it: part of you in exile
for the rest of your life.

> (Bronwen Wallace)

42b | Capitalize proper nouns and words derived from them

Proper nouns name specific persons, places, and things (*Louis Riel, Great Bear Lake, Parliament*). Proper nouns and their derivatives are capitalized. Common nouns name persons, places, and things in general (*a leader, a lake, a governmental assembly*) and are not capitalized unless part of a specific name, as in *Great Slave Lake*.

1 Capitalizing the names and titles of people

- Capitalize the names, nicknames, and initials of real and imaginary persons, and words derived from names: *Pierre E. Trudeau, Trudeauesque, Trudeaumania, Maurice Richard, Rocket Richard, the Rocket, Minnie Mouse.*

- Capitalize races, nationalities, geographic groupings of people, languages, and words derived from them: *French, Greek, South African, Irish, American, Polish, Cantonese.*

- Capitalize civil, military, religious, and professional titles immediately preceding a personal name: *Prime Minister St. Laurent, Pope Paul XXIII, Queen Elizabeth II, General Wolfe, Professor Bird.* Capitalize titles used in place of names in introductions, toasts, and direct address: *Dear Colonel.* Do not capitalize titles following a name: *Abraham Lincoln, sixteenth president of the United States; Victoria, queen of England.*

Karen Redman, ~~Member~~ member of Parliament for Kitchener, will chair the committee.

Patricia McLean has just been reappointed ~~Director~~ director of the Port Authority Board.

- Capitalize kinship names followed by a given name or used in place of the name; otherwise, use lower-case letters. Compare these examples:

This year **Aunt Jennifer** is helping to pay my tuition.

Rebecca's ~~Father~~ father has just been admitted to the hospital.

- Capitalize abstract words if they have been personified with the attributes of people; otherwise, use lower-case letters.

Said Grass, "What is that sound / So dismally profound . . .?"
(Bliss Carman)

. . . I bid my spirit pass / Out into the pale green ever-swaying grass . . .
(Archibald Lampman)

2 Capitalizing religious terms

Capitalize the names of religions, deities, holy persons, holy writings, religious groups and movements, religious events and services, and words derived from these terms.

Islam, Islamic	the Bible	Holy Communion
the Lord, our Lord	the Koran	the Sermon on
Christ, the Saviour	the Ten	the Mount
the Blessed Virgin	Commandments	the Dead Sea Scrolls
Buddha, Buddhism	Catholicism	God
the Prophet	the Baptist Church	Manitou
(Muhammad)	the Crucifixion	the Almighty

Note: Bible is usually not capitalized in its adjective form (biblical) or when it is used as a synonym for "authoritative book": *When Eva is looking for synonyms, her thesaurus is her bible.*

3 Capitalizing cultural and historical terms

Capitalization of cultural and historical terms varies; check your dictionary. In general, capitalize the names of historical, political, and cultural events and documents; capitalize historical periods only when proper nouns or to avoid ambiguity.

Confederation	the Fall of Rome	*but:* ancient Rome
the War of 1812	the Renaissance	*but:* the sixteenth century
the Crusades	the Roaring Twenties	*but:* the twenties
the Russian Revolution	the Great Depression	*but:* the thirties

A note on archeological periods: Capitalize time periods recognized by archeologists and anthropologists: *Bronze Age, Neolithic era, Paleolithic times.* Lowercase recent periods: *the space age, the cold war, the civil rights era.*

A note on philosophic and artistic terms: Capitalize philosophic, literary, and artistic terms derived from proper nouns; otherwise, use lowercase letters: *Platonism* but *existentialism*; a *Gothic* novel but a *horror story.*

4 Capitalizing geographic regions, place names, and structures

■ Capitalize geographic names for countries, regions, and continents: *Spain, Europe, the Arctic, the Southern Hemisphere, the Prairies, the New*

World, the Tropic of Capricorn, the Maritimes, New England. Do not capitalize words that name direction only (although you will capitalize any abbreviations for such directions as *NNE, SW,* and so on):

When they retire, Peter and Becky plan to move ~~South~~.
^south^

- Capitalize the names of cities, counties, regions, empires, colonies, locales, and popular place names: *Winnipeg, the Beaches, Yorkville, Chinatown, Metro, the Klondike, the Gatineau, the Golden Horseshoe, Parliament Hill, the Twin Cities, the Eternal City, the Roman Empire, Soweto Township, the Land of the Midnight Sun.*

- Capitalize the names of rivers, lakes, oceans, islands, and other specific geographic places: *the Thompson River, Churchill Falls, Siwash Rock, the Indian Ocean, Anticosti Island, Nootka Sound, the Red River Valley, Lake of the Woods.*

- Capitalize the names of buildings, streets, highways, bridges, and monuments. *Uniak House, Casa Loma, the Pyramids, Tunnel Louis-Hippolyte, King Street West, Sussex Drive, West Edmonton Mall, Peace Bridge, the Eiffel Tower.*

A note on generic place names: Generic place names that precede a name or stand alone are usually lowercased.

The ~~City~~ of Dartmouth sponsors an annual book fair.
^city^

5 Capitalizing the names of objects

- Capitalize the names of celestial bodies: *Earth, the North Star, Halley's comet, the constellation of Orion, the Big Dipper.*

- Capitalize the names of ships, trains, aircraft, and spacecraft: *the Bluenose, the Orient Express, Spirit of St. Louis, Voyager 2.*

- Capitalize trademarks and brand names but not the generic products associated with them: *Coca-Cola, Coke,* but *cola; Levi's jeans; Kleenex tissue; Tylenol,* but *aspirin; Xerox photocopier; GMC trucks.*

When I was a kid, all I wanted was a CCM ~~Bicycle~~.
^bicycle^

6 Capitalizing dates and time designations

Capitalize days of the week, months, and holidays: *Tuesday, July, Hallowe'en, Lent, Ramadan, Passover, Labour Day, Thanksgiving, St. Jean Baptiste Day.* Lowercase the seasons, decades, centuries, and time zones that are spelled out: *spring, the nineties, the twentieth century, eastern standard time.*

My favourite season is ~~Autumn~~. *autumn*

7 Capitalizing the names of organizations

Capitalize the names of companies, civic organizations, institutions, and government agencies: *Hudson's Bay Company, the 4H Club, the Fraser Institute, the House of Commons.* Lowercase generic organization names and plural generic names used with organization names: *citizenship court, the prime minister's cabinet, the Anglican and United churches.*

8 Capitalizing academic terms

Capitalize the names of specific courses: *I'm taking two literature courses: Commonwealth Literature and American Fiction.* Lowercase school terms (*spring semester*), generic degrees, and the names of academic subjects except languages: *bachelor's degree, political science,* but *English.*

9 Capitalizing the names of plants, animals, and medical terms

Capitalization is varied; see your dictionary. Generally capitalize proper nouns that are part of a name; otherwise, lowercase them: *Prairie crocus, Virginia creeper, Peace rose, a Morgan horse, an Irish setter, Hodgkin's disease, Down's syndrome,* but *rottweiler, cocker spaniel, rheumatic fever.*

10 Capitalizing acronyms

Acronyms are abbreviations set in full capitals with no periods, formed from the first letters of words. They include the names of organizations, government agencies, companies, and institutions (*OPEC, SPCA, CUSO, IBM*); technical, scientific, and military terms (*CD-ROM, HIV, AIDS, CFB*); and radio and television call letters (*CHUM-FM, CBLFT-TV*).

42c Capitalize the first, last, and all major words in the titles of works

1 General guidelines

- Capitalize the titles and subtitles of written works such as books and essays, performances such as plays, visual works such as painting and sculpture, and media productions such as television and radio programs:

  Fifth Business   *West Side Story*
  Home Truths: Selected Canadian Stories   the *Mona Lisa*
  "The Murders in the Rue Morgue"   *Star Trek*

- Capitalize first words, last words, and major words. Do not capitalize articles (*a, an, the*), prepositions (*in, of, toward, according,* and so on), co-ordinating conjunctions (*and, but, for, yet, so, or, nor*), and the *to* in infinitives (*How to Succeed in Business without Really Trying*).

- Always capitalize the first word of a compound in a title (*The Modern City-State*); capitalize the second word only if it is important. Compare *Twenty-First Century Drama* or *A-Bomb* with *C-sharp Minor, Spanish-speaking,* and *Re-education.*

- Do not capitalize, italicize, or underline *the* before a newspaper name.

  My father enjoys doing the cryptic crosswords in ~~The~~ *the* *Globe and Mail.*

  In news story titles as actually published, usually only the first word and proper nouns are capitalized: *"Late snowstorm reveals split over snow removal philosophy."* But when you give the title in your writing, capitalize according to the preceding guidelines: *"Late Snowstorm Reveals Split over Snow Removal Philosophy."*

2 APA guidelines

These are the American Psychological Association guidelines for writing in the social sciences.

- When you cite titles in the text of your writing, capitalize the first and last words. Also capitalize all words of four letters or more and both words of a hyphenated compound: *Communities and Social Policies in Canada.*

- Lowercase articles (*a, an, the*). Also lowercase prepositions and conjunctions of one to three letters (e.g., lowercase *to, in, and,* but capitalize *Toward, Into,* and *When*).

■ When citing titles in references, capitalize only the first word of a title, the first word of a hyphenated compound, the first word after a colon, and proper nouns: *Communities and social policies in Canada; The prosperous community: Social capital and public life.*

42*d* | Avoid unnecessary capital letters

1 **Avoiding capitals with** *a, an,* **and** *the*

Do not capitalize the articles *a, an,* and *the* before proper nouns unless they are the first or last words of a title. Compare these examples:

Gene Kelly did his best dancing in *An American in Paris.*

Today there are few genuine luxury liners like ~~The~~ the Queen Elizabeth II.

2 **Avoiding capitals for emphasis**

Do not capitalize words for emphasis, even in e-mail.

Fantasia is the ~~GREATEST~~ greatest cartoon ever produced by the Disney studio.

[Create emphatic sentences by rewording and rearranging: *The greatest cartoon ever produced by the Disney studio is* Fantasia.]

3 **Avoiding capitals with common nouns derived from**

proper names

Do not capitalize personal, national, or geographic names when used with special meanings. Adjectives derived from proper nouns are usually not capitalized: *french fries, manila envelopes, diesel engines,* and *venetian blinds.* But other such words are capitalized: *Arabic and Roman numerals, Caesar's salad, German shepherd ,* and *Swiss cheese.* With verbs, too, there is disagreement: *anglicize* and *italicize* use lower case; *Canadianize* keeps its capital. See your dictionary for correct capitalization.

chapter
43 Italics/Underlining

In typed or handwritten papers, use underlining whenever italics would appear in printed works. If your computer has the capability and its italic type is easily recognizable, italicize. But note that the Modern Language Association and American Psychological Association recommend underlining. In academic writing, use the following guidelines.

43a Italicize or underline the titles of separately produced works

1 Italicizing written works

Italicize or underline the titles and subtitles of books, pamphlets, the names of magazines and newspapers, and long poems.

The Stone Diaries or <u>The Stone Diaries</u>

Maclean's or <u>Maclean's</u>

the *Edmonton Journal* or the <u>Edmonton Journal.</u> (The article *the* is not italicized or underlined in English newspaper names; however, it is italicized or underlined in French: *La Presse* or <u>Le Devoir.</u>)

2 Italicizing visual and performing arts

Italicize or underline the titles and subtitles of movies and plays, television and radio programs, painting, sculpture, and cartoons: *Evita* or <u>Evita</u>, *Star Trek* or <u>Star Trek</u>, Picasso's *The Bather* or <u>The Bather</u>, *For Better or For Worse* or <u>For Better or For Worse.</u> (Specific episodes of television and radio programs are enclosed by quotations and neither italicized nor underlined: "The Trouble with Tribbles.")

3 Italicizing long musical compositions, recordings, and choreographic works

Italicize or underline long musical compositions, recordings (records, tapes, or compact discs), and choreographic works: *Sgt. Pepper's Lonely Hearts Club Band* or <u>Sgt. Pepper's Lonely Hearts Club Band</u>, *Swan Lake* or <u>Swan Lake.</u>

Note: Individual song titles are enclosed by quotation marks: "You Needed Me." Do not italicize, underline, or use quotations around musical compositions identified by form, number, or key: Beethoven's Symphony no. 5 in C minor.

4 Exceptions

Do not italicize or underline the titles of sacred writings (including all books and versions of the Bible), titles of legal documents, descriptive titles, or the titles of your own writing.

the King James Version of the Bible	the Canadian Charter of Rights
Genesis	and Freedoms
the Talmud	Lincoln's Gettysburg address
the Koran	the War Measures Act

43*b* Italicize or underline the names of ships, trains, aircraft, and spacecraft

the *Bluenose* or the <u>Bluenose</u>	*Spirit of St. Louis* or <u>Spirit of St. Louis</u>
the *Turbo* or the <u>Turbo</u>	*Apollo 8* or <u>Apollo 8</u>

43*c* Italicize or underline foreign words and phrases

Italicize or underline foreign words or phrases, whether part of a quotation or your own words. Translate or explain foreign words if readers may not know them.

Special effects in the ancient Greek theatre included the *deus ex machina* ("the god from the machine"), an actor suspended above the stage by a crane.

Exceptions: (1) Do not italicize or underline foreign words used frequently in English: ad hoc, cliché, laissez-faire, per diem, sauerkraut, status quo, versus, and so on. (2) Do not italicize or underline non-English titles enclosed in quotation marks.

43*d* Italicize or underline letters, words, and numbers used as themselves

With grade inflation, *A*'s have become as common as *B*'s and *C*'s.

Freud's term *narcissism* has nothing to do with the flower; it refers to the myth of the Greek youth Narcissus who fell in love with his reflected image.

The number 3 has symbolic meaning in many religions.

A note on quotation marks in place of italics or underlining: Quotation marks are sometimes used to set off words used as words: "narcissism." (See 40e.)

A note on italics, underlining, and the plurals of letters, words, and numbers Do not italicize or underline the apostrophe or *s* following letters, words and numbers used as themselves: *p*'s and *q*'s or p's and q's; 7's or 7's; *yea*' or *nay*'s, yea's or nay's. (See 39c.)

43*e* | Occasionally italicize or underline for emphasis

Many travellers are uncomfortable when foreign countries feel like *foreign* countries.

Note: Too much emphatic italicizing or underlining will make you writing sound false or strained. Find emphatic words and sentence patterns that emphasize important ideas. (See 25.)

chapter

44 Abbreviations

Abbreviations consist of shortened versions of words (*vol., intro., inc.*) words from which the middle is omitted (*Mr., Mrs., Jr., dept.*), and acronyms formed from the first letters of words (*RCMP, CFL, CAA, AFL CIO, CBC*). Because abbreviations and acronyms may be puzzling to readers, generally avoid them in the body of your writing.

44*a* | General guidelines

1 Using abbreviations correctly

- In the text of most formal writing, use abbreviations only in parenthetical statements. Compare:

  The first insecticides were naturally occurring plant products, **for example,** pyrethrum from dried chrysanthemum flowers.

  The first insecticides were naturally occurring plant products (**e.g.,** pyrethrum from dried chrysanthemum flowers).

- You may use familiar abbreviations in the text of your writing: *CD-ROM, HIV, CAT scan,* and so on.

- Use abbreviations for repeated names and technical terms. For the first use, write out the term completely and include the abbreviation in parentheses. From then on, use the abbreviation alone.

The **Old Age Security (OAS)** program has been in place in Canada since 1952, and in 1966 the federal government added a **Guaranteed Income Supplement (GIS)** for those with little income outside the **OAS** pension.

- Use abbreviations in tables, graphics, notes, and documentation. (See 48b3 and 4. For MLA documentation, see 54a. For APA documentation, see 56b.)

2   Punctuating abbreviations and acronyms

- Personal names. Use a period and a space following initials: *H. L. Mencken.*

- Abbreviations. Neither the International System of Units (SI) nor the metric system uses periods after abbreviations, whether upper or lower case: cm³, hL, km/h, Pa. (See also 44f2.) For imperial abbreviations and other abbreviations ending in lower-case letters, use a period: sq. ft., gal., lb., pp., e.g., fig.

- Acronyms. Do not use periods or spaces between the letters of acronyms: GST, IQ, MBA, CNCP, rpm, PhD.

44*b* | Titles with personal names

Generally avoid titles in academic writing except to give the qualifications of people whose opinions or information you use. You may use titles frequently in other kinds of writing.

1   Abbreviated titles

- Always abbreviate *Mr., Ms., Mrs.,* as in *Mr. Edward O'Connell* or *Mr. O'Connell, Ms. Nora Chang* or *Ms. Chang.*

- Abbreviate titles before or after full names. *Prof. Jay Macpherson, Maj.-Gen. J. M. Baril, Dr. Norman Bethune, the Rev. Enid Ashton, the Hon. Paul Martin, St. Francis Xavier, Gail Cuthbert Brandt, Ph.D., Martin Luther King, Jr., G. M. Garboll, MD.* Do not use abbreviations without names; avoid redundant titles.

The speaker at this year's convocation will be Dr. Barbara

Hickey/~~Ph.D.~~

2 Unabbreviated titles

Spell out titles used with surnames (last names) alone: *Professor Macpherson, Major-General Baril, Doctor Bethune, the Reverend Ashton*, but also *the Honourable Paul Martin, Saint Francis Xavier*. Do not abbreviate given names: write *Charles Dutoit*, not *Chas. Dutoit*.

44*c* Dates and time

1 Abbreviating conventional date and time markers

Always abbreviate *a.m., p.m., AD, BC, BCE* (*Before the Common Era*), and *CE* (*Common Era*). Place *AD* (*anno Domini*, or "year of our Lord") before the date: *AD 1066*; place *BC* ("before Christ") following the date: *461 BC*. Use conventional date and time abbreviations only with specific times and dates: *3:30 p.m.; 1066 CE*.

2 Spelling out months, days, and other time designations

- In the text of formal writing, spell out months and days: *Thursday, October 31*. Exception: In notes and documentation, abbreviate months and days except May, June, and July.

- Spell out words like *seconds, minutes, hours, days, weeks, months*, or *years* in the text of your writing. Do not abbreviate *Christmas* as *Xmas*, or use short forms for other holidays.

44*d* Geographic terms and place names

1 Spelling out names and addresses in text

In the text of your writing, spell out the names of continents, countries, territories, provinces, states, other words in addresses, and place names: *North America, Saudi Arabia, South Africa, the Northwest Territories, Prince Edward Island, North Dakota, Selkirk Avenue, Confederation Parkway, National Arts Centre*. The three exceptions follow the article *the*: *the USA, the UK*, and *the EU*.

2 Abbreviating place names in notes and documentation

In notes, documentation, and addresses, use standard abbreviations: *Ont.* for *Ontario, Ecua.* for *Ecuador, Gr.* for *Greece*, and so on.

44e | Organization names

1 Abbreviating familiar organizations

Use familiar organizational abbreviations in the text of your writing: *YMCA, YTV, CAW, CUPE.* Spell out the names of organizations unfamiliar to your readers: *Royal Newfoundland Constabulary (RNC), International Brotherhood of Teamsters (IB of T), Canadian Industrial Innovation Centre (CIIC). Incorporated* is usually written *Inc.* or omitted.

2 Abbreviating notes and documentation

In notes and documentation abbreviate consistently for *Assoc., &, Co., Corp., Bro., Bros., Inc., Ltd., RR,* and so on: *Nova Corp., Smith Bros.*

44f | Units of Measure

1 Spelling out in-text units of measure

When you spell out units of measure in the text of your writing, respect singular and plural endings: inches, cubic foot, kilograms, metres, megabytes, ounces, and so on. Use standard abbreviations for imperial measures in scientific writing and notes. (See 44a2.)

2 Abbreviating in scientific or technical writing and notes

Follow standard metric and the International System of Units (SI) abbreviations:

mm	millimetre	g	gram	N	newton
cm²	square centimetre	kg	kilogram	V	volt
m	metre	t	tonne	W	watt
km²	square kilometre	mHz	megahertz	M	nautical mile
ha	hectare	kPa	kilopascal	s	second
mL	millilitre	A	ampere	min	minute
L	litre	J	joule	h	hour
m³	cubic metre	K	kelvin	d	day

44g | Scholarly, technical, and Latin terms

Avoid Latin and other scholarly abbreviations in the text of your writing, unless they appear in material enclosed in parentheses. Such abbreviations are appropriate in tables, notes, and documentation. In text, use the

English equivalents of the Latin terms, and spell out ordinary English words. (See also 54b and 56b3.)

c.	*circa,* "around"	MS, MSS	manuscript, manuscripts
cf.	*confer,* "compare"	NB, n.b.	*nota bene,* "note well"
e.g.	*exempli gratia,* "for example"	n.d.	no date of publication
et al.	*et alia,* "and others"	n.p.	no place of publication, no publisher
f., ff.	that or those following	p., pp.	page, pages
i.e.	*id est,* "that is"	vs., v.	versus, "against"
l., ll.	line, lines		

chapter

45 Numbers

45*a* Write numbers as words or figures according to the following guidelines

1 Spelling out numbers that begin sentences

Spell out a number that begins a sentence. If the number is large, rewrite or rearrange the sentence. Compare these examples:

Three hundred students visited Upper Canada Village on their field

trip.

The strike involves

465 employees ~~are on strike~~

2 Using Modern Language Association guidelines for numbers

- Spell out large whole numbers expressible in two words, and spell out whole numbers from one to ninety-nine, including zero if it would be confusing to write the figure "0": *seven, eighteen, twenty-six, two hundred, fifteen thousand.* Use a hyphen for the numbers twenty-one to ninety-nine. Exceptions: When using numbers in technical or business writing, use figures for all numbers except those beginning a sentence. Always use figures in addresses: *PO Box 14, 15 West 43rd Street.*

- Use figures for numbers expressed in more than two words: *340*; *1,650*; *2,989,000*. Use commas to separate groups of three digits, except in addresses (*11460 Yonge Street*), telephone numbers (*613-372-2729*), dates (*1999*), and page numbers (*p. 1048*).

3 Using American Psychological Association guidelines for numbers

- Spell out the numbers one to nine.
- Use figures for numbers over nine: *10*; *68*; *3,462*.

4 Punctuating numbers

- Traditionally, commas have separated groups of three digits (see 2 above). But, because the Metric System uses the comma as a decimal, Canadian style prefers leaving a space to using the comma with groups of three digits: *12 964*; *3 297 567*. This practice also applies to large decimals: *3.141 59*. You will see the substitution of the space for the comma in all government documents, the exception being financial statements and fiscal records.

- With four-digit numbers, the space (or the comma) is optional: *4004* or *4 004* or *4,004*. If your text includes larger numbers, however, punctuate your four-digit numbers just like the larger numbers.

5 Using numbers for time, dates, and time periods

- Time. Spell out the time except when using *a.m.* or *p.m.*: *seven o'clock in the morning, twelve midnight, half past four, 6:30 a.m., 9:45 p.m.*

- Decades. Spell out decades or use figures: *the nineties, the '90s, the 1990s*.

- Centuries. Spell out centuries; hyphenate when used as adjectives.

  In the **twentieth century,** major wars were fought in nearly every decade.

  Next semester I'm taking a **twentieth-century** American history course.

- Historical dates with abbreviations. Use figures with AD, BC, BCE (Before the Common Era), and CE (Common Era): *AD 1066, 461 BC, 32 BCE, 1456 CE*. Notice that *AD* (*anno Domini* or "year of our Lord") precedes the date; BC ("before Christ") follows.

- Inclusive dates. For inclusive dates, write both years in full unless they are in the same century: *1895–1910* but *1941–45*.

6 Writing fractions, ordinal numbers, and ratios

■ Common fractions and ordinal numbers. Spell out common fractions (*one-half, two-thirds*) and the ordinal numbers *first* to *ninth*.

Nearly **one-half** of our employees have been sick since the **first** of the year.

■ Decimal fractions, numbers followed by fractions, and ratios. Write decimal fractions, numbers followed by fractions, and ratios as figures: *a 10.3 grade average, a hat size of 7 and ⁷/₈ , a ratio of 4:1* [or *four to one*].

7 Writing numbers with abbreviations and symbols

Use figures with abbreviations and symbols.

$34.97	65 km/h	62.7 cm	35–mm film
16%	9 V battery	4″ x 6″	4 h 10 min 07 s
4 MB	50 lbs.	32°-43°	49°N lat.

An MLA note: If your writing contains few numbers, spell out one-, two- and three-word percentages and amounts of money: twenty-six percent, sixty-nine cents, four hundred dollars.

8 Writing well-known phrases containing numbers

Generally, spell out well-known phrases containing numbers: *the Ten Commandments, the Twelve Apostles, the Fourth of July.*

9 Writing page numbers and divisions of written works

Use figures for page numbers, book divisions, and acts, scenes, and lines of plays: *page 7, p. 47, volume 5, chapter 16;* Hamlet *3.2.46* or Hamlet *III.ii.46.*

An MLA note: To cite inclusive page numbers, give the second page number in full, through *99: 7–23, 85–96.* For larger numbers, give the last two digits of the second number unless more are necessary to prevent confusion: *122–34, 200–05, 1220–32* but *98–103, 287–303, 1238–1342.*

An APA note: When citing inclusive numbers, give all the digits of both numbers: *23–32, 458–467, 1152–1158.*

45b | When one number modifies another, write one as a figure, the other as a word

1 Writing large rounded numbers

Write large rounded numbers as a combination of figures and words.

The population of China today is **1.25 billion.**

Damages from the flooding were estimated at **$2.4 million**.

2 Writing back-to-back numbers

Write back-to-back numbers as a combination of figures and words.

Last year Maria taught a class of **34 ten**-year-olds.

The order requests **seventy-five 8 x 10** glossy prints.

The **first 10** customers were given a potted plant.

45*c* Write related numbers alike, as words or figures

Related numbers that appear together in the same sentence or paragraph should be written alike, as words or figures. If, according to the guidelines in 45a, you write some numbers as figures, be consistent and write all the numbers in your series as figures.

Within two decades, the university enrolment has grown from

~~ten thousand~~ *10 000* to 25 550 students.

chapter

46 The Hyphen

Type a hyphen as one keystroke, with no space before or after: *self-starter*. Do not confuse a hyphen (-) with a dash (—). (See 41a.) To use hyphens correctly, note how your dictionary lists words:

- Use a hyphen to join words listed with a hyphen (*half-life*).
- Compounds listed as two words (*half note*) are written without hyphens.

46*a* Avoid word division at the end of a line

The Modern Language Association and American Psychological Association guidelines forbid word division at the end of a line, and this is good advice for most writing. If a whole word won't fit, leave the line a little short and begin on the next line. Most word-processing programs have automatic "word wrap" to do this for you.

If you run out of space when writing longhand, you may be obliged to divide a multisyllable word. Refer to your dictionary to divide the word at a syllable (marked by a dot). The word **har·mo·nize** can be divided *har-monize* or *harmo-nize*. If you have to divide an already hyphenated word or personal name, follow these guidelines.

- Divide already hyphenated words only at the hyphen.

  Downhill skiing became more frightening than exciting for me after my ~~brother in-law~~ broke his leg in a bad fall. ^brother-in-law^

- Divide personal names (1) between first and last names: Emily / Carr; (2) after the middle initial: Jean J. / Charest; (3) if necessary, between initials and the last name: k. d. / lang. Never divide between initials.

46b | Use a dictionary to hyphenate compounds

A compound is a word made up of two or more words. Compounds may be hyphenated (*cross-examine, cross-reference, cross-stitch*), written as separate words (*hot cross bun, cross section, cross street*), or written as one word (*crossbar, crossroads, crossword*). Your dictionary will show you the correct forms. If you don't find a compound listed, write it as two words.

46c | Hyphenate compound adjectives before a noun but not following a noun

Compare the following pairs of sentences.

I've written a **first-rate** essay. My essay is **first rate.**

Darrell uncorked a **seven-year-old** bottle of wine. Darrell uncorked a bottle of wine that was **seven years old.**

The film received **less-than-enthusiastic** reviews. The reviews were **less than enthusiastic.**

A note on -ly *adverbs:* Do not hyphenate a compound modifier consisting of an -ly adverb and an adjective or participle.

Heavily/travelled mountain paths contribute to significant soil erosion.

A note on hyphenated adjectives in series: In a series of hyphenated adjectives, suspend the second word of each compound until the last: *Whether we rent a two-, three-, or four-bedroom cottage will depend on our finances.*

46d Hyphenate following the prefixes *all-*, *ex-*, *great-*, *self-* and before the suffix *-elect*

all-star athlete   great-grandmother   self-respect
ex-husband   great-great-grandson   self-fulfilling prophecy
ex-mayor   president-elect

46e Hyphenate spelled-out fractions, numbers twenty-one to ninety-nine, and combinations of figures and words

one-half   forty-seven   100-yard dash
two-thirds   fifty-two   mid-1800s
seven-eighths   eighty-eight   pre-1960

46f Hyphenate to prevent misreading

Without hyphens, some words might be misread or confused with other words.

> Until a fertilized ovum is implanted in the uterus, it exists in a
> pre-embryonic
> ~~preembryonic~~ state.
> ^
>
> [Without a hyphen, readers may pronounce one long *e* sound instead of a long *e* followed by a short *e*.]

> re-sign
> The lawyer asked her client to ~~resign~~ the agreement.
> ^
>
> [Without a hyphen, *re-sign*, "to sign again," could be confused with *resign*, "to relinquish."]

Spelling and Document Formatting

47 Spelling

47a | Follow Canadian spelling practices

Thirty years ago, no one could have foreseen the tremendous influence our neighbours to the south would have on our spelling. Now, with satellite television and electronic word processing, only a few important differences remain to characterize Canadian spelling, some of which are almost a matter of national pride. When writing for a Canadian audience, then, ignore the spell checker on your word processor if it questions words that you have found in your Canadian dictionary. Although some alternatives are more common than others, you can generally count on the following preferred Canadian spellings:

- *aesthetic, axe, cheque, plough* (farm implement), but *snowplow*

- *analyze, colonize, criticize, organize, realize, recognize, specialize, synchronize,* but *advertise, apprise, chastise, surprise*

- *armour, behaviour, clamour, colour, favour, flavour, glamour, honour, humour, labour, neighbour, odour, vigour,* but *ardor, coloration, decor, honorary, humorous, odorous, vapor, vigorous*

- *buses* [noun], *bussed* [verb], *focuses* [noun], *focusses* [verb], *gases* [noun], *gassed* [verb], *licence* [noun], *license* [verb], *practice* [noun], *practise* [verb]

- *calibre, centre, fibre, litre, lustre, manoeuvre, metre, sabre, theatre*

- *cancelled, councillor, counselled, jewellery, kidnapping, labelled, panelling, pedalled, rebelled, signalled, travelled, worshipped*

- *catalogue, demagogue, dialogue, monologue,* but *analog*

- *defence, offence, pretence*

- *enrolment, fulfilment, instalment, skilful,* but *enrolled, fulfilled, installed, skilled*

How to...

How to Edit Spelling

If you don't have a dictionary, spell checker, or spelling guide available, use these tips to figure out the correct spelling of words.

1. Compare spellings. Write out alternative spellings to compare. Correctly spelled words often look and feel right.

2. Disassemble words. Divide them into syllables and sound them out. Try to see and hear the word as you've actually spelled it. Is it *tra-deg-y* or *tra-ged-y*? *lon-li-ness* or *lone-li-ness*? *nec-cess-ary* or *ne-cess-ary*? *di-satisfied* or *dis-satisfied*? *tom-morrow* or *to-morrow*? [The second in each set is correct.]

3. Find related words to help you spell the unaccented vowels that often sound like *uh* no matter what their spelling.

   comp ? tition + comPETE
     = competition
   compar ? tive + compaRAble
     = comparative
   democr ? cy + demoCRATic
     = democracy
   exhil ? rate + hiLARity
     = exhilarate

   infin ? te + fiNITE
     = infinite
   mir ? cle + mirACulous
     = miracle
   monot ? nous + monoTONE
     = monotonous
   prev ? lent + VALue
     = prevalent

4. Use memory aids. Make up phrases or sentences to associate with the correct spelling of words—like "The princiPAL is my PAL." How about "I get all *A*'s in grAmmAr" or "There is A RAT in sepARATe." You can think of others.

When you've finished revising, focus on spelling as you proofread. Read your writing backward, from the end to the beginning, to help you look at each word. Lay a straight edge beneath each line. To spot omitted or sound-alike words, point at each word with a pen or pencil.

47b | Use a word guide, electronic dictionary, or spell checker

As you edit your writing, look up any words not part of your everyday writing vocabulary. Use one of the following aids.

1 Using word guides

Word guides such as *Webster's Instant Word Guide* are pocket-sized books that list words without definitions, pronunciations, or grammatical information. Because they show only how words are spelled, they're quick and easy to use. If you're sometimes so unsure of a spelling that you can't look up the word, consider consulting a word guide that lists words alphabetically by incorrect as well as correct spellings. Both *phantasy* and *fantazy* will lead you to the correct spelling—*fantasy*.

2 Using electronic dictionaries

Pocket-sized electronic dictionaries such as the *Franklin Wordmaster* will confirm an accurate spelling, correct a misspelling, or provide alternatives for unrecognized words you've typed in. Remember, however, that these are American and will occasionally disagree with Canadian usage. (See 47a.) Look for one with a word list of at least 80 000 words. Test it by misspelling a hard or unfamiliar word like *subpoena*. If the dictionary doesn't recognize your error, try another model or brand.

3 Using spell checkers

If you write with a computer, your word-processing program probably has a spell checker, perhaps one that underlines questionable words as you type. Use it to point out mistakes that result from hasty typing as well as words spelled incorrectly. If available, select the Canadian dictionary setting. But to guard against the limitations of even the most up-to-date programs, always proofread your writing carefully when you finish.

 Computer Tip:

Using Spell Checkers

1. Spell checkers do not distinguish between sound-alike words. If you type *their* when you mean *there*, your spell checker will not correct you.
2. Spell checkers do not correct mistakes that produce correctly spelled words. If you mean to type *now* but type *not* or *no*, your spell checker will not recognize your mistake.

47*c* | Make a checklist of your spelling errors

Make your own personalized spelling checklist to help you avoid errors. Buy a small alphabetically arranged address book or a pocket notebook. Find out which words you misspell and list them there. Write the word down, first as you misspelled it (to help you spot errors as you proofread) and then correctly spelled. To help you see the error, underline it.

WRONG	RIGHT	WRONG	RIGHT
acco<u>mo</u>date	accommodate	occa<u>ss</u>ional	occasional
cemet<u>a</u>ry	cemetery	privile<u>dg</u>e	privilege
con<u>c</u>ensus	consensus	pron<u>o</u>unciation	pronunciation
embar<u>a</u>ssment	embarrassment	s<u>e</u>ige	siege
envir<u>o</u>ment	environment	su<u>c</u>ess	success
ex<u>h</u>orbitant	exorbitant	tempe<u>rm</u>ent	temperament

47*d* | Learn the most important spelling rules

1   Putting *i* before *e*

Almost everyone has heard the beginning of this rhyme; not everyone knows the second line:

> *i* before *e* except after *c*
> or when pronounced *a*, as in neighbour and weigh

- *i* before *e* = *believe, chief, field, relief, siege, yield*

- except after *c* = *ceiling, conceive, deceive, receive*

- [except] when pronounced *a* = *eight, freight, neighbour, vein, weight*

- *i* before *e* exceptions: *conscience, financier, science, species, sufficient*

- *e* before *i* exceptions: *counterfeit, either, foreign, forfeit, heifer, height, leisure, neither, seize, sheik, sovereign, weird*

2   Adding silent *e* at the end of a word

English generally requires a silent *e* at the end of a word to keep a preceding vowel long in sound: *mat/mate, met/mete, kit/kite, hot/hotel, cut/cute*. To add a suffix to a silent *e* word, follow these rules.

- Drop the silent *e* when the suffix begins with a vowel: *cute/cutest, desire/desiring, fame/famous, imagine/imaginary, love/lovable, prime/primal, retrieve/retrieving*. Exceptions: *ageing, mileage*.

- Keep the silent *e* when a suffix begins with a consonant: *achieve/achievement, care/careful, live/lively, lone/lonely, sincere/sincerely.* Exceptions: *argument, awful, truly, duly, wholly.*

- Keep the silent *e* when a word ends in *-ce* or *-ge* and the suffix begins with *a* or *o*: *service/serviceable, change/changeable, courage/courageous.*

- Exceptions to avoid confusion or mispronunciation: *dying/dyeing, towing/toeing, shooing/shoeing, singing/singeing.*

3 Changing *y* to *i*

- When a word ends in a consonant + *y*, change *y* to *i* and add the suffix: *busy/business, community/communities, embody/embodiment, lonely/loneliness, modify/modifier, penny/penniless.* Exceptions: *babyish, cityless, fairylike.*

- When the suffix is *-ing* or *-ist*, do not change the *y* to *i*: *copy + ing = copying, essay + ist = essayist, lobby + ing = lobbying, study + ing = studying.*

- When a word ends in a vowel + *y*, add the suffix: *boy/boyish, buy/buyer, obey/obeying, sway/swayed, valley/valleys.* Exceptions: *daily, laid, paid, said.*

4 Doubling consonants

Double the consonant at the end of a word when the word meets all three of these tests:

- The word ends in a vowel + consonant: *begin, cut, fog, glad, occur, prefer, regret.*

- The suffix begins with a vowel: *-ed, -en, -ing, -y.*

- The word has one syllable or is accented on the final syllable: *beginning, cutting, foggy, gladden, occúrrence, preférring, regrétted.* Don't double the consonant if two vowels come before it or if the word is accented on the first of two or more syllables: *bénefited, concealed, gláddened, labouring, préference.*

5 Adding the suffix *-ly*

- When a word ends with one *-l*, add *-ly*. Do not drop the *-l* at the end of the word: *casual/casually, formal/formally, real/really, usual/usually.*

- When a word already ends in *-ll*, add only *-y*: *chill/chilly, full/fully, hill/hilly.*

6 Adding suffixes to words ending in *-ic*

- When a word ends in *-ic* and the suffix begins with *-e, -i,* or *-y*, add a *-k* before adding the suffix: *trafficked, picnicking, panicky.*

- Some words ending in *-ic* take the suffix *-ally*: *artistically, classically, comically, heroically, logically, tragically,* but not *publicly*.

7 Forming plurals

- To form the plural of most nouns, add *-s* to the singular: *boat + s = boats, glove + s = gloves, shoe + s = shoes, Johnson + s = Johnsons.*

- When a noun ends in *-s, -sh, -ch, -x,* or *-z,* form the plural with *-es*: *Jones + es = Joneses, dish + es = dishes, church + es = churches, box + es = boxes, buzz + es = buzzes.*

- When a noun ends in a consonant + *o,* the plural varies:

ADD -*S* ONLY	ADD -*ES* ONLY	ADD -*S* OR -*ES*
autos	echoes	buffalos, buffaloes
cellos	heroes	cargos, cargoes
concertos	mosquitoes	dominos, dominoes
librettos	potatoes	halos, haloes
memos	tomatoes	mottos, mottoes
pianos		zeros, zeroes

- When a noun ends in *-f* or *-fe,* add *-s* to some words: *roofs, safes, chiefs.* To form the plural of others, change the *f* to *v* and add *-es*: *half/halves, hoof/hooves, leaf/leaves, life/lives, shelf/shelves, thief/thieves, wife/wives.*

- Some words have irregular plurals: *child/children, ox/oxen, goose/geese, mouse/mice.*

- Some words have the same form for singular and plural: *aircraft, beaver, deer, moose, sheep.*

- To form the plural of letters, add an apostrophe + *-s*: *the three R's, dot your i's and cross your t's.*

- To form the plural of numbers and abbreviations (including acronyms), add *-s* without an apostrophe, unless one is needed to prevent confusion: *CDs, 1990s.*

- To form the plural of most compound nouns, add *-s* to the last word unless the first word is more important: *handfuls, hand-me-downs, run-ins, U-turns, vice-principals,* but *editors-in-chief, hangers-on, mothers-in-law, passers-by.*

- To form the plural of most English words that originally were Latin, Greek, or French words, use the plural from the original language:

SINGULAR	PLURAL	SINGULAR	PLURAL
analysis	analyses	erratum	errata
antenna	antennae	medium	media
basis	bases	phenomenon	phenomena
chateau	chateaux	psychosis	psychoses
crisis	crises	radius	radii
criterion	criteria	thesis	theses

chapter

48 Formatting Your Writing

48a Give your writing a professional, easy-to-read appearance

To communicate effectively, your academic, business, and public writing must be neat, easy to read, and appropriately formatted. Two formats for academic writing, the Modern Language Association (MLA) and the American Psychological Association (APA), are described later in this chapter. (See 48c and d.) Other formats are described in the style manuals listed in 59. (For business formats, see 63.) To determine appropriate manuscript form, check with your instructor.

The following principles apply to all manuscript methods:

- *Presentation.* Print or write your work on one side of the page only.

- *Margins.* Leave 2.5 cm margins at the top, bottom, and both sides of the page. If asked to submit the paper in a binder, leave a 3.5 cm left margin.

- *Line justification.* Line up (justify) your left margins, but leave the right margins ragged (unjustified). This is the format used in some parts of this handbook (this list, for example).

- *Spacing.* Always double-space (leave every other line blank) to make your text easy on the reader's eyes. Do not double-doublespace to start a new paragraph or section. Indent the first line instead, or use a heading, without any changes to the spacing.

- *Punctuation.* Never begin a line with a comma, colon, semicolon, hyphen, dash, end punctuation, or part of an ellipsis. Never end a line with opening quotation marks, parentheses, or brackets standing alone, disconnected from a word.

- *Binding.* Staple the pages of your writing. Do not use paperclips, pins, or braids. Do not punch holes in your writing and/or include it in a duotang, binder, or other presentation folder unless expressly requested to do so.

1 Writing with computers

- *Paper.* Use high-quality white 21.5 x 28 cm computer paper. If you use continuous-form paper, remove the perforated edges, separate the pages, and put them in order before turning in your work.

- *Printers.* Ink jet or laser printers are always acceptable. Some readers object to dot-matrix printers. Find out before you begin. If you use a dot-matrix or print-wheel printer, be sure your ribbon is fresh and the paper properly aligned to produce correct margins. If necessary, set your printer to letter-quality or near letter-quality printing.

- *Fonts.* Use standard 10- or 12-point fonts: Times Roman, Courier, Geneva, or Helvetica. Avoid cursive and other fancy fonts.

- *Formatting.* Set automatic formatting commands in advance, including spacing, margins, line justification, automatic paging, word wrap, and headers (most word-processing programs do this for you). Use italics, underlining, and boldface sparingly (see 43), and avoid stylistic flourishes that may distract readers.

- *Corrections.* Proofread your final draft carefully. Run your spell checker, correct, and reprint. Give your paper a last check to be sure everything has printed correctly.

2 Writing with a typewriter

- *Paper.* Use standard-sized white 75 g/m^2 typing paper. If you use erasable paper to make typing easier, turn in a clean photocopy of your final draft, not the erasable draft, which will smudge and probably frustrate your reader.

- *Ribbon.* Use a fresh ribbon, and be sure the typeface is clean.

- *Fonts.* Use 10- or 12-point standard fonts: Times Roman, Courier, Geneva, or Helvetica. Avoid cursive fonts and the all-capitals format.

- *Corrections.* Use correction fluid. Insert corrections by hand or typewriter. If you make numerous or lengthy corrections, retype the page. (For proofreading symbols, see 4d2.)

3 Writing by hand

If possible, avoid handwritten work. Your school or local library probably has typewriters or computers for your use. See your Writing Centre head or a librarian for information. If you must do a take-home assignment by hand, make sure your instructor approves, then follow these guidelines:

- *Paper.* Use high-quality, wide-ruled white paper, 21.5 x 28 cm. Do not use spiral notebook paper. Write on one side of the paper only.
- *Ink.* Write in blue or black ink. Form your letters carefully. Don't run words into each other, and guard against smudges. If your handwriting is difficult to read, then print, but do not use all-capital letters.
- *Spacing and margins.* Write on every other line to the right of the ruled vertical margin. Leave 2.5 cm right and bottom margins.
- *Corrections.* Make corrections neatly, using correction fluid produced for pen and ink. (For a list of proofreading symbols, see 4d2.)

48*b* Use headings, lists, tables, and graphics to clarify ideas

Computer word-processing programs give writers powerful tools for enhancing ideas. Even without a computer, you can add headings, lists, tables, and graphics to your writing. But be aware that too many extra features can break continuity and distract readers. To be effective, visual aids should

- add to, rather than duplicate, your text
- convey information, not be merely decorative
- be easy to understand
- make your subject easier to understand

A note on format: Specific subject areas may have differing formats for visual aids. Ask your instructor.

1   Formatting in-text headings

Essays and many other kinds of writing do not require headings. However, reports and other technical documents such as proposals and grant requests are divided by headings that identify topics and guide readers. If headings are appropriate for your writing, use the following format based on American Psychological Association (APA) guidelines:

- *Heading levels.* Use from one to five levels of heading, depending on the complexity of your writing. The following headings are arranged from most to least important and show the position and capitalization style to use. (See 42 c.)

NATIONAL PARKS IN THE NEW MILLENIUM

Tourist Traffic and Environmental Deterioration

<u>Effects on Birds and Animals</u>

<u>The Plover and Other Coastal Birds</u>

<u>Disturbance to nesting habits:</u> The text of the essay immediately follows the heading on the same line.

Note that the first heading is centred and all capitalized. The second, third (underlined) and fourth (underlined, flush-left) headings are capitalized in the style of titles, whereas the fifth (paragraph indent) heading is capitalized in the style of sentences.

- *Numbering.* Headings are not numbered except in scientific writing.

- *Punctuation and capital letters.* Do not end centred and flush-left headings with a period. For run-in headings at the beginning of paragraphs, capitalize the first letter of the first word, lowercase the remaining words, and end with a period. Underline as in the preceding examples.

- *Spacing.* Double-space above and below headings that appear on a line by themselves. Double-space within multi-line headings.

- *Length and consistency.* Keep your headings brief and grammatically parallel. Headings at a particular level should have the same grammatical form: noun phrases, verb phrases, questions, and so on. (See 21.)

- *Grammar.* Make the grammar of a heading suggest the contents of the section. Use nouns or noun phrases to introduce information or explanation (e.g., *Exotic Species*); *-ing* verbs to introduce processes, actions, or events (e.g., *Preserving Native Species*); commands to introduce instructions (e.g., *Reintroduce Natural Predators*); questions to interest readers (e.g., *How Can We Save Endangered Songbirds?*).

- *Format.* Do not begin a new page for each heading. But if a heading comes at the bottom of a page, move it to the next page unless it is followed by at least two lines of text.

2 Formatting lists

Use lists to clarify steps in a process, materials, ingredients, parts, advice, or items to be covered. To make a list, follow these guidelines:

- Write an introductory sentence followed by a colon, as in the sentence just above.

- Precede each item in a list with a marker: a dash or a bullet (•) followed by a space, or a letter or number followed by a period and two spaces.

- Begin each item flush with the left margin. If the item is longer than one line, indent the second and subsequent lines five spaces to make a hanging paragraph.

- Make items grammatically parallel: use balanced words, phrases or other grammatical forms. (See 21.)

- Do not use periods after items in a vertical list unless the items are all complete sentences.

3 Formatting tables

Tables present information in a systematic way, usually in columns. Use tables sparingly to avoid complex, number-filled text. Place each table close to its first mention in the text. Give each title a number: *Table 1, Table 2,* and so on. Briefly introduce each table in a sentence or refer to it in parentheses: (*see Table 1*). Here are the Modern Languages (MLA) guidelines for tables. (See Table 1, p. 319.)

- Double-space throughout each table. Do not use all capital letters.

- Position the Table number (e.g., *Table 1*) flush-left on a line by itself. Then double-space and provide a descriptive caption, also placed flush left. If the caption is long, indent each additional line two spaces from the left. Double-space the captaion. Don't use all capital letters.

- Between ruled lines, insert headings for each column.

- Arrange each column beneath its heading.

- Two spaces below the table, make a ruled bottom line.

- Two spaces beneath the bottom line, after the word *Source* followed by a colon and a space, give the source of the table, if there is one. Indent any additional lines, two spaces.

- Use raised lower-case letters (e.g., [a, b, c,] and so on) for notes to the table.

An APA note: Underline the descriptive caption preceding the table (e.g., <u>1991 Distribution of Population by First Language in the Atlantic Provinces</u>). After the table, in place of the word *Source*, use *Note* underlined and followed by an underlined period and then two spaces (<u>Note.</u>). Cite the source of the information according to APA format. (See 56c.)

Table 1

1991 Distribution of Population by First Language in the Atlantic

Provinces

Province	Total[a]	English	French	Other
Newfoundland	563 345	555 645	2 770	4 930
P.E.I.	127 740	120 590	5 590	1 560
Nova Scotia	887 820	830 120	36 635	21 065
New Brunswick	711 745	460 540	241 565	9 640

Source: Adapted from Statistics Canada, Catalogue no. 93-333.

<http://www.statcan.ca/Documents/English/Pgdb/People/

Population/demo18a.html, February 4, 1997>.

[a]Totals include only those speakers who identified themselves as

unilingual, not bilingual.

4 Displaying graphics

Graphics or figures include charts, drawings, maps, graphs, and pho-tographs. Use them to reveal relationships among data, to draw attention to details, and to dramatize important points. Draw them by hand, cut and paste reproductions, or use a computer graphics program. Introduce each graphic and place it appropriately on the page near related text. Give ap-propriate documentation following the graphic. These are the MLA guide-lines:

- Double-space below your graphic. Flush left, write the label "Fig." and an Arabic numeral followed by a period (see Figure 1 on p. 320).

- On the same line, write a capitalized caption, followed by a comma and documentation of the source. Double-space throughout.

- See the examples of a drawing, a pie chart and a line graph that follow (pages 320–321). See also the bar graph in the sample MLA research paper (p. 409).

An APA note: Below the graph, write and underline the word *Figure,* the numeral, and a period, (Figure 1.). Then leave two spaces and write a caption, using sentence-style punctuation. If necessary, type "from" and document the source of the graphic, using the appropriate APA citation format (see 56c).

A drawing that represents relationships

Fig. 1. Maslow's Needs Hierarchy, from Abraham H. Maslow, <u>Motivation and Personality</u>, 2nd ed. (New York: Harper, 1970).

A pie chart that reveals proportions

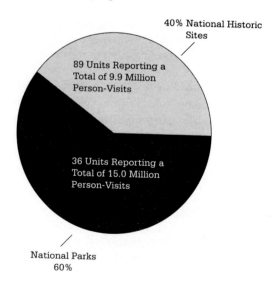

Fig. 2. Parks Canada Attendance by Program (1998–99).

A line graph that reveals related information and changes over time

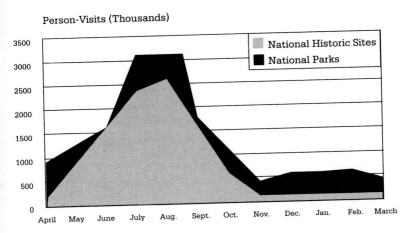

Fig. 3. Parks Canada Attendance by Program (1998–99).

48c Use the Modern Language Association format for writing in the humanities

The following format, based on the *MLA Handbook for Writers of Research Papers*, 5th ed. (New York: MLA, 1999), is appropriate for writing in English composition, literature, and foreign language courses; it is also used in the humanities, philosophy, religion, and history.

Note: See 48a for general information on computerized writing and on typewritten and handwritten work. To determine the appropriate format for your papers, check with your instructor.

1 Formatting the identification heading and title

Most short assignments do not require a title. Use an identification heading instead. On your first page, 2.5 cm from the top and left margins, list your name, your instructor's name, course, section number, and date, double-spacing throughout. Double-space to reach the title line; centre your title. If your title runs more than one line, double-space the lines. Use a colon between a title and subtitle. Capitalize the first and last words and all words except articles, prepositions, conjunctions, and the *to* in infinitives (e.g., *to Write*). Do not use underlining, italics, and quotation marks unless your title contains another title or a direct quotation. Double-space between your title and the first line of text. (See 4f, 55, and 60g for sample papers in the MLA format.)

2 Formatting the title page

If your instructor requires a title page, centre your title one-third of the way down the page. In the centre of the page, write "by," double-space, and give your name. Two-thirds down the page and centred on separate lines, write the course name, your instructor's name, and the date, double-spacing between lines. On the first page of text, repeat your title, centred on the first line. Double-space between the title and the first line of text. (See the sample title page in 55.)

3 Indenting

- Indent the first word of a paragraph five spaces from the left margin. If you write by hand, indent 2.5 cm.

- If a prose quotation runs more than four typed lines, indent 2.5 cm or ten spaces from the left margin, none from the right. If an indented quotation runs longer than one paragraph, indent the first line of successive paragraphs an additional three spaces. Indent more than three lines of poetry 2.5 cm or ten spaces from the left margin, or centre the poetry so that it looks balanced on the page. (See 52d.)

4 Spacing

Double-space between all lines, including titles, headings, indented quotations, and outlines. Space once after a colon and after end punctuation (periods, question marks, and quotations). Leave no space between end punctuation and closing quotation marks, parentheses, and brackets. Space once after periods following initials or abbreviations and after periods within bibliographic citations.

5 Paging

If your paper does not have a title page, begin numbering with Arabic numeral one (1) on the first page. In the upper right corner, about 1 cm from the top of the page, put your last name followed by a space and the page number (e.g., *Lopez 1*). Do not use the word *page,* the abbreviation *p.,* parentheses, dashes, or other punctuation. Number consecutively to the end of your paper, including notes and documentation. Double-space beneath the page heading, or position the first line of text 2.5 cm from the top of the page.

If your paper has a title page and other preliminary pages such as an outline, leave the title page unnumbered and use lowercase roman numerals for the other preliminary pages. Count the title page as page 1, but begin page-numbering on the following page, which is page ii. In the upper right corner, about 1 cm from the top, put your name followed by one space and the roman numeral two (e.g., Lopez ii). Use lowercase Roman numerals for all of the preliminary pages ii, iii, iv, and so on. Then, on the first page of text, begin a new series of numbers with Arabic numerals; put your last name followed by a space and the number 1 (e.g., Lopez 1). Double-space beneath the page heading, or position the first line of text 2.5 cm from the top of the page.

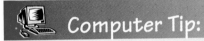

Computer Tip:

Using Headers

Create a page header to insert your name and page numbers automatically at the top of each page. If necessary, turn on the consecutive page numbering feature.

6 Headings

Identify the parts of your paper by appropriate section headings: Outline, the paper's title on the first page of text, Notes, and Works Cited. Centre the heading 2.5 cm from the top of the page, and capitalize it correctly. Double-space to the first line of text. (See the sample research paper in 55.)

In-text topic headings that divide the body of a paper are seldom necessary for essays. However, they may be useful or required for complex technical writing such as reports. (See 48b1.)

7 Ordering pages

Arrange your paper in this order:

Title page, if required
Acknowledgments page, if required
Outline, if required
Body of the paper
Notes, if necessary
Works Cited, if necessary

48d Use the American Psychological Association format for writing in the social sciences

The following format, based on guidelines for student writing in Appendix A to the *Publication Manual of the American Psychological Association,* 4th ed. (Washington, DC: APA, 1994), is appropriate for writing in the social sciences, education, business, linguistics, biology, and earth sciences. Note that the APA format for student papers differs slightly from that of papers to be published in APA journals. Ask your instructor for the appropriate format for your writing.

Note: See 48a for general information on computerized writing and on typewritten and handwritten work.

1 Formatting the title page

Prepare a title page for your paper. (See the APA sample report in 56d.)

- *Page head.* In the top right corner, 1 cm from the top of the page, put a short form of your paper's title (the page head) followed by five spaces and the page number. The page head and page number must appear at the top of all pages of your paper. If you use a computer, you can probably insert the heading and page numbers automatically.

- *Title.* Centre your full title in the middle of the page. Capitalize the first and last words and all words of four letters or more. If your title runs more than one line, double-space; use a colon between a title and a subtitle.

- *Identifying information.* On separate, double-spaced lines beneath the title, put your name, the course title and section number, your instructor's name, and the date.

2 Formatting the preliminary pages

In addition to the title page, you may be required to include some other preliminary pages: acknowledgments, a table of contents, a list of tables and figures, or an abstract. On each preliminary page, type your page header and page number at the top right. Centre the heading for each page, typed in capital and lowercase letters: *Table of Contents, Abstract,* and so on. Double-space beneath the heading.

3 Formatting the abstract

An **abstract** is a brief, comprehensive summary (100–120 words) of your paper. Write the abstract after you have written the paper itself. Report rather than evaluate or comment. Do not use *I* or *we.* Define all terms and abbreviations; write all numbers as figures. Type the abstract in one double-spaced paragraph beginning two lines beneath the heading (*Abstract*). Do *not* indent the first line. (See the example in the sample APA report in 56d.)

4 Indenting

- *Paragraphs.* Indent the first word of a paragraph five spaces from the left margin.

- *Long quotations.* If a quotation runs more than forty words, indent five spaces from the left margin, none from the right. If an indented quotation runs longer than one paragraph, indent the first line of successive paragraphs an additional five spaces. Do not use quotation marks unless they appear in the original.

5 Spacing

Double-space throughout, including titles, headings, quotations, tables, graphics, captions, notes, and references. Space once after commas, semicolons, colons, and after punctuation at the end of a sentence. Leave no space between end punctuation (periods, question marks, and quotations) and closing quotation marks, parentheses, and brackets. Space once after periods following a person's initials and within reference citations.

Note: If your instructor permits, you may single-space within titles, headings, and references to improve readability. You may triple-space or quadruple-space before major in-text headings and before and after in-text tables.

6 Placing tables and figures

Unless instructed otherwise, place tables and figures in the body of your paper, near the text they illustrate. (See also 48b3.)

7 Paging

Unless instructed otherwise, number the pages of your paper consecutively, beginning with the title page and continuing to the end, including notes, references, and appendixes. Use Arabic numerals (1, 2, 3, and so on). At the right margin, 1 cm from the top of the page, put the page header of your paper followed by five spaces and the page number. Double-space beneath the page number.

A note on preliminary pages: Your instructor may require that you use lowercase Roman numerals (i, ii, iii, and so on) for preliminary pages such as the title page and abstract.

8 Formatting in-text headings

APA-style papers frequently contain in-text section and topic headings. (See 48b1 for placement and capitalization information.)

9 Arranging the order of parts

Arrange an APA paper in this order:

Title page
Acknowledgments page, if required
Table of Contents, if required
List of Tables and Figures, if required
Abstract, if required
Text of the paper
References
Appendixes, if required

48*e* Create a Web site for academic or personal use

An increasingly popular assignment in writing classes is the composition of Web sites. As your Internet interests expand, you may even want to create a Web site for personal use. To begin with, a basic Web site consists of three parts: (1) text written by you, (2) links to other Web sites, and (3) interesting and appropriate graphics. Advanced pages may include animation, sound, movies, tables, and frames. However, you should try these only when you are more comfortable with simpler pages.

The code needed to produce Web pages (called *HTML* for *HyperText Markup Language*) is not difficult to learn, but it is easier to use a commercial Web site layout program to produce your page. Such programs enable you to make the page look the way you want it to, and then the software writes the necessary HTML code for you. In fact, most modern word processing programs can turn a word-processed document into HTML.

1 Creating the Site

Composing a Web site is similar in many ways to composing any other piece of writing. You need to plan your page beforehand, write a rough draft, and then revise it until you have it the way you want it. To plan your site, follow these guidelines:

- *Consider your purpose and audience.* Be sure you actually have a purpose—that is, be sure that you're adding something of value to the Internet. Ask yourself, does anyone really want to see pictures of your cat or your bicycle?

- *Sketch out the contents of your entire Web site*—that is, all the interlinked screens or pages you'll be creating. What information needs to be on the opening page, the **home page**? What needs to be on other pages linked from the home page?

- *Decide on the text you'll include.* Research the Web for other sites to link to. Either create or find the graphical material you'll use. Now you're ready to work on creating the actual site.

- *Begin composing the rough draft of your site.* Text on a computer screen is more difficult to read than text on paper. For this reason, make your pages easy to understand at a single glance. Keep them short (one or two full screens at most), with lots of white space and carefully chosen graphics. Think of Web sites as interlinked pages (links to related pages—your own or others), not as long essays. Write in short paragraphs and relatively short sentences.

- *Make effective use of the tools that HTML provides you:* headings of various sizes, indented blocks of text, centred text and images, bulleted and numbered lists, and horizontal rules to make the structure of your page immediately apparent to the reader. Treat your text with the same care you treat the text in other academic papers: carefully revise it until it reads the way you want it to for your audience. (For more formatting tips, see 48b.)

- *Add your graphics.* Use graphics sparingly but effectively. And try to keep them small, because in the split-second world of the Internet, readers will not wait minutes for images to appear, no matter how wonderful they are. Finally, avoid using images that move, flash, or blink. They may distract or even annoy your reader.

- *Create links.* A link is the *hot* text (usually shown in blue and underlined) which transports the reader to another Web site somewhere else on the Internet. A link to another Web site looks like this: **http://www.abacon.com**. Consider linking your site to other pages within your own Web site and to useful e-mail addresses. Be sure to make navigation easy and to provide links back and forth to all other levels (pages) of your site.

- *Use* mailto *tags.* One variation on the link is the *mailto* tag. Instead of providing the user with an *http://*-type Web address (called a *URL,* for *Uniform Resource Locator*), you provide an e-mail address, usually your own. Then, when a reader clicks on this link, a message is automatically preaddressed to that e-mail address. The reader only needs to compose his or her message and send it directly to you. A *mailto* link looks like this: **mailto:jcormier@carletonu.ca**.

- *Add the date and your address.* As a matter of etiquette, at the bottom of the first page, provide the date the page was created or most recently changed, and include your own e-mail address.

- *Keep revising and testing.* Test everything continuously. Is the page attractive and simple to grasp? Is the writing clear and effective? Do all the links work? When you answer these questions affirmatively, you're ready to upload your complete Web site—all linked pages and graphics—onto your Web server.

2 Some final tips

Since pages will look slightly different when viewed in different browsers, test and refine your page on both Macintosh and Windows computers, using both Netscape Communicator and Microsoft Internet Explorer browsers.

The Web changes rapidly. You must maintain your Web site after creating it. Update it frequently. Keep all content up to date. Recheck all links. For a guide to establishing your own Web site, look at <http://www.sitelaunch.net>.

For a complete discussion of writing for the Web, look for help at <http://www.htmlhelp.com>. For a sample site illustrating the principles of Web design covered in this section, see the Allyn & Bacon Web site opposite.

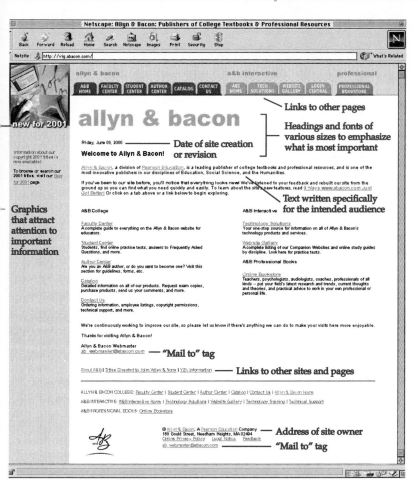

Site designed to move users from left to right and top to bottom
Sparing use of simple, easy-to-understand graphics

49 Choosing a Topic, Finding Sources, Preparing a Bibliography

The research project is such an efficient method for gathering and presenting reliable information that it is a frequent assignment in school and other environments where facts and ideas are important. The research papers you write will be similar to those written by professionals: reports, reviews of other researchers' findings, thesis-support essays, and literary research papers. The following guidelines will help you meet the special challenges of these projects.

49*a* | Choose a "researchable" topic

1 Identifying possible topics

In most respects, choosing a research paper topic is like choosing any topic. The topic you choose should interest you and stimulate your curiosity. (See the guidelines for choosing topics in 2a5.) Research projects, however, follow an additional guideline: your topic must be genuinely researchable, with reliable information and trustworthy opinions available to you. To identify appropriate topics, here's what to do:

- *Ask the experts.* If you don't already have a list of topics given to you as part of an assignment, ask your professor or other experts for recommendations.

- *Check reference sources.* Read about interesting topics in encyclopedias or other reference works. Look for problems, questions, or controversies that have stimulated the writing of scholars and others. A librarian will help you locate these sources.

- *Check source lists.* Skim bibliographies, indexes, and other source lists in your library. The titles of books and articles may suggest topics that have received the serious attention necessary for your research.

- *Think critically about current popular topics.* Before you choose a current popular topic like abortion, the legalization of marijuana, or same-sex marriages, ask yourself whether you have significant questions to answer or serious opinions to test. If you choose a topic only because everyone else is talking about it, your research project may end up boring your readers—and you. Also consider the sources of information available on popular topics. Newspapers, magazines, and the Internet may be filled with them, but their information may be unreliable. Look for topics that appear to have dependable information sources available. (See 1a3 and 51a and b for guidelines to evaluate information and information sources.)

Computer Tip:

Using Internet Subject Directories

Classified subject directories are Internet search tools that group information sources according to topics (see 50a1). Look up topics that interest you to find sources on your topic. The sources' titles alone may suggest problems, questions, or controversies worth investigating.

2 Narrowing and focussing your topic

Professional researchers rarely investigate a whole topic in one project. They choose a part, a single issue, or a key question to investigate in depth in the time available. Do the same. Once you have a topic, narrow it and draw the line of inquiry you'll follow in your research.

- *Writing baseline notes.* Before you begin research, write brief notes exploring your current thinking about your topic and establishing a baseline for investigation. Write down what you feel, believe, and know. Remind yourself where your ideas have come from. Are your sources trustworthy? Your notes may raise research questions for you to answer. They may also reveal assumptions that influence your thinking. Knowing your biases will help you evaluate information more objectively.

- *Reading background material.* If you haven't already read encyclopedias or reference sources, do so now. Look for enduring issues, questions, or problems having to do with your topic. Your librarian will help you locate these sources.

- *Posing key questions or describing a problem.* Pose questions to answer. (They may combine the reporter's six questions: *who, what, when, where, why,* and *how.*) Or briefly describe a problem for your research to solve. For example:

The popularity of our national parks has a negative effect on the environment and the wildlife. Are there any solutions?

- *Stating your purposes.* Your purposes may change as you investigate a topic, perhaps transforming you from a reporter of information to an advocate for a position. But thinking about your purpose will reveal what you're looking for and why. Write a brief statement about why you're investigating your topic. For example:

My purpose is to investigate interpretations of Sinclair Ross's "The Painted Door" to consider the impact of nature on the main characters.

- *Writing a tentative thesis.* What do you expect to discover by your research? If you know little about your subject, you'll have little to say here, but if your purposes are critical or argumentative, you may already have opinions. Research may lead you to revise your thesis, even disprove it, but stating it now will point the direction of your investigation. Write your thesis as a declarative sentence. It will fill the blank in the following pattern:

I am convinced that _____ .

I am convinced that the parallels in Sinclair Ross's "The Painted Door" present human nature as ultimately more destructive than nature itself.

How to Focus a Research Project

How to . . .

At the beginning of a research project, many things about your project will seem unclear—especially if you've not written many research papers. Help yourself focus your project by writing the following exercise. Complete as many items as possible.

1. My general subject area:
2. My specific research topic:
3. My key question:
4. My purposes (to report, explain, evaluate, or persuade):
5. My tentative thesis (if possible):
6. What words in my topic, question, or thesis are vague or unclear? What opposing opinions or questions could be offered in response to my thesis? Do my stated purposes fit the language of my questions or thesis?
7. The date this project is due:
   a. Number of days for researching:
   b. Number of days for organizing:
   c. Number of days for writing:
   d. Number of days for revising and preparing the final draft:

49*b* | Choose a variety of appropriate sources

Good research projects use a variety of sources that provide different kinds of information and differing viewpoints. As you begin a search for sources, consider what will meet your needs.

1 Locating primary and secondary sources

Primary sources provide the raw materials of a subject, unfiltered and unexplained. Sinclair Ross's short story "The Painted Door," like all literary works, is a primary source. So are the annual records of fish caught off the east coast and estimates of their remaining numbers. So, too, are interviews, eyewitness accounts, personal papers, court records, news stories, and the results of surveys and experiments. Part of your work as a researcher is to give raw materials the evaluation and explanation that will make them meaningful.

Secondary sources explain and interpret primary sources, and present opinions. A scholar's essay evaluating "The Painted Door" is a secondary source, as is an article arguing for a continuing moratorium on cod fishing in the Maritimes. Secondary sources use primary source information to help fulfill their purposes.

In your research, you'll use both kinds of sources, perhaps secondary more than primary. But whenever possible, use primary sources to form your own opinions.

2 Locating balanced sources

If you've chosen a controversial topic, such as smoking bans or provincial funding of private schools, look for sources to represent all sides. The best correction for undue bias in one source—which you may not see if you read only one side of an issue—is a voice from the other side. Divide your research among competing opinions. Read those you disagree with as well as those you agree with. You'll end up with a fairer, clearer presentation of your topic and opinions.

3 Locating electronic sources

With the rapid development of computer technology, a vast number of sources are now available electronically. CD-ROM publications will, among other things, provide you with reference sources, indexes such as the *Academic Index,* and encyclopedias such as *Encarta.* Sources available through a computer network and the Internet include electronic books and periodicals, government documents and information services, scientific and meteorological databases, business documents, announcements by special-interest organizations, mailing lists, and personal communications.

There are electronic sources for nearly every researcher. (For more on searching the Internet, see 50a–d.)

4 Using a checklist of sources

The following list indicates the range of sources available to you. Look it over at the beginning of your project, and check off appropriate sources. Come back to the list later, in the middle of your research when you know more about your topic, to identify other possibilities.

_____ *Bibliographies, abstracts, indexes, and Internet subject directories.* These references provide the publication information necessary to locate books, articles, and other sources on your topic. Examples: *MLA International Bibliography* and various academic abstracts like those in the *Social Sciences Index.* Available in print or electronically.

_____ *Encyclopedias.* General encyclopedias such as the *Encyclopedia Britannica* will provide background information on your topic. Specialized encyclopedias such as the *Encyclopedia Canadiana, Encyclopedia of Psychology,* and *Encyclopedia of Biological Sciences* provide more specific information. Available in print or electronically.

_____ *Other references.* Similar to encyclopedias are biographical guides such as the *Dictionary of Canadian Biography;* abstracts, almanacs, and yearbooks such as *Facts on File* or *World Almanac and Book of Facts;* atlases such as the *National Geographic Atlas of the World;* and dictionaries.

_____ *Books.* Indispensable for most academic research, books give long and broad views of a subject. Classic literary works are increasingly available electronically. On the Internet, see Project Gutenberg and IPL (International Public Library).

_____ *Essays in anthologies.* Scholars frequently compile the best essays on a particular topic and publish them together in book form. Published conference proceedings and papers are another worthwhile source. Such collections are frequently available on literary and controversial topics.

_____ *Book reviews.* Book reviews are available in periodicals, in electronic versions of periodicals, and in summarized form in *Book Review Digest, Book Review Index to Social Science Periodicals,* or *Current Book Review Citations.* Check back issues of *Quill & Quire* as well. Check all these sources in print or on the Internet to evaluate a book's quality and coverage of a topic.

_____ *Articles.* Periodical articles are often more current and focussed than books. When possible, rely on scholarly articles in academic journals, written by experts for experts, instead of articles in popular magazines written for general audiences. Available in print and electronically. Refer to the *Canadian Periodical Index.*

_____ *Newspapers.* Complete editions of major newspapers, such as the *Globe and Mail* and the *New York Times,* are available at your library in microfilm form. Daily editions are available electronically. Individual news stories from local newspapers are available through *Canadian News Disc,* available on CD-ROM.

_____ *Information services.* Professional and commercial services such as Dialogue, Nexis/Lexis, and ERIC provide publication information on a vast number of topics. They frequently provide abstracts or full texts of the documents they list. Available electronically, usually through the computers in your library's reference section.

_____ *Government documents.* Government sources contain legislative and judicial information, scientific reports, statistics, cultural and historical information, recreational and health information, and practical how-to information. Available in print and electronically.

_____ *Archival materials.* Most libraries have special collections of letters, diaries, rare books, and local historical materials. Check the *Catalogue of the Public Archives in Canada.*

_____ *Audiovisual materials.* Maps, charts, photos of visual art, films, musical recordings, tapes, or recorded television and radio programs may be appropriate for your topic. Many are available both in print and electronically.

_____ *Special on-line sources.* E-mail, computer bulletin boards, news group subscription services, and discussion groups may provide you with expert or personal sources of information. Use these sources with care. (See 50e and 51b.)

_____ *Businesses, government agencies, and other organizations.* Businesses and other special-interest organizations may provide you with print or electronic sources of information related to your topic, or experts to interview. For an overview of what's available, check *Canada's Sourcebook,* also available on CD-ROM.

_____ *Surveys and interviews.* You may develop your own sources of information by conducting interviews or surveys.

49c Follow a systematic search strategy to identify sources

1 General search guidelines

- *Consult reference librarians.* Whenever you have a research question you can't answer on your own, turn to reference librarians. They are experts on the library and research.

- *List key words.* List key words for your topic that you'll use to search for sources; for example, key words for research on Sinclair Ross's

"The Painted Door" might include his name and the title of the story, *alienation* (one of the topics of the story), and *prairie writing* (the genre of the writing).

- *List synonyms and related terms.* As you list key words, think of synonyms to expand or narrow your search. Research on national parks might use such related terms as *government lands, federal lands, national forests, wilderness, conservation,* or *environmentalism.*

- *Use library guides.* The *Library of Congress Guide to Subject Headings,* a multi-volume work available in your library's reference section, identifies subject headings for the classification system used internationally. For uniquely Canadian topics, consult the National Library of Canada's *Canadian Subject Headings.* Your reference librarian will show you how to use these sources to identify key search words.

- *Expand or narrow the search.* If key words are not leading to sources, expand your search with more general words, or narrow it with more restrictive ones. A researcher getting nowhere using "The Painted Door" as a search term might expand his search using the author's name. Another researcher, not finding what she wants using the term *national parks,* might narrow her search to specific parks like Banff or Yoho.

- *Learn the abbreviations for search terms.* Nearly every search tool, print or electronic, uses abbreviations in its description of sources. Learn what these stand for by checking introductory glossaries or help screens.

- *Take advantage of special library services.* Many libraries will reserve sources for you on request or order them through interlibrary loan. See your reference librarian early in your research process.

2 Special guidelines for electronic searches

- *Find help electronically.* Most electronic search tools come with instructions for their use. Look for introductory screens, welcome messages, help screens, or files with names like "?", "Readme," "About . . . ," "FAQ [frequently asked questions]," or "Formulating a search with . . . ."

- *Use word variations.* In addition to key words and synonyms, try singular or plural word forms, different word combinations (*parks, national parks, government land,* and so on), different disciplines (botany instead of biology, psychology instead of literature), and truncated words in which an asterisk (*) or a pound sign (#) replaces part of a word (*environ** will help you search for sources containing key words such as *environment, environmental, environmentalist, environmentalism,* and *environmental movement*).

- *Use Boolean searching.* A **Boolean search** (named after George Boole, a nineteenth-century mathematician and logician) uses the terms **AND, OR, NOT** and **NEAR** (written in all capital letters) to expand or restrict a search.

  AND. If you tell an electronic search tool to look for *national parks* alone and *pollution* alone, it will list all works having to do with either subject. But if you tell it to search for *national parks **and** pollution,* it will narrow your search to only those sources in which both terms appear.

  OR. If you wish to expand a search, use *or.* Telling a search tool to look for *preservation or conservation* will lead to all sources that contain either term.

  NOT. Using *not* will narrow a search. Telling a search tool to look for *national parks **not** Banff* will lead to all sources about national parks except those mentioning Banff National Park.

  NEAR, ADJACENT, or **FOLLOWED BY**. In some electronic search tools, especially those used for searching the Internet, you can use **NEAR, ADJACENT,** or **FOLLOWED BY** to narrow a search. Telling a search tool to look for *National Parks **NEAR** pollution* will lead you only to those sources in which these terms appear within a few words of each other.

- *Check accuracy.* If you're not getting anywhere, check your typing for correct spelling and accurate search commands. Also note that not all electronic search tools recognize the Boolean operators described above. Some use symbols like plus or minus signs: + or – (see 50c3).

- *Check abstracts.* Some search tools, especially those on CD-ROM, include abstracts briefly summarizing sources. Check these to decide whether a source is worth reading.

- *Access sources.* Many electronic databases provide options for viewing all or part of a source, downloading it to your computer, or printing it out as hard copy.

49d | Use library search tools to identify sources

1 Using card catalogues and microfilm files

If your library uses cards in drawers or files on microfilm to catalogue its holdings, each source will be listed at least three times—according to subject, author, and title. Look for a heading at the top of each card. If yours is a literary topic, look up the author's name to find information about the work you're studying. Microfilm catalogues may permit you to print publication information.

2 Using computerized catalogues

If you use a computerized library catalogue, you will be presented with a series of successively restricted screens, beginning with an initial search screen, then lists of subject categories, followed by lists of sources, and finally a screen containing detailed publication and availability information about a single source.

See the sample screen below and notice the kinds of information it contains to help you find the source and evaluate its suitability for your research project. *A bibliography note:* When you list publication information for a library source that you intend to use in your paper, arrange it in the appropriate format. (See 54a and b for the MLA format and 56b and c for the APA format.)

Computer Catalogue Screen: Details for a Book

Title:	Best practice guidelines for public use measurement and reporting at parks and protected areas : draft 1 for discussion/ Kenneth E. Hornback, Norm McIntyre, Paul F.J. Eagles.
Authors:	<u>Hornback, Kenneth E.</u> <u>McIntyre, Norm.</u> <u>Eagles, Paul F. J.</u>
Publisher:	Waterloo, Ont.: World Commission on Protected Areas, [1997]
Type of Material:	Book
Format:	Printed Material
Status:	Not Charged
Call Number:	SB48.H674x 1997
Location:	UW Porter, Book Stacks. 6th-10th Floors.
Number of Items:	1
Subject(s):	Parks—Public use. Natural areas.
Description:	52 p. : ill. ; 30 cm.
Notes:	"April 1997." Includes bibliographical references.

- *Use subject, author, and title searches.* Search electronic catalogues for sources as you would a print catalogue, according to subject, author, or title.

- *Expand or narrow a search.* To expand or narrow your search you may combine search terms and use the Boolean operators **AND, OR, NOT,** and **NEAR**. (See 49c2.)

- *Use partial title or author names.* You can search for sources even when you have only a partial title or name. Type in what you know, and the catalogue will list all sources with titles or author names that contain what you've typed.

- *Check availability.* After you've recorded or printed complete publication information for a likely source, use the computer to check for availability (whether it's on the shelf or checked out) and location (in the main stacks, on reserve, or at another library).

3   Using CD-ROM indexes

Indexes contain lists of sources arranged alphabetically. Some, like *The Reader's Guide to Periodical Literature,* list only periodical articles; others, like *The Academic Index,* include books, articles, and other sources. Some, like *NewsBank,* list sources on a broad range of topics; others, like the Modern Language Association's *International Bibliography,* are devoted to one general subject area.

Be sure the index you're searching lists the kinds of sources you want. For example, in the *Humanities Index* you would probably find few sources about national parks, but you will find some in the *Canadian Index.*

Many of these indexes are available on CD-ROM disks read by personal computers in your libary's reference section. These electronic indexes contain publication information to help you locate the source and often an abstract or brief summary of it or even its full text. See the sample screen for a source listed in a periodical index (opposite). *A bibliography note:* When you write publication information for a source listed in an index, arrange it in the appropriate format. (See 54a and b for the MLA format and 56b and c for the APA format.)

- *Years of coverage.* CD-ROM indexes usually cover several years of publication, making them more comprehensive than a single print volume of an index. If a CD-ROM index does not go back far enough for the sources you need (e.g., for literary or historical research), use the print versions of the index.

- *Search strategy.* Search for sources as you would in any electronic catalogue, by key words, title, author, or combinations of these.

- *Viewing and recording information.* Generally, you can print publication information from CD-ROM indexes, and many will also permit you to view and print abstracts or complete copies of articles.

Forum for Applied Research and Public Policy
Spring 1997 v12 n1 p6(9)

Paradise lost in parks? (problems of national
parks) *William R. Lowry*

Subjects Covered:
 national parks
 management
 pollution
 ecology
 funding

Abstract: Several problems have plagued
national parks in recent years. Water and air
pollution and nearby developments could eventually threaten a park's ecology. The fate of park
policies and programs is at the mercy of politicians. Funding is another problem with the
government's failure to increase funds to
improve park services despite the 30% rise in
total visitors since the 1980s.

Periodical title and publication information: date, volume, issue, page number and length

Article title, sub-ject, and author

Topics covered in the article

Summary of the article

4 Using print indexes

Print indexes, usually found in the reference section of a library, are issued annually, listing publications for a single year. To investigate what has been published over a number of years, you have to search several volumes. Search for sources as you would in any index—by subject, author, or title.

49e | Compile a bibliography of sources

A **bibliography** is a systematic list of sources. You'll use this list to locate sources and, as you write your paper, to document borrowed information.

Computer Tip:

Using A Bibliography Generator

A computer program known as a bibliography generator, such as BiblioCite or EndNote, can arrange publication information for you in the appropriate bibliographic style.

1 Noting bibliographic information

As soon as you identify a source on your topic, record publication and location information for it. At the beginning of your research, you may simply print this information from electronic catalogues and indexes. Later you'll turn it into bibliographic notes written in a format appropriate to your discipline or subject area.

- *Write note cards.* If you write bibliographic information by hand, use cards instead of lists on sheets of paper. Individual cards, each with a single source, will be easier to use as you search for titles, add and drop sources, and arrange the cards for documentation. Here's a shortcut: Divide sheets of notebook paper into quarters, write a citation in each quarter, and cut the sheets into individual slips when you begin searching for the sources themselves.

- *Use a computer.* If you write with a computer, you may compile bibliographic information in a file that you alphabetize, update, and correct as you go along. You won't need note cards. At the end of your project, you can rework this file to become the works cited or list of references accompanying the final draft of your paper.

- *Decide what to include.* Note the author's name, title of the individual work, other relevant identifying information such as editor and edition, publication information, page numbers, and call numbers for locating a source in the library. If it is an electronic source, note the medium—for example, *CD-ROM* or *online*—the computer service; the date of your search; and the URL, or electronic address.

- *Deal with incomplete information.* If a catalogue or index does not provide complete information, leave blanks to be filled in later when you have the actual source.

- *Follow documentation styles.* As you write bibliographic notes, follow the documentation style assigned by your instructor or preferred by the discipline in which you are writing. Use the Modern Language

Association (MLA) style for papers in the humanities, including literature, history, religion, and the arts. (For sample MLA citations, see 54b.) Use the American Psychological Association (APA) style for writing in the social sciences. (For sample APA citations, see 56c. For a list of style manuals in other disciplines, see 59.)

- *Compare publication information.* When you actually locate a source, compare the publication information on its title page or in preliminary matter with the publication information in your notes. Correct or complete your citation.

Below are bibliographic notes for a book and an Internet source. The notes are written in the MLA documentation style.

2 Writing a working bibliography

At the beginning of your research, your instructor may ask you to prepare a **working bibliography** listing all the sources you plan to read. When you've finished your paper, you'll use an updated and corrected version to prepare the works cited or reference list to accompany your finished project.

To prepare a working bibliography, arrange your note cards in the order required by the documentation system you're using and copy your entries on a sheet of paper following the appropriate format. If you've

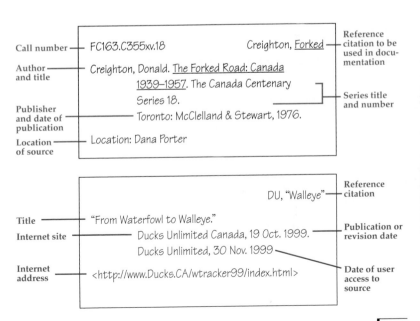

Call number — FC163.C355xv.18   Creighton, <u>Forked</u> — Reference citation to be used in documentation

Author and title — Creighton, Donald. <u>The Forked Road: Canada 1939–1957</u>. The Canada Centenary Series 18. — Series title and number

Publisher and date of publication — Toronto: McClelland & Stewart, 1976.

Location of source — Location: Dana Porter

Title — "From Waterfowl to Walleye."   DU, "Walleye" — Reference citation

Internet site — Ducks Unlimited Canada, 19 Oct. 1999. — Publication or revision date
Ducks Unlimited, 30 Nov. 1999

Internet address — <http://www.Ducks.CA/wtracker99/index.html> — Date of user access to source compiled a computerized bibliography file, format your citations appropriately and print them. See 54a for Modern Language Association guidelines and the sample MLA papers in 6d and 55. See 56b for American Psychological Association reference list guidelines and 56d for a sample reference list.

3 Writing an annotated bibliography

Your instructor may assign you to write an **annotated bibliography**, a list of sources in which each entry is followed by a brief descriptive and evaluative paragraph. Such a bibliography will inform readers of the content, relevance, and quality of the sources you cite. To prepare an annotated bibliography, do the following:

- Select sources that provide a variety of perspectives on your topic.
- Cite each work in the appropriate documentation style, such as MLA or APA style.
- After each citation, write a brief descriptive paragraph in which you evaluate the credentials of the writer, identify the intended audience, compare the work to similar works, and explain what it contributes to your topic.

chapter

50 Searching the Internet

If you use a computer for research, sooner or later you'll come to the **Internet**, an expanding global network of millions of computers. It contains many lists of sources and often the sources themselves, which you can read on screen, print, or, perhaps, transfer to your own computer. You can learn more about this vast electronic world of information by connecting to the Internet and investigating for yourself. For the basics, see "The Teacher's Lounge" at <http://educ.queensu.ca/~hudsonp>. For additional information, see "Links to Online Sources for Help Using the Internet," at <http://www.mont.ib.md.us/tutor.html> or the government of Canada's guide to the Internet at <http://www.connect.gc.ca>.

50*a* | Learn to navigate the Internet

1 Connecting to the Internet

To see Internet sources like these just listed, you'll need a computer with a telephone modem, an Internet service provider such as one made available by your college or university, and, for much of your Internet searching, browser software like Internet Explorer or Netscape Communicator. When you click with your mouse on the "Search the Internet" icon of your service provider's start screen (an image of a globe or flashlight), you'll bring up the **home page**, the first screen of your browser program, and see the following:

- An "Address" or "Go to" box: Type an Internet address to take you to a specific site.

- Back button: Back up to a previous site.

- Forward button: Move forward to return to the site you just moved back from.

- Print button: Print the current page.

- Refresh or reload button: Reload the current display on your monitor.

- Bookmark or Favourites menu: Set an electronic bookmark so that you can return to an interesting site without having to go through other sources or sites to get to it.

- History option: From the Go or Window menu, return to recent sites you have visited.

- Lots of advertisements or announcements: Don't let these distract you.

2 Visiting Internet sites

To read Internet sources like the ones listed at the beginning of this chapter, you will have to visit their individual sites at specific Internet addresses. In the "Address" or "Go to" box, you'll type the sometimes lengthy combination of letters and occasional numbers that make up an address, then click "Enter" or "Return." Suppose you are searching for information about Canada's national parks. You might visit the Parks Canada site at <http://www.parkscanada.pch.gc.ca>. Try typing this address in the "Address" box of your browser screen; omit the angle brackets (< ... >), which are used only to enclose Internet addresses in printed text. When you press the "Enter" or "Return" key, you'll be carried to the Parks Canada home page, a display of images, text, and options for visiting other sites.

345

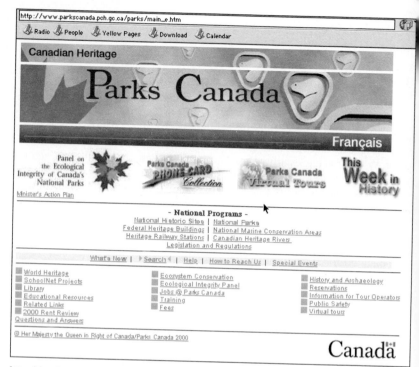

http://parkscanada.pch.gc.ca/parks/main_e.htm © Her Majesty the Queen in Right of Canada/Parks Canada 1999. Reproduced with the permission of the Minister of Public Works and Government Services Canada, 2000.

3 Using hypertext links

On most Internet pages or screens, you'll see special images or high-lighted or underlined text known as "links." You can tell whether some-thing is a hypertext link by using your mouse to move the arrow across the screen. If a hand appears when you move across an image or text, that is a link. Click on it and you'll be taken from the site where you are now to another related site. (Click on the "Back" button to return to your original site.) Hypertext links are the most obvious way in which Internet sites form a network.

For example, if you are viewing the Parks Canada English language home page and move the arrow over the map of Canada and the words

"Virtual Tours," you'll see the little hand appear, telling you that you are on a link. Click on that link and you'll be led to another site with optional links to videos and information on all Canada's national parks. If instead you click on the link "Environmental Agenda," you'll be led to a page connecting you to the March 31, 1999, press release announcing revisions to the National Parks Act and funding for eight new national parks.

Using the Internet in this way, clicking on hypertext links in one source to carry you to links in another containing links to still other sites, is what is known as "surfing the 'Net."

4 Managing Internet addresses

The addresses that enable you to navigate the Internet are also known as **URLs (Uniform Resource Locators)**. They are composed of three parts: a "protocol" identifying the computer language used to gain access to a site, the "domain" identifying the owner of a site, and a "directory path" indicating where this address leads on the Internet. Here are the parts of the address for Parks Canada's English language home page:

protocol   domain   directory path
http://www.parkscanada.pch.gc.ca/parks/main_e.htm

Because these addresses are often difficult to locate and even harder to remember, it's important to keep track of them as you make your way from site to site. Luckily, your computer will help you out in three ways:

- You can set an electronic bookmark. Select the "Add Bookmark" option from the Bookmark menu in Netscape Communicator or the "Add to Favourites" option from the Favourites menu in Internet Explorer. Communicator immediately adds the address to the Bookmark menu. Explorer pops up a window that allows you to edit the address and organize your bookmarks into folders.

- Go to the "history file," which you'll find by clicking on the "Location" arrow in Netscape Communicator or through the "Open History Folder" option in the Internet Explorer's Go menu. Here you'll find recorded all the addresses of recently visited sites.

- When you print an Internet file, many browsers will automatically print the address of that file on each page. With Netscape and some others, you must choose this feature from the "Preferences" file. However, if your browser does not print the address, be sure to copy it accurately for later reference.

As you find interesting sites, add their addresses to your "Book-marks" or "Favourites" file and make written notes of the other important information you'll need to document this source in your paper: (1) author's name, if available, (2) publication information for print and online versions of a source, (3) the Internet address (URL), (4) the date of publication, and (5) the date you gained access to the site. Because Internet sources frequently change content and location, this last date is important. If you go back to a site at a later date, it may be quite different from the site you visited on an earlier occasion—or it may no longer be there. (For more on documenting Internet sources, see 54b3 for MLA guidelines and 56c3 for APA guidelines.)

5   Writing Internet addresses

- _Using URLs in the text of your writing._ Enclose Internet and e-mail addresses in angle brackets. Do not leave internal spaces or drop internal punctuation or capitalization.

  Information about the 2001 census may be found at the Statistics Canada Web site at <http://www.statcan.ca/english/census2001/index.htm>.

- _Using URLs in bibliographies._ Do not italicize or underline URLs or e-mail addresses in Works Cited. Enclose them with angle brackets. For example, <http://www.edf.org>.

- _Breaking addresses._ If you must break a URL or e-mail address, follow these MLA guidelines: (1) Break only after a slashmark (/). (2) Never add a hyphen when you must break an address. (3) Do not break the protocol (_http://_). (4) Add a period after a URL at the end of a sentence.

  Population figures for 1999 are now available at <http://www.statcan.ca/english/Pgdb/People/Population/demo10a.htm>.

6   Reading and saving Internet sources

When you find a site that looks promising, you have several options.

- Read the source on screen and take notes. Take computerized notes by creating a file in your word processor and splitting your computer screen between the Internet site and the notes file. Switch between them as you read. (See the computer tip in 2e.)

- Print the source and read it later, highlighting the text or taking notes. To save time (and printer ink or toner), turn off any images in the text by clicking the appropriate link.

- Copy the source, then cut and paste it into a file in your word processing program by using the commands in your Edit menu. Be aware that you'll probably have to reformat your borrowing when you make such a transfer. Even more important, to avoid plagiarism to sure to document your borrowing of this now-quoted material. (See 52e.)

■ You can save many sources on your own computer by performing a "download" using your browser software. You'll use the "Save" or "Save As" commands in your File menu. Saving other sources is trickier, and you may need special FTP (File Transfer Protocol) software such as *WSFTP* for Windows and *Fetch* for the Macintosh. Remember to reformat text that you download.

7   Learning the basics of Internet research

Learning to use the Internet is a lot like learning to drive a car. What you learned in driver training about skilful and safe driving was probably not as useful as what you learned behind the wheel. So, too, with the Internet. Reference librarians and computer lab personnel are ready to answer your questions, and you can consult books such as *Casting Your Net: A Student's Guide to Research on the Internet* (Allyn & Bacon, 1997). But you'll gain the most useful information and skills while actually searching the Internet.

Many Internet sites have help screens or answers to "Frequently Asked Questions" (FAQs). There are even a number of master sites to link you to introductions to the Internet, guides to research, and search tools for locating information sources. For a list of these sites, see the Appendix. Try them out. Experiment; practise; be patient if you don't always find just what you're looking for. The following pages will help you develop your searching skills.

50b | Search the World Wide Web

If the Internet is something like a virtual continent-sized nation with a complex network of electronic highways connecting all parts of the country, then the World Wide Web is the largest province in this country, a vast region (Internet "space") of millions of computers and millions upon millions of Web sites containing text, graphics, or sound—whatever can be sent electronically. Because of its size, ease of use, and the kinds of information it pulls together, the Web is currently the most popular path to gain access to and utilize the Internet.

You can locate sources on the Web in two ways. If you know a site's URL (address) because it has been given to you, you can type it into your brower's "Address" or "Location" box (Web addresses always begin "http://"). The other method, which you'll probably use more often, is to use one of the electronic search tools described in the following sections. The tool you choose will depend upon how focussed your research topic is and the kind of information you're looking for. To learn to use these tools and to see how they differ, try the same search on several different tools.

1 Using search engines for key word searches

If you have a clear idea of your research topic and have key terms to describe it, then you should do a key word search using a search engine like Excite!, AltaVista, Lycos, or HotBot. A **search engine** scans the texts of documents in its database looking for key words you've told it to search for. (See the Appendix, p. 473–475, for a list of search engines and the master sites that will connect you to them.)

If, for example, you tell a search engine to look for sources about *bilingualism* and *French immersion*, it will give a list of all sources containing these key words. The sources are arranged in order of their relevance to your topic: how many times a source uses your key words or how closely a source matches what you're looking for. When you first use a particular search engine, be sure to check its FAQs file ("Frequently Asked Questions") or help screens for guidance to its use.

2 Using classified subject directories for browsing

If you're hazy about a topic or unsure of its key words, then you should use a search engine with a subject directory like Yahoo! or AltaVista. (Since 1999, most search engines offer such directories.) A subject directory will carry you down through a series of menus from general to more narrow topics until you find the specific topic you want to investigate and a list of sources written about that topic. (See the Appendix, p. 473, for sites to take you to these tools.)

If, for example, you are investigating the effects of visitors on national parks but are unsure how to look for sources, you might turn to Yahoo! In your brower's address box you'll type its URL and be taken to its home page. There you will see a number of hypertext topic links: *Art & Humanities, Government, News & Media, Society & Culture*, and so on. Beneath each of these are more specific topic links. For example, under *Society & Culture* are *People, Environment, Religion*. Click on *Environment* and you'll be taken to a list of even more specific topic links, all having to do with the environment, among them, Environmental Studies, Parks, and Pollution.

Browsing through Yahoo! in this way, moving through successively restricted topic lists, you'll eventually come to individual Internet information sources, such as "Monitoring for Gaseous Pollutants in the Parks," which you can read on-screen or download to your computer.

3   Using other search tools

- If you have the time, search for sources on your topic using both the search engine and its subject directory. Or choose a multi-engine (also

How to Search the World Wide Web

Use these tips and guidelines to search the Web successfully:

1. Click on the "Find" button or "Search the Internet" icon of your browser (NetFind, Netscape Navigator, or Internet Explorer) and you'll be taken to the home page of a default search engine like Excite! If you wish, type in the URL (address) or another search tool, like Yahoo!, in the "Address" or "Go to" window of your browser. Use the links to search tools listed in Appendix A2.

2. Create bookmarks for your favourite search tools or collect their addresses in a folder. See 50a4.

3. To make a keyword search using a search engine like Excite! or Infoseek, do the following. Type your key words into the query box and then click on the "Find," "Search," or "Seek" button. Use the scroll bar to examine the list of sources. Read the brief descriptions that follow. Then click on the highlighted hypertext of an interesting title or address and be taken directly to the source. Examine the source to see whether it meets your needs. If so, give it a bookmark (see 50a4); then read it, print it, or save it (see 50a6).

4. To browse a subject directory for specific topics and sources, do the following. Type the address of a subject directory like Yahoo! in your browser's address box, <http://www.yahoo.com>. Be sure to omit the angle brackets. From the list of topics displayed, choose one that interests you, click on it, and examine the list of subtopics that appear. Choose increasingly specific topics until you find a topic that suits you. Use the scroll bar to examine the list of references. Click on titles to see full documents. Bookmark an interesting source (see 50a4); then read it, print it, or save it (see 50a6).

5. To make a multi-engine search for sources, try a tool such as SavvySearch. In the "Address" window of your browser, type the following address without the angle brackets: <http://www.savvysearch.com>. Then follow the instructions for making a keyword search (see item 3 above).

6. If your search is unsatisfactory, try another search tool. None lists all sources on the Internet, and each tool searches in a different way. If you want to focus your search on Canadian sources only, try the Canadian versions of search engines and directories (see Appendix).

called a "meta-search") tool like MetaCrawler, Dogpile, or ASKJeeves. A note on multi-tool searching: Because no search tool, not even a multi-search tool, lists all the sources on a topic and because no two search tools list the same sources, you should always use more than one search tool. The more search tools you use, the greater the chance of your success finding sources.

- Librarians have access to specialized databases and search tools that may provide the quality sources you need. Tell them your topic and ask whether they have special resources to help you.

50c | Use effective search techniques

The Internet is vast, constantly changing, and lacking an overall organization. Therefore, searching for sources is more challenging than looking for a book or magazine article in the library. You'll improve your online searches if you practise the following techniques.

1 Using help screens and FAQs

Develop an understanding of the search tools you use. Every search tool comes with guides to its use. Examine the home page or first screen for links to a help screen or a "Frequently Asked Questions" (FAQ) file. Also, the Internet has many master sites to help you learn the tricks of online searching. (See the Appendix.) As you experiment with a search tool, don't be intimidated by links called "advanced," "super search" or "expert searching." Try out the hints they provide.

2 Focussing and narrowing your search terms

Large Web search tools like Excite! and HotBot have so many documents in their databases that they are difficult to use unless you have unusual or specific key words to cue your search. At the beginning of a search spend a few minutes thinking about the best key words for your topic.

- Avoid general terms except when they are modified by more specific ones. Searching for "parks" will give you millions of sources. "National parks" will limit your sources somewhat, but you'll still get citations for parks in the US, New Zealand, and Australia, as well as Canada. Limiting yourself to "Canadian national parks" will focus your search better.

- Use Boolean search operators to link key words (see 49c2). Searching Banff AND overcrowding will lead to a focussed search. Whenever possible, use a unique phrase as your search term; you'll see listed only those documents in which that phrase appears.

- Search for organizations associated with your topic. They will provide you with hypertext links to other sites containing additional information. If your topic is controversial, however, remember to search for organizations on all sides of an issue. For example, search for both Right to Life and the Planned Parenthood sites.

- Narrow the field of your search. When appropriate to your topic, click on the buttons that allow you to restrict your search by date or geographic location.

3 Using search operators with Internet search tools

In Chapter 49c2, you learned to use Boolean search operators to narrow a search for sources: *AND, OR, NOT, NEAR,* and so on. Be sure to type these operators in all capital letters between the terms you're searching for. Be aware that not all search tools will accept these operators; some use punctuation marks or symbols instead. See the search tool help screens for further information. AltaVista gives you the most detailed assistance; Hotbot, the most concise.

- Use double quotation marks (" ... ") to treat a group of words as a phrase, for example, "*automobile pollution in national parks.*"

- If your search tool accepts them, use "+" (plus) as you would the Boolean AND; use "–" (minus) as you would the operator NOT. For example: "*Canada's parks*" *+pollution –automobile.*

- Use an asterisk "*" to truncate a key word to its base and enable you to search for variants of the word. For example shorten *pollution* to *pollut** to search for variants like *pollution, pollute, polluter, polluting,* and so on.

4 Solving common search problems

Some search problems appear so often for so many researchers that you need to be aware of what they are and how to solve them.

- *Typing URLs correctly.* It's easy to mistype a computer address. If you're not finding the source you're looking for, check the address to be sure you've typed all the letters, numbers, and punctuation correctly. Look carefully for incorrect capitals and unnecessary spaces.

- *Narrowing a topic that is too broad.* If your topic is too broad, begin by searching in a subject directory. When you find a more restricted topic, switch to a key word search. You'll limit yourself to the last topic category and produce a shorter list of sources to examine.

- *Coping with too many sources.* If your search is leading you to too many sources, concentrate on the top ten or so. Examine them to see whether their hypertext links will lead you to more relevant sources.

- *Coping with too few sources.* If your search is not leading to enough sources, broaden it by omitting the least required word.

- *Coping with lengthy files.* If you want to print or download a lengthy file and if you can live without the graphics, click on the "text only" option if it exists at that site. You'll get only the text of the file, and you'll get it more quickly.

- *Guessing relevant sites with unknown addresses.* If you are unable to find relevant sources, try to guess the URL (address) of an organization associated with your topic. In the "Address" box of your browser, type in a basic Web template beginning *<http://www>*. Then add the name or abbreviation of a relevant organization. Conclude with the appropriate domain suffix: *.ca* (for Canadian sites), *.com* (for commercial sites), or *.org* (for non-commercial, non-profit organizations). For example, if you are investigating endangered species, you might guess that the URL of the Canadian Parks and Wilderness Society would look something like <http://www.cpaws.ca> and you'd be right.

- *Locating sites that have moved.* Not infrequently, Internet sources move from one host computer to another. When they do, their addresses change. Often, there will be an automatic link to the new address, but sometimes you'll be told there is no such address at all. Before you give up, type the URL into a browser "Address" box, but then delete parts of it, beginning at the right and stopping at each slash mark. If, for example, you're searching without success for an article on fire management in the national parks which was originally located at <http://www.parkscanada.pch.gc.ca/library/Fire/Fire_e.htm>, begin by omitting Fire/Fire_e.htm to see whether you can locate the article at another site.

- *Locating publication information.* Sometimes it is difficult to locate all the publication information necessary to document Internet sources. For authors and publication dates, look in headers and footers. Also, authors may have included e-mail addresses containing their names (look for the @ symbol appearing in all e-mail addresses). For titles, look at the top of your browser screen window or in the upper corner of text. If a title seems incomplete, go to the Document or Source Information window. If a document is untitled, create an appropriate title enclosed in square brackets [...]. For information about publishers, see the "About this Site" or home page link. Or you may be able to reach a home page by shortening the URL to the domain name. For example, if you can't locate publication information at <http://www.mla.org/main_stl.htm>, shorten the address to <http://www.mla.org>.

50d | Search other Internet spaces

As it rapidly expands, the World Wide Web is adding to its search capabilities and to the sites to which you can gain access. It is now possible to get to non-Web sites through Web "gateways," Web addresses that connect to non-Web sites. However, the Web has not yet colonized the whole Internet, and because many non-Web sites are potentially useful to researchers, you need to know about them.

1 Visiting Gopher sites

Developed at the University of Minnesota, Gopher once enabled users to "go for" text-based Internet sources by burrowing through a series of hierarchically arranged menus. Now such access is available through the Internet. To see a subject directory of Gopher files, go to "Gopher Jewels" at <http://galaxy.einet.net/GJ/index.html>.

2 Visiting FTP sites

FTP (short for "File Transfer Protocol") represents an archive of Internet sites. You can access FTP sources directly with addresses beginning "ftp://." Better yet, investigate FTP sources through the Web at <http://www.info.net/Public/ftp-list.html>.

50e | Using e-mail and discussion groups to communicate with people

1 Communication by e-mail

When you send messages by e-mail, you turn the Internet into an electronic post office. Now you can communicate directly with experts and others involved with topics of interest or join group discussions of important issues. You might, for example, write to testing experts at a distant university to gather opinions about the presence of bias in standardized tests. With the "attachments" option built into most e-mailing software, you and your addressees can attach documents to e-mail messages and exchange files as part of your dialogue.

To send and receive e-mail messages, you and those you communicate with will need a modem, a browser like Netscape Navigator or Internet Explorer, and an e-mail address, usually available through the service provider that connects you to the Internet. An e-mail address looks like this:

user name   electronic address
jewinski@renison.ca

To send mail, you'll need e-mail software, which is usually a part of your browser. To search for e-mail addresses and locate people online, use a "people finder" program such as Knowbot, Lycos, People Find, or Switchboard. (Use the address under "Internet Searching" in the Appendix to take you to links to these tools.)

2   Participating in news groups

News groups are electronically connected groups of people and their collections of messages, called "postings." These postings are made available, usually for a week or so, to interested people through a network variously called Usenet or Netnews. If, for example, you are investigating overcrowding in national parks and looking for visitor anecdotes and experiences, you might search for them on the World Wide Web with a Usenet search tool like DejaNews. With it, you can browse through menus of general-to-specific topics, in this instance, from "Recreation" to "Travel" to a specific discussion topic: "Should you visit Ellesmere Island?" Following the topic question, you would see responses to it grouped as a discussion "thread." You can simply read these responses or join the discussion yourself and, using your e-mail address, post a reply.

To find other discussions relevant to your topic, you might also conduct a key word search of the Usenet database. The many thousands of discussions are organized under broad topic headings. Seven of the major ones and their abbreviations used in addresses are these: (1) alternative topics that don't fit other categories (*alt*); (2) computer topics (*comp*); (3) miscellaneous topics related to the news itself (*misc news*); (4) recreational activities and hobbies (*rec*); (5) scientific topics (*sci*); (6) social, political, and religious topics (*soc*); and (7) opinions (*talk*).

To participate in a news group, you'll need news reader software, probably available as part of your browser. Or you can access news groups through the Web's "HyperNews" at <http://union.ncsa.uiuc. edu/HyperNews/get/hypernews/html>. Or search for topics at DejaNews (<http:// www.deja.com/>).

A cautionary note about news groups: Evaluate news group postings with great care. Anyone and everyone can join a news group and add his or her two cents to a discussion. The quality of the contributions, therefore, varies widely from contributor to contributor. (For guidelines on evaluating information sources, see 51a and b.)

3   Subscribing to listservs

A **listserv** is a special kind of news group, a subscription-based e-mail discussion of a particular topic. The postings of each subscriber are sent by a list owner to the e-mail addresses of all other subscribers, who may then reply to one or more of these messages, creating a topic "thread." The many thousands of these groups are divided into "public" or "open" discussions, open to anyone who wishes to subscribe, and "private" or "closed" discussions. To subscribe to a "private" group, you must apply to a moderator for permission to participate and describe your interests.

To search for listservs, begin with the World Wide Web CataList Reference site for public lists at <http://www.lsoft.com/lists.listref.html>. CataList allows you to search for discussion groups in a variety of ways. For example, to locate listservs focussing on language learning, you might do a keyword search using "bilingualism." You'll discover a group called "Forum for Discussion of Research on Bilingualism and Bilingual Education" <BILING@LISTS.ASU.ED>. If you wish, you can subscribe and receive the postings of the group members.

To join a listserv that interests you, send a subscription message to the listserv's subscription e-mail address, usually accompanying the name of the discussion list itself. If you want to join the Bilingualism listserv, for example, the subscription address is <LISTSERV@LISTS.ASU.ED>. In the body of the message, not the subject heading, include the word *SUBSCRIBE* in all capitals. For example, in your message subscribing to the Bilingualism listserv, you'll type "SUBSCRIBE BILING" plus your name and e-mail address. To receive reference cards containing general user commands, or to ask questions, you'll include the words *HELP* or *INFO*.

Two cautions: (1) Never send a subscription message to the listserv e-mail address itself; that is reserved for the listserv discussion. Send your subscription queries to the subscription address. (2) Evaluate listserv contributions as carefully as you would the remarks in a news group posting, especially those that appear in public or unmoderated listservs. (For guidelines for evaluating information sources, see 51a and b.)

4 "Real-time" communicating via MOOs, MUDs, and IRCs

When you communicate by e-mail or join a news group or listserv, the recipients of your messages may not be online when you type them. Your communication is **asynchronous**: you send a message at one time and they receive it at another. But when you join a MOO ("multi-user domain, object-oriented") group, MUD ("multi-user domain"), or IRC (Internet relay chat"), you enter an Internet space in which all writers are present at their computers. Here the communication is **synchronous**, in real time. Such Internet spaces are useful for classes, seminars, and special interest groups whose members meet with one another at specific times.

If you are part of a MOO, MUD, or IRC, you will join the discussion using Telnet, an Internet language that lets you log on to another computer from your computer. Telnet addresses always begin "telnet://." To learn more about these spaces, see the "Telnet Help Sheet for Mooing" at <http://daedalus.com/net/telnet.html>.

A cautionary note: Evaluate MOO, MUD, and IRC groups with great care. Participants' remarks may or may not be trustworthy or authoritative. (For guidelines for evaluating information sources, see 51a and b.)

5 Writing effectively online

To communicate effectively, successfully—and happily—on the Internet, observe the following guidelines, often referred to as **Netiquette**.

- Before you participate in a newsgroup or listserv, spend time familiarizing yourself with the discussion. Read the FAQs that almost always accompany these groups to get an idea of the subject matter and level of conversation.

- Use the subject line of an e-mail to identify your topic.

- Begin your e-mail message with a brief greeting to set the tone: *Hi Annie* or *Dear Dr. Masood*. Include a brief appropriate close: *Bye* or *Sincerely*.

- Keep your messages short and to the point.

- Adjust your formality to fit the occasion. Online messages addressed to friends and co-workers are often as informal as casual conversation, with all the slang, abbreviations, and sentence fragments you would expect to hear in speech. But online messages addressed to strangers or anonymous readers should sound somewhat more formal, suitable to your topic and purpose for communicating. For example, if you sent an e-mail to an educational researcher, asking about the benefits of home schooling, you would be more formal than when discussing the same topic with friends in an online chat. To create the appropriate formality for your messages, follow the guidelines in 32.

- Send plain text only, avoiding tabs and other computer commands you would use to format print documents.

- Observe these punctuation guidelines:

Underlining. Use a single underlining mark before and after text that you would italicize or underline in a print document.

Henry David Thoreau's_Walden_recommends simple living but not poverty.

Asterisks to replace italics and underlining. If your e-mail provider does not support italics or underlining, use asterisks.

Poverty is *not* what Thoreau had in mind.

Hyphens and Internet addresses (URLs). Never add a hyphen when you must break an Internet address at the end of a line. The MLA guideline is to break only after a slashmark (/). (See also 50a5.)

Angle brackets (< … >) *and Internet addresses* (URLs). In the text of your message, enclose Internet addresses, including e-mail, in angle brackets: <http://www.infocan.gc.ca>. Do not put additional punctuation within the angle brackets.

- Edit online communication as the occasion requires. Because online communication is often as spontaneous and informal as speech, readers are generally tolerant of minor errors and typos. But you should always reread your messages to see that you've said what you intended and that your formality fits the occasion. Then check to see that your writing is relatively free of error. If your e-mail program has a spell checker, run it.

- Never send a message when you're angry or upset. Online name calling and other outbursts, known as "flaming," are an especially vivid display of poor online manners. Avoid all-capital words for emphasis, a practice known as "shouting."

chapter 51 Evaluating Print and Electronic Sources, Writing Research Notes

51*a* Evaluate sources with the "CASE" method

In Chapter 1a3, you learned to evaluate the quality of information and opinions before using them in your writing. At the same time, you should be evaluating the sources of information and opinion. Not all will be of equal value. Some may not suit your purposes; others may be flawed or unreliable. If you can't trust the quality of your sources, you can't trust their contents.

As you evaluate sources, think of the word *case*. In order to make your case and support your thesis, be sure that each of your sources meets the standards represented by the letters C-A-S-E: Currency, Authority, Suitability, and Ease of use. To make an evaluation, answer the questions in the following sections.

1 Currency: Is this source up to date?

When was this source published? Is it a first edition, reprint, or revision? For most research topics, you want sources that contain the most recent information and opinion. Look for a recent publication or revision date, or an indication that a work has recently been reissued in a new edition. Currency is not always a relevant standard with literary and historical topics. You may be reading primary sources published hundreds of years ago, and secondary sources published decades ago may still provide valuable insights. But for technical and social science topics, in which information and opinion are changing rapidly, currency is an important standard of quality.

2 Authority: Is this source authoritative and trustworthy?

- What are the author's credentials for writing about this topic? Is this person an expert or eyewitness? What political, religious, or social beliefs may influence this person's view of the facts or objectivity? What organizational affiliations reveal this person's point of view? A biased source is not necessarily a bad source, but you need to know what these biases are and how they influence objectivity.

- Is the publication source (e.g., a university press, scholarly journal, or major publisher) known for publishing reliable information? Are submissions to this publication source checked for their quality—"refereed"—by a panel of experts?

3 Suitability: Does this source meet your needs and those of your readers?

- Does this source contain the materials that you want and your readers need: facts, explanation, opinion, statistics, examples, eyewitness accounts, narratives? What are its main idea, thesis, and major supporting points? Will they lead you away from your topic?

- What is the purpose of this source: to inform, entertain, evaluate, or persuade? Does its purpose match your own or the needs of your readers? If a source aims to persuade, does it do so with facts, reasoning, or emotion? Which of these help you make a case appealing to your readers?

- Do you and your readers share the point of view or outlook of this source? A source that your readers may reject as biased will probably not suit your purposes.

- What is this source's coverage of your topic? Is it broad in scope, presenting detailed background information? Is it narrow in scope, focussing on a specific topic? Does it present its topics in depth or superficially? Is it complete or partial in its coverage? Answering these questions will help you decide whether a source has the kinds and amount of information suitable for you and your readers.

4 Ease of use: Will you and your readers find this source and its contents easy to use?

- Can you locate this source, read it, and understand it in the time available for your project?
- Who is the audience for this source, experts or general readers? Is it written at a level appropriate for your readers? Will they be able to understand its contents if you quote or summarize it in your writing?

51*b* Evaluate Internet sources with special care

To evaluate Internet sources, use the "CASE" standards (currency, authority, suitability, and ease of use) you use to evaluate other sources. But with Internet sources, you will sometimes have difficulty finding what you need for an effective evaluation. The following information and tips will help you.

 Computer Tip:

Internet Evaluation Sites

Some Internet sites claim to evaluate online sources, but they are often concerned with whether a site is "cool," fun to use," or visually appealing, not whether its information is accurate or complete. Such standards aren't of much use to serious researchers.

1 Currency: Is this source up to date?

Most Internet sources have three dates associated with them: a publication date, file date (when they are placed on a particular host computer), and revision date. Look at the beginning or end of a file for publication and revision dates. Prefer sites with the most recent dates.

2   Authority: Is this source trustworthy?

Because the Internet, news groups, and e-mail are open to anyon
with a computer and a little technical knowledge, online sources var
widely in authority—the expertise of their authors. With few editorial re
view boards in cyberspace to vouch for quality, you must use these source
with care. To locate an author's name within a document, look at the be
ginning or end of the file. To decide whether an author is trustworthy, d
the following:

- *Examine addresses for their domain.* An abbreviation in a site's URL can
  identify the type of organization that stands behind a source. For example, distinguish between sites ending **.com** (a commercial enter-
  prise) and **.org** (a non for-profit organization). Some designations
  point to American sources: **.gov** (government), **.edu** (educational institution), **.mil** (military) or **.net** (network management). The abbreviation **.gc.ca** indicates Government of Canada sites, but the
  designation **.ca** alone indicates only that the source is in Canada. Can
  you find a statement that a sponsoring organization approves of the
  site in question? The domain of a source doesn't guarantee quality,
  but it may suggest purpose or point of view, or the likelihood that a
  source has been checked for accuracy.

- *Check an author's home page.* Use an author's name to search for his or
  her home page, which may contain autobiographical information
  you can use to evaluate trustworthiness. Look for organizational
  affiliations that suggest point of view or bias. *Note:* a ~ (tilde) in a
  URL indicates a personal Web site.

- Send an e-mail message. Online authors often include e-mail
  addresses with their names. Explore their qualifications or the
  background of their opinions. *Note:* you can locate e-mail addresses
  with a people finder program. (See the Appendix for links to these
  programs.)

- *Trace an author's postings.* Evaluate the trustworthiness of an author by
  tracing his or her various contributions to a news group or listserv.
  Check whether the news group or listserv has a moderator to screen
  postings for quality and suitability.

- *Follow hypertext links.* See whether the source you are viewing is
  linked to other quality sites. Do these sites verify the claims of the
  source you are considering? Do they have the same outlook? *Note:*
  Two sites connected by hypertext links are not equally authoritative.
  And one source does not necessarily authorize another. Evaluate each
  site separately.

- *Check grammar, spelling, and punctuation.* Poorly written sources may
  indicate a source with untrustworthy or incorrect information.

How to ...

How to Evaluate Sources

Evaluate sources with the "CASE" method, checking for Currency, Authority, Suitability, and Ease of use. Follow these tips and guidelines:

1. Skim information at the beginning and end of a source.
   Print sources: For information about book authors, examine book jackets, author descriptions, and title pages. With periodicals, check the footnotes at the beginning or end of an article, or the list of contributors, usually appearing at the beginning or end of the periodical. For information about publication dates and editions, check the copyright pages of books (immediately following title pages) and the title pages of magazines.
   Internet sources: Examine the headers and footers of a file for information about authors, contact persons, institutional sponsors, home pages, and dates of creation, copyright, or revision. Use search engines or people finders to search for information about an author. (See the Appendix.)

2. Read reviews, abstracts, and annotated bibliographies. Many print and Internet sources exist primarily to describe and evaluate other sources.
   Print sources: Check for book reviews in *Book Review Digest* or *Book Review Index*. Read author biographies in the various "Who's Who" biographical guides such as *Current Biography*.
   Internet sources: For reviews of Internet sites, use The Argus Clearinghouse at <http://www.clearinghouse.net/> or The Internet Public Library at <http://www.ipl.org/>.

3. Note red flags that signal sources to avoid. One or two red flags may not prevent you from using a source, but more than a few should make you very cautious.
   - No publication date, no recent revision date, or an old date for information known to change rapidly.
   - Lots of negative reviews.
   - Counter-scenarios or explanations that spring readily to mind as you read a source. If you can think of other, more plausible explanations, then the reasoning of a source may be suspect.
   - Wild claims and broad generalizations. Most logical assertions sound reasonable, and trustworthy authors usually support their assertions.
   - Facts and statistics without source citations. Trustworthy authors usually give the sources for information they use.
   - Charged or biased language.
   - Poor writing, incorrect grammar, spelling, and punctuation.

3 **Suitability: Does this source meet your needs and those of your readers?**

Like a print document, an Internet site should have a purpose and topic coverage suitable for you and your readers. To evaluate suitability, do the following:

- Identify the type of site: Is it informational, business or marketing, news, advocacy, or personal? Is this type of site likely to have the information you need? Do the purpose and outlook suit your readers' interests and outlook?

- Examine the body of the source. Does this source's coverage suit you and your readers?

4 **Ease of use: Will you and your readers find this source and its contents easy to use?**

To make this evaluation, answer the following questions.

- Do you, and if necessary your readers, have the equipment and software necessary to gain access to the source?

- Is the site user friendly? Do you understand how to gain access to the site and use it to its fullest capacity? Can you make your way through it easily, using hypertext links or keyword searches?

- Is this site linked to other up-to-date, authoritative, and suitable sites?

- Do you and your readers have the background information necessary to understand the contents of the site?

51c | Follow effective strategies for gathering information

1 Reading for research

As you read your sources, take notes on whatever seems relevant. If you're like most researchers, you'll end up taking more notes than you need, especially in the beginning. The deeper you dig into your subject, however, the more perceptive you'll become about what is right for you.

- *Where to begin.* Before you begin reading, arrange your sources according to difficulty. Read general or introductory sources first, as background for more specialized or technical sources.

- *Preview your reading.* Before you begin reading a source, even if you're going to read only a chapter, say, or a paragraph or two, put your reading in context by skimming the table of contents, the introduction, and surrounding paragraphs. See how the part fits into the whole document. Use the guidelines and questions in 1b1.

- *What to look for.* Look for facts, of course, but also for explanations or interpretations, expert opinions, evaluations, and examples that illustrate ideas. *A note on conflicts:* Take note of any controversies involved with your topic. If you already have an opinion, pay attention to the other side. Use this opportunity to test the quality of your opinion or to make up your mind.

- *Read by the paragraph.* Finish reading a paragraph before taking a note about something you've found in it. In this way you'll see how the information that interests you fits into its context.

- *Think critically as you read.* To understand your reading, use the methods of critical thinking described in 1a: analysis (to see how things fit together), interpretation (to find the meaning of your reading), evaluation (to measure quality), and synthesis (to see how sources fit together and suit your purposes).

2 Gathering information with surveys and interviews

- *Conduct surveys.* Plan survey questions carefully to avoid personal bias or charged language. Avoid asking "yes or no" questions whenever possible; they are often not very informative. Guard against overly personal questions that may hinder respondents from answering truthfully. Ask one question at a time; don't combine two or more questions in one sentence.

- *Interview.* Make appointments with your sources and be prompt. Be clear about your purposes for the interview. Prepare your questions in advance using the guidelines above. Ask clarifying or follow-up questions as necessary. As you listen, take careful notes; doublecheck quotations to be sure they're accurate. If necessary, ask your sources whether they're speaking "for the record" and may be cited by name. Tape sources only with their permission. Offer to send them a copy of your completed project. Thank them sincerely.

51d | Take notes in an easy-to-use format

1 Taking notes on paper or with a computer

For brief papers involving only a few sources, you can gather information informally, photocopying or highlighting important information, jotting ideas in margins or on a sheet of paper. But if you have more than a few sources and if your paper is longer than a page or two, you'll want to take individual notes to handle your information effectively.

- *Size.* Make note cards easy to sort by using only one size. Avoid cards too small for complete notes or so large you may write too much on one card. Buy a package of 10 x 15 cm cards, or make your own by dividing notebook sheets into four.

 Computer Tip:

Taking Notes

Make a template for a "Notes" file by creating and saving properly sized columns or boxes. Adjust margins as necessary. Print and cut these computerized notes when you finish your research.

- *Length.* Generally, the shorter the note, the better. Put one piece of information in each note. More than one idea makes a note difficult to sort and organize. When in doubt, divide an idea in two and put each in a separate note. Never write on the backs of cards. If you have a long note that won't fit on one card, write *Note 1 of 2, Note 2 of 2,* and so on on the appropriate cards.

- *Plagiarism.* Use quotation marks around all word-for-word quotations. Compare summaries and paraphrases with their original to be sure they are complete and you haven't quoted unintentionally. (See 52e.)

2 Formatting notes

Every note should contain the following information, which you'll use as you think about your topic, organize your paper, write your paper, and document your borrowing.

- A subject heading to identify the topic of the note.
- A reference citation for identifying the source of the note parenthetically in the text of your paper (the author and a short version of the title).
- A page number, if a print source.
- An introduction that provides a context for the note: *who, what, when, where, why,* or *how.*
- The note itself: quotation, summary, paraphrase, or a combination.

■ Your comments on the note, if necessary, explaining it or telling how you intend to use it.

Here is a sample note card citing from Northrop Frye's 1991 book, *The Double Vision*.

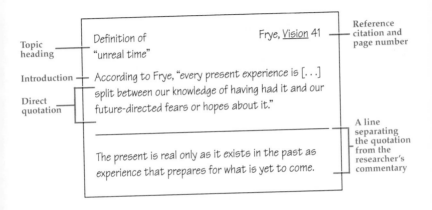

Topic heading → Definition of "unreal time"

Frye, <u>Vision</u> 41 — Reference citation and page number

Introduction → According to Frye, "every present experience is [. . .]

Direct quotation → split between our knowledge of having had it and our future-directed fears or hopes about it."

The present is real only as it exists in the past as experience that prepares for what is yet to come.

A line separating the quotation from the researcher's commentary

51*e* | Take notes by an appropriate method: quotation, summary, or paraphrase

1 Note-taking by direct quotation

A direct quotation is a word-for-word reproduction of an original source. Quote often but briefly as you take notes. Remember that long quotations may be difficult to weave into a paper and difficult for readers to use. What to quote:

■ *Key points.* Quote passages that sum up a key point in a condensed, emphatic way.

■ *Expert opinions.* Quote sources when they offer an expert's opinion.

■ *Powerful passages.* Quote dramatic, memorable, or well-known passages.

■ *Subtle ideas.* Quote passages whose meaning may be lost in a summary.

■ *Concise passages.* Quote passages whose meaning cannot be expressed in fewer words.

For a sample direct quotation note card, see 51d2. To quote effectively, you'll need to know how to use quotation marks (see 40a–d), commas and colons to introduce quotations (see 36g and 38a), brackets to insert editorial comments within a quotation (see 41c), and the ellipsis points to signal omitted words (see 41d).

2 Note-taking by summary

> ### How to Write a Summary
>
> Follow these tips and guidelines to write effective summaries.
>
> 1. When you come to a passage you want to summarize, consider the surrounding sentences or paragraphs. Avoid taking information or opinions out of context; avoid distorting the author's purpose to suit your own.
> 2. Read the passage carefully and then look away to write your summary. In your own words and sentence style, present the author's main ideas and most important details. Usually omit examples, explanations, and statistics.
> 3. Compare your summary to the original to be sure that your words accurately and completely reflect the original.
> 4. Check to see whether you have quoted from the original. If you must quote single words or phrases from the original, enclose them in double quotation marks (see 40a and b).

A summary condenses an original in your own words, reducing a passage as short as a sentence or as long as a paragraph or a chapter to its central meaning and essential details. Summarize the following:

- Background information
- Commentaries, explanations, and evaluations
- Arguments or a line of thinking
- Facts
- In literary works: description, events, episodes, and lengthy speeches or dialogue

Here is an original passage about the role of trained grief counsellors and a note summarizing the passage.

In the long run, professional grief counsellors are crucial, as the loss of a child is frequently a major factor that leads to family breakdown. Spouses are sometimes inclined to blame each other and act out their grief in other ways that include drinking, social isolation, refusal to discuss the problem, or fixation on the death. If these actions take place, they can create serious difficulties for the other spouse and surviving children. Grief counsellors are fully aware of the short- and long-term consequences of loss, and can provide valuable strategies for maintaining the integrity of the family in stressful situations.

(M. Nagler, *Yes You Can: A Guide for Parents of Children with Disabilities*, p. 79)

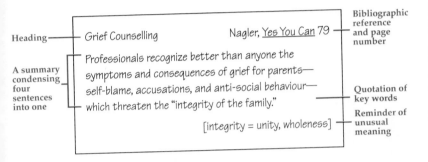

Heading — Grief Counselling   Nagler, <u>Yes You Can</u> 79 — Bibliographic reference and page number

A summary condensing four sentences into one — Professionals recognize better than anyone the symptoms and consequences of grief for parents— self-blame, accusations, and anti-social behaviour— which threaten the "integrity of the family." — Quotation of key words

[integrity = unity, wholeness] — Reminder of unusual meaning

3   Note-taking by paraphrase

A **paraphrase** restates a passage in your own words and phrasing. Usually about as long as the original, it includes examples and explanations from the original. Paraphrase what readers might otherwise misunderstand. Avoid a word-for-word "translation" of the original into your words and phrases, for that is plagiarism. (See 52e.) If you quote key words or phrases, enclose them in quotation marks. Here is an original passage about the role the land plays in the natural life cycle and a note paraphrasing it.

Land, then, is not merely soil; it is a fountain of energy flowing through a circuit of soils, plants, and animals. Food chains are the living channels which conduct energy upward; death and decay return it to the soil. The circuit is not closed; some energy is dissipated in decay, some is added by absorption from the air, some is stored in soils, peats, and long-lived forests; but it is a sustained circuit, like a slowly augmented revolving fund of life.

(Aldo Leopold, *A Sand County Almanac*, p. 212)

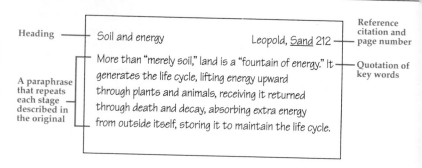

| Heading | Soil and energy — Leopold, <u>Sand</u> 212 — Reference citation and page number |

Heading — Soil and energy   Leopold, <u>Sand</u> 212 — Reference citation and page number

A paraphrase that repeats each stage described in the original — More than "merely soil," land is a "fountain of energy." It generates the life cycle, lifting energy upward through plants and animals, receiving it returned through death and decay, absorbing extra energy from outside itself, storing it to maintain the life cycle. — Quotation of key words

chapter

52 Planning, Writing, Using Sources, and Revising

Planning and writing a research project are much like writing other kinds of papers. (See the guidelines to planning, writing, and revising in 3–4.) The following guidelines will give you tips for meeting the special challenges of research writing.

52a As you finish your research, take stock of it

1 Making planning notes

As you do research, your initial thoughts about your topic and paper will change. That's natural. You should expect to change your mind as the result of new information. To keep your thoughts straight and keep track of changing plans for your paper, write them down in planning notes. What should you write down?

- New ideas. Keep track of your new thinking as the result of research.
- New versions of key questions or statements of your problem.
- New versions of your thesis. Rewrite your thesis until it fits your research. Avoid overly general or incomplete thesis statements. If you're writing a formal report, draw conclusions about the results of your research. (See 63d.)
- Organizing plans. Write lists of ideas or brief sketch outlines to help you organize your research.

- Good lines. Write brief passages you might use to begin your paper, introduce parts, or explain key ideas.

Your aim is to write down as much as possible about your paper before you write it. The more you write now, the less you'll have to think of later as you write a draft.

52*b* Plan your strategy

1 Organizing

One of the biggest challenges of a research paper is organizing all your materials to support your thesis or, if you're writing a report, to lead logically to your conclusion. Avoid organizing source by source, one after another. Your paper is about the point you want to make, not about your sources. Its design should support that point and reflect the logic of your thought. Here are organizing patterns traditionally used by researchers. See whether one is right for you.

- *Thesis support.* State your thesis early and then support it systematically, point by point.
- *Classical organizing patterns.* Arrange your ideas by *order of importance, classification, part by part* (*analysis*), *cause/effect,* or *comparison/contrast.*
- *Persuasion.* If you aim to persuade readers to change their beliefs or behaviour, see the organizing patterns in 6a3.

How to . . .

How to Refocus Your Research Project

As you near the end of your research, use the following exercise to help you refocus your thinking and see your project more clearly.

1. I can now state my specific research topic as:
2. My key question or problem to be solved is now:
3. What I've discovered about my topic from my sources:
   a. What did I expect to find? What have I found instead?
   b. What are the controversies? Who agrees with whom?
   c. Which sources are the best? Why? What sources do I have left to check? (Reconsider the checklist in 50a4.)
4. My tentative thesis: "What I want to prove/explain/demonstrate/ show about [my topic] is that. . . . What I mean to say is that . . . " If you're writing a formal report, say: "My conclusion about [my topic] is that . . . "
5. I now have _____ days left to organize, write, and revise my paper.

- *Review of research.* If you're writing a survey of research, classify your sources into groups, explain their differing views, and then evaluate them to determine the most informative, insightful, and useful.

- *Problem/solution.* First describe the problem in detail, then propose a solution for it, if necessary explaining how the solution might be implemented (*process*) or showing how it is better than an alternative (*contrast*).

- *Historical overview.* Give necessary background information and then trace the unfolding of an event from one episode to the next. Be sure to show how each relates or leads to the next. Conclude by describing the consequences of the event.

- *Formal report.* For guidelines to organizing a formal report, see 63d2. I your report will use in-text subject headings, see 48b.

A note on outlining. For a paper as complex as a research project, outlining is usually essential for discovering an effective pattern of organization (See 3c for guidelines.)

2 Planning for readers

Focussing intently on their work, researchers sometimes lose sight o who their audience is, what their readers need to know, and what will be of interest to that audience. (See 1c3.) Here are the essentials for satisfying a reader.

- *An introduction.* Many kinds of introductions are appropriate for research projects. (See 8c1.) Be sure that your topic and purpose are clear from the outset. Unless you have good reasons for doing otherwise, your opening should lead directly to your thesis, key question, or problem.

- *Illustrations.* Plan for examples and, if necessary, visual aids to explain or dramatize your ideas. (For more on visual aids, see 48b2-4.) Consider figurative language, especially analogies. (See 8b7 and 31c.)

- *Conclusions.* The following are appropriate ways to conclude research projects: warn about the need to act on your topic; offer solutions or make recommendations; show how your topic relates to some larger subject; identify a path that future researchers should take. (See 8d1 for other strategies.)

52_c_ Integrate source materials into your project

Your paper should weave other people's words and ideas so smoothly into your own that readers feel they are following one unbroken thread as they read. The following tips, based on the Modern Language Association style.

will help you achieve this effect. (For tips on the American Psychological Association style, see 56a.)

1 Presenting borrowed material

Generally, presenting borrowed materials is a four-step process. With practice you'll learn to vary it in artful, interesting ways.

■ Step 1: Use a signal statement. Whenever you quote, give another's opinions, or provide disputed information, write signal statements to introduce your borrowing. Use them to earn readers' acceptance of a source or to help readers understand or see the value of a source. To write a signal statement, do one or more of the following in an introductory phrase or sentence: identify the author or sponsor of the source; summarize the writer's credentials; give the title; announce the subject matter of the borrowing; provide its context; suggest the writer's purpose; evaluate the contents of the borrowing. Consider these sample signal statements:

Dr. Pringle points out that ... [credentials, author, purpose]

Barry Herr, president of Bio-Systems International, assumes ... [author, credentials, purpose, and an implied evaluation]

Parks Canada has recently confirmed the alarming numbers of wild animals killed yearly by motorists on national parks roadways ... [sponsoring source, purpose, subject matter, evaluation]

... warns Aldo Leopold in *A Sand County Almanac*, one of the most important documents of the environmental movement. [purpose, author, title, evaluation]

To signal a writer's purpose accurately, choose from the following list of verbs.

acknowledge	claim	emphasize	object	report
add	comment	endorse	observe	respond
admit	compare	explain	offer	reveal
advise	confirm	grant	oppose	say
agree	consider	hint	point out	state
allow	contend	hold	present	suggest
analyze	criticize	hope	propose	support
answer	declare	illustrate	reason	tell
argue	define	imply	recognize	think
assert	deny	indicate	refute	urge
assume	describe	insist	regard	warn
believe	discuss	interpret	remark	wonder
charge	dispute	note	reply	

- Step 2: Insert the quotation, summary, or paraphrase.
- Step 3: Document the borrowing. Provide enough information about the source to guide readers to complete publication information in the works cited or list of references at the end of your paper. (See the MLA style, 54a and b; the APA style, 56a and c; endnotes or footnotes, 57a; or the appropriate style manuals listed in 59.)
- Step 4: Explain the borrowing. If readers may not understand the meaning or purpose of your borrowing, explain it. Don't assume readers will see what you do or get your message without assistance.

For example:

	Canadians are constantly surprised to be told that they have a
	quaint pronunciation of *about* (to many ears, it rhymes with either
Signal phrase	*a boot* or *a boat*). As linguistics professor Jack Chambers explains
Direct quotation	it, the "difference in the two *ou* sounds is systematic, and known
	[. . .] as Canadian Raising. Because of it, Canadians have a
Parenthetical documentation	different *ou* sound in *house* and *houses*, and in *lout* and *loud*" (qtd. in McCrum 267). This is one of the main features distinguishing
Explanation	Canadian speech, almost as characteristic as the *eh?* that is
	recognized worldwide.

2 Taking credit for your ideas

Occasionally you'll have an idea about your topic and then find that a source has had a similar idea. To take credit for original thinking and yet be fair to others, present your source's version of your idea, quoting if necessary, but also give your version, if necessary explaining how yours differs.

	It is difficult to motivate people to change when they do not
	feel the necessity for change, or if they feel that the need is
An idea that the writer shares with a source	contrived. The result is resistance and apathy. Yet a person's refusal to participate may just as easily reflect frustration and
	despair. Community organizers should heed James Dittes'
Citation of the source and a quotation	warning that "some groans are [. . .] unambiguously articulate" ("Poverty" 21), that they may well be cries for help and for action.
Explanation	Those organizers who take a person's "no" at face value may
	therefore not be hearing the plea for help behind the "no."

3 **Working with several sources at once**

Occasionally, you will present several sources together.

- *Present one source at a time.* The standard procedure is to present your sources one at a time, documenting each as you borrow from it, as in the preceding examples.

- *Summarize sources as a group.* A second method, useful when sources agree, is to summarize all of them at once, without mentioning names. After the summary, document them in one citation. But be aware that lengthy citations can be distracting.

> Most usage experts now begrudgingly acknowledge that "hopefully" can be a synonym for "it is hoped" (Blackburn, "Lost" 89; O'Conner 84–85; Swan 299).

- *Select a spokesperson.* A third method is to select a spokesperson to speak for all your sources. Document the person you quote or summarize.

> That usage experts acknowledge "hopefully" as a synonym for "it is hoped" does not mean they like it. Bob Blackburn speaks for many when he says tersely, "The misuse is well established" ("Lost" 89).

4 **Quoting briefly**

Quote whenever you need a source's exact words. But be brief; use only the words you need. More may only mislead. Try to keep quotations to a sentence or less, punctuate them correctly, and connect them grammatically to your own words. (See 40b.) Here are two examples, the first quoting a phrase, the second a complete sentence.

> Children who care only about getting presents are, in the words of Miss Manners, "skilled extortionists" (Martin 33).

> According to Stephen Baetz, managers should watch how they use the word *but*: "Used as a bridge between praise and criticism, this word comes across as a slap in the face after a pat on the head" (2).

A note on quoting excessively: Many people object to reading numerous quotations one after another, especially numerous long quotations. Such a pattern becomes monotonous. It may also suggest that you haven't thought carefully about the meaning of your borrowing or that you have not synthesized information effectively.

5 Using ellipsis points to signal omissions

Use three evenly spaced periods to signal that you have omitted words from a quotation. *Note:* The Modern Language Association requires that square brackets enclose ellipsis points inserted in quotations, as in the example below. (See 41d.)

- *An omission of less than a sentence.* Use ellipsis points for omissions within a sentence or at the end. The remaining words must themselves be grammatically complete. Do not use ellipsis points before or after fragmentary quotations or for an omission at the beginning of a sentence.

  In his article in *Second Language Dynamics*, Rem Kooistra makes his point metaphorically: "The teaching of 'cultural context' is not [. . .] the icing on the language cake" (167).

  [The writer has omitted twelve words: *the sugar coating on the pill of grammar study, nor is it.* The remaining words make a grammatically complete sentence.]

- *An omission of more than a sentence.* If you omit more than a full sentence, place a period before the three bracketed ellipsis points.

  David Suzuki's warning is urgent: "Like the Amazon rain forest, coastal Canadian rain forests are being cleared faster than they can be replaced. [. . .] These unique and irreplaceable watersheds appear ready to disappear within this generation." (n. pag.)

6 Using brackets for insertions

Use typed or hand-drawn brackets (not parentheses) to insert your words into a quotation to explain a reference or complete the grammar of the sentence. (See 41c.)

Nature writer Wallace Stegner believes that "recreation could be as dangerous [to wilderness areas] as logging or extractive use" (43).

52d | Indent long quotations of prose and poetry

1 Indenting prose quotations

These are the Modern Language Association guidelines for long quotations. (For American Psychological Association guidelines, see 48d4.)

- *Length.* To make quotations longer than four typed lines easy to read, set them off in an indented block, separate from your words.

- *Introduction and punctuation.* Introduce the quotation in your own words. If your introduction is an independent clause that could be punctuated as a complete sentence, follow it with a colon. If it is a signal statement such as *According to economist Dian Cohen,* follow it with a comma. If no grammatical break occurs between your words and the quotation, use no punctuation.

- *Indentation.* Indent 2.5 cm or ten spaces from the left margin and none from the right.

- *Quotation marks and spacing.* Do not enclose indented quotations with quotation marks. The block format signals word-for-word quotation. Double-space the quotation.

- *Paragraphing.* If you quote part of a paragraph or only one paragraph, do not indent the first line more than the rest. To quote two or more paragraphs in block format, indent first lines an additional three spaces (a total of thirteen spaces from the left margin). Following a block quotation, begin a new paragraph of your own writing only if you change subjects.

- *Documentation.* One space after the punctuation ending the quotation, cite the source parenthetically. (For more on MLA in-text documentation, see 53b.)

> The portrait of Thomas Gradgrind that Charles Dickens presents in <u>Hard Times</u> satirizes defects in the nineteenth-century philosophy of utilitarianism:
>
>> Thomas Gradgrind, sir. A man of realities. A man of facts and calculations. A man who proceeds upon the principle that two and two are four, and nothing over, and who is not to be talked into allowing for anything over. [. . .] With a rule and a pair of scales, and multiplication tables always in his pocket, sir, ready to weigh and measure any parcel of human nature, and tell you exactly what it comes to. (2)

A note on omitted words: If you omit words from a quotation, signal the omission with ellipsis points [. . .]. (See 41d.)

2 Indenting quotations of dialogue in fiction

If you quote exchanges of dialogue between two or more speakers, use the indented quotation format and follow the paragraphing of the original, even if you quote fewer than four typed lines. One space after the quotation, cite the source parenthetically. (See 53b9.)

3 Indenting quotations of dialogue in drama and film

If you quote dialogue between two or more speakers, use the indented quotation format. Indent 2.5 cm or ten spaces from the left margin. Introduce each speaker by his or her name written in capitals followed by a period: *OTHELLO.* Use quotation marks only if they appear in the original. Indent subsequent lines in a character's speech an additional three spaces. When a new character speaks, start a new line 2.5 cm or ten spaces from the left margin. One space after the quotation, cite the source parenthetically. (See 53b9.)

> As Iago incites him, Othello plots Desdemona's murder:
>
> OTHELLO. Get me some poison, Iago, this night. I'll not expostulate
>   with her, lest her body and beauty unprovide my mind again. This
>   night, Iago!
>
> IAGO. Do it not with poison. Strangle her in bed, even the bed she hath
>   contaminated. (4.1.200–204)

4 Indenting quotations of poetry

For quotations of more than three lines of poetry, use the indented quotation format.

- *Indentation.* Indent 2.5 cm or ten spaces from the left margin. If the poem looks unbalanced on the page, indent more or less as necessary.

- *Spacing and formatting.* Double-space the quotation and arrange the passage to look as much like the original as possible. If a quotation begins in the middle of a line, follow the alignment of the original and do not shift the line to the left or right.

- *Line length.* If a long line would extend beyond the right margin, continue it on the next line, indenting an extra three spaces.

- *Quotation marks.* Use quotation marks only if they appear in the original.

- *Line numbers.* Include line numbers in parentheses one space after the last line.

- *Omissions.* If you omit words or lines from a quotation, use ellipsis points. (See 41d.)

William Blake's "The Tiger" questions the origins of that part of creation that is not innocent but not necessarily evil, either.

> Tiger, Tiger, burning bright
>
> In the forests of the night,
>
> What immortal hand or eye
>
> Could frame thy fearful symmetry? (1–4)

A note on brief quotations: If you are quoting only two or three lines of poetry, incorporate them in your text, using a slash (/) to indicate the start of a new line (see 41e).

52e | Avoid plagiarism

When you use a person's words or ideas or mention facts that are not common knowledge, you must credit your sources, first by giving in-text documentation and then by listing your sources in a Works Cited or Reference list at the end of your paper. Newspaper reporters and magazine journalists are not always required to document their sources of information, but in academic writing, you must acknowledge your sources.

Failure to document your borrowing is **plagiarism,** a form of theft and a serious breach of the researcher's code of ethics. On the other hand, frequent, fair, and accurate documentation will give credibility and authority to your writing. (For the MLA style of documentation, see 53 and 54; for the APA style, see 56. For other styles, see 57–59.)

A note on recycling papers: It is unethical to submit the same paper in more than one course. Never do so.

A note on collaborative writing: In school and on the job, writers are increasingly required to write collaboratively. This is especially true of computer documents such as Web pages. Fairness, graciousness, and even policy statements require you to acknowledge the work of your collaborators and other assistance you receive. You may do so with an acknowledgements page preceding the text of your writing or in a note at the end. In either case, acknowledge collaborators by name, identify their contributions, and thank them. (For an example of an acknowledgement, see the end of the preface to this book, p. xiv.)

1 Documenting common knowledge

Always document the sources of direct quotations, opinions, explanations, and interpretations, but facts and ideas are sometimes difficult to handle. A fact or an idea is "common knowledge" if educated men and women would be expected to know it or when experts repeat a fact or idea from one source to the next without documentation.

That the Red River Valley is prone to flooding is a fact that requires no documentation. But what should a researcher do with the fact that such flooding reduces rather than increases the fertility of fields? If many sources cite this result without an outside reference, it is common knowledge and does not need to be documented. If, however, only one of your sources introduces it, the fact is original to that source and must be documented. Always document when in doubt.

Of course, if you quote or paraphrase one writer's statement or interpretation of common knowledge, you must provide documentation.

2 Documenting quotations

Enclose direct quotations with quotation marks and document your borrowing.

■ The original source:

The pesticides could have some deleterious effects on Lake Winnipeg's wildlife, but scientists say the huge quantity of water rushing northward should dilute them.

> (Stephen Strauss, "Ecosystem May Profit From Disaster," *Globe and Mail*, April 28, 1997, p. A9)

■ Unfair borrowing (plagiarism emphasized):

Pesticides may cause *some* damage to *Lake Winnipeg's wildlife, but* it is likely that these chemicals will be dissipated by *the huge quantity of water rushing northward* (Strauss A9).

[Even though this example is documented, the writer has used half of the original words without using quotation marks. Take care that your summaries do not drift into plagiarism.]

■ Fair use:

Stephen Strauss admits that "pesticides could have some deleterious effects on Lake Winnipeg's wildlife," while offering the reassurance that "the huge quantity of water rushing northward should dilute them" (A9).

3 Documenting key words

Even if you take only one or two key words from a source, you must enclose them with quotation marks and document your borrowing.

■ The original source:

Poetry is a matter of rhythm and the poetry of Hopkins particularly so. It seems to have an internal dynamism, a driving force inside it that explodes into every kind of dislocation.

> (Peter Levi, "The Case of Gerard Manley Hopkins, S.J.," *Grail*, March 1997, p. 17)

- Unfair use (plagiarism emphasized):

  Students of poetry must be alert for "internal dynamism," which determines and controls the rhythm of verse.

  [Even though the borrowed words are enclosed in quotation marks, the writer has not documented the source.]

- Fair use:

  Students of poetry must be alert for what critic Peter Levi calls "internal dynamism," which determines and controls the rhythm of verse (17).

4   Documenting opinions

You must document an author's opinion or line of thinking. Writers have rights to their ideas as well as their words.

- The original source:

  Publicly funded libraries are not free bookstores but rather thermometers of social dynamics. Their healthy presence declares social equality is underpinned by intellectual equality: all knowledge is freely available, all inquiries are legitimate.

  (Mary Beaty, "To the Barricades!" *Quill & Quire*, March 1997, p. 15)

- Unfair use:

  One of the best reasons for maintaining the funding of public libraries is that they are not bookstores. In remaining accessible to everyone, they promote literacy—anything less is like slamming school doors in the face of the less fortunate.

  [Although this passage is in the writer's own words and even imaginatively written, the first sentence depends heavily on the original and the pro-library argument is that of the original source and must be documented.]

- Fair use:

  One of the best reasons for maintaining the funding of public libraries is that they are, as Mary Beaty argues, "not free bookstores but rather thermometers of social dynamics" (15). In other words, in remaining accessible to everyone, they promote literacy—anything less is like slamming school doors in the face of the less fortunate.

5   Documenting a paraphrase

To paraphrase effectively, restate the author's words and phrasing in your own words and phrasing. Avoid the mere substitution of synonyms for the author's original.

- The original source:

  Low-income families are seldom able to cross town to take advantage of one-time shopping specials; nor can such families normally stock up on bargain items.

  (D. P. Ross, E. R. Shillington and C. Lochhead,
  The Canadian Fact Book on Poverty, 1994, p. 19)

- Unfair use (bordering on plagiarism):

  Lower-income families cannot easily travel from store to store to shop the specials, nor can they afford to buy in bulk when things are on sale (Ross, Shillington and Lochhead 19).

  [The writer has documented the source of the original but has merely substituted synonyms for the original words and retained the original sentence structure.]

- Fair use:

  Lower-income families are often unfairly criticized for paying full price instead of spot-shopping for specials and for not buying in bulk. What their critics forget, of course, is that low-income families have neither the resources nor the disposable income for enjoying such savings (Ross, Shillington and Lochhead 19).

 Computer Tip:

Avoiding Internet Plagiarism

If you cut an excerpt from an Internet file and paste it into your paper, be sure to enclose it in double quotation marks (see 40a and b), introduce it with a signal statement (see 52c1), and document your borrowing at the end.

How to Revise and Edit a Research Project

Use the following questions to guide your revision and editing. Or ask fellow students to read your draft with these questions in mind and answer the most important. (For more on revision, see 4b and c.)

1. Does the paper's thesis appear somewhere in the introduction? Is it clear and complete? Does the introduction to a formal report describe a problem or pose a key question?
2. Does the paper include all the information, explanation, and interpretation needed to support its thesis or, in a formal report, to justify its conclusion? Will your support satisfy your readers' needs and interests?
3. Does the paper introduce and explain borrowed materials? Is the documentation complete and appropriate to the discipline in which the paper is written? Are all direct quotations enclosed by quotation marks?
4. Do the paper's ideas make sense and fit together logically and smoothly? Does the paper follow its outline? If not, which is more logically organized, the paper or the outline? Would another design improve the paper?
5. If the project uses subject headings, as in a report, are they formatted correctly? Do headings clearly identify the sections they introduce? (See 48b1.)
6. Is the language appropriate to research writing: accurate, precise, objective, and appropriately formal? (See 32a and c.) Is the style appropriate for the intended audience?
7. Does the paper include appropriately formatted drafts of a title page, outline page, acknowledgments, or abstract, if required? (See 48c for MLA format, 48d for APA format.) Is there a comprehensive Works Cited or Reference list? (See 54a to prepare an MLA Works Cited list or 56b to prepare an APA Reference list.)

For a sample MLA research project with title and outline page, see 55.

53 Writing MLA In-Text (Parenthetical) Citations

In papers for humanities courses, the preferred way to cite borrowed materials is the Modern Language Association (MLA) system of in-text citation. (For the American Psychological Association's author-date system, see 56. For footnotes or endnotes, and a citation-sequence system, see 57 and 58. For a list of style manuals used in various fields, see 59.)

53a Follow MLA citation guidelines

As you write a first draft, document your borrowing at appropriate places in your paper.

- *In a signal statement.* Name your source in an introductory signal phrase when you quote directly or borrow an explanation, opinion, interpretation, or disputed fact. Give the author's full name for the first references and the last name only thereafter. (See also 52c1.)

- *In a parenthetical citation.* In parentheses, following your borrowing, provide enough information to guide readers to full publication information in the Works Cited list at the end of your paper. Give page numbers if your sources have them. Place the citation after the borrowing, following quotation marks, but before the period at the end of a sentence.

  In block or indented quotations, place the parentheses one space after the last punctuation mark.

- *In the Works Cited list.* At the end of your paper, in a list titled **Works Cited**, provide full publication or source information for each source you've used.

53b Follow parenthetical citation formats

The following guidelines will show you how to match signal statements with appropriate citation formats.

1 Naming an author in a signal statement

If you name an author in a signal statement and use only one source by that author, cite the page number of your borrowing in parentheses.

Applying psychoanalytic theory to her analysis of Conrad's *The Secret Sharer*, Esther Rankin suggests that "the preamble may reflect [the captain's] separation or alienation from something as yet unnamed [. . .]" (52).

2 Naming a corporate author in a signal statement

Cite a corporate author as you would a person.

The Vanier Institute of the Family cites projections that almost half of a year's marriages "will end in divorce" (24).

3 Omitting an author name and a signal statement

If you do not name the author in a signal statement and use only one source by that author, cite the author's last name and the page number in parentheses. No punctuation separates the author's name and the page number.

Although it is counterproductive to point out and demand correction of every error, it is worth devoting some time each week to revision and editing (Prokop 35).

4 Citing two or more sources by the same author

If your paper includes two or more sources by the same author, follow these guidelines to parenthetical citation.

- *Author named in a signal statement.* If you name the author in a signal statement, give a short form of the title and the page number in parentheses. Enclose article titles in quotation marks; underline book titles.

  Annie Dillard compares the dynamics between writer and writing to "what happens between a painter and the canvas" (<u>Writing Life</u> 56).

- *Author and title in a signal statement.* If a signal statement includes the author's name and title of the source, give only the page number in parentheses.

  In <u>Anatomy of Criticism</u>, Frye draws tidy parallels between literature and mathematics, especially as represented by "the metaphor and the equation" (352).

■ *Author and title not named in a signal statement.* If you do not give the author or title in a signal statement, include both in the parenthetical citation separated by a comma. Write brief titles in full; give shortened versions of longer titles.

Censorship, whether the result of nationalist fervour or heightened religious fundamentalism, still threatens democracy (D'Souza, "Censorship?" 41).

5 Citing more than one author of a source

■ If a source has two or three authors, name them in the signal statement or parenthetical citation.

As springtime tourists know only too well, Northern Ontario is "prime blackfly country, perhaps the world's most notorious" (Bennet and Tiner 76).

■ If a source has four or more authors, you may indicate multiple authorship in your signal statement (Dr. Peters and her colleagues reported …) or give only the first author's name followed by *et al.* ("and others") in the parenthetical citation.

Jacob *et al.* warn primary school educators of the "poor track record" of conventional approaches to educational reform (255).

6 Citing an unknown author

If an author's name is not given in the source, use the complete title in a signal statement or the first key words in the parenthetical citation.

The five or so species of cacti in Canada survive because they dehydrate in the fall to grow and swell with the warm spring rains ("Cacti" 72).

7 Citing authors with the same last name

If you cite two or more authors with the same last name, include each author's first and last name in signal statements or in parenthetical documentation include each author's first initial (full first name if the initial is shared, too) and last name.

In 1939, the former Edward VIII accepted the post of Governor of the Bahamas, silencing speculation that he was a Nazi sympathizer (Josephine Ross 171).

8 Citing a multivolume source

If you cite more than one volume of a multi-volume source, give the volume number followed by a colon, a space, and the page number in the parenthetical citation.

> In chronicling the evolution of Canadian heraldry, I. L. Campbell's <u>The Identifying Symbols of Canadian Institutions</u> defines arms as "marks of honour granted to Canadian individuals, corporations or institutions" (1: 231).

9 Citing literary works

Provide enough information in the parenthetical citation to enable readers to locate the material you are citing even if they use an edition different from yours. For **undivided** works such as short stories, include the page number in the parenthetical citation. For works **divided** into chapters, acts and so on, provide additional information.

- *Novels.* Parenthetically cite the page number in the edition you used, followed by a semicolon and the part, section or chapter number.

> In <u>Light in August</u>, novelist William Faulkner traces the complex process by which his protagonist's childhood memories are transformed into knowledge and then belief: "Memory believes before knowing remembers" (104; ch. 6).

- *Poetry.* For poetry that is divided into books or other numbered sections, give the part and line numbers.

> Birney describes David's sudden falling with striking sibilants:
>
> > [Without] A gasp he was gone. I froze to the sound of grating
> > Edge-nails and fingers, the slither of stones, the lone
> > Second of silence, the nightmare thud. Then only
> > the wind and the muted beat of unknowing cascades.
>
> > (7. 97–100)

- *Plays.* Cite modern plays as you would a book, including page numbers. Cite verse and classic plays by act, scene, and line. Use Arabic numerals unless instructed otherwise.

> As Othello plots Desdemona's murder, he confesses her enduring power over him: "I'll not expostulate with her, lest her body and beauty unprovide my mind again" (4.1.200–201).

10 Citing an indirect source

If you quote a writer whose words appear in a source written by someone else, name the source you are quoting in a signal phrase. Begin the parenthetical citation with *qtd. in* ("quoted in") and identify the source where you found the quotation.

> As early as 1923, the <u>Toronto Star</u> recognized Hemingway's "genius for
>
> newspaper work [and] for the short story" (qtd. in Brian 40).

11 Citing an entire source

To cite an entire work, give the author's name and the title, if necessary, in a signal statement or parenthetical citation.

> John Robert Colombo's <u>Canadian Global Almanac</u> is an indispensable annual
>
> compendium of Canadian facts and figures.

12 Citing two or more sources in one citation

When citing two or more sources in parentheses, separate the citations with a semicolon. Remember, however, that multiple references may be distracting. For other ways to handle multiple sources, see 52c3.

> Many who oppose restricting access to national parks profit economically
>
> from that access (Coates, "Comfort" 14; Stapleton 34).

13 Citing an interview

To document an interview, name the source in a signal statement or parenthetical citation.

> Toronto poet Allan Jevons points out impishly that many of the most
>
> memorable quotations have anonymous sources.

14 Citing Internet sources

Cite Internet sources as you would print documents. Include enough information to direct readers to the appropriate citation in your Works Cited list. If an Internet source includes section headings, page numbers, or paragraph numbers, include them. (*Pars.* is the abbreviation for *paragraphs*; *chs.* for *chapters*.) Do not include page numbers from printouts because they may vary from one printout to another.

Terry McGuide, Parks Canada's Highways Manager, describes plans to

monitor the effectiveness of "wildlife overpasses" designed to reduce

accidents between vehicles and animals ("Phase Illa," pars. 4-5).

53c Include content and bibliography notes when necessary

Use notes in an MLA-style research paper only when you must provide additional information that cannot be worked into the text of your paper. Put raised numbers in your text to refer readers to a **footnote** at the bottom of the page or to an **endnote** on a page headed *Notes* immediately preceding the list of Works Cited. Number your notes consecutively throughout the paper. (For more on the use of notes, see 57.)

1 Writing content notes

Use content notes for definitions, formulas, explanations, and translations that would interrupt the flow of ideas if placed in the text of your paper.

- Text:

    In 1991, Canada's national parks received more than 13 million visitors, almost two-thirds, 8.4 million, visiting the five most popular parks.[5]

- Note:

    [5] These parks were visited the most: Banff, 4.2 million; Jasper, 1.4 million; Kootenay, 1.2 million; Prince Edward Island, 930 000; and Yoho, 690 000.

2 Writing bibliography notes

Use bibliography notes to cite several sources at once without a lengthy parenthetical citation, make cross-references, or refer readers to sources relevant to a topic.

- Text:

    Most usage experts now begrudgingly acknowledge that "hopefully" can be used, at least informally, as a synonym for "it is hoped."[4]

- Note:

    [4] For detailed commentary on the acceptability of "hopefully," see Blackburn, "Lost" 89; O'Conner 84–85; Swan 299; Johnson 255–56; and E. B. White, qtd. in <u>Webster's Dictionary of English Usage</u> 513.

chapter

54 Preparing the MLA Works Cited List

54*a* | Follow the MLA general guidelines

A list of Works Cited gives full publication information for all sources cited in an MLA-style research paper. (See the example in 55.) Your instructor may ask you to also provide a Works Consulted list that includes all the works you've read, whether you cite them parenthetically or not.

1 Placement of the Works Cited list

Begin the Works Cited on a separate page at the end of your paper, after other concluding materials. (See 48c7 for the order of pages in an MLA paper.)

2 Format of the Works Cited list

- *Title.* Centre the title Works Cited (without italics, underlining, or quotation marks) 2.5 cm from the top of the page. Continue page numbers from the text of your paper.

- *Spacing.* Double-space before the first entry and throughout all entries.

- *Indentation.* Begin each entry flush with the left margin. Indent second and successive lines 1 cm (five spaces).

- *Numbering.* Do not number the entries.

- *Alphabetical order.* Arrange entries alphabetically according to the author's last name as it appears on the title page of your source. Use square brackets to identify the true name when a pseudonym is given: *Mark Twain [Samuel Langhorne Clemens].* If an entry has no author, alphabetize according to the first word of the title, ignoring *A, An,* and *The.*

  Interpretation and Tourism: Ottawa '88. Proc. of a Conference on Heritage

  Interpretation 13–17 Apr. 1988. N.p.: n.p., n.d.

  Leighton, Douglas. "Helping the Animals Cross the Road." Canadian

  Geographic Aug.–Sept. 1988: 22–28.

  Ministry of Environment. Parks Canada Policy. 18 Feb. 1997. Parks Canada. 4

  Mar. 1998 <http://www.parkscanada.pch.gc.ca>.

3 Citation formats

See 54b for sample MLA citations.

■ *Two or more sources by the same author.* List two or more sources by the same author alphabetically by title. List the author's name for the first entry only. For the remaining entries, in place of the name type three hyphens followed by a period.

> Frye, Northrop. <u>Anatomy of Criticism: Four Essays</u>. Princeton: Princeton UP,
>
> > 1957.
>
> ---. "Haunted by Lack of Ghosts: Some Patterns in the Imagery of Canadian
>
> > Poetry." <u>The Canadian Imagination</u>. Ed. David Staines. Cambridge,
> >
> > Mass.: Harvard UP, 1977.
>
> ---. <u>Reading the World: Selected Writings, 1935–1976</u>. Ed. Robert D. Denham.
>
> > New York: Lang, 1990.

■ *Punctuation of entries.* Place a period followed by one space after each part of a citation:

> Author. Title. Publication information.

■ Publication dates. For books, use the most recent publication date. For periodicals, abbreviate all months except May, June, and July.

■ *Page numbers.* For inclusive page numbers, give only the last two digits unless more are necessary, e.g., *1–21, 88–93, 95–121, 141–61, 1198–213.* When a periodical or newspaper article is not printed on consecutive pages, give the first page number and a plus sign, (e.g., *36+).*

■ *Incomplete entries.* If an entry is incomplete, use the following abbreviations in the appropriate places: *n.p.* = no publisher given; *n.p.* = no place of publication; *n.d.* = no date of publication; *n. pag.* = no page numbers.

54*b* | Sample citations

1 Citing books

The basic citation for a book:

> Author's last name, first name. Title and subtitle underlined or italicized.
>
> > Place of publication: publisher, date of publication.

Shorten names of publishers to the publisher's last name (e.g., *Knopf* for *Alfred Knopf*) or to one or two key words, dropping *Books* or *Press* (e.g., *Black*

Moss for *Black Moss Press*). Abbreviate *University Press* as *UP* (without periods).

■ **A book with one author**

Berton, Pierre. <u>The Great Depression 1929–1939</u>. Toronto: McClelland and

  Stewart, 1990.

■ **Two or three authors.** List authors in the order in which they appear on the title page; reverse the name of only the first author. Use commas to separate three authors' names.

English, John, and Kenneth McLaughlin. <u>Kitchener: An Illustrated History</u>.

  Toronto: Robin Brass, 1996.

■ **Four or more authors.** Cite all authors in the order in which they appear on the title page, or cite only the first author, followed by *et al.* ("and others").

Frampton, Merle E., et al. <u>Forgotten Children</u>. Boston: Sargent, 1968.

■ **Corporate or institutional publication**. Give the name of the corporation or institution as the author, even when it is also the publisher.

Canada Council. <u>Provincial Essays</u>. 8 vols. Toronto: Coach House, 1984–89.

■ **A book title within a title.** If a book title appears within the title of another book, do not underline or italicize the shorter title. If the shorter title is normally enclosed with quotation marks, retain the quotation marks and underline the complete longer title.

Bowering, George, ed. <u>Sheila Watson and</u> The Double Hook. Ottawa: Golden

  Dog, 1985.

Callaghan, Morley. <u>"Now That April's Here" and Other Stories</u>. New York:

  Random, 1936.

■ **An introduction, foreword, preface, or afterword.** If you borrow from an introduction, foreword, preface, or afterword, begin with the author of the element being cited; then identify the element. Place the author of the book after the title.

Suzuki, David. Preface. <u>The Last Wilderness: Images of the Canadian Wild</u>. By

  the Canadian Nature Federation and Freeman Patterson. Toronto: Key

  Porter, 1990.

■ **An author and an editor.** Cite the author's name, the title, and then the editor. Use *Ed.* for one or more editors.

Nichol, Barry P. <u>Selected Writing</u>. Ed. B. P. Nichol and Jack David. Vancouver:

  Talonbooks, 1980.

■ **An editor or editors.** Give the editor(s), followed by *ed.* or *eds.*

Dearden, Philip, and Rick Rollins, eds. <u>Parks and Protected Areas in Canada:</u>

<u>Planning and Management</u>. Toronto: Oxford UP, 1993.

■ **An edition other than the first.** Include the number of the edition following the title and the name of the translator or editor, if any.

Newlove, John. <u>Moving in Alone</u>. 2nd ed. Lantzville: Oolichan, 1977.

■ **A republished edition.** Give the original publication date before the place of publication.

Haliburton, Thomas Chandler. <u>History of Nova Scotia</u>. 1829. Belleville: Mika,

1973.

■ **A book in a series.** Following the title, include the name of the series and series number.

Traill, Catherine Parr. <u>The Canadian Settler's Guide</u>. 1855. New Canadian

Library 64. Toronto: McClelland and Stewart, 1969.

■ **A translation.** Following the title, write *Trans.* ("translated by") and the name of the translator.

Blais, Marie-Claire. <u>Tête-Blanche</u>. Trans. Charles Fullman. Toronto:

McClelland and Stewart, 1961.

■ **Unilingual and bilingual editions.** Record a title in its original language, followed by a translation in square brackets. Write the title out in full if it appears in two languages. For simultaneous publication by two publishers, list comprehensive information for both.

Racine, Claude. <u>L'anticléricalisme dans le roman québécois 1940–1965</u>

[<u>Anticlericalism in the Quebec novel 1940–1965</u>]. Montreal: Hurtubise,

1972.

Godbout, Jacques, and John Robert Colombo, eds. <u>Poésie 64/Poetry 64</u>.

Montreal: Les Editions du Jour/Toronto: Ryerson, 1963.

■ **A multi-volume work**. Give the number of volumes before the place of publication.

Costain, Thomas B. <u>The Tontine</u>. 2 vols. New York: Doubleday, 1955.

■ **A volume in a series.** If you borrow from only one volume of a multi-volume series, give its number and the series to which it belongs (following *of*) before the place of publication. Give the total number of volumes following the date of publication.

Durrell, Lawrence. <u>Mountolive</u>. Vol. 3 of <u>The Alexandria Quartet</u>. New York:

Dutton, 1959. 4 vols.

■ **A selection in an anthology.** Give the author and title of the selection, followed by the title of the book, the editor's name, the edition if appropriate, and the publication information.

Cohen, Matt. "The Eiffel Tower in Three Parts." <u>The Oxford Book of</u>

<u>Canadian Short Stories in English</u>. Ed. Margaret Atwood and Robert

Weaver. Toronto: Oxford, 1986. 370–75.

■ **A selection reprinted in an anthology.** If a selection in an anthology was originally published elsewhere, cite the original source first. Follow with *Rpt. in* ("reprinted in") and a citation for the anthology. Original publication sources are usually listed on acknowledgment pages at the beginning or end of a book or at the bottom of the first page of a selection.

Urquhart, Jane. "The Death of Robert Browning." <u>Storm Glass</u>. Erin:

Porcupine's Quill, 1987. Rpt. in <u>Likely Stories: A Postmodern Sampler</u>.

Eds. George Bowering and Linda Hutcheon. Toronto: Coach House,

1992. 283–97.

■ **Cross-references to an anthology.** If you cite more than one source from an anthology, provide full publication information for the anthology in its own citation. Cross-reference individual selections, giving author, title, editor's last name, and page numbers.

Atwood, Margaret, and Robert Weaver, eds. <u>The Oxford Book of Canadian</u>

<u>Short Stories in English</u>. Toronto: Oxford, 1986.

Cohen, Matt. "The Eiffel Tower in Three Parts." Atwood and Weaver 370–75.

Thomas, Audrey. "Kill Day on the Government Wharf." Atwood and Weaver

296–304.

■ **Anonymous or unknown author.** Alphabetize the entry according to the first word of the title, except for an initial *A, An,* or *The.*

<u>Sir Gawain and the Green Knight</u>. Ed. J. A. Burrow. Baltimore:

Penguin, 1972.

■ **Encyclopedia or dictionary.** Give the author of the entry, if any, followed by the entry title, title of the encyclopedia or dictionary, edition number if any, and the date.

"Hopefully." <u>Webster's Dictionary of English Usage</u>. 1989.

■ **Publisher's imprint.** If a book was published by an imprint of a publishing company, give the name of the imprint followed by a hyphen and the publisher's name.

Engel, Marian. <u>Sarah Bastard's Notebook</u>. Toronto: Paperbacks-General, 1968.

2 Citing periodicals and newspapers

■ **Article in a monthly magazine.** Give the author's name, the title of the article enclosed by quotation marks, the name of the magazine underlined or italicized, the month and year of publication, and the page numbers on which the article appears. If the pages are not consecutive, cite the first page number followed by the plus sign (+).

Findley, Timothy. "Old Dogs Teach New Tricks." <u>Harrowsmith Country Life</u>
Aug. 1996: 80.

■ **Article in a weekly magazine.** Cite the exact date of publication, not only the month.

McDonald, Marci. "Picturing History." <u>Maclean's</u> 20 Jan. 1997: 60–61.

■ **Article in a journal paged by volume.** For scholarly journals paged consecutively throughout the volume, give the volume number after the name of the periodical and then the date in parentheses.

McNairn, Jeffrey L. "Publius of the North." <u>The Canadian Historical Review</u>
77 (Dec. 1996): 526–48.

■ **Article in a journal paged by issue.** For scholarly journals paged separately by issue, give the issue number following the volume number.

Handscombe, Richard. "WHAT English?" <u>The English Quarterly</u> 11. 2 (1978):
147–56.

■ **Signed newspaper article.** Cite the author, title, name of the newspaper, and date of publication as you would an article in a weekly magazine. If an edition is given on the masthead of the paper, include it in your citation following the date. If each section of the paper is numbered separately, include the section number or letters before the page number.

McArthur, Douglas. "Banff's Future: National Park or Upscale Mall?" <u>Globe</u>
<u>and Mail</u> 18 Jan. 1997. Weekend ed. F1+.

■ **Unsigned magazine or newspaper article.** If no author is given for an article, begin the citation with the title.

- **Editorial.** Identify the element by writing *Editorial* following the title.

  "Our Children Walk Close to the Edge." Editorial. <u>The Record</u> 15 Mar. 1997:

    A14.

- **Letter to the editor.** Write "Letter" following the author's name.

  Purves-Smith, Mike. Letter. <u>Saturday Night</u> Feb. 1997: 11.

- **Review of a book, movie, or play.** Following the author and title of the review, write *Rev. of* and then name the work reviewed. Give important information about the work reviewed such as the author (preceded with *by*) or the director (preceded with *dir.*).

  Hughes, Susan. "The Wealthy Boomer." Rev. of <u>The Pig and the Python</u> by

    David Cork. <u>Quill & Quire</u> Jan. 1997: 29.

3   Citing Internet sources

In a 1998 Internet posting, the Modern Language Association published a master template to guide students and scholars when citing Internet sources. As you prepare an MLA-style Works Cited list, include as many items from the following list as are relevant or can be found. The sample citations illustrate various applications of this template.

For information about writing URLs, see 50a5. For tips on locating publication information in an Internet source, see 50c4. For more information about MLA Internet citations, see <http://www.mla.org> or the *MLA Style Manual and Guide to Scholarly Publishing*, Second Edition (MLA, 1998).

1. Author, editor, compiler, or translator of the source (last name first, followed by an abbreviation such as *ed.* or *trans.* when appropriate).
2. Title of article, short story, poem, or chapter (in quotation marks); or the title of a posting to a news group, listserv, or other discussion group (taken from the subject line and put in quotation marks), followed by the description *Online posting*.
3. Title of book or report (underlined).
4. Editor, compiler, or translator (if not cited earlier), preceded by an abbreviation such as *Ed.* or *Trans.* when appropriate.
5. Publication information for print versions of the source (arranged according to the guidelines elsewhere in 54).
6. Title of periodical, professional or personal site, database, or scholarly project (underlined); or for an untitled professional or personal site, a description such as *HomePage*.
7. Editor of the database or scholarly project (if available).

8. Volume number, issue number, or other identifying number for a journal; or the version number of a source when it is not part of the title.

9. Date of electronic publication, of the latest update, or of posting.

10. The name of the news group, listserv, or other discussion group.

11. The number range or total number of pages, paragraphs, sections, or chapters, if they are numbered.

12. Name of any institution or organization sponsoring or associated with the site.

13. Date when the researcher accessed the source. Do not use a period between this date and the electronic address which follows.

14. Electronic address (URL) of the source (in angle brackets, followed by a period). For guidelines to citing Internet addresses, see 48a5.

■ **A book or other lengthy document**

Thoreau, Henry David. "Where I Lived and What I Lived For." <u>Walden.</u> 1854. <u>Project Gutenberg</u>. Jan. 1995. U. of Illinois. 1 Sept. 1998 <ftp://uiarchive.cso.uius.edu/pub/gutenberg/etext95/waldn10.txt>.

[This example includes the author, chapter title, title of the work, date of original publication, title of the scholarly project, date of electronic publication, organization sponsoring the site, data of access, and URL.]

<u>Journals of the Senate: Issue 23</u>. 16 Dec. 1999. 11 pp. The Senate of Canada. 28 Dec. 1999 <http://www.parl.gc.ca/36/2/parlbus/senate/jour-e/23jr-e.htm>.

(This example includes the title of the work, publication date, total number of pages, organization, access date, and URL.]

■ **Articles in scholarly journals and in magazines**

Townsend-Gault, Charlotte. "First Nations Culture: Who Knows What?" <u>Canadian Journal of Communications</u> 23.1 (1998). 30 Nov. 1998. 30 pars. Simon Fraser University. 14 Oct. 1999 <http://www.cjc-online.ca/backissues/23.1/townsend.html>.

[This example from a scholarly journal includes the author, article title, journal title, original publication date, latest Internet update, number or paragraphs, sponsoring organization, access date, and URL.]

Lawton, Millicent. "ETS Dispute Charges of Gender Bias." <u>Education Week</u> 14 May 1997: 1+. 3 June 1998 <http://www.edweek.org/we/vol-16/33ets.h16>.

[This example from a magazine includes the author, article title, magazine title, print publication date, page number indicating non-sequential paging, access date, and URL.]

■ **Articles at professional, scholarly, business, and organization sites**

"Longer Working Hours and Health." <u>The Daily</u>. 16 Nov. 1999. Statistics Canada. 12 Dec. 1999 <http://www.statcan.ca:80/daily/english/991116/d991116b.htm>.

[This example includes the article title, bulletin title, release date, organization sponsoring the site, access date, and URL.]

- ## Professional, scholarly, business, or organizational site

  <u>Canada's Role in Fighting Tuberculosis</u>. Saskatchewan Lung Association. 4 Nov. 1999. 15 Dec. 1999 <www.lung.ca>.

  [This example includes the name of the site, the organization sponsoring the site, the date of last update, access date, and URL.]

- ## Newspaper articles

  Ruttan, Susan. "The Facade of Official Bilingualism." <u>National Post Online</u> 22 Jan 2000. Commentary. 29 Jan. 2000 <http://www.nationalpost.com/commentary.asp?f + 000122/ 183870.html>.

  [This example includes the author, article title, newspaper title, print publication information, access date, and URL.]

- ## Articles in a reference database such as an encyclopedia

  "Jericho." <u>Encyclopedia of the Orient</u>. 1997. Centre d'Information Arabe Scandinave. 4 Jan. 1998 <http://I-cias.com/e.o/jericho.htm>.

  [This example includes the article title, title of the reference source, date of electronic publication, sponsoring organization, access date, and URL.]

- ## Posting to a newsgroup, listserv, or discussion forum (MOOs, MUDs, and IRCs)

  To, Caron. "Re: Icebreaker for Students with a New Teacher." Online posting. 18 Mar. 1996. TESL-L listserv. 31 Mar. 1996 <http://www.tesl-l.cuny.edu/log961803/ICEBREAKER.txt>.

  [This example includes the author, the title of the posting, the description of the posting, the posting date, the name of the forum, access date, and URL.]

- ## Literary works such as poems or short stories in a scholarly project or database

  Gilman, Charlotte Perkins. "The Yellow Wall-Paper." 1892. <u>The "Yellow Wall-Paper"</u> *Site*. Ed. Daniel Anderson and Nick Evans. 3 Sept. 1996. 1 May 1997 <http://www.cwrl.utexas.edu/~daniel/amlit/wallpaper/ wallpapertext.html>.

  [This example includes the author, the title of the short story, the original publication date, the name of the scholarly project, the editors of the project, the latest update, the access date, and URL.]

- ## Personal site

  Rehm, Stefan. Home Page. 23 Sept. 1999 <http://www.uoguelph.ca/~srehm>.

- **Electronic mail.** To cite electronic mail, give the sender's name, a description of the document that includes the recipient, and the date of the document.

Buss, Pauline. "Choosing a New Computer for Your Office." E-mail to Joseph

Sternberg. 18 Jan. 1996.

4   Citing other electronic and print sources

- **Periodical sources published on CD-ROM and also available in print.** Many electronic sources are published at regular intervals, as magazines are, and also have print counterparts. For these, give the name of the author, if available; publication information for the printed source; the title of the database underlined; the publication medium (*CD-ROM*); the name of the vendor or distributor (if any); and the electronic publication date.

Lacayo, Richard. "This Land Is Whose Land?" <u>Time</u> 23 Oct. 1995: 68-71.

   <u>Academic ASAP</u>. CD-ROM. Infotrac. Dec. 1995.

- **Nonperiodical sources published on CD-ROM, diskette, and tape.** Some CD-ROM sources and those published on diskette or magnetic tape are issued only once, as books are. For these, give the author's name, if available; the title underlined or in quotation marks, as appropriate; the title of the product underlined; the edition, release, or version; the publication medium (*CD-ROM*); and the city of publication, publisher; and date of publication.

"Parks Canada Attendance." <u>Canada Yearbook 1997</u>. CD-ROM. Ottawa:

   Statistics Canada, Nov. 1996.

- **Pamphlet.** Cite a pamphlet as you would a book.

<u>The Golden Age of Justinian</u>. Art Gallery of Ontario. 1976.

- **Government publications.** The formats for government publications are many. The order of an entry is as follows:

Government body. Subsidiary body. <u>Title of Document</u>. Type and number of

   document. Publication information.

If you know the author's name, place it at the beginning of an entry or after the title, following the word *By*.

Ontario. Ministry of Education and Training. <u>Excellence in Education: High

   School Reform</u>. A Discussion Paper. n.p.: Queen's Printer for Ontario,

   1996.

Canada. Department of Industry, Trade and Commerce. <u>Annual Report,</u>

<u>1981–1982</u>. Ottawa: Queen's Printer, 1983.

■ **Legal references.** Do not italicize or underline the titles of laws, acts, or legal documents or enclose them with quotation marks; give the section and, if appropriate, the year. Italicize or underline the name of cases in the text of your paper but not in the Works Cited.

Health Care Consent Act, 1996, S.O. 1996, c. 2, s. 37(1)

Rodriguez v. British Columbia, [1993] 3 S.C.R. 519

■ **Dissertations.** Give the author and title as you would for a book, followed by the abbreviation *Diss.*, the university granting the degree, and the date it was granted.

Hurst, Robert O. <u>The Enzymatic Degradation of Thymus Nucleic Acid</u>. Diss.

University of Toronto, 1952.

■ **A dissertation abstract.** Give the author's name followed by the dissertation title in quotations, the abbreviation *Diss.*, the name of the university granting the degree, the date granted, the abbreviation *DA* or *DAI* (*Dissertation Abstracts* or *Dissertation Abstracts International*) as appropriate, the volume number, date of publication, and page number.

DiPierro, Marianne Elizabeth. "The Utopian Vision in the Works of

Wollstonecraft, Gilman, and Chopin." Diss. U of South Florida, 1994.

<u>DAI</u> 54 (1994): 3737A.

■ **Published proceedings of a conference.** Cite a selection from the published proceedings of a conference as you would cite a book. After the title of the publication, give information about the conference. Then give the editor's name if available, followed by the publication information.

Brandt, Gail. "Organizations in Canada: The English Protestant Tradition."

<u>Women's Paid and Unpaid Work: Historical and Contemporary</u>

<u>Perspectives</u>. Proceedings of the Workshop on the History of Women's

Collective Work, OISE, May 1984. Ed. Paula Bourne. Toronto: New

Hogtown, 1985. 79–95.

■ **Lecture or speech.** Name the person making the speech, followed by its title in quotation marks, the name of the conference or sponsoring organization, the location, and date. If not all of this information is available, provide as much as possible.

Matthews, The Rt. Rev. Victoria. "Searching for Canada's Soul." Speech to

the Empire Club of Canada. Toronto. 20 Oct. 1994.

■ **Interview.** To cite an interview you have conducted, name the person interviewed followed by *Personal interview* or *Telephone interview* and the date. To cite a radio or television interview, name the person interviewed followed by *Interview* or *Interview with* and the name of the interviewer.

Miller, Judith. Personal interview. 4 May 1996.

Oates, Joyce Carol. Interview with Terry Gross. <u>Fresh Air</u>. Natl. Public
   Radio. WHYY, Philadelphia. 3 Aug. 1993.

Purdy, Al. Interview. <u>Arc</u> 8, 9. Ed. Christopher Levenson. (Summer 1983):
   78–84.

■ **Personal letter.** Cite a letter by identifying sender and receiver. If the letter is to you, write *Letter to the author*.

Le Corbusier. Letter to Max Du Bois. 10 Apr. 1915.

■ **Radio or television program.** When appropriate, identify those involved with the production preceded by the following abbreviations: *Narr.* (narrator), *Writ.* (writer), *Dir.* (director), *Perf.* (performer), *Introd.* (introducer), *Prod.* (producer).

"Tornado!" <u>Provincewide</u>. Narr. Daiene Vernile and Mike Yaworski. CKCO,
   Kitchener, Ont. 19 Apr. 1997.

■ **Play performance.** Give the title underlined, followed with *By* and the author's name, *Dir.* and the director's name, *Perf.* and the leading actor's name.

<u>The Country Wife</u>. By William Wycherley. Dir. Douglas Campbell. Perf. Tom
   McManus. Festival Theatre, Stratford, Ont. 10 Sept. 1995.

■ **Film or video recording**

<u>Shall We Dance</u>. Dir. Edward Everett Horton. Perf. Fred Astaire and Ginger
   Rogers. 1937. Videocassette. RKO Radio Pictures, 1987.

■ **Musical composition**

Mendelssohn, Felix. Symphony no. 4 in A Major, op. 90.

Tchaikovsky, Peter. <u>The Nutcracker Suite</u>.

■ **Record, tape, or CD**

Layton, Irving. "The Birth of Tragedy." <u>Six Montreal Poets</u>. LP. Folkways,
   1957.

- **A work of art**

  Kosuth, Joseph. <u>L'essence de la rhétorique est dans l'allégorie</u>. Montreal
  Museum of Fine Arts.

- **Map or chart**

  <u>Manitoba</u>. Map. Manitoba: Surveys and Mapping Branch, 1990.

- **Cartoon.** Give the cartoonist's name, followed by the name of the cartoon or its caption if any, the label *Cartoon,* and appropriate publication information.

  King, Allan. "Check Out 11:00 a.m." Cartoon. <u>The Canadian Forum</u> 58
  (June–July 1978): 38.

chapter
55
MLA Research Project with Title and Outline Pages

The writer of the following problem/solution project was instructed to include title and outline pages. The paper follows MLA guidelines for parenthetical in-text documentation and the Works Cited (See 53 and 54). Marginal notes indicate important features of research projects and MLA documentation. For an MLA paper without a title page or an outline page, see 6d.

Modern Language Association format, with title and outline pages added.

THE NATURE OF NATURE: PROBLEMS OF ESTABLISHING

AND MAINTAINING CANADA'S NATIONAL PARKS

Centre title
one-third
down
the page

by

Heather Sparling

97259816

Double-space

Include ID #
if you have
one

Geography 101

Professor J. R. Talbot

November 30, 20--

Centre
course
information
two-thirds
down
the page

Sparling i

Use lower-case roman numerals for preliminary pages

Centre heading 2.5 cm from top of page

OUTLINE

Thesis: Canada's national parks are important for wilderness preservation but are difficult to establish and maintain.

   I. National parks are crucial to wilderness preservation.

        A. Irreversible damage is prevalent.

        B. National parks have multiple uses.

        C. Goals have been set but not yet met.

  II. Establishing national parks is problematic.

        A. Official establishment is a lengthy process.

        B. Acquiring land can be difficult.

            1. Provincial governments must relinquish land.

Note lettering and numbering for topics and subtopics

            2. Parks must respect Aboriginal land claims.

        C. Proposed parks are frequently opposed.

            1. Industry wants to develop resources.

            2. Existing residents do not want to move.

 III. Existing parks have problems.

        A. Urban centres within parks affect wilderness areas.

        B. Tourism causes damage.

            1. Animal behaviour changes.

            2. Tourists are unaware or inconsiderate of needs.

Double-space throughout

 IV. Effective management can prevent some problems.

        A. Establish parks with naturally limited access.

        B. Charge admission.

        C. Use zoning to establish less sensitive areas.

  V. Individuals can influence the success of national parks.

        A. Participate actively in park establishment and management decisions.

For guidelines to formal outlines, see 3c

        B. Change thinking to put environment first.

Sparling 1

THE NATURE OF NATURE: PROBLEMS OF ESTABLISHING AND MAINTAINING CANADA'S NATIONAL PARKS

Only recently have we begun to recognize the damage that we are doing to our planet. Global warming is inevitable, acid rain and dead lakes are commonplace, and the extinction of countless species is a sad reality. And these are not problems affecting "other people."

In an economically driven society like Canada, concerns for wilderness preservation are of relatively low priority (Aniskowicz 26) compared to, for example, national debt reduction. But we must remember that humans are not external to nature: we are an integral part of it. David Suzuki believes that there is "a genetic record of our companionship with [all other organisms] and thus the human need for wilderness is real, profound and biological" (n. pag.).

National parks are an important part of wilderness preservation and are relevant to our identity, not just for "the beauty of the natural environment and the richness of our history," enshrined in Parks Canada Policy. Paul Eagles stresses that parks offer a comparison of wilderness and lands altered by human activity ("Management" 157). They permit both recreation and education. Economically speaking, they provide tourist revenue and opportunities for generating sustainable development (Nelson, "Beyond Parks" 48). Finally, they provide sanctuary for animals and plants, many of which are endangered. Kevin McNamee reminds us that Parks Canada's priority is "to protect natural resources" (40).

Canada has a long history of national parks: the first, Banff National Park, was opened in 1885. Today, Canada has 36 parks, preserving 2% of Canada's land. This is far short of Parks Canada's goal of preserving 12% of Canada's land

Title centred and double-spaced, if necessary, and typed 2.5 cm from top of page

Dramatic plea to reader, anticipating the forthcoming appeal to "we"

Personal appeal with "we"

An expert source compels our participation

Brackets indicate an explanation within the citation

Citation of an author who provides more than one source for this paper

A paraphrase of a source's comments

A direct quotation from a source named in a signal phrase

Sparling 2

by the year 2000. In addition, it has failed to keep its promise to represent 39 of Canada's natural regions—Wayne Lynch admits that only 22 were represented by 1992 (26). Because these goals were not attained by 2000, McNamee fears that "opportunities to do so have all but disappeared" (38).

The difficulty lies in establishing and maintaining national parks. For each park, a significant natural area must be identified, then an area proposed, its feasibility assessed, an agreement negotiated and its establishment legislated (Rollins 81). Because national park land is federally owned, the relevant provincial government must release the land in perpetuity (Bryan 291). Provincial governments are reluctant to relinquish potential resource development revenues and thus hesitate to comply.

Proposed park sites frequently incorporate Native reserves and therefore involve negotiations with Aboriginals, too. National parks are subject to Aboriginal land-claim agreements, and current policy suggests a movement towards joint management. Northern national parks now allow Aboriginals to continue to live, hunt, trap, and fish on national park land (McNamee 34), but some people question the justice of making exceptions to the non-hunting policy in parks. Subsistence use and joint management are not yet guaranteed (Berg, Fenge, and Dearden 235).

In addition to provincial and Aboriginal negotiations, resource industries oppose park designations, viewing them as a threat to development of forestry, hydroelectric power, and agriculture (Rollins 78). Once a park is established, industries often create an island of the park by continuing resource development to its very boundaries. This has ramifications for the wildlife that may be used to roaming beyond the park's perimeter. Dearden and Rollins point to

Writer's name and page number typed 2.5 cm from top of page

Specific statistical support

Part II: Problems of establishment

An author named in the citation because he is not named in a signal phrase

Double-space throughout

Citation of a source by three authors

Paraphrase

Joint authors named in a signal phrase

Sparling 3

another drawback: industries bring acid rain, climatic change, and altered water quality (6–7).

Existing housing on proposed park land has also posed problems. Until the 1970s, property was simply expropriated. McNamee cites the creation of Forillon National Park, when more than 200 families were forcibly removed (32). Now "private land can [. . .] only be acquired for parks purposes if the owner is willing to sell the land" (33).

Some parks that have been built around existing towns, such as Banff, Jasper and Lake Louise, have their own special problems. Banff National Park was originally established to protect federal rights to exploit its hot springs. As these springs became a popular tourist attraction, the town grew. Banff's population is currently under 8 000, but daytime populations can swell to 30 000 during the peak tourist season, according to Douglas McArthur (F10). Animals can adapt to the presence of humans, even in such numbers, but in so doing, they alter their natural patterns:

> Elk congregate in the town to avoid attacks by wolves. As a result, tourists are being attacked by aggressive bull elk in the fall rutting season and by females protecting calves in the spring. (F1)

The Trans-Canada highway between Lake Louise and Banff has been another issue. The traffic disturbs and kills wildlife. To protect animals, fencing has been installed for 26 km and eleven bridges or culvert underpasses have been provided for crossings. Road kill has decreased by 90% (Leighton 25), but there are concerns regarding the cost and maintenance, aesthetics, and altered wildlife patterns: fewer elk cross the road with the current fencing system (Leighton 28).

Point Pelee National Park, some 2 500 km to the east, receives over half a million visitors per year, reports

Ellipsis points signalling an omission of a part of a sentence

Part III: Problems of maintenance

A block quotation

Documentation to follow final punctuation

Examples supporting the main point

Deliberate link from paragraph to paragraph

Sparling 4

B. T. Aniskowicz (25). Large numbers of tourists damage the wildlife they come to see: the very people that seek a wilderness experience help destroy both the environment and the experience they cherish so much (26). Experts in national park wildlife "agree that many animals are aware that they are in a wildlife sanctuary and therefore no longer retain their innate fear of humans and are more frequently met" (Bryan 269). Because animal behaviour has been altered artificially, just as in Banff, it can also be dangerous.

Tourists who ignore park signs endanger wildlife regularly. As John Sylvester explains, P.E.I. National Park is the nesting ground for approximately 560 of 2 000 pairs of breeding plovers left in the world (38). Their endangered designation means that nesting beaches are cordoned off. Unfortunately, these are close to popular recreational beaches, and strollers frequently ignore the signs, and boaters land on the apparently empty beaches, causing the nesting plovers to desert their eggs (38). Students must be hired during the peak summer season to patrol the beaches daily. Even so, plover populations continue to decline as a direct result of encroachment on their territory (40).

There are a number of ways to prevent human interference in national parks. Limited visiting is especially viable in the north where there are few urban centres and parks have limited access. Aulavik National Park is accessible only by chartered aircraft. It offers "what national parks were primarily designed for: a wilderness environment unaltered by humanity, where an individual can rejoice in the workings of the natural world" (Lynch 33). Pukaskwa National Park is accessible only by Pukaskwa River and canoeable only one month per year. The fact that it "can barely be used is a conundrum to its administrators" (Barber 61). In 1983, therefore, an area of Pukaskwa Park was

Reminder of a previous point

Unworkable present solution

Solution 1: Limit visits

Pros and cons

Sparling 5

designated for a marina. There was considerable public outcry: Barber speaks of the naturalist who complained that Parks Canada was "spending money to destroy a wilderness area" (61). The plans were cancelled. Limiting visitors is a proposed solution for southern parks but is certain to frustrate tourists who have travelled some distance only to be turned away at the gate. Yet according to Parks Canada statistics, the number of visitors to national parks has stabilized over the past few years.

One expert's response

Implications

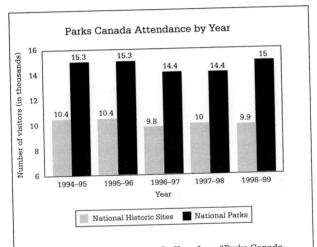

Fig. 1 Parks Canada Attendance By Year, from "Parks Canada Visitor Profiles," 1999, Parks Canada, 4 Nov. 1999 <http://www.parkscanada.pch.gc.ca/library/Indexe.htm>.

These figures suggest that simply limiting the number of visitors will do little to reduce the present levels of environmental damage.

Rorke Bryan sees an advantage to charging admission: paid entries cause a visit to be valued (278). The regulation of admission booths, however, is expensive. The amount of

Solution 2: Charge admission

Sparling 6

admission is also debated. Some suggest that foreign tourists should pay more than Canadians since we already help to fund parks through our taxes. On the other hand, Bryan warns, this may be interpreted to mean that our resources are for sale to the highest bidder (279). In addition, admission charges exclude low-income families (278).

Pros and cons

To protect and preserve sensitive areas, Parks Canada has adopted a zoning policy that determines recreational levels in various areas of a park. Five different zones designate land—from primarily wilderness areas with strict controls on human participation to urban sites used for visitor service centres (Nelson, "Wildlands" 710). Bryan argues that zoning must consider the future and not cave in to current public pressure merely for more recreational facilities (285). National parks cannot "satisfy the complete recreational [. . .] needs of our society. National parks should not be called upon to satisfy a demand which can be satisfied equally well by parks of provincial or local status" (286).

A warning

What can we, as individuals, do to help Canada's national parks? The National Parks Act requires public participation (Eagles, "Legislation" 60), so we can start by actively contributing to the decision-making process. We can think through the solutions presented here and offer new ones. We can write to our MPs to tell them of our concern for national parks. We can donate to wildlife associations, especially the Canadian Parks and Wilderness Society, the watchdog society for Parks Canada. And we can alter our thinking about the environment.

Transition to Part V: A question

A warrant (a government policy) that calls for participation

The answer: What readers (we) can do

Reference to Introduction

Part of our problem is that our study and understanding of wildlife has been reductionist in nature. That is to say, we "have studied life downward, from species to DNA structure, but not upward" (Theberge 142). We have a lot to learn from studying the interrelationships of species and vegetation.

Expert rebuttal of opposing arguments, explaining an error in approach

Sparling 7

Actions affecting an individual lifeform may have far-reaching
implications which we do not currently understand. Perhaps
our mindset should be one not of determining the minimum
amount of space required to be set aside for national parks,
but of "consider[ing] the whole environment as park and to
allow, on a case-by-case basis, only enclaves of disturbed
areas within it" (Theberge 149).

    Our participation ensures that national parks are truly
national in nature. By taking interest in national park
legislation, we ensure that national parks remain a priority in
Canada's future.

*Use square
brackets to
mark an
editorial
adjustment*

*Conclusion:
The benefits
of heeding
the writer's
plea*

Sparling 8

WORKS CITED

Aniskowicz, B. T. "The Environment, Tourism and Interpretation."
    Interpretation and Tourism: Ottawa '88. Proc. of a Conference
    on Heritage Interpretation. 13–17 Apr. 1988. n.p.: n.p., n.d.
    25–27.

Barber, John. "North Shore Solitudes." Equinox Sept.–Oct. 1988:
    55–62.

Berg, Lawrence, Terry Fenge, and Philip Dearden. "The Role of
    Aboriginal Peoples in National Park Designation, Planning
    and Management in Canada." Dearden and Rollins 225–55.

Bryan, Rorke. Much Is Taken, Much Remains: Canadian Issues in
    Environmental Conservation. North Scituate, Mass: Duxbury
    Press, 1973.

Dearden, Philip, and Rick Rollins, eds. Parks and Protected Areas
    in Canada: Planning and Management. Toronto: Oxford UP,
    1993.

- - -. "The Times They Are A-Changin'." Dearden and Rollins
    1–16.

Sparling 9

Eagles, Paul F. J. "Environmental Management in Parks." Dearden
and Rollins 154–84.

- - -. "Parks Legislation in Canada." Dearden and Rollins 57–74.

Leighton, Douglas. "Helping the Animals Cross the Road."
<u>Canadian Geographic</u> Aug.–Sept. 1988: 22–28.

Lynch, Wayne. "Aulavik." <u>Canadian Geographic</u> Mar.–Apr. 1995:
24–33.

McArthur, Douglas. "Banff's Future: National Park or Upscale
Mall?" <u>Globe and Mail</u> 18 Jan. 1997. Weekend ed. F1+.

McNamee, Kevin. "From Wild Places to Endangered Spaces: A
History of Canada's National Parks." Dearden and Rollins
17–44.

Nelson, J. G. "Beyond Parks and Protected Areas: From Public
Lands and Private Stewardship to Landscape Planning and
Management." Dearden and Rollins 45–56.

- - -. "Canada's Wildlands." <u>In the Canadian National Parks: Today
and Tomorrow: Conference II: 10 Years Later</u> 2. Ed. J. G.
Nelson et al. North Scituate, Mass: Duxbury Press, 1973.
707–23.

"Parks Canada Visitor Profiles," 1999, Parks Canada, 4 Nov. 1999
<http://www.parkscanada.pch.gc.ca/library/Indexe.htm>.

"Preserving Canada's Heritage: The Government's Environmental
Agenda." 28 Apr. 1999. 38 pars. Parks Canada. 3 Nov. 1999
<http://www.parkscanada.pch.gc.ca/library/77_e.htm#details>.

Rollins, Rick. "Managing the National Parks." Dearden and Rollins
75–96.

Suzuki, David. Preface. <u>The Last Wilderness: Images of the
Canadian Wild</u>. By The Canadian Nature Federation and
Freeman Patterson. Toronto: Key Porter Books, 1990. n. pag.

Sylvester, John. "Privacy Please!" <u>Canadian Geographic</u> Apr.–May
1991: 37–40.

Theberge, John B. "Ecology, Conservation, and Protected Areas in
Canada." Dearden and Rollins 137–53.

APA Documentation

chapter 56 | Using the APA In-Text Citation Style

The American Psychological Association (APA) recommends an author-date style of documentation for papers written in the social sciences. This style is also used in anthropology, the biological sciences, business, economics, education, linguistics, and political science.

56a | Follow APA citation guidelines

1 Citing a summary or paraphrase

To summarize or paraphrase a source, use a signal statement containing the author's last name followed by the publication date in parentheses, or give the author's name and the date in parentheses at the end of the borrowed material, preceding the period. Use the past tense with signal verbs: *explained, reported,* and *argued* (see 15b1).

- *Author and date preceding the borrowing:*

  Sanchez (1993) reported that students from small, often rural schools do not fare as well on standardized tests as students from urban areas with large economic bases.

- *Author and date in parentheses following the borrowing.* Use a comma between items in parentheses.

  Students from small, often rural schools do not fare as well on standardized tests as students from urban areas with large economic bases (Sanchez, 1993).

2 Citing a quotation or specific reference

To quote directly or refer to a specific part of a source, include page numbers in the parenthetical citation, preceded by *p.* or *pp.* ("page" or "pages").

  In its statistical sense used in standardized testing, bias refers to "constant or systematic error as opposed to chance errors" (Anastasi, 1988, p. 194).

3 Citing authors' names

- *A source by one author.* Follow the examples given in 56a1 and 2.

- *A source by two authors.* For a source by two authors, give both last names in all signal statements and parenthetical citations. In parentheses, join the two authors' names with an ampersand (&).

Aptitude tests have assisted "students who vary in significant respects from the traditionally academically successful students" (Tyler & Wolf, 1974, p. 47).

- *A source by three to five authors.* For a source with three to five authors, give all last names in the first signal statement or parenthetical citation.

Elder, Lopez, Smith, and Breen (1993) have systematically documented the social bias in standardized tests.

In later citations, give the last name of the first author, followed by *et al.* ("and others").

Elder et al. (1993) have proposed greater minority involvement in the design of standardized tests.

- *A source by six or more authors.* When a work has six or more authors, give the last name of the first author followed by *et al.* in signal statements and parenthetical citations.

- *Corporate authors.* Spell out corporate names generally. Always spell out all corporate names in the reference list at the end of your paper. If corporations have well-known abbreviations, spell out the name in the first citation and abbreviate thereafter:

First citation: (Institute for Public Policy Research [IPPR], 1994)

Subsequent citations: (IPPR, 1994)

- *Unknown author.* When the author of a work is not identified in the source, use the complete title in a signal statement or the first few words of the title in a parenthetical citation.

Standardized testing puts students from rural, often poor areas at a great disadvantage ("Opportunity for All," 1995).

- *Two or more sources in one parentheses.* To cite two or more sources in one citation, put them in the order in which they appear in the list of references at the end of the paper. Separate them with semicolons.

(Anastasi, 1988; "Test Bias," 43; Tyler & Wolfe, 1974)

If two or more sources are by the same author, give the author's last name once followed by the dates of publication in chronological order.

(Anastasi, 1988, 1991)

- *Authors with the same last name.* When two or more authors have the same last name, include initials in all signal statements and parenthetical citations:

(G. B. Dukes, 1991)

(L. K. Dukes, 1989)

■ *Personal communication.* To cite personal communication, such as a letter or e-mail, give the author's initial(s) and last name, followed by the words *personal communication* and the date.

W. Hine (personal communication, October 8, 1995) has proposed three reforms for standardized tests.

56*b* | Prepare the APA reference list

The reference list gives full publication information for all sources cited in a research paper. See the sample citations in 56c and the complete reference list at the end of the sample research project in 56d.

1 Placement of the reference list

Begin the reference list on a separate page at the end of your paper.

2 Reference list format

■ *Title.* Centre the title "References" (without italics, underlining, or quotation marks) at the top of the page. Continue page numbers from the text of your paper.

■ *Spacing.* Double-space throughout, unless instructed to single-space within entries.

■ *Indentation.* Begin each entry flush with the left margin. Indent second and successive lines up to 1 cm or from three to five spaces. In projects sent to APA journals for publication, first lines are indented and successive lines typed flush left. If you are uncertain which format to use, ask your instructor. (For more on indentation, see the *APA Publication Manual*, 4th ed., pp. 251 and 331–32.)

■ *Alphabetical order.* Arrange entries in alphabetical order according to the last names of first authors or corporate names. If the author is not given, alphabetize by the first word of the title, ignoring *A, An*, and *The*.

■ *Two or more works by one author.* If you use two or more works by the same author, arrange them by date of publication, with the earliest first.

3 Citation formats

■ *Author names.* Invert the names of all authors: write the last name first followed by a comma and the person's initials, separated by one space. With two or more authors, use the ampersand (&) instead of *and*. Separate three or more names with commas. Write the names of all the authors; do not use *et al.*

- *Date of publication.* Put the date of publication in parentheses following the author's name.

- *Punctuation.* Space once after punctuation within an entry. Underline periods and commas following the titles of books, the names of periodicals, and volume numbers.

- *Quotation marks and underlining.* Do not enclose article titles in quotation marks. Underline book titles and the names of periodicals. Underline the volume number of periodicals.

- *Capitalization.* Capitalize the names of periodicals as you would ordinarily. Capitalize only the first word of article and book titles, the first word of a subtitle (if any) usually following a colon, and proper nouns.

   Periodical: <u>Canadian Journal of Sociology</u>.

   Article: A new work agenda: Social choices for a healthy society.

   Book: <u>Unemployment , welfare and social work policy in Canada.</u>

- *Abbreviations.* Use standard bibliographic abbreviations when appropriate: *chap.* (chapter), *Ed.* (editor), *ed.* (edition), *n.d.* (no date), *p.* or *pp.* (page or pages), *Rev. ed.* (revised edition), *Trans.* (translator), *Vol.* (a single volume), *Vols.* (number of volumes), *No.* (number).

- *Publishers' names.* You may shorten publishers' names, as long as they are recognizable.

- *Page numbers.* Write out inclusive page numbers in full: *341–344* (not *341–44*).

56c Sample APA citations

The APA keeps an up-to-date list of frequently asked questions (FAQ) on-line:

     http://www.apa.org/journals/faq.html

1 Books

- **One author**

   Guest, D. (1985). <u>The emergence of social security in Canada.</u> Vancouver:

        UBC Press.

- ### Two or more authors

    Pulkingham, J., & Ternowetsky, G. (1996). <u>Remaking Canadian social policy: Social security in the late 1990s.</u> Halifax: Fernwood.

- ### Corporate or institutional author

    Canadian Medical Association. (1990). <u>The Canadian Medical Association guide to prescription and over-the-counter drugs.</u> Montreal: Reader's Digest.

- ### An unknown author

    <u>Chronicle of Canada.</u> (1990). Montreal: Chronicle Publications.

- ### Edited book

    Baines, C., Evans, P., & Neysmith, S. (Eds.). (1991). <u>Women's caring perspectives in social welfare.</u> Toronto: McClelland and Stewart.

- ### An edition other than the first

    Frideres, J. S. (1993). <u>Native people in Canada: Contemporary conflicts</u> (4th ed.). Scarborough: Prentice Hall.

- ### Source in an anthology or a chapter in an edited book

    Gorlick, C., & Pomfret, A. (1993). Hope and circumstance: Single mothers exiting social assistance. In J. Hudson and B. Galaway (Eds.), <u>Single parent families: Perspectives on research and policy</u> (pp. 147–186). Toronto: Thomson Educational.

- ### Translation

    Tremblay, M. (1977). <u>Stories for late night drinkers</u> (M. Bullock, Trans.). Vancouver: Intermedia. (Original work published 1966).

- ### Multi-volume work

    Shepard, L. A. (Ed.). (1991). <u>Encyclopedia of occultism and parapsychology</u> (3rd ed., Vols. 1–2). Detroit: Gale Research.

2   Periodicals and newspapers

- ### Journal article, one author, journal paged by issue

    Kraft, R. J. (1992). Closed classrooms, high mountains and strange lands: An inquiry into culture and caring. <u>Journal of Experiential Education, 15</u> (3), 8-15.

- **Journal article, two authors, journal paged by volume**

  Bartlett, D., & Bartlett, J. (1973). North with the snow goose. <u>National Geographic, 144.</u> 822–847.

- **Journal article, three, four, or five authors**

  Nickle, M. N., Flynt, F. C., Poynter, S. D., & Rees, J. A., Jr. (1990). Does it make a difference if you change the structure? School-within-a-school. <u>Phi Delta Kappan, 72,</u> 148-152.

- **Magazine article**

  Twatio, B. (1996, Fall). The Red Baron reconsidered. <u>Airforce, 20.</u> 34–36.

- **Signed newspaper article, discontinuous pages.** If an article appears on discontinuous pages, give all page numbers, separated by commas.

  Greenspon, E., & Sallot, J. (1995, October 31). Too close for Ottawa's comfort. <u>Globe and Mail.</u> pp. A1, A11.

- **Review**

  Smyth, R. (1995, Winter). Readings in second language acquisition [Review of the book <u>Readings in second language acquisition</u> edited by H.D. Brown & S.T. Gonzo] <u>TESL Canada Journal, 13,</u> 95–100.

- **Letter to the editor**

  Longstaff, B. (1976, February). Riel and Dumont [Letter to the editor]. <u>Canadian Forum,</u> p. 24.

3   Internet sources

The following guidelines and examples are based upon the American Psychological Association's *Publication Manual*, 4th ed. (APA, 1994) and "How to Cite Information from the Internet and the World Wide Web," available at <http://www.apa.org/journals/webref.html>.

1. For sources with print counterparts, cite the print publication and the location of the Internet version.
2. When necessary, identify the type of document or source in square brackets […].
3. Do *not* enclose Internet addresses (URLs) with angle brackets (<…>); do not end URLs with periods.
4. *A note on breaking URLs:* As of 1999, the APA had not given guidelines on breaking URLs. Others who have applied the APA style to electronic sources recommend that punctuation such as hyphens and slashes be retained at the end of a line. For more information about URLs, see

"Web Extension to American Psychological Association Style" at <http://www.beadsland.com/weapas/>.

■ **An electronic text such as a book**

London, J. (1905). <u>The people of the abyss</u> [Textfile]. Retrieved September 2, 1998 from the World Wide Web: http://sunsite.berkeley.edu/~emorgan/ text/literature/american/1900-/london-people-205.txt

[This example includes the author, date of original publication, title, type of source in brackets, and a retrieval note identifying date of retrieval, Internet space, and URL.]

■ **A report from a government body, university, or private organization**

National Research Council. (1999). <u>The state of Canada's forests</u> [Online textfile]. Ottawa: Author. Retrieved November 14, 1999 from the World Wide Web: http://www.nrcan.gc.cca/cfs/proj/ppiab/sof/sof99/brief.shtml

[This example includes the name of the organization, publication date, title of the report, type of source in brackets, place of publication, publisher (Author indicates that the organization is the publisher), and a retrieval note identifying date of retrieval, Internet space, and URL.]

■ **An article in an online periodical**

Skrzeszewski, S., and Badger, D. (1995). A national vision for Canada's information infrastructure. <u>Government Information in Canada/ Information gouvernmentale au Canada</u> [Electronic journal], <u>1</u> (4) [6 pages]. Retrieved February 12, 1997 from the World Wide Web: http://www.usask.ca/library/gic/v1n4.html

[This example includes two authors' names, date of original publication, article title, journal title, volume number, original pages, and a retrieval note identifying date of retrieval, Internet space, and URL.]

■ **A newspaper article**

Cooper, M. (2000, February 3). Spirited goodbye: Barrett quits after out-of-body experience. <u>The Edmonton Sun</u>, p. A1 [Newspaper, selected stories on line]. Retrieved February 3, 2000 from the World Wide Web: http://www.canoe.ca/Edmonton Sun/front1.html

[This example includes the author, original publication date, title, name of the newspaper, page number, type of source in brackets, and a retrieval note identifying date of retrieval, Internet space, and URL.]

■ **A source in an Internet information service or database**

National Clearinghouse on Family Violence. (1993). <u>Gender and violence in the mass media</u> [Online textfile republished from a printed source]. <u>Health Canada/Santé Canada</u>. Ottawa: Health Canada. Retrieved January 21, 2000 from the World Wide Web: http://www.hcsc.gc.ca/hppb/ familyviolence/html/1gender.htm

[This example includes the name of the organization that produced the information, the date of publication, title, type of source in brackets, name of the site, place of publication, publisher, and a retrieval note identifying date of retrieval, Internet space, and URL.]

■ **An abstract of an article**

Weingardt, K. R. et al. (1998, September). Episodic heavy drinking among

college students: methodological issues and longitudinal perspectives

[Abstract]. <u>Psychology of Addictive Behaviors</u>, 12, 155–167. Retrieved

September 2, 1998 from the World Wide Web: http://www.apa.org/

journals/adb/998ab.html#1

[This example includes the name of the first of six authors, publication date, title, type of source in brackets, journal title, volume, page numbers, and a retrieval note identifying date of retrieval, Internet space, and URL.]

■ **Discussion group posting**

Hamilton, K. (1998, August 12). Forget nature vs. nurture—do parents

matter? [Online news posting]. <u>Deja News</u>. Retrieved September 1, 1998

from the World Wide Web: http://www.dejanews.com/[ST_chan=soc]/

channels/soc/soc_fpl.shtml

[This example of a news group posting includes the author, posting date, title of the discussion group, type of source in brackets, the owner of the site, and a retrieval note identifying date of retrieval and listserv web address.]

■ **E-mail.** Because e-mail is not easily recoverable, it is not cited in the reference list. Cite personal communications only in the text of your paper. (See 56a3.)

4 Other sources

■ **Abstract on CD-ROM**

Rubin, D. (1992, May). Cultural bias undermines assessment [CD-ROM].

<u>Personnel Journal, 71</u> (5), 47-50. Abstract from: Infotrac File: Academic

ASAP Item: 12422735

■ **Data file or database on tape or CD-ROM**

Software services gain ground, IBM says. (1994, September). Info Canada, 19

(9), p. 2. <u>Canadian Business and Current Affairs 1988–November 1996</u>

[Electronic database], KR-OnDisc. Micromedia Ltd.

■ Abstract on database

Kwok, D.C., & Lytton, H. (1996). Perceptions of mathematics ability versus
actual mathematics performance: Canadian and Hong Kong Chinese
children [Electronic database]. British Journal of Educational Psychology,
66 (2), 209–222. Abstract from: PsycLIT Journal Articles 1/90–12/96.
PC-SPIRS 3.40ZU.

■ Government reports

Parsons, L.S. (1993). Management of marine fisheries in Canada. Ottawa:
National Research Council and Dept. of Fisheries and Oceans.

■ Published proceedings of a conference or symposium. Present the regularly published proceedings of a conference as you would a periodical.

Aniskowicz, B. T. (1988). The environment, tourism and interpretation.
Interpretation and tourism: Ottawa '88. Proceedings of a conference on
heritage interpretation. Ottawa. 13–17 April 1988, 25–27.

■ Dissertation abstract

Queen, J. M. (1990). The nature of substantial being: An examination of
Aristotle's view of living substance. (Doctoral dissertation, University of
Guelph, 1990). Dissertation Abstracts International, 52 (11–12), 4356A.

■ Videotape

LeLorrain, E., & Shannon, K. (Producers) & Nash, T. (Director). (1982). If you
love this planet [16 mm movie & videotape]. National Film Board.

56*d* A sample APA research project

The following report has been written in the APA manuscript format for
student papers (see 48d), with APA in-text documentation and a reference
list. (For more on reports, see 63d. For more about the headings often used
in reports, see 48b1.)

Children and Bilingualism:

Original Views of Language Acquisition

Kellie Siegner

9275742

Psychology 101, Section F

Dr. Hsiao d'Ailly

November 19, 2000

American Psychological Association (APA) Format

Page header and number 1.5 cm from top of page

Number pages consecutively from the title page to the end of the paper, including references

Centre everything else

Abstract

Psychologists and linguists alike have grappled with the problem of language acquisition in children. Numerous theories have developed in response to the question of why it is so much easier for a child to learn a new language than it is for an adult. Followers of Chomsky claim children are biologically programmed for learning. Proponents of behaviourist theory prefer to think that children learn language through social reinforcement and exposure. Process theory combines aspects of both. Notions of ideal timing for second language learning and the effect of interference by the child's first language also have an impact. Although each theory has been the focus of years of research and study, there is always contrary evidence. Still, theories of second language acquisition are engaging. They do help explain why children acquire language seemingly effortlessly while their parents continue to struggle.

An abstract is a block paragraph of 100 to 150 words

Children and Bilingualism:

Original Views of Language Acquisition

Living in an officially bilingual country, a great many Canadian school children are exposed to French and English from an early age. In fact, as recent census numbers confirm, because over 15% of Canada's population comes from other language backgrounds, it is not surprising that so many Canadians speak two or more languages (Statistics Canada, 1997). As Prokop (1993) points out, "there are more students registered in bilingual and immersion programs in Canada than there are in the United States or Europe" (p. 21). Indeed, it has always been clear that children can learn new languages much more rapidly and accurately than their parents. Whether that is the result of some innate ability or simply a matter of being exposed to the proper environment is an issue that has been extensively examined by linguists and psychologists alike. This paper considers some of the original thinking about second language acquisition, recognizing how inconclusive any theory can be.

① The Theories

② Critical Period Hypothesis

③ Chomsky. In studies of language acquisition in children, Noam Chomsky (1957) was convinced that language learning is a matter of the maturation of an innate capacity. In other words, children's ability to learn language is a direct result of biological preprogramming. This innate capacity expires at the onset of puberty, as Balkan (1970) recognized, noting that older children had more difficulty handling the English that they were learning. When the timing is right, children acquire language not so much through daily experience as through their general capacity for knowledge. It is not a step-by-step process but rather the result

Side notes:

2.5 cm margins; page header 1.5 cm from top of page

APA citation of a source not mentioned in a signal phase

Introduction raises a research issue

Thesis

Headings: (1) primary centred; (2) secondary underlined, flush left; (3) tertiary underlined, run-in

Bilingualism   4

of a formulation of a theory of grammar on the basis of limited data. This theory of language acquisition was, as McLaughlin (1978) made clear, greatly dependent on the "critical period"—between the ages of two and puberty.

Crystal. During this critical period, conceptual processes are already developed enough that they support "un apprentissage linguistique quasi indigène [next to native speaker proficiency]" (Balkan, p. 47), without actually inhibiting the child. In the first year or so of life, the child's brain has not yet developed the capacity for such learning. After puberty, the brain loses its cerebral plasticity, thus making it more difficult to acquire another language. During puberty, the nature of the language learning process alters dramatically, as Crystal (1976) showed. At the onset of adolescence, the child has many fragmented "selves," which enhance the language learning capacity; soon after, these "selves" come together, fusing the child's identity culturally as well as intellectually (p. 49).

> Direct quotation in the original language; translation included in square brackets

Leopold. In interpreting studies of human behaviour, W. F. Leopold pointed out that acquisition of a new language relies on discovery procedures: "In the process of learning, the child utilizes the limited material acquired with supreme disregard for establishing practices, striking wildly out of bounds in every direction but in the same manner as adults do with less freedom of action" (Bar-Adon & Leopold, 1971, p. 11). Positive as well as negative information is required in order to learn language. As Naiman, Forhlich, Stern, and Tedesco (1978) observed, the best language learners take such ambiguity in their stride.

> Citation of a source with two names linked by an ampersand

> Citation of a source with multiple authors, all named; next reference uses *et al.*

Binet. The critical period hypothesis remains very much a hypothesis. Some evidence exists of differential ability to learn other languages pre- and post-puberty. This is rather indirect, however, given the difficulty in controlling such variables as motivation (Crystal, p. 49). Binet (1975) made the point that language acquisition is dependent on strong self-discipline, family support, and sufficient intellectual development. Less is demanded from the child in terms of linguistic competence: as McLaughlin (1978) put it, "children are considered fluent when they can communicate at a level appropriate for their age" (p. 68). This is yet another reason why it is easier for a child to become "fluent" in a second language than it is for adults.

Connection to thesis

<u>Behaviourism and Imitation</u>

The classic explanation put forth by behaviourists for language acquisition takes the basic form of stimulus-response theory, as outlined in the studies of B. F. Skinner. When children use a new language, they do so in conjunction with actions they perform or with objects they can see, reach, or touch. In early stages of childhood, parents are often heard echoing their child's utterances and making the grammatical corrections, thus acting as language models for children. This social reinforcement helps children explore a language, learning from mistakes.

And yet, if imitation were the governing principle behind language acquisition, one would expect children to produce rather different patterns in their language than they actually do (Crystal, p. 34). If "stimulus-response" applied to language acquisition unilaterally, it would be expected that children would use more adult, complex speech than "gibberish." When a child makes a grammatical error and is corrected, it would be expected that the child would immediately pick up and use this corrected phrase. A child who uses "I goed" did not learn that phrase from an adult.

Contrast signal

Process Model

With internal cognitive processes his concern, linguist David McNeill is reported by McLaughlin to suggest that language acquisition in children can be explained by combining aspects of both Skinner's and Chomsky's theories. Unlike Chomsky's transformational model, McNeill's process model is concerned with language behaviour occurring in real time—other linguistic models are static. Linguistic models aim at accounting for the speaker's competence in language; the process model is concerned with what it is that people do in comprehending and producing (McLaughlin, p. 25). According to this theory, children are born with innate abilities to learn rather than an innate set of ideas. The child's mind is receptive to learning language, and each child progresses at his or her own pace, which, as Nicholas (1985) argued, is the ideal approach to language learning.

A primary source cited in a secondary source. The reference is to the secondary source.

Second Language Mastery

According to studies completed by Theodore Andersson (1960) and reported in Balkan (1970), the ideal time to begin learning another language is between four and eight years of age. At this age, the unconscious formation of speech habits has an important role in the learning. Young children's powers of speech development are more readily directed towards conversation than towards discursive reasoning. The ability to master a second language before completing the acquisition of their first language occurs because lateralization of the brain is not yet permanent. According to studies done by Scovel in 1969 (and reported by McLaughlin), it is during adolescence that an individual's accent becomes permanent, marking the beginning of brain lateralization.

Major heading indicates shift to second major section

First Language Interference

A major problem with acquiring a second language is the possibility of interference from the child's first language. The older the child is, the more fixed the grammar rules of the first language. In acquiring a second language, the child does not have to build knowledge from the ground up, having already been exposed to grammar rules in the native language. Hakuta's (1986) study of a Japanese girl learning English reveals primary language interference. For example, she would confuse the English noun "mistake" with the Japanese equivalent "machigau," a verb. Therefore, she would use such phrases as "Oh no, I mistake. Don't give me more because you're mistaking [. . .] because I mistake it" (p. 14). These examples offer solid evidence of one language's interference with a child's acquisition of another.

An ellipsis to signal omission of part of a sentence

Benefits

Balkan (1970) reported studies on the effects of bilingualism on intellectual maturity and on the individual's sociability. Studies reported by R. Trites (1984) showed that "French immersion programming did not have negative effects upon cognitive development" (p. 96). Prokop (1993) reported similar results, commenting that students in immersion or double language programs do have superior vocabularies and communication skills. While early immersion has enjoyed considerable success, factors such as age, stage of cognitive development, and attitudes are also to be considered. Because all children receive the same education, Binet (1975) argued, they are all taught similarly: those who have a good memory are treated just like those with a poor one. No allowances were made for different learning styles in those days.

Managing two languages produces a loose link in the child's mind between the word and the object. Thus "bilingualism [. . .] helps to break down the intimate association between form and content. A bilingual child will pay more attention to things referred to, situations and actions described and ideas expressed than to phonetic forms pronounced" (Bar-Adon & Leopold, 1971, p. 301). In terms of speed of acquisition, features that correspond to linguistic universals are the first to be acquired.

Conclusions

What lies ahead? No matter how difficult it is to determine how any language is assimilated, what remains true is the Canadian commitment to bilingualism in general. It is a commitment that has seen the number of bilingual teenagers almost double Canada-wide since 1981 ("Bilingual Teens," 1999). It is, altogether, a commitment that prepares for what Prokop calls "fluency and accuracy" (p. 35) in children, who obviously can learn much more easily than their parents.

Conclusion pointing out the current application of the theories presented in the paper

References

Balkan, L. (1970). <u>Les effets du bilinguisme français-anglais sur les aptitudes intellectuelles.</u> [The effects of French-English bilingualism on intellectual aptitudes.] Bruxelles: Aimav.

Bastien, H. (1938). <u>Le bilinguisme au Canada</u>. Montréal: Editions de l'ACF.

Binet, A. (1975). <u>Modern ideas about children</u>. San Francisco: Suzanne Heisler.

Canadian Parents for French. (1999, March 21). Bilingual teens almost double in Canada over past 15 years [Online press

Reference list arranged alphabetically

A source written in another language

APA guidelines for students: First line of citation is typed flush left, following lines are indented 5 spaces

Bilingualism   10

release]. <u>CCNA News Service</u>. Retrieved October 14, 1999 from the World Wide Web: http://ccna.ca/cpf01.html

<u>Child language: A book of readings.</u> (1971). A. Bar-Adon & W. F. Leopold, (Eds.) Englewood Cliffs, NJ: Prentice Hall.

Chomsky, N. (1957). <u>Syntactic Structures</u>. The Hague: Mouton.

Crystal, D. (1976). <u>Child language, learning and linguistics.</u> London: Billing & Sons, Ltd.

Hakuta, K. (1986). <u>Mirror of language.</u> New York: Basic.

McLaughlin, B. (1978). <u>Second language acquisition in children.</u> Hillsdale: Laurence Erlbram.

Naiman, N., Frohlich, M., Stern, H. H., Tedesco, A. (1978). The good language learner. <u>Research in education series 7,</u> Toronto: OISE.

Nicholas, H. (1985). Learner variation and the teachability hypothesis. In K. Hyltenstam & M. Pienemann (Eds.), <u>Modelling and assessing second language acquisition.</u> San Diego: College Hill, pp. 23–75.

Prokop, M. (1993). Teaching for accuracy in a communicatively oriented curriculum: An elusive objective? In J. Ainsworth (Ed.), <u>Second language dynamics: Essays for teachers.</u> Waterloo: University of Waterloo, pp. 21–42.

Statistics Canada. (1997). Population by mother tongue, Canada, the provinces and territories, 1996. Statistics Canada. (1997, December 2). 1996 Census: Mother tongue, home language and knowledge of languages [Online textfile]. <u>The Daily</u>. Ottawa: Author. Retrieved February 4, 1998 from the World Wide Web: http://statcan.ca/Daily/English/971202/ d971202.htm

Trites, R. L. (1984). Early immersion in French at school for anglophone children: Learning disabilities and prediction of success. In M. Paradis & Y. LeBrun (Eds.), <u>Early Bilingualism and Child Development. Neurolinguistics 13.</u> (pp. 95–133). Lisse, Holland: Swets and Zeitlinger.

Annotations (right margin):

- An edited book that has been a major source
- A book with one author
- A source with four authors
- A source from an edited book, including pages
- An on-line source
- A chapter in an edited book that is part of a numbered series

Other Styles

57 Using CM Style

The preferred style for papers in the humanities is the in-text parenthetical system of documentation outlined by the Modern Language Association. (See 53 and 54.) But in business, the humanities, and the fine arts, endnotes and footnotes are often used to cite the sources of borrowed materials. This system of documentation is sometimes called CM style (after the University of Chicago's Manual of Style, where it is presented in detail). If you use endnotes or footnotes, you will likely also include a bibliography. (See 57c.)

57a | Choose an endnote or footnote format

Use endnotes at the end of your paper unless you are instructed to place footnotes at the bottom of a page of text.

- *Placement.* Endnotes appear on a separate page headed *Notes* at the end of your paper, following the text and preceding the bibliography. Double-space between them and within them. If you must use footnotes, place them at the bottom of the page, four spaces below the text. Single-space footnotes; double-space between them. If a note continues to the next page, type a solid line two spaces below the text on the new page, continue the note two spaces below the line and place new notes immediately after it.

- *Numbering.* Number notes consecutively from the beginning to the end of your paper. Do not assign each source its own number. Use a new number for each citation even if several numbers refer to the same source. In the text, at the first break after a summary, paraphrase, or quotation, write a raised, or superscript, Arabic numeral outside all punctuation except dashes.

  Marshall McLuhan describes "the television generation [as] a grim bunch."[9]

- *Indentations.* Indent the first line the same number of spaces as other paragraphs in your paper, generally five spaces. Make second and succeeding lines flush with the left margin.

- *Formatting the note numbers.* The number preceding each note should be the same size as your text (not superscript), followed by a period and one space.

- *The first reference to a source.* When you cite a source for the first time, give complete publication information in the note. Begin each note with a capital letter and end with a period. Do not use internal periods. Give the author's name in normal word order. For books, enclose the place of publication, publisher, and date of publication in parentheses. Always give the exact page number(s) of a borrowing.

1. Margaret Visser, *The Rituals of Dinner* (Toronto: Harper Collins, 1991), 289.

■ *Subsequent references to a source.* In second and later references to a source, give the author's last name, or a short form of the title if no author's name is given, followed by the page numbers of the borrowing. This information will allow readers to locate complete information for a source in an earlier reference or in the bibliography.

2. Visser, 121.

6. "Report," 14.

■ *Subsequent references to an author of more than one source.* If you use more than one source by an author, use the author's last name and a short form of the title in subsequent references to distinguish one source from another.

12. Richler, "Woolly Thinking," 37.

13. Richler, "Write Stuff," 41.

$57b$ Sample first references to a source

1 Citing books

■ **Basic reference to a book.** Cite two or more authors in the order given on the title page of the book. Use commas to separate the names of three or more authors. Use *and* before the second or final author's name. For a corporate publication, cite the corporation as the author. After a book title, include information such as the translators or editors (if any), the number or description of the edition (other than the first); and the name of the series (if any). Cite a pamphlet as you would a book. Note that the Chicago style uses complete publisher names (Random House).

1. Linda McQuaig, *The Wealthy Banker's Wife* (Toronto: Penguin, 1993), 97.

■ **An introduction, foreword, preface, or afterword**

2. M. H. Scargill, preface to *A Dictionary of Canadianisms* (Toronto: Gage, 1967), vii.

- **One volume from a multi-volume work.** Place the volume number following the general title. If a particular volume is titled separately, include the individual title after the volume number.

    3. *Bernard Shaw Collected Letters 1874–1897*, vol. 1, edited by Dan H. Laurence (London: Max Reinhardt, 1965), 133–34.

- **Titled parts of a book**

    4. Carl Berger, "Reorientation and Tradition" in *The Writing of Canadian History* (Toronto: Oxford University Press, 1976), 205.

- **An encyclopedia or dictionary.** Begin with the name of the reference work followed by the edition, *s.v.* (an abbreviation of *sub verbo*, "under the word"), and the item cited, which is capitalized if a proper noun and otherwise written in lower case.

    5. *The Canadian Encyclopedia*, 2nd ed., s.v. "pornography," 1724.

2   Citing periodicals and newspapers

Write out the names of months in publication dates. Do not capitalize the names of seasons: (*fall 1996*).

- **Article in a weekly or monthly magazine**

    6. Ian Pearson, "Growing Old Disgracefully," *Saturday Night*, March 1993, 49.

- **Article in a scholarly journal.** If the periodical is paged by issue, include the issue following the volume number of the journal.

    7. Kathleen O'Donnell, "François Hertel: The Unprecedented Voice," *Canadian Literature 66* [autumn 1975]: 86.

- **Review of a book, movie, or play**

    8. Brian D. Johnson, "A Skin-Deep Portrait," review of *The Portrait of a Lady* (movie) directed by Jane Campion, *Maclean's*, 20 January 1997, 69.

- **Newspaper article.** To cite a signed newspaper article, begin with the author's name. To cite an unsigned newspaper article, begin with the title. When appropriate, include the edition, section number, and page number.

    9. "The Poet Cop," *The Toronto Star*, 23 June 1973, Saturday edition, sec. 6, p. 69.

3 Citing electronic sources

The Chicago Manual of Style, 14th edition, provides only brief instructions for citing Internet sources. Its publisher, University of Chicago Press, recommends that writers use the more detailed guidelines presented by Andrew Harnack and Eugene Kleppinger in *Online! A Reference Guide to Using Internet Sources* (New York: St. Martin's, 1998) as a supplement. The following examples are based on Harnack and Kleppinger's guidelines.

- **An Internet document.** Provide the author's name (if known), the title of the document in quotation marks, the title of the complete work (if applicable) in italics or underlined, date of publication or last revision (if known; otherwise use *n.d.*), the URL in angle brackets, and the date of access in parentheses.

  10. Office of Consumer Affairs, "Biotechnology: What Is It All About?" Consumer Quarterly 1, no. 3 (July 1996),<http://www.strategis.ic.gc.ca/SSG/ca00040e.html> (26 July 1997).

- **Internet information service.** Provide the author's name (if known), the title of the document in quotation marks, the name of the service, identifying numbers of the document, the URL in angle brackets, and the date of access in parentheses.

  11. Childs, Ruth Axman, "Gender Bias and Fairness," ERIC Digest, December 1990, ED328610, <http://www.ed.gov/databases/ERIC_Digests/ed328610.html> (31 July 1998).

- **Electronic mail.** Provide the author's name (if known), the author's e-mail address in angle brackets, the subject line from the posting (in quotation marks), date of publication, type of communication (personal mail, distribution list, office communication), date of access (in parentheses).

  12. Tom Norton, <tnorton@efpd.maff.gov.uk>, "Library Lesson Plans," 13 May 1996, personal e-mail (15 May 1996).

- **Listserv message.** Provide the author's name (if known), the author's e-mail address in angle brackets, the subject line from the posting (in quotation marks), date of publication, address of listserv (in angle brackets), date of access (in parentheses).

  13. Denis Arbel, <denis.arbel@wanadoo.fr> "The Rise and Fall of the Euro," 12 October 1999, <econinfo@wlu.ca> (1 November 1999).

- **Newsgroup message.** Provide the author's name (if known), author's e-mail address (in angle brackets), subject line from posting (in quotation marks), date of publication, name of newsgroup (in angle brackets), date of access (in parentheses).

14. Maria de Marco, <mdimarco@canoe.ca>, "Tobacco Fascists," 19 June 1998, <can.legal> (2 July 1998).

- **Synchronous communication (MOOs, MUDs, IRCs).** Provide the name of the speaker (if known), or the name of the site, title of the event (if appropriate) in quotation marks, date of event, type of communication (group discussion, personal interview) if not indicated elsewhere in the entry, address (using a URL in angle brackets or command line directions), date of access in parentheses.

15. Jerome Stone, "Seminar on Environmental Ethics and Eco-Terrorism," 1 November 1997, <telnet://kcsumoo.edu:8888> (1 November 1997).

4 Citing other sources

- **Government publications.** The format for government publications follows this sequence: government body, subsidiary body, title of document, individual author if given, identifying numbers, publication information (in parentheses), page number(s).

16. Department of External Affairs and Northern Affairs and National Resources, *The Columbia River Treaty: A Presentation* (Ottawa: Queen's Printer, 1964), 15.

- **A dissertation.** If you are citing a published dissertation, follow the title with *Ph.D. diss.*, the institution granting the degree, the date it was granted, publication information, and page number. If you are citing an abstract, follow the title with a reference to *Dissertation Abstracts* or *Dissertation Abstracts International*.

17. George Roger Taft, "Socialism in North America: The Case of British Columbia and Washington State" (Ph.D. diss. Simon Fraser University, 1983), abstract in *Dissertation Abstracts International* 46 (1985): 1418A.

- **A letter**

18. Max Du Bois, letter to author, 10 September 1988.

- **Lecture or speech.** To cite the printed version of a lecture or speech, give the page numbers from which you have borrowed.

19. Henry Friesen, "Reshaping Health Research in Canada: An Initiative Whose Time Has Come" (Speech to the Canadian Institute of Academic Medicine, Montreal, 14 February 1999), 3.

- **Interview**

20. Joyce Carol Oates, interview by Terry Gross, *Fresh Air*, National Public Radio, WHYY, Philadelphia, 3 August 1993.

- **Film or video cassette**

    21. *The Sweater* [after a story by Roch Carrier], prods. David Verrall, Marrin Canell and Derek Lamb, dir. Sheldon Cohen, 10 min. 50 sec., National Film Board, 1980, videocassette.

- **Recording**

    22. Rick Avery and Judy Greenhill, "The Blackfly," on *Harbour Grace: Songs of Eastern Canada*, J + R Records 1981 [CAPAC] JR001.

57c Prepare a bibliography

If a bibliography is required to accompany your project, follow these guidelines.

- *Placement.* Place the bibliography on its own page immediately following the endnotes or, if you have used footnotes, following the text of the paper. Centre the heading *Bibliography* 2.5 cm from the top of the page. Continue page numbering from the notes page or text of the paper.

- *Spacing.* Double-space throughout.

- *Indentation.* Do not indent the first line of an entry. Indent following lines five spaces.

- *Alphabetical order.* Do not number the entries of a bibliography. Arrange them in alphabetical order according to the author's last name or the first word of the title, ignoring *A, An,* and *The.*

    Banting, Keith. *The Welfare State and Canadian Federalism.* 2nd ed. Kingston and Montreal: McGill/Queen's University Press, 1987.

    Campaign 2000. *Investing in the Next Generation: Policy Perspective on Children and Nationhood.* Toronto: Child Poverty Action Group, 1994.

- *Punctuation.* Separate the major parts of an entry with a period and one space.

- *A titled part of a book.* Cite the pages of the part immediately following the title and the editor.

    Atwood, Margaret. "Canadian Monsters: Some Aspects of the Supernatural in Canadian Fiction." In *The Canadian Imagination: Dimensions of a Literary Culture*, edited by David Staines, 97–122. Cambridge, Mass.: Harvard University Press, 1977.

58 Using CBE Style

A frequently recommended style for scientific papers (in biology, chemistry, engineering, medicine, physics, and so on) is outlined in a publication issued by the Council of Biology Editors. The most recent edition is *Scientific Style and Format: The CBE Manual for Authors, Editors and Publishers*, 6th ed. (New York: Cambridge University Press, 1994). If an assignment calls for CBE style, here are some rough guidelines.

58*a* | Choose a referencing system

As long as you are consistent, you can follow either one of the CBE approved referencing systems.

1 The citation-sequence (C-S) system

The **citation-sequence** (C-S) system allows for exhaustive in-text references by superscript numbers, determined according to their first appearance in the paper. Thus, your first reference work will be identified by the superscript numeral [1] whenever you refer to it in the text of your paper, and it will appear as the first (1.) of the references you name at the end. The next citation takes the number 2, and the rest follow in sequence, thus the name.

The convenience of referring to several sources unobtrusively keeps your reader from being distracted. For multiple references, separate the numbers with commas if the sequence is not continuous; otherwise use a hyphen:

Fehrenbach[1] proposes a system for assessing tasks undertaken by an

integrated robot manipulator . . . .

[This is a reference to the first work in the reference list, and it will retain this number throughout the paper.]

The procedure has proven effective[2, 4, 6–8] in reducing the concentration of

purine in patients with gout.

[This is a reference to the second, fourth, sixth, seventh, and eighth works in the reference list.]

2 The name-year (N-Y) system

The **name-year** (N-Y) system is quite similar to APA style (see 56a and b), which includes authors and dates in the text of the paper with no superscripts. In the reference list at the end of the paper, however, you do not put the dates in parentheses. The ordering of references at the end of the paper is alphabetical, as with other styles, but you put multiple works by the same author in chronological order in CBE style (where other styles would alphabetize them by title).

Multiple in-text references may be distracting, so provide only as much information as necessary to avoid ambiguity: use initials only to distinguish two authors with the same last name, and use chronological order to refer to multiple publications by the same author:

Most micromanipulative procedures produce abnormally celled embryos

(Babuik and Phillips 1989).

The principal investigators (Graham and Prevec 1990; King GA and others 1991; King RW 1991; Vining and others 1992; Jensen 1993) confirmed

Hawthorne's hypothesis.

[The advantage of the C-S system is that it cites these references much more compactly: The principal investigators[5, 7–9, 13] confirmed Hawthorne's hypothesis.]

As Morales' groundbreaking series of experiments (1991, 1993a, 1993b, 1994)

reveals. . . .

[Note: Morales published two reports in 1993.]

58*b* Model your end-of-text references on these examples

Just as you would for a bibliography, CBE style calls for you to compile a list of references at the end of your paper. If it seems appropriate, you can divide these into cited references and additional references. Here are some general principles:

- Use Arabic numerals only. Do not indent lines.
- Use initials, without spaces or periods, to replace authors' first names. For multiple authors, list the first ten names in their order of appearance on the title page, separating them with commas, then put *and others*.
- Use periods only to separate fields of information:

C-S: author(s)/editor(s). title [type of work]. publishing information; year. pages. availability statement.

N-Y: author(s)/editor(s). year. title [type of work]. publishing information. pages. availability statement.

- Capitalize only the first word of a title, except for proper names. Do not underline or italicize titles.

- Note the different uses of **p.** To indicate the total number of pages, put **p.** after the number (673 p.), to point to the actual page(s), put **p.** first (p. 673). For more than one page number, use **p.** followed by the beginning and end numbers without unnecessary repetition: *p. 1427–31, p. 1427–565.*

- For dates, put the year first, followed by the month (always use a three-letter abbreviation without punctuation) and the day.

- Use **nr** as the abbreviation for number in contracts, patents, etc.

1 The C-S reference list

The following works have been listed as if they were cited in this order in the text of a paper. Whenever the author refers to the Hall and Brown text, for example, the superscript 3 ([3]) would appear in the paper.

- **One author—A journal article**

  1. Reeder M. Exterior powers of the adjoint representation. Canadian journal of mathematics 1997 Feb; 49(1): 133–59.

- **Multiple authors—A journal supplement**

  2. MacLean DR, Petrasovits A, Nargundkar M, Connelly PW, MacLeod E, Edwards A, Hesswel P, CHHSRG. Canadian heart health surveys: a profile of cardiovascular risk. CMAJ 1992 Jun 1; special supplement: 1–56.

- **Multiple authors—A book**

  3. Hall IR, Brown G. The black truffle. Mosgiel NZ: Invermay Agricultural Centre; 1988. 73 p.

- **Organizational author—A book**

  4. [CPHA] Canadian Public Health Association. A resource manual for AIDS educators. rev. ed. Ottawa: CPHA; 1992. 168 p.

- **A bibliography**

  5. Abdelmalek NN, compiler. Robotics bibliography: 1981–82, Part A: Applications of industrial robots. Ottawa: National Research Council; 1983. 155 p. Available from: Division of Electrical Engineering NRCC; nr ERB-9959, NRCC 22602.

- **A dissertation**

  6. Kay PA. Post-glacial history of vegetation and climate in the forest-tundra transition zone Dubawnt Lake region, Northwest Territories, Canada [dissertation]. Madison: University of Wisconsin-Madison; 1976. 143 p. Available from: University Microfilms International, Ann Arbor, Mich; 77–8793.

- **Conference proceedings**

  7. Gao QG, Wang RX. Extracting structure-tokens of cephalograms. In: Intelligent systems for the 21st century. Proceedings of the 1995 IEEE international conference on systems, man and cybernetics. Vol. 5; 1995 Oct 22–25; Vancouver BC. Piscataway NJ: IEEE; 1995. p. 4268–72.

- **An abstract**

  8. Roney JM. New results from LEP [abstract]. In: CAP congress; 1997 Jun 8–11; Physics in Canada 53 (3); 1997 May/Jun. p. 63. Abstract nr EH3.

- **A patent**

  9. Schemenauer RW, inventor; Bourgault Industries Ltd, grantee. Master/slave hydraulic system for farming implements. Can. patent nr 2 015 835; 1997 Jul 22.

- **An audio-visual source**

  10. CANDU reactor [overhead transparency]. Corbeil J-C. Atomic energy of Canada. Toronto: Stoddart; 1986. Available from: 34 Lesmill Rd. Toronto M3B 2T6. VD-648.

- **An Internet document**

  11. Bergman RA, Afifi AK, Miyauchi R. Illustrated encyclopedia of human anatomic variation [Online]. Available from: The Virtual Hospital, University of Iowa. <http://vh.radiology.uiowa.edu/Providers/Textbooks/ AnatomicVariants/ AnatomyHP.html> Accessed 1997 Jun 5.

- **E-mail message**

  12. Winegarden O. <owine@medtronix.org> 1998 Oct. 25. Hodgkins disease [personal e-mail]. Accessed 1998 Oct. 26.

2   The N-Y reference list

The following list contains the twelve works that would be numbered in the C-S system. In the N-Y reference list, they appear in alphabetical order with the year appearing directly after the first piece of bibliographic information. Note the indentation of the second and subsequent lines.

Abdelmalek NN, compiler. 1983. Robotics bibliography: 1981–82, Part A: Applications of industrial robots. Ottawa: National Research Council. 155 p. Available from: Division of Electrical Engineering NRCC; nr ERB-9959, NRCC 22602.

Bergman RA, Afifi AK, Miyauchi R. 1997. Illustrated encyclopedia of human anatomic variation [online]. University of Iowa: The Virtual Hospital. <http://vh.radiology.uiowa.edu/Providers/Textbooks/AnatomicVariants/ AnatomyHP.html> Accessed 1997 June 5.

CANDU reactor [overhead transparency]. 1986. Corbeil J-C. Atomic energy of Canada. Toronto: Stoddart. Available from: 34 Lesmill Rd. Toronto M3B 2T6. VD-648.

[CPHA] Canadian Public Health Association, 1992. A resource manual for AIDS educators. rev. ed. Ottawa: CPHA. 168 p.

Gao QG, Wang RX. 1995. Extracting structure-tokens of cephalograms. In: Intelligent systems for the 21st century. Proceedings of the 1995 IEEE international conference on systems, man and cybernetics. Vol. 5; 1995 Oct 22–25; Vancouver BC. Piscataway NJ: IEEE. p. 4268–72.

Hall IR, Brown G. 1988. The black truffle. Mosgiel NZ: Invermay Agricultural Centre. 73 p.

Kay PA. 1976. Post-glacial history of vegetation and climate in the forest-tundra transition zone Dubawnt Lake region, Northwest Territories, Canada [dissertation]. Madison: University of Wisconsin-Madison. 143 p. Available from: University Microfilms International, Ann Arbor, Mich; 77–8793.

MacLean DR, Petrasovits A, Nargundkar M, Connelly PW, MacLeod E, Edwards A, Hesswel P, CHHSRG. 1992. Canadian heart health surveys: a profile of cardiovascular risk. CMAJ Jun 1; special supplement: 1–56.

Reeder M. 1997. Exterior powers of the adjoint representation. Canadian journal of mathematics 49(1): 133–59.

Roney JM. 1997. New results from LEP [abstract]. In: CAP congress; 1997 Jun 8–11; Physics in Canada 53 (3). p. 63. Abstract nr EH3.

Schemenauer RW, inventor; Bourgault Industries Ltd, grantee. 1997. Master/slave hydraulic system for farming implements. Can. patent nr 2 015 835. Jul 22.

Winegarden O. 1998. <owine@medtronix.org> Hodgkin's disease [personal e-mail]. Accessed 1998 Oct 26.

chapter

59 A List of Style Manuals

Every discipline has a preferred manuscript form and system of documentation. Below is a list of recommended style manuals for a variety of fields.

- Biology. Council of Biology Editors. *Scientific Style and Format: The CBE Manual for Authors, Editors, and Publishers.* 6th ed. New York: Cambridge UP, 1994.

- Chemistry. American Chemical Society. *The ACS Style Guide: A Manual for Authors and Editors.* Washington: ACS, 1997.

- Engineering. Michaelson, Herbert B. *How to Write and Publish Engineering Papers and Reports.* 3rd ed. Phoenix: Oryx, 1990.

- English and the humanities. Gibaldi, Joseph. *MLA Handbook for Writers of Research Papers.* 5th ed. New York: Modern Language Association, 1999.

- Law. *The Bluebook: A Uniform System of Citation.* Comp. Editors of Columbia Law Review et al. 15th ed. Cambridge: Harvard Law Review, 1996.

- Linguistics. Linguistic Society of America. *LSA Bulletin,* Dec. issue, annually.

- Mathematics.

  American Mathematical Society. *A Manual for Authors of Mathematical Papers.* 8th rev. ed. Providence: AMS, 1990.

  Kranz, Steven G. *A Primer of Mathematical Writing.* Providence: AMS, 1997.

- Music. Holoman, D. Kern, ed. *Writing about Music: A Style Sheet from the Editors of 19th-Century Music.* Berkeley: U of California P, 1988.

- Physics. American Institute of Physics. *AIP Style Manual.* 4th ed. New York: AIP, 1990.

- Psychology. American Psychological Association. *Publication Manual of the American Psychological Association.* 4th ed. Washington: APA, 1994.

- General.

  The Chicago Manual of Style. 14th ed. Chicago: U of Chicago P, 1993.

  Department of the Secretary of State. *The Canadian Style: A Guide to Writing and Editing.* Toronto: Dundurn Press and the Government Publishing Centre, Supply and Services Canada, 1997.

60 Writing about Literature

You're reading literature at school for the same reasons you might read while relaxing at home, for the pleasures of escape, vicarious experience, suspense, and surprise. But you're also reading for the deeper pleasures that come from an enlarged understanding of yourself and the world. The writing you do in response to your reading may be notebook or journal entries, in-class writing, essays, reviews, research projects, or creative assignments. Their form will depend on your focus, whether on the work itself, on your responses, or on the context (historical or biographical) in which the work was written. In any case, you are writing to enlarge your understanding, explore your feelings, develop your creative powers, and share your responses with others.

60a | Reading the elements of literature

See 1b for general guidelines for critical reading. Here are some additional ones to help increase your pleasure in reading and add to your insights. As you read, look for the literary elements writers use to create their art. These elements open a doorway to response and understanding.

- *Characters.* Greet literary characters as you greet real people you're meeting for the first time—with healthy skepticism. Don't believe everything they say. What do they know, exactly? Are they reliable observers? Compare words to deeds and to other characters' remarks.

- *The narrator.* Every work of fiction and poetry has a narrator, a person who tells the story or presents the poem, even if there is no *I* in the work. Narrators do not necessarily speak for the author. Unless they earn your trust, treat narrators with the same healthy skepticism you would any other character in the work.

- *Stylistic devices.* Look for the stylistic devices writers use to dramatize their message: **irony** (discrepancies between words and deeds, between your expectation and what actually happens, between what a character says and what you know to be true), **symbols** (things, places, or people that have meaning beyond themselves), and **figurative language** (metaphor and simile). (See 31c.)

- *Mood.* As you read, be sensitive to the feeling expressed in the work toward the subject (serious, humorous, mocking, amused, and so on). Mood is expressed by the narrator's point of view, details of characterization, the course of events, and the way events and settings are described.

- *The title.* Decide what the title suggests about the mood, subject, or message of the work.

- *Key passages.* Look for key passages in which the narrator or another character seems to step back and comment on the subject or action.

- *Layout and staging.* Consider white space between passages and stanza forms as clues to structure or meaning. When you read drama, stage directions and descriptions of set design help you imagine settings, events, and the personalities of the characters. Note the instructions for characters' actions or speeches that suggest personality, motivation, and conflict.

60b | Choose your options for writing about literature: analysis and interpretation

Readers use analysis and interpretation to understand a work, their response, or the historical context. **Analysis** is the systematic description of literary elements (character, setting, plot, imagery, and so on) and the way they work together to form your opinions as you read. **Interpretation** focusses on elements in a work that are not immediately apparent (for example, the hidden causes of an event or the reasons for two characters' conflict) and then, using evidence and logic, tries to clarify these elements (see 1a1 and 2).

1 Selecting literary elements to analyze and interpret

Adapt the questions after each of the following elements to your chosen literary work. Your answers will provide material for your writing.

- *Character.* Explain your opinion of a character by answering one or more of these questions: What kind of person is this? (Consider appearance, dress, speech, action, thoughts, feelings, flaws, relationships, and motives.) Does this character change? If so, how? What is the secret of the relationship between this character and another? Why do these characters engage in conflict? How are conflicts resolved? What is this character's role in the work: main character (protagonist), antagonist, confidant(e), or foil (a character whose personality sheds light on a main character's personality)?

- *Setting.* Describe the setting of the work—natural, social, political, or cultural. What does setting contribute to the mood, your understanding, or your evaluation? What force does it exert on the characters?

- *Plot and structure.* Describe the change taking place in the course of the narrative. What are the causes and consequences of this change? What mood or message is expressed by the arrangement of events? Consider the use of flashback. What patterns of imagery, language, dialogue, or poetic form do you see? What does each contribute to mood or message?

- *Symbols.* Identify and explain literary symbols. What characters or details of setting seem to be symbolic? What ideas, values, or conditions do they symbolize?

- *Mood.* Explain the overall feeling or attitude expressed in the work about its subject. What do the characters, setting, plot, imagery, and style contribute to this mood?

- *Style.* Describe the style of the work and the contributions of this style to the work's mood or theme. Consider formal or informal word choice (see 32a), metaphor and simile (see 31c), and complex or simple sentence structure (see 12c).

- *Point of view.* Point of view is the narrator's vantage point for presenting the action of a literary work. Who is the narrator: an actual character in the work (an *I* telling his or her story or someone else's) or a disembodied voice writing in the third person (*he* or *she*)? What does the narrator know or not know? Do you trust this narrator? Why or why not? How do the narrator's knowledge, values, and relationships with other characters affect the structure, mood, and message of the work?

- *A key passage.* Explain how a brief key passage sums up the mood or message of a work.

2 Defending a theme

In a broad sense, a **theme** is the message of a work but more than simply a moral. A moral says "Do this; don't do that." A theme says, "Life is like that." A theme is a message or judgment a work dramatizes about its subject. Present the theme of a work, and show how it is embodied by the characters, plot, imagery, mood, and style. Follow these guidelines for writing theme statements:

- *A formula for writing theme statements.* Use this formula to write a tentative theme statement: "The message of _____ is that _____ . "

- *A generalization.* A theme is a generalization about life; therefore, it does not identify characters by name but makes statements about people in general or certain types of people.

- *A complete sentence.* A theme is a complete declarative sentence, not a fragment or question.

- *A stated or implied theme.* A theme may sometimes be located in an actual statement in a work. Or it may only be implied, and you'll express it in your own words.

- *An insightful statement.* A theme statement for a serious work of literature will always be more insightful than pronouncements on "the moral of the story" or a trite saying ("Love conquers all").

- *A unifying statement.* As a unifying statement, a theme should not be contradicted by any major details of a work.*

Here is an example: *In* Sunshine Sketches of a Little Town, *Stephen Leacock's apt but gentle humour ridicules the narrow, provincial, hypocritical values of the people he depicts.*

60c Choose your options for writing about literature: the review

Analysis and interpretation *explain* a literary work or some part of it. A **review,** on the other hand, *evaluates* a work or some part of it. But a review does more than present one reader's personal preferences. Skillful reviewers rely on widely shared standards of value and recognized points of comparison to decide the value of their subjects (see 1a3).

1 Applying standards of value

There are three kinds of standards for evaluating literature.

- Reviewers apply **technical** and **aesthetic standards** to judge how well a work achieves its intended effects. Is a humorous story humorous; is a tragedy tragic? What explains a work's success or failure in achieving its aims: point of view, structure, plot, characterization, or style? How well constructed is it in comparison with others of its type?

- Reviewers use **psychological** and **social standards of personality and behaviour** to evaluate the plausibility of characters and their world. How "real" are these characters? Or how well do they express the conventions of their literary type?

- Reviewers use **ethical standards** to evaluate the morality of a work and its contents. What values does the work seem to endorse? Do you share them?

---

*For these guidelines to theme statements, thanks go to Laurence Perrine's *Literature,* 5th ed. (New York: Harcourt, 1988).

2 Writing a review

The thesis for a review will be your dominant impression, your overall judgment of the work or the feature you've chosen to evaluate. You may focus your review in two ways, drawing from the standards in 60c1 to make your judgment.

- Evaluate a literary work or some feature of it. How effectively does the writer handle characters, setting, plot, structure, or style? Is the work believable, consistent, appropriate to its type, well constructed?

- Evaluate the ideas or values expressed in a literary work. What does the work dramatize as useful, valuable, desirable, or virtuous? What does the work suggest about the way things should be? Consider description, dialogue, and the narrator's comments. Do you agree with what the work seems to favour? Why or why not?

60*d* | Choose your options for writing about literature: personal and creative responses

1 Writing a personal response

- *Respond.* Write an essay in which you explain your responses to a literary work. Answer these questions: What in the literary work prompted your responses? What were your feelings, memories, or associations as you read? What personal experiences, observations, or beliefs explain these responses?

- *Compare.* Explore the relationship between art and life by writing a comparison. Use your experiences to help you explain something in a literary work: character, setting, plot, theme. Or use something from the work to help make sense of something in your own life.

- *Examine then and now.* Responses and opinions change as readers reread and discuss a literary work. Trace the evolution in your thinking by answering these questions: What did I originally think or feel and why? What made me change? What do I now think and feel?

2 Writing a creative response

Use literary techniques to dramatize your feelings or opinions about a work or some part of it. Imagine a revealing scene that the author has not presented. Or dramatize the thoughts of a character in a soliloquy (a monologue in which a character expresses thoughts or feelings that would otherwise be unspoken). Or narrate events that might have occurred "off-stage." Or present an episode in a character's life from before or after the events described in the literary work. Whichever strategy you choose, try to remain faithful to the characters, plot, mood, theme, and style as the original author expressed them.

60*e* | Choose your options for writing about literature: the research project

Many literature classes require some form of research paper. (For guidelines, see 49–52.)

- *Writing a review of research.* Your project may expand on one of the preceding options, using scholars' interpretations to enrich your own. With whom do you agree? Why? How has your research changed your thinking?

- *Writing a biographical project.* Investigate a writer and his or her work. How does this writer's work reflect his or her life? How did he or she come to write this work? What is the history of the work's reputation?

- *Writing about historical context.* Investigate the historical context of a work or some part of it. What does this work reveal about the culture and period in which it was written? How accurately does it present historical figures, conditions, or events?

60*f* | Write a literary paper using these guidelines

1 Preparing to write

- *Focus.* Write a key question about your topic or a tentative thesis to provide focus as you reread your chosen work and gather ideas for your paper. (See 2b3 and 2d.)

- *Take notes.* To support your thesis, take notes as you reread. Provide a context for each note: Who's speaking to whom? What's happening where and when? (See 51c and d.)

- *Refocus your thesis.* When you've finished rereading and taking notes, reconsider your thesis to see whether it fits what you've discovered. (See 3a.) Beware of "So?" statements, incomplete assertions. Revise to make assertions about the causes, consequences, or importance of your topic.

Laura Sheridan, of Katherine Mansfield's short story "The Garden Party," lives in a dream world/until her visit to the grieving Scott family, when she awakens from her dream and discovers what it means to be fully alive.

[The original leaves the reader saying "So? So, what's the point about Laura and her dream world?" The revision answers the question.]

- *Organize to support your thesis.* In an important sense, your paper is not about your chosen literary work. It's about your thesis. Organize so that everything in your paper follows from or leads to your thesis.

2 Writing and revising

- *Identify author and title.* Identify the author and title of your literary work early in your essay, even in the first sentence. Use quotation marks around the titles of poems and short stories ("The Garden Party"). Italicize or underline the titles of novels, plays, and films (*Hamlet* or Hamlet). (For quotation marks, see 40d; for italics or underlining, see 43a.)

- *Avoid an all-summary paper.* Unless instructed otherwise, assume that the audience for your paper is your instructor and the other members of your class. They've probably read your chosen work and won't want to read a report-style summary. But they may not understand the work as you do or remember the small details you have in mind. Summarize briefly to present evidence supporting your opinions.

- *Use the present tense for summaries.* Use the present tense to write about an author's work and to summarize action in the work. The original may read: *As Laura walked up to the workers, she blushed and tried to look severe.* But you would write: *As Laura **walks** up to the workers, she **blushes** and **tries** to look severe.* Events occurring before the opening of a work should be summarized in the past tense. (See 15b1.)

- *Use quotations.* Quote often but briefly to explain and illustrate. (See 40a and b.) Indent long quotations of more than four typed lines. (See 52d.) Use ellipsis points to signal omissions from quotations (see 41d) and brackets to insert clarifications (see 41c).

- *Follow the proper format.* Format the final draft of your paper according to Modern Language Association guidelines for writing in the humanities. (See 48c.)

60*g* A sample literary essay

The following essay was written by student Leslie Kelly in an introduction to literature course. Her assignment was to write a character study of the narrator of William Stafford's poem "Traveling Through the Dark." To make her interpretation, she considers the narrator's personality and the

How to . . .

How to Revise and Edit a Literary Essay

Use the following questions to guide your revision and editing. Or ask your peers to read your draft with these questions in mind and answer the most important. (For more on revision, see 4b and c.)

1. A question for peer reviewers: Describe the thoughts and feelings you had as you read this paper. Do your responses to the literary work agree with the writer's? If not, where do you differ? Can you explain the differences?

2. Identify this paper's purpose: analysis, interpretation, evaluation, or personal response. Point out any passages that may not fit this purpose.

3. Point out or summarize the thesis of this paper: Does it seem to be a "So?" thesis? Does the paper include another version at the end? Is that statement clearer? Does it better fit the evidence of the paper? (See 4b4.)

4. Does the paper present enough evidence (quotation, summary, and explanation) to support the thesis? Point out places where more support is needed.

5. Can readers follow this essay from beginning to end? Does its design follow the order of events in the original literary work (summary order) or the order of ideas in the thesis (logical order)? What design is clearest and most appropriate?

6. Does this paper follow the format for literary essays? (See 60f.)

poem's setting, imagery, and style. She concludes by explaining how the narrator embodies the poem's theme. (For guidelines to the format of a literary essay, see 60f2.)

"Traveling Through the Dark" by William Stafford

Traveling through the dark, I found a deer
dead on the edge of the Wilson River road.
It is usually best to roll them into the canyon:
that road is narrow; to swerve might make more dead.

By glow of the tail-light I stumbled back of the car
and stood by the heap, a doe, a recent killing;
she had stiffened already, almost cold.
I dragged her off; she was large in the belly.

My fingers touching her side brought me the reason—
her side was warm; her fawn lay there waiting,
alive, still, never to be born.
Beside that mountain road I hesitated.

The car aimed ahead its lowered parking lights;
under the hood purred the steady engine.
I stood in the glare of the warm exhaust turning red;
around our group I could hear the wilderness listen.

I thought hard for us all—my only swerving—
then pushed her over the edge into the river.

Dark Necessity
by Leslie Kelly

An opening that identifies the author and title of the literary work

A general statement of the thesis

Topic sentence introducing the first part of the essay

The use of brackets to insert a clarification into a quotation

Quotations from the poem woven into the text of the essay to support the writer's interpretation

A topic sentence to introduce another trait of the narrator's personality

An interpretation of poetic language

On a first reading of William Stafford's "Traveling Through the Dark," the narrator of the poem appears admirable, a hero even. He is a good Samaritan, sensitive but in control of his feelings, thoughtful, and capable of decisive action. Who wouldn't trust him to be the driver on a journey down a dark, dangerous, lonely road? And yet a careful rereading reveals that there is more to this man and his actions than first appears.

Make no mistake. He is a good man doing the right thing for the right reasons. From the first stanza, as soon as he sees the dead deer, he shows his concern for others and their safety. You or I might whiz by, unseeing, indifferent, or pressed for time. But he sees that if he does not act, because the "road is narrow," other travellers might swerve to avoid the carcass and turn into the path of oncoming traffic or over the edge into the river. Three times he acts. He "dragged her [the dead doe] off" the road. He "thought hard" about what should be done after he discovers that the dead doe's unborn fawn is alive. Then, deciding what must be done, he "pushed her over the edge into the river."

He acts decisively, in part, because he thinks so clearly. Nearly every stanza reveals his logic. In the first, he reasons about what he has discovered—the dead deer, the narrow road, and the potential consequences of a swerve. In stanzas 2 and 3 he reasons inductively. Already stiffened, "almost cold," the deer was a "recent killing," but "large in the belly" and "her side [still] warm." The "fawn lay there waiting." He knows from common sense that there is no saving this fawn. Reasoning by analogy, he knows that to pause in pity is a "swerving" as dangerous as the actual swerve of a car.

Throughout, however, his logic is tempered by sensitivity. "Her fawn lay there waiting,/alive, still, never to be born." The word "still" seems to mean both "yet," as in "yet alive," and "quiet" or "unmoving," as one might expect of an animal connected by umbilical cord to its dead mother. There is paradox and enormous awareness in these lines. As he thinks of what to do, he personifies the silence of the wilderness into listening attention. In these connections between life and death, self and wilderness, he understands the importance of his decision. How often do we think and act so decisively but with such understanding and awareness?

And yet . . . even if the narrator is as admirable as these details make him appear, there are other details to be accounted for. Consider the title. The narrator is not driving through the dark; he's "traveling." This word suggests more than a drive in the country, not the fact of a journey so much as its condition. He may be driving his car, but to no near destination.

Here is a man whose condition is being in the dark. In such darkness, some things are difficult to see. One is the world of the poem. It is a pair of parallel universes existing simultaneously in the same space. There is, first of all, the natural world of night, mountain, river, canyon, dead doe, and dying fawn. The other world penetrates, dominates, and finally destroys the former. Its features are the human name for the river, the road, the man, the darkness of the poem's title that refers to more than night, and, most vivid of all, the narrator's car. In contrast to doe and fawn, it lives in images of "the steady engine" that "purred" "under the hood," in the breath of "warm exhaust turning red," in its readiness for purposeful action as it "aimed ahead its lowered parking lights." Given these powerful differences, the human, technological world must displace the natural as it does in the narrator's last, symbolic act, when, with an energy not called for in the first stanza, he does not "roll [the deer] into the canyon," he "*pushed* [emphasis added] her over the edge into the river."

He pushes despite his feelings for the fawn because he stands apart from the natural world. His first response, in stanza 1, is to the social code covering such encounters with the natural world: "It is usually best to roll them into the canyon." The deer is a "heap" *before* it is a "doe" ("the heap, a doe"), the descriptive word suggesting debris more than a "recent killing." He does not perceive the presence of the fawn directly. Instead, "my fingers touching her side brought me the reason," as if his fingers were intermediaries between the natural and human world of reason and technology. Throughout, of course, he thinks and acts "by glow of the tail-light." The only sound the wilderness can hear as he thinks and it listens is the purr of the car, the sound of the life that directs his life and decides his choice.

Given his character and the nature of his world, what other choice does he have? He may think hard, but his concern for the fawn is only a "swerving"—a dangerous reflex from a civilized point of view. Viewed in the dim tail-lights of the car, "roll" comes naturally to "push," and "shove" is not far behind. Stafford's poem dramatizes the force of civilized life in the natural world. However much human pity may give pause, its effects are inevitably disregarding, brutal, destructive.

Marginal notes:

A transition to the second part of the essay

An interpretation of a key word from the title

An interpretation of the setting that reveals a contrast between the narrator's civilized world and the natural world

The narrator's behaviour explained in terms of the values of his world

A conclusion that states the theme of the poem as the writer of the essay understands it

chapter

61 Writing for Oral Presentation

For many, making a presentation to an audience is much more intimidating than preparing a paper or an essay to hand in. It's often a question of experience—classes in school rarely allow the opportunity for regular speeches and oral presentations. There just isn't enough time for everybody to be heard. In those cases where individual presentations are possible, a few ground rules can help you overcome your anxiety.

61a | Prepare for your presentation

Get yourself organized in the same way that you would for preparing something in writing.

1 Identify your audience

In preparing for your oral presentation, you first need a clear idea of who your audience is going to be. What is its overall size? (Sometimes, the smaller the group, the more informal you can be.) What do you know about the members of the audience? Do they know you? Do they know your subject? By determining their attitude to you and your subject before you begin to plan the presentation, you will know which areas to avoid and which ones to emphasize. You will also have an idea of how to persuade your audience to be sympathetic to your point of view.

One point to keep in mind: giving an oral presentation is still quite different from writing a formal paper. Rather than worry about whether your audience is going to like you, take advantage of the opportunities that speaking provides. After all, even though you may not have much experience speaking in a formal setting, speaking is still something you do every day.

- You can ignore such details as punctuation and spelling, because nobody can hear the difference between a comma and a semicolon and no one cares whether or not you can spell correctly.

- You can address your audience as "you," while referring to yourself and your opinions with "I." (Note the rapport you can establish by including your audience with "we.")

- Your tone of voice and body language can enhance your presentation. Use your voice, face, and gestures to make the meaning clear.

- You can rely on your audience for immediate feedback. When people look puzzled, you can take the time to expand a point or repeat it. That's an opportunity you'll never get as a writer.

2 Determine your purpose

Unless your topic has already been chosen for you, you should select a subject you are interested in, one you know something about. Knowing who your audience is allows you to determine your purpose in addressing the group: Are you informing, persuading, instructing or entertaining? *Note:* although you may never be expected to play the part of the stand-up comic, there is no rule that prohibits an audience from enjoying a presentation. Always look carefully at a subject to identify its possibilities for humour.

3 Collect and organize your material

Putting together material for a presentation is no different from planning a paper. Sometimes you already have a firm idea of what you need. Most of the time you will need to do some digging to find support for your main ideas. Reinforce your points with appropriate quotations from experts on the topic, with concrete examples, analogies, anecdotes.

Plan to write your presentation out in full, whether or not you plan to read it to your audience. The better organized you are, the less nervous you will be.

While you are planning the text of your talk, determine how you will be presenting it: impromptu (you speak from memory with few notes, if any), controlled (your note cards are comprehensive), or formal (you read the prepared text of your paper). Be aware of potential problems with reciting or reading a speech: if you present from memory, you will have to master the fear of forgetting; if you read your text, you will have to work especially hard to establish rapport with your audience.

Knowing how much time is allotted for your presentation will determine how much material you will need to include in support of the main point. Generally speaking, you can count on taking a minute or two to read a single double-spaced page of text. (After all, you want to take your time and let your points sink in.) You will be surprised how quickly ten minutes will pass.

In preparing the text of your presentation, pay careful attention to the special expectations for each section.

- *Introduction:* You want your audience to become immediately interested in what you have to say. The time you take to develop a catchy introduction is worth it. Begin with a related story, pose a provocative question, make a startling statement, tell an unusual joke—all these are popular ways of grabbing the audience's attention and piquing their curiosity. At the same time, you will want to avoid the clichéd openings that are the butt of comedy: "A funny thing happened to me on my way to . . . ." or "But seriously folks." You should also avoid any kind of introduction that sounds as if you are speaking from a soapbox. Catch your audience's interest first, before you start preaching.

- *Discussion:* The main part of your presentation will follow a clear organization, just as it would in writing. Because of time limits, however, you cannot get carried away by the details. Arrange to have the specifics available on handouts and on overheads. Your job is to summarize what the information means, not to read it together with your audience. Be careful about how much new information your listeners can take in. Your audience will be grateful not to be overwhelmed by all your research. At the same time, you will want to take advantage of transitional signals that let your audience know where you are heading in your presentation: *First, Then, Next, Finally, On the other hand, Indeed, Therefore* are wonderful clues.

- *Conclusion:* Use the remaining minutes of your presentation to let the audience know you are winding down. Don't take too long, however, or people will become restless. The conclusion is designed to summarize and reinforce the main point of your presentation—memorably if possible. Leave your audience with a sense of finality by echoing what you said in your introduction. Remind everyone of the relevance of the story you began with, give an answer to your original provocative question, emphasize how your opening statement is now actually not so startling, tell the point of your initial joke. Make the ending sound like an ending, and your audience will be both grateful and impressed.

4 Choose effective visual aids

When you are presenting information to a group, you are the centre of attention, like it or not. One way of sharing this focal point is to take advantage of visual aids like handouts, blackboards, whiteboards, flip charts, posters, overhead transparencies, power point technology (if you have a laptop), even short videos. To control your material and your presentation, pay careful attention to how you use your visual aids:

- Keep them simple. Your charts and diagrams must be easy to understand and involve a minimum of explanation. They are there to supplement your discussion, not to take over.

- Make sure that everything can be seen by your audience. (Long before you give your presentation, check that the print on transparencies, posters, and power point projections can be read by someone in the back of the room. If it can't, you need to fix it.)

- During your presentation, move around at the front of the room so you are not permanently blocking anyone from seeing your visual aids. If you are projecting anything on a screen, do not stand in its way.

- Audiences appreciate being able to take handouts away with them. Make handouts practical by keeping them to a single sheet and by using point form. Include your name, title, and the date of presentation in the upper right-hand corner, so that the handout will retain its relevance long after your presentation.

5   Practise your presentation

To increase your confidence, deliver your presentation at least once before you address the intended audience. If you can't practise in the actual room where you will be giving your talk, choose a room that is similar. Rehearse with someone who is reasonably objective, and take advantage of any feedback to make improvements in your delivery.

- Speak slowly and clearly. Make sure your voice can be heard at the back of the room.

- Time the reading of your presentation. Be sure that you keep within your time limit. Be ruthless about cutting out sections if you go overtime. Mark those parts of your discussion that can be dropped during the actual presentation if time is tight.

- Practise looking around the room so that you will make eye contact when you have a real audience. Look at three areas of the room—left, right, and centre. Then, when you are actually presenting, deliberately look at a member of the audience in each area. By reducing your audience size to three in this way, you will appear more personable and less wooden when at the podium.

61*b* | Examine a model speech

Topic: The value of education

Audience: Senior business students

An opening that immediately engages the reader with a question and an I-you focus

Do I think education is valuable? You bet I do. Take a look at this $20 bill. It's not enough to pay for a textbook any more, but it certainly has value as a wager. In fact, I'm willing to bet this $20 that nobody here really questions the value of an education. You might question the worth of a *kind* of education, but you wouldn't question the principle itself. Yes, education is valuable.

You can help me prove the point. You just have to answer a couple of questions. For this $20 would you run across a four-lane highway without looking? If I gave you this money, would you

Repetition of
questions for
rhetorical effect

I + you = we

Quotations for
humour and
support

Informal
language
appropriate to
conversational
tone

Personal appeal
with emphasis
on "I"

Humorous
anonymous
quotation

Us vs them
focus empha-
sizes the audi-
ence is on the
right side of the
issue

Repetition for
effect

stick a screwdriver into an electrical outlet? Would you eat rhubarb leaves? Would you willingly trade it for a pair of socks that you could buy at Zellers for $2.69 + tax? No. You wouldn't do any of these things because you are too educated to be fooled. Our knowledge of highways, electricity, oxalic acid and the value of money reveals how very educated we really are. No argument.

What we might argue, and often do, is the *form* this education takes. Mention education, and everybody thinks of school first. This is the education Mark Twain was talking about when he said "Training is everything. The peach was once a bitter almond; cauliflower is nothing but a cabbage with a college education." Mark Twain also said, "Soap and education are not as sudden as a massacre, but they are more deadly in the long run." Now he wasn't contradicting himself, just referring to the kind of formal schooling that props notetakers up in desks for hours a day so that they can eventually be labelled successful. This kind of education has its value, too. After all, everyone learns to live with it. And living with and through things is a side benefit of education that we use much more often than we trot out concepts of polynomial distribution or the dates of people's coronations.

Ask people about their education, though, and they'll inevitably tell you how long they've been going to school. But all the diplomas and certificates and whatnot mean nothing if you stop learning once you get them. The really valuable education is the one you get by keeping your eyes and ears open all the time. It's what you learn about *how* the world works—not just what people who write textbooks say you should know—that is valuable, more valuable, I believe, than the grounding you get in the first twenty years or so of your life.

I'm using the word "grounding" deliberately. What gets packed into your head during your years of formal schooling ought to give you a good basis for starting a productive life, but it is only a start. Whoever said that "education is what you have left over once you've forgotten everything you've learned" meant that your real education, the one we're calling valuable here, begins only once you forget about all the theories and concentrate on the practice.

This practical education, which is informal and ongoing, is one that will last you a lifetime.

People who limit themselves to the view that education takes place only in school have forgotten the central role of education in society. School is but one place where learning can begin. The next time you double-check your bank balance to make sure there are no irregular service charges, the next time you apply for a loan, the next time you grouse about how tuition fees are escalating, remember this: you can do all this because you are able to apply some of that knowledge you have gained, whether you knew you were getting it or not.

Signal that end
is near

Echo of
introduction of-
fers sense of
completeness
and questions
answered

So your ability to cross streets safely, avoid electric shocks, eat right and save money are all fundamental givens that really bring home my point. No matter how straightforward or complicated the highway of our lives, it is our formal backgrounds along with our informal experience that give us our sense of where we are going and why. This is an education that is worth infinitely more than the $20 I've been waving around. Best of all, it's an education you don't have to spend a penny to get. Thank you.

61c | Collaborate on presentations

The assignment of a group presentation can be frustrating for the individuals involved, whether or not they know each other well. Everyone is understandably worried about how much time and effort the work is going to call for. Team projects require meetings, not all of which may be productive. More important, people want some guarantee the work will be shared equally and the quality will be consistent. The fear is, understandably, that one person will end up doing the work of someone else—and not getting the credit.

When you have to work as a team, whether at school or on the job, the key ingredient is organization. If you take the time to plan ahead, your project stands a much better chance of success. Once you are sure of your assignment, follow these steps to good management:

- Always begin with a strategy meeting. As soon as the project is assigned, choose a time when you can all get together for at least one hour uninterrupted. Designate someone as leader, and establish an agenda beforehand. As soon as you have a statement of purpose for your project, develop a general outline of work to accomplish. At this point, delegate responsibilities to each member. Do so in writing, not just so everyone knows what's expected of him or her but, more important, so you can confirm, as a group, that every aspect of the subject is covered. (Gaps in research are best identified at the outset, when something can still be done, rather than when it is too late.) Give everyone a planning sheet to complete for your next meeting. You can model yours on the chart on the next page.

- At your second meeting, everyone reports on progress. Have someone collect and collate the planning charts to determine what's there and what's missing. Now is the time to confirm deadlines. Be sure to leave enough time to put the presentation together, and to practise it, before it is due. Determine who among you will be responsible for editing and preparing the final manuscript. Be sure the work is distributed fairly. Arrange for someone to collect the sections, for someone else to verify their continuity, and for someone else to manage

Date due: _____   Position in outline: _____

Section title: _____   Number of pages: _____

Author: _____   Phone: _____

Statement of purpose of section: _____

_____

_____

Key points:

- _____

- _____

- _____

- _____

Graphs, charts, supporting documentation:

- _____

- _____

- _____

quality control. Now is the time to do the first draft editing as a group to identify deficiencies and gaps in your research—and to resolve them.

Of course, it would save time if everyone were to have his or her section on disc already formatted appropriately. If, on the other hand, the presentation is not expected in print, you can leave it up to the members of your group whether they should present their material formally or informally. Although it is always important to be very well organized, it is often inconsequential whether the material is read out loud or delivered off the cuff. Indeed, it is wise to leave the decision up to the individual. Some people are much more comfortable than others in front of an audience.

- At your final pre-presentation meeting, be sure that there are several copies of each person's contribution, so that you can "cut and paste" the manuscript and designate two efficient writers to share the crucial responsibility of polishing the final version if the project is to be turned in. This final editing will confirm its quality:

  - One style is consistent throughout.
  - All requirements have been met.
  - Every item is specific.
  - Every item relates to the overall message.
  - The text is readable (see 4d2).
  - The grammar is accurate.
  - Charts and graphs are consistent and understandable.

Someone else should be arranging for handouts to be proofread, then printed. Take the time to have one final dress rehearsal before your presentation day. If you invite non-members of your group to be members of the rehearsal audience, they may offer helpful feedback, or they may simply praise you for all your hard work. Your organization and planning and revisions will certainly be worthwhile when your group presentation goes off without a hitch.

chapter

62 Essay Examinations

Essay exams will usually ask you to demonstrate three skills:

- *Recall.* You'll show your grasp of the facts by recalling information.

- *Clarification.* You'll demonstrate your understanding of facts (their meaning, causes, consequences, sequences, relationships, points of comparison, and priorities) by clarifying and organizing information.

- *Argument.* You'll apply your knowledge to new situations by constructing arguments that use factual information to prove a point. (See 5.)

Your instructors know at least as much as you do about the subject you are being examined on. But don't take their knowledge for granted and leave out information you assume they know. Treat them as intelligent, curious readers who are interested in your subject. Provide them with whatever they need to understand you.

62*a* | Decide what a question calls for

When you receive an essay exam, study each question carefully before you begin writing.

- Look for **topical terms** identifying the subjects you'll cover in your answer. Frequently nouns, they identify people, events, issues, and concepts.

  List the most prominent Canadian politicians of the 1860s. Discuss their contributions to the confederation movement.

  [Topical terms here are *politicians, 1860s, contributions,* and *confederation movement.*]

- Locate **operators** to decide what skills the question calls for. Frequently verbs, these terms will tell you what to do with your information: inform, clarify, or argue. In the sample question above, students are asked to *list* (recall) and *discuss* (recall and clarify)—in other words, to describe what each politician did, identify influence, and evaluate achievement or importance. Here is a list of operators that appear frequently on essay exams. Note the accompanying definitions and synonyms.

  Analyze: divide into parts, explain features, describe the structure or operations.
  Argue: make a point and prove it with evidence.
  Classify: divide into groups based on shared characteristics.
  Comment: describe, analyze, or explain.
  Compare: show similarities and differences.
  Contrast: show differences.
  Criticize: evaluate positively or negatively, giving reasons.
  Defend: support a statement with facts, statistics, authorities, and logic.
  Define: tell what something is, how it works.
  Describe: present features, parts, or details about a subject.
  Develop: explain, analyze, or present details involved with the subject.
  Discuss: explain, trace, analyze, or make a subject clear.
  Enumerate: list, using numbers (first, second, third).
  Evaluate: present and defend a judgment about a subject.
  Exemplify: present examples that illustrate or explain a subject.
  Explain: make clear by description, definition, or enumeration.
  Identify: describe, list, explain, or offer examples.
  Illustrate: present examples.
  Interpret: analyze, explain, or present and defend your opinion.
  Judge: evaluate.
  Justify: explain, prove, or defend.
  List: recall.
  Outline: give steps or stages; identify major points or topics.

Persuade: argue; support a statement with evidence and reasoning.
Prove: argue.
Provide information: give facts and figures.
Rebut: oppose a statement with evidence and reasoning.
Refute: oppose with proof.
Review: summarize, explain, or provide information.
Show: explain, illustrate, or prove.
Summarize: give the main points of your reading, observation, or study.
Trace: identify the steps or stages in a process; describe causes or effects.

- Look for **modifiers** indicating how to organize or focus your answer. Usually these will be adjectives or adverbs: *most important, primary, briefly, thoroughly,* and so on. In the sample question earlier, *most prominent* indicates that students must decide who were the most important politicians and focus on their *contributions only.*

- Here are some more essay questions. Before you read the accompanying analysis of each question, try to identify their topical terms, operators, and modifiers.

Describe the operation of the adrenal glands.

[This recall question asks students to provide details about the adrenal glands before describing how they operate.]

Briefly define and illustrate the concept of determinism.

[This question's first word, *briefly,* provides a clue that this is primarily a test of recall and understanding. Students are being asked to state the meaning of a key term—presented in class discussion or a textbook—and summarize examples that illustrate the way *determinism* works.]

Analyze the characters of the Duke and Duchess of Ferrara in Robert Browning's poem "My Last Duchess." Trace the Duke's growing disenchantment with his wife, and evaluate his reasons for his actions.

[To answer this question successfully, students would have to do more than summarize the poem. To *analyze,* they must describe the personalities of the Duke and Duchess and then support their opinions with details from the poem. To *trace,* they must describe a process. To *evaluate,* they must judge the quality of a character's reasoning.]

62*b* | Plan and write your answer

If scratch paper is available, use it. Even if you're well prepared, the answer to a complex question may not spring to mind fully formed.

- *Brainstorming and exploring.* Make lists, jot down ideas, freewrite.

- *Noting your main idea or thesis.* Write out the main idea or thesis of your essay. Be sure that this most important part of your essay includes key topical terms from the question to keep you on course as you write. Consider this thesis:

Determinism is the philosophical doctrine that every event, human or natural, can be explained as the result of earlier events. Everything is caused; there is no such thing as free will; no event is purely accidental.

[This thesis gives the definition called for by the question. The following explanatory sentence clarifies the definition by telling what *determinism* is not and lists the areas from which the writer will draw the examples called for by the question: examples of causality, the absence of free will, and the absence of chance.]

- *Writing a sketch outline.* To complete your plans, sketch an outline of your answer. Think of your answer as a pyramid with the thesis or main idea at the top and your facts and explanations spreading out beneath, following a line of reasoning and providing support.

- *Manuscript form.* If permitted, write in pencil so that you can erase. Write on every other line, allowing generous margins. (Check with your instructor before bringing a laptop computer to an exam.)

- *Organization.* Don't waste time with introductions. Get to the point. Follow your outline.

- *Rereading.* If you have time, read your answer twice—once to make sure you've actually answered the question, a second time to check grammar, punctuation, spelling, and legibility.

chapter

63 Business and Professional Writing

Computer Tip:

Creating Templates for Business Documents

Your word processing program may already have a "templates file," containing a variety of templates for familiar business documents such as letters and memos. You can customize them to suit your needs. Or you can create your own templates using the fonts, styles, header, and format commands of your word processor. Note, however, that ornate, "over-produced" documents will distract readers.

63*a* | Write effective business letters

1 Following the conventions for writing business letters

- *Paper.* Use good-quality, heavy white bond paper. Letterhead paper makes the best impression. Do not use business letterhead for personal correspondence or job applications, however.

- *Typescript.* Type your letters or use a computer. Use a black ribbon and standard typeface. If you use a computer, note that many readers object to dot matrix printers. (See 48a.)

- *Length.* Whenever possible, limit letters to one page. If you write a longer letter, put second and successive pages on plain white paper.

- *Balance.* Make your letter look easy to read by centring it on the page. Keep paragraphs relatively brief; doublespace between them. Provide ample white space surrounding your text. To help readers keep track of important information, use indented lists, bullets, or enumeration. (See 48b2.)

- *Format.* Among letter formats, one of the most common and attractive is the modified block, illustrated by the sample letter on page 428. Near the right margin, place the return address, the date, complimentary close, and signature section. All other parts begin at the left margin. When you have letterhead, use the full block format: all parts lined up along the left margin with double-spacing between the parts and the paragraphs.

- *Salutations.* Whenever possible, address readers by name or specific title: *Dear Mr. Li, Ms. Black, Mrs. Shaw, Dr. Singh, Prof. Szczinski,* and so on. Check with a receptionist to find out your reader's preferences. When you cannot find these out, or you do not have names, address the reader by title alone: *Dear Editor, Personnel Manager, Director of Admissions,* and so on. Do not use first names unless you know your reader personally. (See 32e.)

- *Envelopes.* Mail business letters in standard business-size envelopes, 10 x 24 cm.

2 Conveying your personality to readers

Whatever your reasons for writing, your readers will usually be reading as part of their jobs. They'll appreciate anything in your letter that makes their work easier, including layout, detailed information, and style.

906 1st Avenue West
Prince Albert, Saskatchewan
S6V 4Y2
March 31, 2001

Dianne L. Garcia
Director of Early Childhood Studies
Woodland Institute of Applied Psychology
3680 Strathcona Place
Prince Albert, Saskatchewan S6V 6G1

Dear Ms. Garcia:

Dr. Phil Merikle, Chair of the Psychology Department at the University of Waterloo, has told me that you have three summer internship openings for Child Care Workers. I would like to apply for one of the positions.

As you will see from my résumé, I am now in my third year of Applied Psychology, with a specialization in Child Development. I am studying to become a child psychologist working with institutionalized children. My minor in English has emphasized writing and communication skills.

Most of my work experience has been with children.

- For the last two years, I worked as a summer counsellor at a camp for children with developmental difficulties. My responsibilities were to provide tutoring, physical therapy, and recreational supervision.

- Before attending university, I worked as a Recreation Supervisor with a Boys and Girls Club. Besides my supervisory and coaching duties, I acted as "big brother" to three pre-teen boys.

- Since last September, I have been volunteering ten hours a week at a local school to help children with low self-esteem. This experience has provided a valuable introduction to institutional work.

Because of my educational background and job experience, I believe I would be an asset to your institute this summer. I will be returning to Prince Albert once my exams end and can come to an interview at your convenience after April 10. Until then, I can be reached by e-mail at mdbryant@watarts.uwaterloo.ca or by voice mail at (306) 763-2671.

Thank you very much for your consideration. I look forward to hearing from you.

Sincerely,

Lucas Bryant
Lucas Bryant

Enclosure: Résumé

Modified block business letter format (return address omitted with letterhead)

Full block format puts date first, two lines above destination address

Formal salutation followed by a colon (use a comma only to be informal)

Put your message first

Block paragraphs highlighting qualifications

Most relevant job-related details of résumé

Specifics make writer easy to contact

Polite closing

Complimentary close

Signature

Writer's name

Be businesslike. Don't sound stuffy, but be as serious as the occasion requires. Avoid the features of an informal style: slang, most contractions, sentence fragments, and inappropriately emotional language. (For more on voice, see 2c and 32a.)

Whenever possible, adopt what business writers call a "you" attitude. Try to see things from your readers' point of view, keeping their interests, needs, and benefits uppermost in your mind. Most public letters are, after all, persuasive. You'll be persuasive if your readers know you're thinking of them as you write.

3 Organizing business letters

Make your letters easy to follow by adopting the standard three-part design. In your opening paragraph, provide necessary background; then identify your subject and purpose. In your middle paragraphs, provide information, explanation, and reasons. Close with a brief paragraph describing the action you want your audience to take. If you have bad news, save it until you've presented all the information and reasons explaining it.

4 Using electronic communications

Neither of the following is confidential. Use them for speed, not privacy.

- *Faxes.* Because faxes are easily lost, advise the recipient that one is coming. Include a cover sheet that gives the recipient's name, company, fax number, date, time, subject, your name, fax number, and the total number of pages, including the cover sheet. If you are mailing the original after you fax it, say so on the cover sheet.

- *E-mail.* E-mail messages are less formal than business letters or even memos; sometimes they seem closer to speech than writing. But as you write, keep your readers in mind: their knowledge, their positions, and your relationship with them. Be courteous—say "please" and "thank you"—and take the time to be sure your language is accurate and that your message will be clear to its reader. Headings for e-mail depend on the network you're using, but you can still address your reader by name and sign off with your name. (See also 50e1.)

63b Write effective résumés

The résumé presents important information about your background, education, experiences, achievements, and references. It is the proof of your qualifications.

1 Preparing a résumé

As you prepare a résumé, be brief but complete. If possible, limit it to one page. Use clipped phrases rather than complete sentences: *Career Objective: To become a child psychologist working with autistic children in an institutional setting.* Group related information to make it easy to locate, and make headings grammatically parallel, such as all nouns or noun phrases: *Education, Experience, References,* and so on. (See 21.) Remember always to include a cover letter, even if you are delivering your résumé by hand.

2 Formatting a résumé

The formats for résumés are varied; make yours look professional and easy to read. Take advantage of models provided by your word processor or by your school's co-operative education department. If you have important achievements, list them first. Follow a chronological order, most recent job first, or describe the functions of your job, most important first. If you're a recent graduate or still in school, place your education first, beginning with your most recent schooling. See the sample résumé on page 465.

63c Write effective memos

A **memo** is a written document sent within an organization to specific persons or departments. Its purposes are to inform, summarize, record, or call for action. Successful memos are usually sensitive to writer-reader relations. (See 1c3 for questions about audience; see 2c for guidelines on voice.) Often customized to suit the needs of a particular organization, memos vary widely in their formats. The sample memo on page 468 illustrates standard memo parts and a common pattern of organization. The sample uses a standard business block format to produce a memo (with no documentation necessary).

LUCAS BRYANT
906 1st Avenue West
Prince Albert, Saskatchewan S6V 4Y2
(306) 763-2671

Position Sought: Child Care Worker—Summer Intern

Career Objective: To become a child psychologist working with autistic children in an institutional setting

Education:

199– to present: University of Waterloo
Major: Applied Psychology, Child Development Option
Minor: English
Overall Average: 86.4%
Recipient of Faculty of Arts scholarships (199– to 199–) and Founders Academic Achievement Award (200–)

Academic history to highlight training

Honours and awards listed

Experience:

200– to present: Volunteer Teacher's Assistant
Notre Dame of St. Agatha Children's Centre, St. Agatha, Ontario
Helped organize and run after-school and Saturday day camps for children aged 6–12

199– and 199–:   Senior Counsellor, Camp Indigo, Benjamin River, New Brunswick
Tutored and supervised recreation for developmentally challenged children aged 8–14

199– to 199–:   Spruce River Boys and Girls Club
Prince Albert, Saskatchewan
Supervised group recreation

Experience listed in reverse chronological order

Extracurricular: Member of UW fencing and handball teams
Regular contributor to *Imprint* (weekly student paper)

Additional activities and accomplishments to confirm applicant's versatility

References and transcripts available upon request.

TO: Michael Wells

FROM: Jean Tarquin *JT*

DATE: February 19, 200–

SUBJECT: January Management Training Program:
           Evaluation and Recommendations

The January Management Training Session was generally successful, with most participants rating the training "very good." Following is a list of the workshop's major strengths as well as recommendations for improvements. These are based on both my own observations and the participants' written evaluations.

Workshop Strengths

- Dividing the topic into two parts, presented on two separate days, gave a useful general-to-specific focus. The first day covered company structure and functions, and the second covered management skills.
- Videotaping the trainees' oral presentations and then soliciting critique from the group helped the trainees identify their strengths and weaknesses as speakers.
- The strong emphasis on interpersonal communication skills (active listening, showing sympathy, interpreting body language) helped trainees feel comfortable and relaxed about the group, the training and the company.

Recommended Changes

- All training sessions should have at least ten trainees for more efficient use of training resources and richer interaction among participants. (The small group of only six trainees seemed less relaxed and enthusiastic than the larger group of twelve.)
- All of our executive speakers should take a few minutes to relate personal stories to illustrate their perception of the company culture. The one speaker who did so was identified by the trainees as the most informative.
- We should do a six-month follow up of trainees and their supervisors to gain insights for designing an advanced management training program.

None of these recommendations is costly or difficult to implement. Such improvements would mean even greater benefits to the company through our successful training program. I suggest we follow through on these recommendations for the July session.

Enclosures: Participants' written evaluations

Annotations in right margin:

Block format

Writer initials memo

Begin body of memo three spaces below subject line

Message

Single space within paragraphs; doublespace between

All paragraphs flush left, no indentation

Past tense reports action that took place

Headings help orient reader

Use bullets for clarity and emphasis

Content is well balanced (general ideas + specific details)

Present tense for factual statements

Action spelled out

Reference area

63*d* Choose your options for writing an effective report

A report is a systematic presentation of information to a specific audience for a specific purpose. The reports you'll write in school and on the job may take several forms: informal memo or letter reports, technical field or lab reports, informative reports, problem/solution reports, progress reports, proposals, and case studies.

1 Preliminary activities

Your preliminary preparations will be similar to those for other investigative writing: surveying the situation (see 1c), posing key questions or describing the problem, and identifying your purpose (see 49a2). You will gather the information for your report from appropriate sources: interviews, minutes, letters, questionnaires, surveys, experimentation, direct observation, published reports, and other documents. (For guidelines to research, see 49–51.) When you finish your investigation, write out your **conclusion,** the point of your report supported by your information (see 2d4).

2 Organizing a report

Prepare an informal report as you would a letter, memo, or essay, with an appropriate beginning, middle, and end. Formal reports generally consist of (1) prefatory parts, such as a cover, title page, letters of authorization or acceptance, acknowledgments, a table of contents, an abstract, and an executive summary; (2) the text of the report, including an introduction, body, and conclusion; (3) supplementary parts, such as an appendix, bibliography, or index. Include all parts relevant to your report and required by your readers. Follow these guidelines to organize the text of your report:

- *Introduction.* The introduction includes all elements necessary to orient your readers and help them understand your information: a statement of the problem or key questions, a description of materials and methods, background or history, definitions, a review of relevant published research, or an overview of the presentation to follow.

- *Body.* The body of a report is often labelled *Results, Data, Findings,* or *Discussion.* The results and discussion may be separated or combined, depending upon their relationship, the length of the report, and your readers' needs. Organize the body of a report according to topics, chronology, importance, or other logical patterns. (See 8b.)

- *Conclusion.* A conclusion summarizes information, makes generalizations about it (comparisons, causes and effects, classifications, estimations, predictions), proposes solutions to problems, makes evaluations and recommendations, or proposes action.

- *Inductive vs. deductive organization.* For readers who need detailed explanation or who may resist your recommendations without a full presentation of the case, organize the text of your report in an *inductive* or "conclusion-last" order: introduction, body, conclusion. For busy readers who may not read the entire report, who will agree with you, or who want your opinion promptly, use a *deductive* or "conclusion-first" order: introduction, conclusion, body.

3 Formatting and style

- *Headings.* Informal reports are usually written as continuous documents, undivided except for paragraphing. The text of formal reports is usually divided by headings into clearly labelled parts: *Introduction, Background, Discussion, Conclusion,* and so on. (For guidelines to effective headings, see 48b1.)

- *Visual aids.* Use lists, tables, and graphics to illustrate and group information as well as to help your readers understand it. (See 48b2–4.)

- *Style.* Generally write in the present tense unless you have a good reason for using the past tense: *This report recommends. . . .* (See 15b1.) Choose concrete, specific words as specialized as the subject requires and as reader understanding will allow. (See 31a and b.) Except in conclusions, avoid generalities. Also avoid emotionally charged words that may make your report sound biased. (See 30b.)

- *Documentation.* Cite the sources of borrowed information in an appropriate format. (For Modern Language Association guidelines, see 53 and 54; for American Psychological Association guidelines, see 56a–c; for other formats, see the style manuals listed in 57–59.)

4 A sample formal report

For a sample formal report written in the American Psychological Association style, see 56d.

Appendix

 Computer Tip:

Locating Internet Resources

It's impossible to keep track of all the Web sites that provide valuable resources for researchers. Fortunately, the ever-increasing reliability of search engines/subject directories permits us to track sites which may have moved. Count on the following to give you a solid start to your research on the Internet, and add new URLs here.

1 Learning the Internet and the World Wide Web

■ *Internet Help Desk.* A list of hypertext links to Internet guides, references, and search tools.

   <http://www.strife.com/helpdesk.html>

■ *Sink or Swim: Internet Search Tools & Techniques.* A detailed guide to search tools and strategies.

   <http://www.sci.ouc.bc.ca/libr//connect96/search.htm>

2 Search Tools

■ *Search.com.* A site linking you to over one hundred specialty search engines world wide.

   <http://www.search.com>

■ *Internet Searching.* December Communications' exhaustive list of sites, resource lists, subject directories, search engines, people finders, and protocol search tools for searching the Web, gopher space, and ftp sites.

   <http://www.December.com/cmc/info/internet-searching.html>

■ *Canadian Search Engines.* A selection of URLs for searching for Canadian content and Canadian sites.

   Altavista Canada: <http://www.altavistacanada.com>

   Excite Canada: <http://www.excite.ca>

   Canadian Online Explorer: <http://www.canoe.ca>

   Yahoo! Canada: <http://www.yahoo.ca>

■ *Catalist.* A catalogue of LISTSERV information providing links to over 33 000 public lists.

   <http://www.lsoft.com/lists/listref.html>

3 Desktop references

- *Britannica.* A searchable compendium of information from the *Encyclopedia Britannica*, including a link to the *Merriam-Webster Dictionary*.

  <http://www.britannica.com>

- *CIA World Factbook.* Details and facts about every country in the world.

  <http://www.odci.gov/cia/publications/factbook>

- *Onelook Dictionary.* Access to a searchable database of dictionaries providing definitions of almost 3 million words.

  <http://www.onelook.com>

- *Quotation Page.* Access to a searchable database of quotations, with links to other quotation collections including *Bartlett's*.

  <http://www.starlingtech.com/quotes>

4 Writing help

- *Allyn and Bacon's CompSite.* An interactive meeting place for teachers and students to share resources and work on projects.

  <http://www.abacon.com/compsite>

- *English as a Second Language Resources.* A good starting point for learning English as a second language online.

  <http://www.aitech.ac.jp/~iteslj/links/ESL>

- *Resources for Writers and Writing Instructors,* by Jack Lynch. A detailed list of hypertext links to writing instruction sites, dictionaries and other reference works, grammar, punctuation, and usage sites.

  <http://www.andromeda.rutgers.edu/~jlynch/Writing/links.html>

5 Canadiana

- *Canadian History Resources.* A searchable collection of more than 3000 books and pamphlets documenting Canadian history from the first European contact to the late nineteenth century.

  <http://www.canadiana.org>

- *Canadian Newspaper Association.* Comprehensive links to Canadian daily papers and the media (searchable).

  <http://www.can-acj.ca>

- *The Canadian Resource Page.* An invaluable compendium of comprehensive links to Canadian sites and information of all kinds.

  <http://www.cs.cmu.edu/Unofficial/Canadiana/README.html>

- *Government of Canada.* The starting point for Canadian information searches, including links to all departments, institutions, and programs administered by the federal government.

    <http://www.canada.gc.ca>

- *Statistics Canada.* A gold mine of information, figures, and statistics, including links to international sources.

    <http://www.statcan.ca>

6 General resources

- *CultureNet.* A guide to cultural information resources on the Internet.

    <http://www.culturenet.ca>

- *The Human-Language Page.* A huge compendium of links to resources in language.

    <http://www.june29.com/HLP>

- *Internet Public Library.* A collection of over 10 000 online texts including links to major newspapers around the world and to over 2000 magazines and e-zines.

    <http://www.ipl.org>

- *Internet Movie Database.* A searchable database of everything you ever wanted to know about movies.

    <http://us.imdb.com>

- *Project Gutenberg.* The continuing project to make text versions of public domain classic literature available online.

    <http://sailor.gutenberg.org>

- *Social Science Information Gateway.* A comprehensive listing of social science information sources available electronically worldwide.

    <http://sosig.esrc.bris.ac.uk>

- *Song Lyrics.* Access to a database of lyrics and information on over 2 million songs.

    <http://www.lyrics.ch>

- *Voice of the Shuttle: Web Page for Humanities Research.* An amazingly comprehensive directory of humanities-oriented Web pages.

    <http://vos.ucsb.edu>

Index

A Guide to Correction and Editing Symbols

Numbers and letters in bold refer to chapters and sections; these are followed by page numbers.
Check abbreviations at the top corners for quick reference.

abbr	check abbreviation, **44**, pp. 298–302
adj	check adjective, **10d**, **20**, **24f**, pp. 96, 152–157, 186–187
adv	check adverb, **10e**, **20**, **24f**, pp. 96, 152–157, 187
agr	check agreement/verb agreement, **11**, **16**, pp. 99–100, 130–137; check noun/pronoun agreement, **10b**, **17**, pp. 91–93, 137–141; check determiner/noun agreement, **10a**, **22**, pp. 90–91, 161–168
apos	check apostrophe, **24e**, **39**, pp. 185, 273–277
aud	check appropriateness to audience, **1c**, **2c**, **4c**, **4d**, **6a**, pp. 13–15, 21–23, 36–40, 57–61
awk	revise awkward construction according to reader's suggestions
cap	check capitalization, **42**, pp. 289–296
case	check case agreement, **19**, pp. 146–152
cliché	rewrite cliché, **31d**, p. 224
coh	check coherence, **3**, **9**, pp. 27–32, 82–87
comp	check comparisons, **20d**, **27c**, pp. 155–156, 204–205
co-ord	check co-ordination, **10g**, **25c**, pp. 97–98, 192–193
cs	revise comma splice, **14a–c**, pp. 114–117
d	check diction (word choice): exact words, **30**, pp. 213–219; vivid words, **31**, pp. 219–223; appropriate words, **24a**, **32**, **34**, pp. 180, 225–233, 239–252
db neg	revise double negative, **20e**, pp. 156–157
det	check determiners, **22**, pp. 163–168
dev	check development, **1**, **2**, **4**, **7**, **8**, **49**, **50**, **51**, **60e–g**, pp. 2–28, 33–42, 66–82, 331–370, 448–451
dm	revise dangling modifier, **28b**, pp. 208–209
doc	check documentation: general, **52c–e**, pp. 372–383; MLA, **53**, pp. 385–390; APA, **56**, pp. 413–421; CM, **57**, pp. 430–435; CBE, **58**, pp. 436–441
emph	add emphasis, **25**, pp. 189–195
ev	add evaluation, **60b**, pp. 444–452
exact	exact wording called for, **30**, pp. 213–220
fig	check figure of speech, **31c**, pp. 221–224
frag	revise sentence fragment, **11**, **12**, **13**, pp. 99–113
fs	revise fused sentence, **14c**, pp. 117–120
hyph	check hyphen, **46**, pp. 305–307
id	check idiomatic usage, **23h**, **i**, **24**, pp. 177–188
ital	check italics, **43**, pp. 296–298
jar	revise jargon, **32c**, **d**, pp. 227–229
log	check logic, **5c**, **d**, pp. 53–57
mixed	revise mixed construction, **27**, pp. 201–206
mm	revise misplaced modifier, **12**, **24f**, **28a**, pp. 103–107, 186–188, 207–208
ms	check manuscript format: general, **48a–d**, **63**, pp. 41–47, 314–321, 463–471; MLA, **48c**, **54**, **55**, pp. 321–323, 391–412; APA, **48d**, **56**, pp. 342–326, 413–429; CM, **57**, pp. 430–436; CBE, **58**, pp. 436–442
nonst	revise nonstandard usage, **15a4**, **23c**, pp. 123–125, 171–172
num	check number format, **45**, pp. 302–305